THE DETROIT TIGERS

D1026923

WRITING SPORTS SERIES
Richard "Pete" Peterson, Editor

The Cleveland Indians
Franklin Lewis

The Cincinnati Reds
Lee Allen

The Chicago White Sox
Warren Brown

Dreaming Baseball
James T. Farrell

My Greatest Day in Football
Murray Goodman and Leonard Lewin

The Detroit Tigers
Frederick G. Lieb

THE DETROIT TIGERS

by

FREDERICK G. LIEB

Foreword by Tom Stanton

The Kent State University Press
Kent, Ohio

Library of Congress Catalog Card Number 2008014195
ISBN: 978-0-87338-958-7
Manufactured in the United States of America

Library of Congress Cataloging-in-Publication Data

Lieb, Fred, b. 1888.
  The Detroit Tigers / Frederick G. Lieb ; foreword by Tom Stanton.
      p. cm. — (Writing sports series)
  Originally published: New York : G.P. Putnam's Sons, [1946]. With
a new foreword and index.
  Includes index.
  ISBN 978-0-87338-958-7 (pbk. : alk. paper) ∞
  1. Detroit Tigers (Baseball team).   2. American League of
Professional Baseball Clubs.   I. Title.
  GV875.D6L5 2008
  796.357′640977434—dc22
                                                        2008014195

British Library Cataloging-in-Publication data are available.

12 11 10 09 08   5 4 3 2 1

CONTENTS

FOREWORD
by Tom Stanton

As a baseball-obsessed boy growing up in Michigan, I savored the sporting stories told by my father and uncles at our family holiday gatherings. Amid the glow of Christmas lights, in air scented by cigarettes and sweet pipe tobacco, with drinks in hand, they laughed of long-ago streetcar rides to the ballpark at Michigan and Trumbull, of scorching afternoons spent in the Navin Field bleachers rooting for Ty Cobb or Harry Heilmann or Hank Greenberg, of Schoolboy Rowe winning sixteen straight, of Charlie Gehringer gliding like a ghost toward the hole, of Mickey Cochrane leading the Tigers to their first world championship—"Boy, he was a good one."

Their tales brought life to magical names, and they fired in me a love for our Detroit team that burns yet, at age forty-seven. My father is now approaching his eighty-eighth birthday, and most of my uncles have died. Those joyous winter evenings when I sat mesmerized as they reminisced about the Tigers of the 1920s and 1930s are, like the players they once talked about, gone. And I certainly miss them.

But in a small way, this Fred Lieb classic helps fill that void. It evokes those wondrous days. Reading Lieb is like listening to a favorite old uncle. You hear the passion and enthusiasm in his words. You sense the good cheer in his tone, and you recognize in him the kindred spirit of another soul who knew and loved baseball.

Born in 1888, Lieb got his first taste on the streets of south Philadelphia. In 1909, at age twenty-one, he pestered the editor of *Baseball Magazine* into allowing him to profile Honus Wagner and Ty Cobb, whose teams would meet in the World Series. Within two years he had landed in New York as the baseball writer for the *Press*. At the time, New York was home to a dozen daily newspapers, and their sports departments glimmered with talent.

In 1911 Lieb shared space in the press box with fellow newcomers Grantland Rice, Damon Runyon, and Heywood Broun. Rice became the nation's best-known sports columnist; Runyon went on to write of guys and dolls;

and Broun, a syndicated socialist commentator, ascended to the famed Algonquin Table. Only Lieb remained on the baseball beat. "I admired them for their accomplishments," he said of his peers. "But never for a moment was I jealous of them. I preferred baseball—it had become part of my life." In New York Lieb covered his favorite sport for a series of newspapers—the *Press, Morning Sun, Telegram,* and *Post.* He served for years as the Yankees' official scorer before making his way to *The Sporting News.* Along the way he authored books on Connie Mack, Judge Kenesaw Mountain Landis, the Phillies, the Pirates, the Cardinals, the Red Sox, the World Series, and this one, about my beloved team.

The Detroit Tigers is a treasure. It spans more than sixty-five years in baseball history—from 1881, when the city entered a team in the National League, through 1947, when the club edged Boston out of second place behind the pennant-winning Yankees. What makes the book special is Fred Lieb. He lived through much of this history. He saw most of these players. He knew them—not only Cobb and Cochrane and Gehringer and Greenberg but also Hughie Jennings and Wild Bill Donovan and Germany Schaefer.

In Lieb's time, in the days when St. Louis qualified as a western team, writers and players traveled together on the trains, shared drinks and meals, played poker against one another, and stayed in the same hotels. That closeness provided access and insight, but it also ensured that local beat writers pondered carefully what to reveal and when to be critical of the hometown crew. The New York writers, for example, were famous for protecting Babe Ruth and polishing his image into mythical proportions.

Sports journalists used to be classified as belonging to either the "Gee Whiz" or the "Aw Nuts" schools. Grantland Rice, with his mostly upbeat stories, was considered part of the first group; the questioning and critical Westbrook Pegler belonged to the latter. Lieb didn't see himself in either faction.

"I wrote first of all to satisfy Fred Lieb the reader of sports pages," he said late in life. "As a reader I wanted honest reporting, and I wanted to know not just who won, but how and why. If I could be made to feel by the writer that I had missed something exciting by not being present, so much the better. It was perhaps natural that as a writer without talents of a creative literary sort—such as the talents of Runyon or Broun—I modeled myself on my own preferences as a sports-page reader."

Lieb's history of the Detroit Tigers concludes in the decade of World War II. Of course, much has happened in the past sixty years that merits mention.

There was, for starters, the 22-year career of Al Kaline, the most popular Tiger of all time, and the World Series championships of 1968 and 1984, which ensured regional immortality for Mickey Lolich, Kirk Gibson, and their respective teammates. There were MVPs for Denny McLain and Guillermo (then known as Willie) Hernandez; batting titles for George Kell, Kaline, Harvey Kuenn, Norm Cash, and Magglio Ordonez; home run crowns for Darrell Evans and Cecil Fielder; no-hitters by Virgil Trucks, Jim Bunning, Jack Morris, and Justin Verlander; shared glory for Alan Trammell and Lou Whitaker; a Hall of Fame performance by Ernie Harwell; and one sparkling season for Mark "the Bird" Fidrych.

The passing decades have seen a parade of optimistic owners (John Fetzer, Tom Monaghan, and Mike Ilitch) and legendary managers (Billy Martin, Sparky Anderson, and Jim Leyland) and witnessed the momentous farewell of a venerable ballpark, Tiger Stadium, and the debut of a new one, Comerica. There have been ups and downs, including a torturous, twelve-year stretch of losing seasons, during which the Tigers set a team record for most defeats in a season. Three years later, in a renaissance sparked by the signing of Pudge Rodriguez, the Tigers found themselves in the World Series. The next year, 2007, they topped the three million mark in attendance for the first time. The heart of metro-Detroit once again beats to the summer sounds of baseball. New heroes have succeeded old ones.

Less than a decade ago, Tiger fans were asked to select their greatest-ever team. Many of the choices were expected, obvious, and inevitable: Cobb and Kaline in the outfield, Greenberg at first, Gehringer at second. Others were debatable. But one selection in particular drew the ire of old-timers and baseball historians. The third outfield position went to Kirk Gibson, a favorite of the 1980s and 1990s who never knocked in 100 runs or hit 30 home runs and only once topped .300. Gibson was chosen over Cooperstown inductees Harry Heilmann, whose lifetime .342 average remains tenth-best in the game's history, and Sam Crawford, whose record 309 career triples has stood for 90 years. Gibson's advantage—aside from his competitive nature and electric personality—was time. Save for the Georgia Peach, the stars of the first quarter of the twentieth century were forgotten or overlooked in favor of the more recent stars.

There are few people alive who saw Ty Cobb play in the major leagues and certainly no one around who witnessed his appearance in the 1907 World Series. Skip forward a few decades. A teenager who watched Goose Goslin and the Tigers defeat the Chicago Cubs in 1935 would be in his eighties now.

The old stories are rapidly disappearing from our collective memory, which makes *The Detroit Tigers* more important than ever. On these pages Fred Lieb devotes chapters to the pennant-winning Detroiters of the early 1900s. Lieb revives the series of 1909, an era in which many major league cities prohibited Sunday games. He recalls the sheets of canvas that were deployed to block the view from the wildcat bleachers beyond the outfield walls: "They flapped noisily when the lake winds took hold of them."

He remembers Harry Coveleski coming to Detroit after being run out of the National League by opponents taunting him with renditions of "Sweet Adeline" . . . Bob "Fat" Fothergill, "a roly-poly fellow" with "an Elmer-the-Great" appetite who grew larger every year until he "looked like a bouncing ball" . . . Tommy Bridges missing a perfect game in 1932 by one out. It's all sweet stuff.

In 1972 the Baseball Hall of Fame bestowed on Fred Lieb the J. G. Taylor Spink Award, the highest honor given to baseball writers. I was eleven at the time, and my uncles were in their glory years of story telling. It wasn't until 1977, when I was edging toward manhood, that I discovered Lieb. That year, as he was nearing ninety, he published his memoirs, *Baseball As I Have Known It,* a lovely, rollicking book, and I became a fan.

Lieb died in 1980. But he hasn't been forgotten. A few seasons back, in his Lou Gehrig book, *Luckiest Man,* author Jonathan Eig painted a colorful portrait of Lieb as a yoga-practicing, reincarnation-embracing, séance-attending, Ouija board–believing friend of Gehrig's. "Fred's knowledge of the game was greater than that of all but a handful of men," wrote Eig.

You're about to see for yourself. Enjoy!

THE DETROIT TIGERS

Ty Cobb Slides Safely into Third in a Spray of Dust and Dirt

⊗ I ⊗

THE MAYOR INTRODUCES
BIG-TIME BASEBALL

I

ALWAYS A GOOD SPORTING TOWN, DETROIT FIRST WAS INTRODUCED to major-league baseball in 1881, the sixth season of the venerable National League, which was launched in the centennial year of 1876. The enterprising Michigan city took over the franchise vacated by Cincinnati, one of the league's charter members, after the 1880 season. A horse-and-buggy town, not much bigger than Saginaw of today, Detroit was hardly big enough to support big-league ball, but the National League of 1881 resembled Ford Frick's flourishing parent major of today about as much as those ramshackle Detroit stands of 1881 resembled the well-equipped, well-manicured present-day baseball palace, Briggs Stadium. In a half-belligerent, half-humorous mood, Bill Terry, former Giant manager, once asked —quite unhappily for himself: "Is Brooklyn still in the league?" Well, in 1881, Brooklyn wasn't even in the league, neither were the Giants. Only Chicago and Boston of the 1946 National League were then represented in the circuit, the league being rounded out by such towns as Providence, R. I., Worcester, Mass., and Troy, N. Y., in the East, and the lake cities of Buffalo, Cleveland, and Detroit in the West. To all intents and purposes, it was a New England–Great Lakes league.

The man directly responsible for bringing major-league ball to Detroit was His Honor, the Mayor, himself. The president of the 1881 club was the Hon. W. G. Thompson, mayor of Detroit, and in the 1882 *Spalding's Guide*, the address of the Detroit club was given as "mayor's office." Mayor Thompson was an early baseball enthusiast, and brought a National League club to Detroit through a sincere love of the game and a sense of civic pride. The club then advertised the town, and was known throughout the nation as "the Detroits." It had no other nickname. Even in the official standings,

3

the club was listed as "Detroits" in contrast to the singular "Chicago," "Boston," "Providence."

The club played its home games at what then was known as Recreation Park, situated in the vicinity of what now is the intersection of Brady and Brush Streets. The centrally located Detroit ball park of today, within walking distance of the downtown hotels, office buildings, and theaters, was then out in the country. In 1880, the population of Detroit was 116,340.

In its first major-league season, the Detroits finished fourth with two more defeats than victories. The club won 41 games and lost 43 for a percentage of .488. Anson's Chicago White Stockings, the pennant winner, the Providence Grays, and Buffalo were the clubs which wound up ahead of the new member. The Detroits got off to a rocky start, but we read in the 1882 *Spalding's Guide* that Michigan fans were treated to a profitable and enjoyable baseball summer. "In July the Detroits began to recover some of the ground lost in May, the July record showing that team to have led all the league clubs by a score of eleven victories for the month's play."

2

Through the years, Detroit has had some of the most colorful characters in the game on the manager's seat. They have been aggressive, hard-driving martinets or free-and-easy chaps who led with tact and diplomacy, but they all have been colorful figures. The first Detroit major-league manager, Frank Carter Bancroft, was no exception. A former Union Army soldier, he bridged the infant game which followed the War between the States with World War I baseball. For over a half century, "Banny" was one of the most lovable characters ever connected with the game. He was father of Cuban baseball, taking a team to the island as early as the winter of 1879, when the Spanish governor wanted to stop his exhibitions on grounds of cruelty. After managing the Detroits for the first two seasons, 1881 and 1882, he led the Providence club to a National League pennant in 1884. From 1890, until he died in the saddle, March 31, 1921, he was the popular and able business manager of the Cincinnati Reds.

Even at the start, Detroit had some good and interesting players. As the season moved on, Mayor Thompson and Banny made some advantageous deals, strengthening the club and accounting for that July improvement. Detroit always has been famous for slugging teams, and it was that way right from the beginning. The fellow who led Cap Anson, the Chicago first baseman-playing manager in the league's 1881 hit parade, was Marty Powell, first sacker for the Detroits.

However, the two most famous names for Detroit in that early aggregation were Catcher Charley Bennett and Center Fielder Ned Hanlon. Both remained with Detroit in its eight years in the National League. Bennett, a native of Newcastle, Pa., was one of the great catchers of the eighties, second only to Buck Ewing, the Mickey Cochrane,of his day. Charley went to Boston after Detroit gave up its franchise in 1888, and suffered a tragic accident on January 9, 1894, while on a hunting trip with his former battery mate, John Clarkson.

The pair were on a train bound for Kansas City, when it made a short stop at Wellesville, Kansas. Charley stepped off the train to speak to a friend. When the train started to pull out, Bennett attempted to board it, but slipped, lost his footing, and fell under the wheels. He was taken to a hospital in Wellesville, where the left foot was amputated at the ankle and the right leg at the knee.

Bennett had made his home in Detroit from the time he had first played there in 1881. He opened a cigar store after his baseball career had been so abruptly terminated, and for years was a familiar figure to Detroit's fans. The early American League grounds in Detroit were named Bennett Park in his honor. Charley died in Detroit in 1927.

Ned Hanlon, the Detroit center fielder, was an Irish Connecticut Yankee from Montville, Conn. Ned never was much of a hitter, but one of the great early fly hawks of the game. On the defense he was the Tris Speaker of his day. Ned could go out for them. He was aggressive and a natural leader, and soon was appointed captain of the Detroits. In those early days, the captain ran the team on the field, while the manager's duties were more like those of the business manager of today. As manager of the famous Baltimore Orioles, National League champions of 1894-5-6, Hanlon developed Hughie Jennings into one of the game's outstanding shortstops. Detroit fans were to know Hughie well in the years which followed.

While the 1881 club had an assortment of pitchers from time to time, the club's "pitching staff" was George Derby. Of Detroit's 88 games, Derby figured in 55 of them, winning 29 and losing 26. George Weidman, John Leary, Frank Mountain, Tony Mullane, and William White pitched at such times as Derby was getting his breath.

Sam Trott helped Bennett behind the plate. Martin Powell and

Lew Brown played first base; Joe Gerhardt and Dasher Troy appeared at second; Sadie Houck, Dan Stearns, and W. F. Riley at shortstop; Frank Whitney and Sam Wise at third; and George Wood, Ned Hanlon, Alonzo Knight, Mike Moynahan, Mike Dorgan, and Dan O'Leary in the outfield.

3

In 1882, the Detroits slipped back from fourth to sixth, and as far as Detroit was concerned the year was outstanding for producing one of the few cases of an errant umpire and for the hometown team's participating in the longest 1 to 0 game decided by a home run.

It often has been said that no umpire in the majors ever has been accused of doing an unrighteous thing. Their record for honesty has been very high, but if the wraith of Mayor Thompson still hovers over Detroit's ball yard, he can't give them a batting average of 1.000. At a special meeting of the National League held in Chicago in June, 1882, President Thompson of the Detroits brought charges against Umpire Higham, accusing him of collusion with pool gamblers, especially a coterie in Detroit. The league upheld Mayor Thompson's charges, and President Hulbert of the National League expelled Higham from the circuit.

On April 26, 1944, Bucky Walters, famous Cincinnati righthander, won a 1 to 0, thirteen-inning pitching duel from Al Jurisich, rookie St. Louis Cardinal pitcher, in which the Reds scored the winning run when First Baseman Frank McCormick hammered a home run over the left-field fence in the thirteenth inning.

That was the longest 1 to 0 major-league game of this century terminated by a four-bagger, and it started a search through musty old records for the longest similar contest since big-league box scores have been compiled. The trail led way back to August 17, 1882, when Providence defeated the Detroits in the Rhode Island town by 1 to 0 in 18 innings. "Old Hoss" Radbourne, one of the pitching immortals of baseball, ended the game with an eighteenth-inning clout over the left-field fence. Oddly enough, Radbourne, who won 49 games that season and 60 in 1883, did not pitch that day, but played right field, where they used to play the "spare tires" in the eighties. The pitchers were John Montgomery Ward for Providence and George Weidman for Detroit.

Old-time Detroit fans still recall that game, as it was discussed for weeks thereafter. In the fifteenth inning, George Wright hit the ball through a carriage gate in the outfield, but Detroit Right Fielder Lon Knight chased the ball under the horses' hoofs, and started a relay to the plate which nipped George. The Providence players argued long and loud that it was a homer, and Providence fans almost jumped out of the stands, but Umpire Bradley sided with Detroit that the ball was playable.

The next three years were poor ones for Detroit fandom, as Joseph H. Marsh succeeded Mayor Thompson to the Detroit presidency and John Curtis Chapman followed Banny as manager. The club wallowed in the lower recesses of the second division, finishing seventh, eighth, and sixth in 1883, 1884, and 1885, respectively. The Detroit management also still seemed to be having trouble with the umpires as we read that Herman Doescher, another arbiter, was expelled by the league on charges of dishonorable conduct preferred by the Detroit club. Herman later got back into baseball's good graces.

Then something happened in 1886 which gave Detroit baseball a real shot in the arm. It was the most sensational baseball news of the year—breath-taking news. They discussed it from ocean to ocean and from the Canadian border to the Rio Grande. The Detroit club purchased the "Big Four" of baseball—First Baseman Dennis "Dan" Brouthers, Second Baseman Hardy Richardson, Shortstop Jack Rowe, and Third Baseman "Deacon" Jim White from the Buffalo club. It was the Deacon's second association with a famous quartet, as he also had been a member of baseball's original "Big Four"—Al Spalding, Cal McVey, Ross Barnes, and Jim White of the early Boston Red Stockings.

Buffalo and Providence had dropped out of the league after the 1885 season to make way for Washington and Kansas City, and Detroit acquired its fabulous "Big Four" for the rather ridiculous bargain price of $8,000. But as far as Detroit was concerned, it was as though in a later day Frank Navin had purchased Connie Mack's old $100,000 infield of Frank Baker, Jack Barry, Eddie Collins, and Stuffy McInnis.

In their 1885 averages, their last year in Buffalo, all had been top-rung batters. Brouthers was second in league hitting with .358 and Richardson fourth with .319, while White and Rowe were well up with .292 and .289. Sam Thompson had come to the Detroit club the previous year, and he already was showing himself one of the great sluggers of the game. He went to right field, a position filled so often in Detroit by one of the game's outstanding maulers.

The acquisition of the "Big Four" was expected to do wonders for

7

Detroit baseball, and it did. In one year, the club leaped from a percentage of .379 to .707. But even that high mark couldn't win. It would be equivalent to winning 109 games under the present 154 game schedule, and still see yourself beaten out. It was an all-season-long battle between the Detroits and Cap Anson's Chicago White Stockings. The City-of-the-Straits was a hotbed of baseball excitement, as the lead fluctuated back and forth. But Cap's club won by two and a half games. The Chicagos won 90 and lost 34; the Detroits won 87 and lost 36.

The club had acquired a new manager, William H. "Wattie" Watkins. He was another colorful figure, and always well thought of in Michigan. He played his early ball at Port Huron as a third baseman, and in 1884, at the age of 29, he was struck on the head with a pitched ball at Bay City and just barely escaped with his life. His hair turned white overnight as a result of the accident. Wattie later became a justice of the peace at Marysville, Mich., and died at the good old age of 82 in Port Huron in 1937.

II

AN EARLY WORLD'S
CHAMPIONSHIP

I

THE DISAPPOINTMENT OF 1886 WAS SOON FORGOTTEN, FOR WATTIE Watkins' Detroits went over the top amid a great display of enthusiasm and civic pride in 1887. The "Big Four" were paying substantial dividends on that $8,000 investment.

The National League had been pretty well made over since Detroit first entered it in 1881, and looked a little more as it does today. Such towns as Providence, Buffalo, Troy, and Worcester had moved out, as had Kansas City after a one-year trial. In many respects, the make-up of the 1887 National League is similar to that of the American League of today, as six cities of the Harridge loop—Detroit, New York, Boston, Philadelphia, Chicago, and Washington—were represented. The other two towns were Pittsburgh and Indianapolis.

As often happened when the Tigers won their early American League pennants, the 1887 Detroits found their main opposition in Philadelphia. The Phillies, led by Harry Wright, one of the famous baseball pioneers, put up a strong fight, and eventually were beaten out by four and a half games. In fact, it was a five-team race most of the way. Though weakened by the sale of Mike "King" Kelly, the most colorful player of the day, to the Boston club, Anson's former Chicago champions still were tough and finished a good third, right on the heels of the Phillies. The New York Giants also were in the thick of the fighting until the late summer, and came home ten games off the pace. Even the fifth place Bostons, strengthened by the acquisition of Kelly, finished over the .500 mark. It was a profitable season for the league and for the Detroits, so much so in fact that the players organized their Brotherhood of Ball Players in the fall of that year, with the idea that the players should share more fully in the fruits of the game.

The make-up of that first championship Detroit team was: Brouthers, first base; Dunlap, second base; Rowe, shortstop; White, third base; Richardson, left field; Hanlon, center field; Thompson, right field; Bennett, Ganzel, and Briody, catchers; Getzein, Baldwin, Weidman, Twitchell, and Conway, pitchers. Though Watkins was manager, Captain Ned Hanlon was responsible for much of the team's strategy and tactics on the ball field and already was setting the foundation for his great managerial career of later days. We read frequently of "Hanlon's splendid handling of the team" and "Captain Ned pulling another smart one on the opposition."

A glance at the 1887 batting averages would make it appear that the entire Detroit club of that year was an aggregation of batting Titans. The club had two .400 hitters with Brouthers, .419, and Thompson, .406, and had eight hitters above .340. Hardy Richardson, Charley Bennett, and Jack Rowe were all bunched together at .363.

But there is a pretty sound explanation. Those batters weren't really that good. The season of 1887 was the batter's paradise. In that season, the scoring rules were changed so that bases on balls were recorded as base hits, and this explains the top-heavy averages. The batters also were permitted four strikes instead of three. Can you imagine what Cobb, Gehringer, and Greenberg would have hit under such conditions? However, after one year's trial, three strikes were restored, and bases on balls were scored only as bases on balls.

In the meantime, the club again had changed hands and in 1888 was owned by Frederick K. Stearns, a whiskered gentleman who was in the wholesale drug business.

2

Fred Stearns wasn't satisfied with his team just winning the National League pennant, even though that was a big honor for Detroit with its population then around 150,000. He wanted his Detroits to be champs of all the universe. The St. Louis Browns, owned by the picturesque Chris Von Der Ahe and managed by the dynamic Charley Comiskey, had won the old American Association's pennant for the third successive year. The Association then was a full-fledged major, and the Browns had won the world's championship from the Chicago White Stockings the previous fall. So Stearns challenged old Chris to a new series, but he didn't want to be beaten in six games as were the White Stockings of 1886. He wanted this one to go fifteen games. With the autumn World's Series such an established American custom today, with rules and regulations covering every possible contingency, Stearns's challenge of 1887 and Chris's acceptance make interesting reading for the fan of today, by contrast:

DETROIT, MICH., September 23, 1887

CHRIS VON DER AHE, PRESIDENT,
ST. LOUIS BROWNS,
ST. LOUIS, MO.

DEAR SIR:

I take this occasion on behalf of the Detroit Baseball Club to challenge you to a series of contests for supremacy, and for the title of world's champions, which was won and is now held by your club. The details of the series can best be arranged by a personal interview at such time and place as may be hereafter mutually agreed upon. I would, however, respectfully offer the following suggestions for your consideration:

First, that the number of games played be not less than fifteen, and not more than one game be played in any one city, with the possible exception of such cities as where both the League and Association clubs exist.

Second, that a purse be made up between us so that each player of the winning team shall receive one hundred dollars.

Third, that seventy-five percent of the proceeds of the series go to the club winning a majority of the games played.

Fourth, that an appropriate championship banner be played for, the cost of which shall not exceed two hundred dollars.

Fifth, that two umpires shall be chosen, one each from the League and the Association, and that they serve alternately.

I would also be pleased to test in a game the plan of having two umpires, one stationed behind the bat to pass judgment on balls and strikes, the other near second base to decide all putouts made on the bases and in the field.

Any suggestions or objections that you have to offer will be gladly received. Trusting that nothing may tend to interfere with this series, being the greatest ever contested, and awaiting your early acceptance, I am yours very respectfully.

F. K. STEARNS
President, Detroit Base Ball Club.

"Der Poss Bresident" of the Browns replied as follows:

St. Louis, Mo., September 27, 1887

Mr. Frederick Stearns, President
Detroit Club, Detroit, Mich.
My Dear Sir:

I am in receipt of your favor in which you, in behalf of the Detroit club, challenge the St. Louis club for a series of games for the world's championship, the title which we at present hold. Though the championship season is not yet at an end, both clubs have practically won the championship of their respective associations, and it is fitting that a series of games for the world's championship now be arranged. As to the number of games that constitute the series in view of your claim that a fair test count cannot be made in seven games as in the St. Louis-Chicago world's series last fall, I agree to your proposition to play fifteen games, to take place at such dates and at such cities as may be agreed upon later. In behalf of the St. Louis club, therefore, I accept the challenge of the Detroit club for a series of fifteen games for the championship of the world, in accordance with the stipulations embodied to your challenge, with the following modifications:

1. That not more than one game be played in any city except St. Louis and Brooklyn, where not less than two be played, and also in Philadelphia, where two games be played, one each at American Association and League grounds.

2. That the umpires chosen representing the American Association and League who are to officiate in the series be clothed with full authority, empowering them to enforce the national playing rules as in regular championship season.

3. That any and all fines imposed upon players for infractions of rules be sustained and donated to charitable institutions in St. Louis and Detroit in the following manner: Fines imposed on the St. Louis players be paid by myself and donated to any charitable institution in Detroit you may name, and a similar disposition made of the fines charged against the Detroit players donated to any St. Louis charitable institution I may name.

Trusting that all details will be satisfactorily arranged and nothing may occur to mar what promises to be the greatest series of games ever played, I remain, yours truly

Chris Von Der Ahe
President, St. Louis Base Ball Club

In view of the plump $6,443 full shares which went to the 1945 Tigers as their bit for trapping the Cubs in seven games, the munificent sum of $100 which Fred Stearns offered to each of the winning players must bring chuckles from the present-day player. Also, with four umpires on the field, and two alternates in the grandstand, at modern World's Series, Stearns's rash suggestion of trying out two umpires in one of the games is also worthy of comment. In fact, in most of the fifteen games which followed, John Gaffney, the crack National League umpire of his day, and Kelly, the American Association man, worked as a two-man team. So, the early Detroit owner was, to quite a degree, the father of the double-umpire system.

As Stearns suggested it, and old Chris acquiesced, they made a traveling circus of the World's Series, and it wandered all over the big-league belt of nearly six decades ago. Fifteen games were played, and though the Detroits won their eighth and clinching victory in the eleventh game, they went on and played out the schedule.

3

The series opened in St. Louis and the Browns easily won the first game, 6 to 1, as Bob Carruthers beat Charley Getzein. "Ve beat you as easy as ve beat Anson's team," chuckled Chris. "No von can beat my vonder boys."

Stearns replied in the 1887 version of: "You ain't seen nothing yet. You know this time the series goes fifteen games."

With Pete Conway enjoying a good day, the Detroits evened it up by winning the second game in St. Louis, 5 to 3. With a rest of only one day, Getzein and Carruthers went at it again in Detroit, and the first World's Series game in the Michigan metropolis produced the best game of the series. The Detroits finally wore down Comiskey's team, 2 to 1, in 13 innings. That gave the Detroits a 2 to 1 edge. "Lady" Baldwin, the lefthander, had been held back until the fourth game, played in Pittsburgh, and he gave Chris and Comiskey some of his southpaw magic, winning an 8 to 0 shutout.

The team from Michigan continued to roll up the victories as the baseball caravan played in Brooklyn, New York, Philadelphia, and Boston. Despite Vondy's insistence on two games in Brooklyn, early home of the Dodgers, only one game was played there. Brooklyn then was still in the American Association, and perhaps Chris figured the grandpappies of present-day Flatbush rooters would give him moral, and vocal, support. Maybe he had something, as the Detroits were stopped in Brooklyn, 5 to 2.

However, by the time they got down to the District of Columbia area, October 21, Hanlon's team needed only one more game to fly that $200-bunting. A morning game was played in Washington, and an afternoon session was on the card for Baltimore. Imagine splitting up a present World's Series in that manner! Maybe the St. Louis lads got more sleep and were wider awake in the morning, as they drubbed the Detroits, 11 to 3, for the edification of Washington's early-morning risers. But, as the show moved to Baltimore for the P.M. performance, it was all Detroit. Getzein took the morning pasting, but Lady Baldwin made everything all right, and won the clinching game with runs to spare, 13 to 3.

Even though the Detroits now led, eight games to three, the remaining games were played as originally scheduled.

4

The twelfth game was scheduled back in Detroit on October 24, and by that time the lake city was pretty cold for baseball. It is difficult to say, at this late day, whether Detroit regretted the fact that the Series already had been decided by the time the baseball circus got back to Detroit. It made the ball game of the 24th little more than an exhibition, though the *Detroit Free Press* of October 25, 1887, gave over two columns on the second page to the ball game and Detroit's welcome to its new world's champions.

At any rate, as the players arrived from Baltimore, the whole town was on hand to greet them, although the "Special," which had hauled the caravan from the Mississippi to the Atlantic, got in so early that it almost ruined the reception. The two teams got in over an hour before they were expected. Captain Ned Hanlon had pulled "inside strategy" on the ball field, and now Owner Fred Stearns had to use some outside strategy. He ordered train attendants to lock the doors of all the cars until the welcoming party of sixty carriages could reach the station.

When the big party, headed by Mayor Chamberlain, eventually arrived, the doors were unlocked and the Detroits were greeted as conquerors and given keys to everything in Detroit. The Browns looked sheepishly on while the victors were being lauded. Both teams then were paraded to the old Russell House on Woodward Avenue, where Detroits and Browns were stuffed with a meal which no players should eat before a ball game. And it spoke well for the sportsmanship of that period that the two clubs, who had fought each other so hard on the field, broke bread together and enjoyed kidding each other as they swallowed chunks of roast, fat juicy chops, game, and other substantial delicacies of the eighties. After this light repast the players of the two clubs climbed into horse-drawn omnibuses for the trip to the ball park.

The *Detroit Free Press* said "a great crowd of 4,000" attended, which wasn't bad considering that by this time the boys were playing for fun. However, they put on a good show, even though they were bulging with food, and the Detroits, with Lady Baldwin pitching, won by a score of 6 to 3, as Bob Carruthers pitched for the losers.

The game was stopped long enough in the fourth inning for a park employee to wheel a wheelbarrow, containing 520 silver dollars, across the field and to the home plate. The dollars were a special gift of the fans to their popular catcher, Charley Bennett. With the whole crowd cheering him on, Charley wheeled his barrow of dollars gaily around the base lines.

The Series eventually came to an end a few days later in St. Louis, with Detroit finally having eleven victories to four for their opponents. At the end of Series, A. S. Stern, president of the Cincinnati American Association, tried to win a new world's championship for sheer brass and audacity. Cincinnati's Stern wired Detroit's Stearns:

INASMUCH AS THE CINCINNATI CLUB WAS THE ONLY TEAM IN THE AMERICAN ASSOCIATION TO WIN THE YEAR'S SERIES FROM THE ST. LOUIS BROWNS, AND YOUR TEAM HAS JUST DEFEATED THE BROWNS IN THE RECENT SERIES, I NOW CHALLENGE YOU TO ONE GAME IN CINCINNATI FOR THE CHAMPIONSHIP.

Stearns wired back to Stern: YOUR CHALLENGE IS REJECTED.

5

Detroit was suffering from a pennant hangover when the 1888 season started. Nobody in all the state of Michigan could see anything to the new National League race but the slugging Detroits. Weren't they the proud champions of all the universe? But there was a lot of grief and anguish ahead, and an early injury jinx worked overtime in knocking out Wattie Watkins' players. By June 9, the Detroits reached second place, and from there on, their followers expected them to regain the old pennant heights. But adversity was ahead; the Detroits fell back, while the New York Giants, led by "We are the people" Jim Mutrie, went on to win the first of their fifteen National League flags.

In Francis Richter's *History of Baseball*, we read it wasn't all due to the letdown of the Detroit players. He writes:

The season was the most prosperous on record for the National League, all the clubs except Detroit, Washington, and Indianapolis making money. The pennant race was confined to four clubs—New York, Chicago, Philadelphia and Boston, and these made a great race, New York finally winning by a magnificent streak of good work, commencing with July and lasting to the finish. The Detroits met with an unparalleled series of accidents to players, which deprived them of all chance for another penannt.

As further evidence of that "unparalleled series of accidents," Sam Thompson, the slugging right fielder, and Hardy Richardson played in only 55 and 57 games, respectively. The club played 131. Rowe and Ned Hanlon each missed 30 games; Charley Bennett caught only half of the team's contests, and the pitching staff was shot. One of the pitchers, Twitchell, was used as an outfielder, and such players as Nicholson, Sutcliffe, Campau, and Beaton were hurriedly picked up to plug the many holes in the infield and outfield.

In reading betweeen the lines of old clippings, the Detroits brought other troubles on their own heads. These often were befuddled, pain-wracked heads from a previous hectic evening. As world's champions, the Detroit players were town heroes, and all of Detroit's sporting fraternity vied with each other for the privilege of setting them up for Watkins' athletes and in offering other entertainment usually frowned upon by managers in all periods of American professional baseball.

6

Spalding's Guide of 1889, discussing the National League season of 1888, has this interesting item on baseball of that era:

The two great obstacles in the way of success of the majority of professional ball players are wine and women. The saloon and the brothel are the evils of the baseball world at the present day; and we see it practically exemplified in the failure of noted players to play up to the standard they are capable of were they to avoid these gross evils. One day it is a noted pitcher who fails to serve his club at a critical period of the campaign. Anon, it is the disgraceful escapade of an equally noted umpire. And so it goes from one season to another, at the cost of the loss of thousands of dollars to clubs who blindly shut their eyes to the costly nature of intemperance and dissipation in their ranks.

We tell you gentlemen of the National League and the American Association, the sooner you introduce the prohibition plank in your contracts the sooner you will get rid of the costly evil of drunkenness and dissipation among your players. Club after club have lost championship honors time and again by this evil, and yet they blindly condone these offenses season after season. The prohibition rule from April to October is the only practical rule for removing drunkenness in your teams.

At all events, from pennant winners, the 1888 Detroits dropped to fifth, though they still were good enough to win five more games than they lost, winding up what proved to be Detroit's last National League season with a percentage of .519.

Stearns gave up the presidency of the club in 1888 to Charles W. Smith, though Stearns retained an interest in the club. Smith was a member of the Detroit shoe firm of Pingree and Smith, and Hazen S. Pingree, the partner, became one of Detroit's greatest mayors. He later was elected governor of Michigan, resigning from his mayor's job in 1897 when the state supreme court ruled he couldn't hold both offices. There is an interesting story in connection with Smith, entirely apart from his brief connection with baseball as president of a National League club. While he was Pingree's partner, he disappeared as completely and mysteriously as did New York's Judge Crater over a decade ago. And as in the case of Crater, no trace of Smith ever was found, though Pingree spent thousands of dollars to solve the mystery of the strange disappearance of his partner.

Smith and Stearns ran short of baseball enthusiasm during the latter months of the 1888 season. In one of the smallest cities of the league, they had one of the largest pay rolls. The players were becoming more belligerent, and the Brotherhood War, which broke in 1890, could be seen in the offing. As Richter related, the club had gone through a poor financial season in a year of prosperity; the Detroit owners saw more financial shoals ahead; and one morning Detroit woke up, rubbed its startled eyes, and learned it had been erased from the big-league map.

Across the lake, Cleveland wanted to get back in the league; it had been out since 1884, and Smith and Stearns paved the way for its return. In a series of sensational sales, reminiscent of the later transactions whereby Connie Mack of Philadelphia and Harry Frazee of Boston sold pennant-winning ball players in wholesale lots, Smith and Stearns disposed of the players on the Detroit roster for $45,000, which in 1889 was important money.

The famous "Big Four" of Buffalo and Detroit finally was broken up. Dan Brouthers and Harry Richardson, along with the two catchers Charley Bennett and Charley Ganzel, were sold to Boston; Pittsburgh got the remaining members of the "Big Four"—White and Rowe—and Ned Hanlon, who was to start his famous managerial career there in 1889. The Phillies purchased slugging Sam Thompson, and he was to remain a star on that club for another decade. John Brush's Indianapolis club purchased the crack pitcher, Charley Getzein, though a year later "Getz" joined the "Detroit colony" in Boston. What was left of players and the National League franchise then was disposed of to Cleveland.

The disposal of the franchise brought an end to Detroit major-league baseball, and it was to be thirteen years before it was to return. Many Detroiters were indignant and intensely disappointed when the franchise was sold, and there was sharp criticism of the men who had scattered the famous 1887 Detroit World's Champions to the four winds.

But Detroit had not only enjoyed, but had profited by, its eight-year sojourn in the National League. The team had given the town much publicity, and the club which beat the Browns in the 1887 World's Series made the word "Detroits" a byword in the nation. The city had a magic growth from 1880 to 1890, 116,340 to 205,875, and while baseball wasn't entirely responsible, it deserved quite a big assist.

Frank J. Navin, "Old Poker Face"
Tiger President, 1908-1933

"Wahoo Sam" Crawford

"Smiling Bill" Donovan

⊝ III ⊝

THE DETROITS BECOME
THE TIGERS

I

FOLLOWING THEIR DISAPPEARANCE FROM THE NATIONAL LEAGUE, the Detroits next bobbed up in the International Association, which later became the Eastern League, until Ed Barrow, one of Detroit's early managers, changed its name back to the International League in 1911. It was a loop built largely around Lake Erie and was truly international in character, being made up of three clubs in Canada—Toronto, London, and Hamilton—and five in the States— Detroit, Buffalo, Toledo, Rochester, and Syracuse. The Detroits won two championships while they were in the International Association, 1889 and 1890, but as the league wasn't of very high stature—even for minor-league ball of that period—those flags are never counted when Detroit talks about its pennants.

Detroit then was without league ball for several years. In 1893, Washington was proving a weak sister in the twelve-club National League, and the league was desirous of finding a stronger town to round out its circuit. There were moves in both Detroit and Buffalo to get back into the league, but Detroit's bid evoked no enthusiasm. In the October 14, 1893, issue of the *Sporting News*, Captain W. W. Kerr of Pittsburgh, a member of the National League committee on membership, doused a bucket of ice water on Detroit's hopes of getting back in the big league.

"Detroit has not the remotest chance of getting back into the big league," said the Captain. "It was no stayer when it was a member of the league and sold out at a considerable profit. Buffalo would be a good city if Washington decides to quit, but I would see no sense in leaving Washington merely to go to Detroit."

The Captain did not exactly bat 1.000 as a prophet. He spoke of not getting back into "the big league," for by this time there was only one, the National League and the American Association having merged in 1892 into the one twelve-club league. Yet that very merger was to pave the way for the return of Detroit to the major-league map.

Around the same time that Pittsburgh's Kerr was belittling Detroit as a "big-league stayer," a young adventurous Cincinnati baseball writer, Byron Bancroft Johnson, had other plans for Detroit. Ban was busy reorganizing the Western League. The league had gone under in 1892, year of the so-called Cleveland panic, and had failed to put teams in the field in 1893. So enthusiastic, cherubic Ban, then a young man of thirty, pulled the loose ends together, and put the league back on its feet for the season of 1894.

This date means a lot to the American League, and it has especial significance for Detroit. Later, with the enthusiastic and valued support of Charley Comiskey, a former Johnson buddy in Cincinnati when Commy was manager of the Reds, Johnson was to change the name of the Western League to the American League, and in 1901 expand it into the present major American League of today.

The reason why 1894 should be of especial interest to the Detroit club and its fans is that, of the cities which Ban had in his first Western League of that year, Detroit is the only one which has been continually in the circuit under the first name or the latter. The cities in the 1894 circuit were Detroit, Toledo, Milwaukee, Minneapolis, Indianapolis, Kansas City, Grand Rapids, and Sioux City. Sioux City was shifted to St. Paul in 1895, where Charley Comiskey took charge.

Detroit's games were played in a small park just outside of what then were the easterly city limits (now well within the city) at Helen and Lafayette Boulevard. We read that "Six thousand saw Detroit win its Western League opening game in Toledo, April 25, the Detroits winning by a score of 8 to 7." On May 2, Detroit had its home opening, and neither the score nor the crowd was so good. This time the report was: "Thirty-two hundred cranks saw the opening game of the Western League in Detroit, and incidentally watched Grand Rapids pull a game out of the fire in the eighth." The Detroits lost this one, 4 to 3.

Two days later, May 4, we read this gem: "Detroit would not have been beaten by Grand Rapids if their pitchers had held up a little stiffer, but the Detroits did lose the game, 14 to 11." Those pitchers had more and more trouble holding up a little stiffer, and from May 13 to June 1 didn't win a game. Then we read that Manager-Captain R. J. Glenalvin came on the field with "a smile lighting up his entire countenance. The man has had so few occasions to smile."

And believe it or not, that early Detroit club had a Cobb, George Cobb, a pitcher. There were a few name players in the club. Billy Kreig, the catcher, and Cliff Carroll had been former Washington National League players. Both had been in the Washington box score when Connie Mack broke in with the capital city team as a big-league catcher eight years before. No one got rich in that early Detroit Western League club, with the league's salary limit of $200 a month, which was strictly enforced by young Ban. When the team closed up its shutters in the fall, the Detroits limped home a poor seventh; the club had had difficulty in meeting expenses and few cared whether they would open the shutters again.

2

George Arthur Van Derbeck was president-owner of the club, and after an advance to fifth place in 1895, he engaged George Tweedy Stallings as manager for the 1896 season, and George moved the club up to third. George Stallings, who later was to manage the miracle Boston Braves of 1914, was to write considerable Detroit baseball history around the turn of the century.

Stallings came from a plantation near Haddock, Ga., and the great Cracker State could produce only one George Stallings, as it later could produce only one Ty Cobb. Incidentally the men were great friends during Stallings' lifetime. The son of a Confederate general, Stallings' ancestral home was pretty well shot up by the damyankees, but the family saved enough from the war to give George a splendid military and medical education. He was graduated from the Virginia Military Institute in 1886, and then studied medicine for several years at the College of Physicians and Surgeons at Baltimore. But he liked the pill of the diamond better than the pill of the laboratory, and rather shocked the old Haddock general when he forsook medicine to sign with the old Phillies as a catcher. He later drifted to the minors and came to Detroit in 1896 from Nashville.

George was the Dr. Jekyll and Mr. Hyde of baseball. He probably was the most handsome manager in baseball ever to get into evening clothes. In that attire, he was a suave, cultured Southern gentleman. However, in his baseball clothes, whether he wore a uniform as he did in Detroit, or civilian bench attire as he did later in Boston, he was often a raving maniac.

He was as profane as a Marine cleaning out a nest of Japs at Saipan and knew words and expressions that were new to such hardened old Orioles as McGraw, Jennings, and Robinson. He thought nothing of getting off his bench during the heat of battle and hurling imprecations on friend and foe alike. As a player and manager, he was as superstitious as a Haitian sugar-plantation field hand. He had charms, voodoos, and hexes to meet any and all occasions. He was terribly afraid of the jinx which would attach itself to his team if there were any bits of paper in front of his dugout. Once Josh Devore, the former Giant outfielder, tore up half a newspaper into little scraps, and scattered them all before Stallings' bench. Shouting all the damnations of Haddock on Devore, and threatening to strangle him if he ever got his fingers around his neck, George got down on his knees and personally picked each scrap of paper out of the dirt.

During the historic 1914 drive of his Braves from the cellar in July to a four-straight world's championship in October, he attributed much of his success to a dime "blessed" by a Negro fanatic of Cuba, who called himself the "Negro Pope." Money blessed by him had ten times its face value among his followers. Shortly before the Braves started on their dramatic spurt, a friend back from Cuba handed George the dime, told of its history, and said: "Here's something to bring you luck." At the end of that season, Stallings wouldn't have traded that dime for an amount equivalent to his World's Series slice.

However, for Detroit fans, Stallings' first managerial tenure is especially noteworthy as it was then that the Automobile City's ball club first was called the Tigers. Many persons—even Detroiters—wrongfully associate the nickname with Ty Cobb's early connection with the present American League team. But they were Tigers long before the advent of Ty. Philip J. Reid, a Detroit city editor of the nineties, is credited with first using the term in print.

Stallings took personal credit for it. "When I was first manager out in Detroit, I changed a lot of things," George once told the author. "Among other things I thought maybe changes of uniforms would change their luck. I put striped stockings on them, black and a sort of yellowish brown. I didn't think of their resemblance to a tiger's stripes at the time, but the fans and some of our early writers noticed it, and soon started calling the club the Tigers, and they have been Tigers ever since."

Stallings' first sojourn in Detroit lasted only one season. He did so well with the Tigers in 1896 that he was given his first managerial opportunity in the major leagues. He was put in charge of the Phillies. George Van Derbeck then selected Frank Graves as keeper of the Tiger cage and under the latter's administration the team slipped back to fifth. Already the Tigers had developed the short-comings which later were to plague many Tiger managers, the very antithesis of Mike Gonzalez' report on a rookie, "Good field. No hit!" These Tigers were "Good hit. No field! No pitch!"

In the issue of the *Sporting News* right after the July 4, 1897, games we read a familiar head: "BATTING LIKE FIENDS. The Detroit Tigers Have Suddenly Developed into Terrific Sluggers." It went on to say: "In four straight games, the Tigers have made a total of 92 hits (that's an average of 23 a game) and Steinfeldt, Hines, and Burnett have made a total of 30 hits in their last three games."

Then that Detroit correspondent, who signed himself F.J.J., made a prediction which Tiger fans had good occasion to remember ten years later. "And right here, the club that gets Harry Steinfeldt will not get a gold brick. He is by far the best infielder in the Western League."

Steinfeldt, of course, later became the famous third baseman on that crack Chicago Cub infield of Steinfeldt, Tinker, Evers, and Chance. In 1907, he was to be tough enough to hit .470 against the Tigers in Detroit's first modern World's Series.

In his gossipy newsletter, F.J.J. also apparently got considerable pleasure out of the fact that the Detroit club had just signed Tom Delahanty, brother of the famous Ed, and one of the five Delahantys to reach the majors. "The thought came to the mind of President Van Derbeck: 'I wonder if we could get Tom Delahanty.' A telegram was despatched to the brother of the mighty Philadelphian. Well, the next day Del was covering second base, and covering it in good shape, too. That was Friday, and by Saturday it was Team Captain Delahanty."

F.J.J.'s closing paragraphs give such a good picture of Detroit baseball of the 90's that they are included:

A funny little instance happened at Grand Rapids on July 5 (the holiday was celebrated that day, a Monday). During the morning game, the heat was intense. The sun was beating down hot enough to burn the hair off a man's head, and Mike Trost (the Detroit catcher) was a sight. The sweat of honest toil was pouring out of Mike in streams and he couldn't stem the flow to save his neck. At the end of the fifth inning,

Mike was seen to disappear around the end of the grandstand and make his way to the gate where Van Derbeck (the boss) was keeping tab on the quarters.

When within a few feet of the magnate, Mike broke out: "Say, got a towel?" "No, what would I want with a towel?" asked Van. "I don't know," came back from the catcher, "but I thought maybe you might have one. Look at me; don't I need one?" Van handed over his handkerchief, and Mike took it with a look of grief and scorn combined that would make a corpse smile. Before the afternoon game, Mike saw to it that every man on the team had a towel.

Even if Steinfeldt, Hines, and Burnett made 30 hits in three games, none of this trio was the batting star of the team. As was the case with Sam Thompson of the early Detroits, the man was to be found in right field, and his name also was Sam—Sam Dungan. He had previously played with Chicago and Louisville in the National League, and came to Detroit in midseason of 1894. He remained until 1900, when he was shifted to Kansas City. After the American League blossomed into a major, Dungan played with Washington and Milwaukee. Like Thompson, this Sam was a hitting fool, and during his stay in Detroit, he either led the league or was the guy the other fellow had to beat. In 1894 and 1895 he hit .447 and .424, respectively, and that was well after the year in which bases on balls were scored as base hits.

Anthony J. Mullane, another colorful chap, was the Tiger manager in 1898. He was known as "Tony" and "The Count," the latter from his big handle-bar mustache and distinguished appearance. Though born in Ireland, he had no taste for Irish whisky and was outstanding in his day because he touched neither liquor nor tobacco. He was an ambidextrous pitcher, who pitched the first no-hit game in the old major American Association and then won a twenty-inning affair in the National League. In addition, he was a hard hitter, and could play any position. But baseball was only one of his accomplishments; he was an expert on skates, either ice or roller, a fine boxer, and an all-round musician. After leaving baseball, he served for years on the Chicago police force, retiring in 1926. The Count retained his interest in baseball until he died at the age of 85 years in 1944.

Mullane's Spanish-American War year was no howling success, and the club fell back another notch, to sixth. The season was mainly interesting to Detroit fans from the fact that it gave them a brief opportunity to see that famous child of nature, Rube Waddell, the game's greatest left-hander, in a Tiger uniform. At that time Louisville, owned by Barney Dreyfuss, was in the twelve-club National League, and they farmed Waddell to Detroit, or sent him there for punishment or reform.

Waddell had been pitching great ball for strong independent clubs in western Pennsylvania in 1897. Fred Clarke, Dreyfuss' manager, heard of him, and offered Waddell a contract. I WON'T PITCH FOR YOU UNLESS YOU PAY ME TWENTY-FIVE DOLLARS A GAME, wired Rube. WE'LL SIGN YOU FOR THE SEASON, AND GIVE YOU FIVE HUNDRED DOLLARS FOR SIGNING WITH US," wired back Clarke. Had he known Waddell as he knew him later, Fred would have been a little more careful with his bonuses.

Anyway, the Rube reported to the Louisville club in the usual Waddell manner—at 2 A.M. in Washington, where the Colonels were playing. The hotel clerk told him the number of Clarke's room, but said he had orders not to disturb him. The Rube took care of that little disturbing detail himself, almost pounding down Clarke's door. "It's George Waddell, your new pitcher," he shouted.

"Go away," yelled Clarke.

"I got to see you; it's important," insisted Rube.

Clarke then had a brilliant idea. "Why don't you go down and introduce yourself to the other players," he said.

Rube was back at 3:30 and pounded Clarke's door again, saying: "I done what you told me. I've waked them all up, and introduced myself to the Colonels. All but one, the man in Room 128. He never heard me. There must be something wrong with that guy; maybe he's dead."

He wasn't dead; the man was Dummy Hoy, the deaf-mute outfielder.

Clarke never had the patience that Connie Mack later had with the eccentric southpaw in Milwaukee and Philadelphia. After the Rube pulled some more of his quaint peccadillos with Louisville early in the season of 1898, Clarke sent him to Detroit, perhaps with the hope that the teetotaler Count Mullane would have a restraining effect on him.

Waddell didn't wear his Tiger stripes long, pitching in only nine Detroit games. He was credited with 4 victories against 4 defeats and struck out 31. Then he got into fresh trouble—a little matter of drinking—and the Louisville club fined him $50. Now Rube wasn't going to let anyone fine him $50 at long range. He skipped across the border, joined a semipro outfit at Chatham, Ontario, and soon Detroit was hearing new stories of his astounding feats. He beat Dunnville, Ontario, 1 to 0, striking out 17, tossing out 9 men at first base, and producing the hit that won the game. He went right back at Dunnville the next afternoon, gave up 3 hits and fanned 20.

Detroit fans were to see much of Waddell in subsequent years, but he then wore the uniform of the opposition.

Stallings' stay with Philadelphia was brief. In his two seasons at the helm of the Phillies, his clubs of 1897 and 1898 finished tenth and sixth, respectively. When he went to the Quaker City, he succeeded Billy Shettsline as manager, and after the 1898 season, the Philadelphia owners, Al Reach and Colonel Rogers, decided to give the job back to Shettsline.

Stallings, later known as the Big Chief, also returned to his old job in Detroit. After two second-division seasons under Frank Graves and Tony Mullane, George Van Derbeck welcomed back the Georgian with open arms. George Tweedy Stallings again effected a decided improvement, as the Tigers advanced to third place in 1899, and Sam Dungan of Detroit led the Ban Johnson hit parade with a reduced average of .347. Fourth on the list was a young left-handed slugger from Wahoo, Neb., Sam Crawford, who played for the Grand Rapids club and hit balls to right field with terrific vigor. Detroit was to get rather well acquainted with Wahoo Sam in the years that followed. Stallings, himself, still felt chipper enough to play 91 games in the outfield.

When Stallings returned from Philadelphia, he brought with him a brash, fresh little infielder, hard as nails and as tough as an Apache. His name was Norman "Kid" Elberfeld. Sam Crane, a New York sports writer, later was to give him a still more descriptive appellation, "the Tabasco Kid." Elberfeld, inserted into the Tiger line-up at shortstop, quickly became a Detroit favorite. The Tabasco Kid probably gave more base runners the hip or shoulder than anyone of his size in the game. "I had to be rough and tough, or everyone would have taken advantage of me and pushed me around," Elberfeld told the writer in Florida, years after his retirement. So, the Kid pushed them around first.

Elberfeld always was proud that a Philadelphia National scout had picked him in preference to the great Honus Wagner. While Stallings was managing the Phillies, one of the pitchers, Con Lucid, was sent to scout Hans Wagner, then shortstop of the Paterson club of the Atlantic League. Con scouted Honus in a game with Richmond, the club for which Elberfeld was the shortstop. Lucid's report was: "Wagner big and clumsy; too awkward to play big-league ball. Recommend purchase of Elberfeld, shortstop of Richmond team. He is fast and aggressive, and should make National League grade." The Phillies passed up Wagner, and purchased Elberfeld.

☙ IV ☙

DETROIT IS BACK IN
A MAJOR LEAGUE

I

BAN JOHNSON, LIVE-WIRE PRESIDENT OF THE WESTERN LEAGUE, BY this time thirty-five years old, began dreaming dreams and seeing visions. At the turn of the century, he could see that his circuit could be of far greater scope and importance than the Western League over which he had presided for six years.

The National League helped along that vision. Led by Andy Freedman, the Tammany politician who owned the New York Giants, the National League was reduced from twelve clubs back to its original eight. "Lop off the dead wood" was Andy's slogan; so the league lopped off Cleveland and Louisville in the West and Washington and Baltimore in the East.

That gave Johnson and Comiskey, his able lieutenant in St. Paul, fresh vigorous ideas. The league officially changed its name from the Western League to the American League; Comiskey moved his St. Paul club to the south side of Chicago and revived the old nickname of White Stockings, while the Grand Rapids franchise was shifted to the vacated territory in Cleveland. Two years before, the league had expanded as far east as Buffalo.

The National League didn't take particularly kindly to the airs of the "old Western under a highfalutin name," as one of the old leaguers put it. In other words, a rose or a stinkweed, under some other name, was still a rose or a stinkweed. There was also a question of veracity between Ban Johnson and Jim Hart, the Chicago National owner, on the right of Comiskey to move into Hart's Chicago domain. Ban said Jim had given his consent, and Hart just as stubbornly denied that he ever had approved St. Paul's transfer. Both gentlemen had more liberal ideas on the subject of liquid refreshment than old Tony Mullane, and when they first threshed it

28

out, they may have decided it was "two other fellows" who did the talking.

There even was talk of a war then and there, but eventually an agreement was signed by the presidents of the two leagues, whereby the transfers to Chicago and Cleveland were approved, Hart was permitted to draft two players from Comiskey's new White Sox, and Ban Johnson promised to support the old National agreement.

Detroit naturally was pleased over the new developments. The American League did not yet claim to be a major league, but the reduction of the National League from twelve clubs to eight threw some seventy-five players on the market, and Ban Johnson's clubs grabbed most of them. Detroit knew the city was in for the best brand of ball since the city was last represented in the National League. The League in 1900 was made up of the following clubs and they finished in the order in which they are named: Chicago, Milwaukee, Indianapolis, Detroit, Kansas City, Cleveland, Buffalo, Minneapolis. Stallings' Tigers finished fourth with a percentage of .514.

Big George pretty well made over his club in accordance with Ban Johnson's new deal for the American League. He brought in such hard-hitting outfielders as Ducky Holmes and Dick Cooley, catchers Lew McAllister and Jack Ryan, and a chunky little third baseman, "Doc" Jim Casey. Doc Casey remained a well-known figure around Detroit for years. A dentist by profession, Doc ran a Woodward Avenue drugstore until the depression caught up with him. At the time of his death in 1936, he was a guard in Detroit's Municipal Building.

Comiskey then managed the new Chicago champions himself, and Connie Mack still had the club in Milwaukee. "Wattie" Watkins of the old Detroit World's Champions of 1887 ran things in Indianapolis. Players who soon were to bring distinction to the Tiger stripes of Detroit came calling in other uniforms, Herman Schaefer and Bill Coughlin with Kansas City and Charley O'Leary in the white socks of Comiskey. Such other 1900 American Leaguers who called in Detroit—Rube Waddell, Socks Seybold, Topsy Hartsel, Roy Patterson, Dave Fultz, Ossie Schreckengost, Mike Powers— showed that even then the league was a quasi-major.

However, the fiery Stallings, in his effort to do well with the Tigers in the expanded league, was in constant trouble with Ban Johnson, who was waging a fight for clean baseball. We read in one place where "George T. Stallings is on the bench in disgrace, paying the penalty for the abuse of the laws of his organization," and in another: "President Ban Johnson is in Minneapolis, looking into an outbreak between Walter Wilmot and Perry Warden. The outlook is that Manager Wilmot will meet the same stern discipline which Manager Stallings got when he brooked the displeasure of the league head."

"Stallings, you've got to let my umpires alone, or get out of this league; I won't stand for your conduct," Ban lectured the Tiger manager.

"I only want my rights," insisted George. "Those fatheads you have working for you are costing me game after game."

"They're only calling their plays as they see them, and not through your prejudiced eyes," replied Johnson. "And do not speak disrespectfully of my umpires in my presence. Remember, I have warned you."

And though Ban Johnson was rather a convivial person, especially around club owners and baseball writers, he was active in driving the rumpots out of the game. The following paragraph appeared in a July, 1900, issue of the *Detroit Journal:* "Ban Johnson is the only baseball magnate who is not afraid to march in the van and be a general. He is advocating strict temperance principles for players and doesn't hesitate to say that the day is not far away when booze will be banished and there will be no place in the game for those who do not control their appetites for stimulants."

2

A real cloud darkened the baseball skies after that first American League season of 1900. It soon was to break into the worst war of baseball history, a war which again would make Detroit a full-fledged big-league town.

There still was a lot of idle big-league territory around, and there was a move on to revive the old major American Association, which had been absorbed by the National League in 1892. A. A. promoters had especially covetous eyes on Philadelphia and the two vacated National League cities in the East, Washington and Baltimore. In fact, John McGraw, then with the St. Louis Cardinals but a former famous Oriole, had been offered an American Association franchise in Baltimore.

No doubt for years Ban Johnson had had his vision of the American League holding its place in the sun as a major-league rival of the National. But these American Association moves stirred him into quick action. He held an important meeting in Chicago, October 14,

1900, which also was attended by Comiskey, Connie Mack, Charles Somers, and Tom Manning. Johnson was not too sure then of Detroit's place in the new setup, and there was no Detroit representative at the meeting. A five-year agreement between the clubs of the old Western League, by this time the American, expired on that date. Ban washed up the affairs of the old league, and on his recommendation a motion was entertained to form a new major American League which would expand into the East.

He announced that new clubs would be placed in Philadelphia, Washington, Baltimore, and in a fourth city in the East to be selected later. Johnson said he would try to get the consent of the National League, but with or without that consent he would move East.

At its November annual meeting in New York, the National League ignored a letter by Johnson, stating the conditions which had impelled him to make the moves, especially beating the promoters who were trying to pump life back into the old Association. That action precipitated the war. The American League moved into Boston as the fourth Eastern city, where Charley Somers took over the franchise. Mack, the former Milwaukee manager, was given the Philadelphia club, and he induced Ben Shibe, a sporting goods manufacturer, to come in with him. McGraw was handed the Baltimore franchise, where he interested a Democratic city boss, John J. Mahon, father-in-law of Joe Kelly, Hanlon's left fielder on the famous Orioles. The Washington club went to Tom Manning. In spreading East, the young American League jettisoned Kansas City, Indianapolis, Minneapolis, and Buffalo.

Johnson ordered raids to start on the National League, and Connie Mack, McGraw, Jimmy McAleer, Jim Collins, and Clark Griffith were his leading raiders. Griff had just jumped from the Chicago Nationals to take over the management of Comiskey's South Side team in Chicago. They came up with some super-dupers, too: such stars as Nap Lajoie, Jesse Burkett, Joe McGinnity, Cy Young, Lew Criger, Lave Cross, Wilbert Robinson, Roger Bresnahan, and Mike Donlin. Stallings, the Detroit manager, also knew many of the National League players, but he already had a pretty good club, and didn't have to start from scratch as did Mack in Philadelphia, Collins in Boston, McGraw in Baltimore, and Manning in Washington. George's biggest acquisitions were Kid Gleason, the second baseman, who jumped the New York Giants; pitcher Frank Owen, who later starred with the White Sox; and the Berlin, Germany-born catcher, Fred Buelow, who had been the property of the St. Louis Nationals in 1900.

Detroit naturally was steamed up over the ambitious and bellicose plans of Ban Johnson and his fighting henchmen. Van Derbeck had faded from the Detroit baseball picture, not entirely of his own choosing, and James D. Burns, a Detroit hotel man and sheriff of Wayne County, was the president-owner as the Tigers returned to big-league ball.

Back in February, 1901, there was considerable talk of a National League-backed American Association team entering Detroit in an effort to block Ban Johnson's team. A man named Koch was its front; he picked up a few well-to-do supporters, and tried to lease a piece of ground for a ball park. On February 16, 1901, a spokesman for the A. A. movement said: "We are going to buy Jimmy Burns out, and not allow another American League game in Detroit." That was somewhat of an overstatement, for by February 23, B. F. Wright, the *Sporting News's* Detroit correspondent, had this to say:

There is no one here who inclines to an American Association club except Van Derbeck, who has an axe to grind, and the board of directors of the D. A. C. The owners of property around the park have united in a petition to the mayor to withhold a license, and have retained counsel to bring injunction proceedings unless the project is dropped. Any one who backed an American Association club in Detroit would have no more chance than a prizefighter in Cincinnati.

We don't know what chance a prizefighter had with the Cincinnati burghers of 1901, but the A. A. backers must have become pretty well discouraged, for a few weeks later, we read that: "Two thirds of the grandstand at Burns Park is sold out for the Tiger opening game of April 24."

3

When Detroit had its coming-out party as an American League major-league city, it saw a game fully fitting to the occasion and to the great ball club which from then on was to make history as "the slugging Tigers." They did more than sell that remaining third of the grandstand, as standees around the park brought the crowd to around 9,000.

The opponents of the Tigers that day were the Milwaukee club, led by Hughie Duffy, who had jumped the Boston Nationals. Hughie's .438 batting average with the 1894 Bostons still is the National League all-time high. For eight innings, most of the Detroit rooters must have voted the contest very much on the dreary side.

Detroit was trailing, 13 to 4, when the Tigers came up to bat for the ninth inning. Every Detroit manager since then should have had that box score nailed in the locker of every player, with the legend: "See what happens if you don't give up," for Stallings' club scored ten runs in its half of the ninth and pulled out the ball game, 14 to 13. It was the greatest opening day rally in baseball history. Detroit knocked out 19 hits that day, with First Baseman Frank Dillon getting 4 doubles. That remains an American League record today, though Billy Werber tied it in 1935.

The Detroit line-up that day was as follows: Jim "Doc" Casey, third base; Jim Barrett, center field; Bill "Kid" Gleason, second base; Bill "Ducky" Holmes, right field; Frank Dillon, first base; Norman "Kid" Elberfeld, shortstop; Bill Nance, left field; Fred Buelow, catcher; Roscoe Miller and Emil Frisk, pitchers. Other 1901 Tigers who rounded out the team were pitchers Joe Yeager, Jack Cronin, Eddie Siever, Frank Owens; catchers Lew McAllister and Al Shaw, and infielder Crackett. That second-base combination of the two Kids—Gleason and Elberfeld—not only was one of the best in the game, but it probably holds the all-time championship for toughness at the midway.

Not much more than a week after the Tigers pulled out their home opener with that spirited ten-run ninth-inning rally, they took part in another historic game, May 2, in Chicago, in which Clark Griffith, later the venerable gentlemanly head of the Senators, was the villain.

Griffith was pitching against Frisk of the Felines and after eight innings, Chicago led, 5 to 2. The Tigers started one of those ninth-inning rallies which were becoming a habit. Everybody was taking a toe hold and driving Griff's dinky curve to the fence. Griffith, who was manager, captain, and pitcher, moaned on the mound, and Stallings jeered from the bench. It was a cool early spring day, and darkness was fast engulfing the park. Five Detroit runs were in, putting the Tigers ahead 7 to 5, when Griffith began stalling for time, perhaps hoping the complete inning could not be played. "Get in there and pitch, you yellow ———," yelled Stallings.

For once the Big Chief had an ally in the arbiter, Tommy Connolly, the single umpire, who was working the game from his position behind Griffith. Tommy tried to get Griff to hurry up; instead he became even more dilatory. There were things he had to discuss with his catcher, his first baseman, and even his right fielder. After several warnings, Connolly forfeited the game to Detroit, 9 to 0.

We'll let the *Chicago Herald-Record* reporter take it on from there:

Griffith, who had twice been benched in the series, rushed forward with angry protests, his right arm raised threateningly. Some of the spectators near said Griffith struck Connolly, but the latter said after the game that he had not been hit. Isbell and other players rushed in, "Issy" grabbing his manager, and the residue forming around the umpire. If "Griff" had any hostile intentions, he changed quickly when he saw the temper of the crowd, and with the others turned toward the shouting throng, among whom a few irresponsible persons were yelling, "Mob him! Lynch the umpire!" and warned them against violence. The policemen on the grounds were by this time on the scene and danger of violence and bodily harm to Connolly quickly subsided.

On the side line, Stallings was having great fun. Having won the game on the field, 7 to 5, and by forfeit, 9 to 0, he was in a mood to enjoy Griffith's rage and discomfiture. "Don't hit the little fellow, Griff. Ban won't like that at all," he taunted Griffith. And, after the police quieted the near riot, George continued to shout: "Now we'll see what Ban Johnson does to his pet."

4

One thing is certain: George Stallings never was Ban Johnson's pet. Though George's Tigers finished a good third, beating out the Athletics for the show place on the last day of the season, Johnson wasn't satisfied with the Big Chief's conduct on the field or the way he ran the Detroit ball club. George's fiery temper got him into one scrape after another. Stallings and John McGraw, manager of the Orioles, were supposedly the leading culprits in Ban's fight for clean baseball and for upholding the sovereignty of the umpires.

There was tension between Stallings and Johnson during most of the season, and then Stallings fell out with his associate, Sheriff Jim Burns. It turned into a beautiful row, with recriminations and accusations on all sides. George accused Jim of putting something over on him, and the Sheriff made the same accusations against the Georgian. The books of the club were exhibited by Secretary McNamara, and the Detroit papers of that period sizzled with red-hot statements by Ban Johnson, Burns, Stallings, and McNamara. "Burns is a hell of a nice fellow, but I am a ———," George was quoted as saying to one newspaperman.

34

Ban Johnson came to Detroit on November 13, and the fur really started to fly. Ban made the immediate positive statement that George Stallings must go. He never had cared for George to begin with; he said that when the Detroit club was taken out of George Van Derbeck's hands, the stock was issued to Jim Burns and not to Stallings, and for that reason George never had been taken into the councils of the American League.

However, the most serious charge that Ban made against the Detroit manager was that in the previous summer Stallings had entertained a proposition for the Detroit club to jump to the National League and wreck the new American League. Upon this point, and the financial charge said to have been made to Johnson by Stallings, a friend of Burns made the following public explanation:

"Stallings put a proposition before Burns for the transfer of the club to the National League, and Burns was very mad about it. That was the origin of all the trouble between Burns and Stallings. Burns then decided to take everything possible into his own hands, and as he was the treasurer, clamped upon the funds. He has got the money put away where it is safe, and it will be produced at the proper time. Stallings will get back every dollar that he put into the club; and that wasn't so very much."

From other sources we hear that Stallings was the majority stockholder, and the club's biggest creditor, and as such threatened to throw the club into bankruptcy. *Sporting Life,* of that period, said he mentioned $22,500 as his price to get out. It reached such a pass that Johnson said that if it became necessary to head off Stallings, he would take the club out of Detroit and shift it to another city. He also explained to Detroit newspapermen that in order to keep objectionable owners and managers out of the American League, 51 per cent of the stock of each club had been placed in his hands, and that there could be no change in the ownership or management of any club without his consent. That condition existed for years, and explained the czaristic powers which Ban enjoyed in his league up to the coming of Judge Landis.

Johnson eventually forced a sale of the stock owned by Burns and Stallings to Samuel F. Angus, a Detroit insurance man and railroad contractor. A liberal cash settlement was made with Stallings, but George remained in Ban's doghouse permanently.

Seven years later, Frank Farrell, owner of the early New York Yankees—then the Highlanders—without advising Johnson, signed Stallings to a New York contract as his manager.

Johnson, who had a memory like an elephant, and was as unforgiving, was furious when he heard about it. He summoned Farrell to Chicago.

"What do you mean by signing that man Stallings to a contract?" he shouted. "You know he isn't wanted in this league."

"That Detroit business happened before I was in the league; it took place during a baseball war, and I thought it long since has been forgotten."

"Forgotten nothing," stormed Ban. "I hope you didn't sign him for longer than a year."

"I signed him to a two-year contract," said Farrell.

"Well, at the end of that period, that contract is not to be renewed under any circumstances; do you understand?" And though Stallings lifted New York's 1908 tail-ender to second in 1910, he was released in the closing weeks of the latter season to make room for Hal Chase, who quickly wrecked a promising Yankee contender. But Ban had had his way.

5

About the time that the old Western League blossomed into the American League, the Detroit club moved from its old park at Helen Avenue and Lafayette Boulevard, and located at Michigan and Trumbull Avenues, the site of present Briggs Stadium. It was the site of the old Haymarket, and originally was paved with cobblestones. Afterwards, it was known as Woodbridge Grove. When it was transformed for baseball purposes, only a few inches of loam were spread over the cobblestones. Balls often took all sorts of crazy bounces and hops, and gave the players plenty of alibis when they failed to come up with grounders. "It hit another cobble," was a familiar expression around the park. The field was named Bennett Field, after the famous early catcher of the Detroits who lost his legs in the railroad accident.

Early Bennett Field had seats for only 8,500, even as late as the championship year of 1907. The club had another worry in wildcat bleachers which were constructed on property fronting on both Cherry Street and National Avenue. The owners cut in on the Detroit club's slender revenue by charging 15 cents for these "outside" vantage points. On some dull days, the charge would go as low as a nickel. The wildcat bleachers eventually were removed as a hazard by the fire marshal.

On Sunday, in the early years of the century the club played its games at what was known as Burns Park, named after the early club president. This park was on Dix Avenue on the west side, just outside of Detroit's westerly line in Springwells County. It adjoined the stockyards, and early fans were treated to the same odors that Comiskey used to throw in with a Sunday admission ticket in Chicago. Michigan then had a law against Sunday ball, and it was strictly enforced in Detroit. Of course, Springwells Township hadn't seceded from the state, but the enforcement officers over the line weren't so particular and winked at the goings on in Burns Park.

The park's grandstand seated only about 1,000; the rest of the crowd sat in the bleachers or stood in the rangy outfield. After a Sunday game virtually the whole attendance descended on the bar at Garvey's Stockyard Hotel, located next to the ball orchard. However, Ban Johnson later discouraged this Sunday bootleg ball in the Detroit suburbs.

⊖ V ⊖

BASEBALL'S

MR. POKER FACE

I

IN SAMUEL ANGUS' INSURANCE OFFICE, THERE WAS A YOUNG BOOK-keeper named Frank J. Navin. When Angus moved into baseball, he brought Frank over with him to help with the Detroit club's books. He always knew how to figure. Navin wasn't a Detroiter by birth, being born in Adrian, Mich., in 1871, but Frank Navin was to become Mr. Baseball in Detroit. No man in the city's baseball history contributed more to the development of the Tigers from one of the poor waifs of major-league ball to the American League's prize breadwinner than this quiet, unassuming son of Adrian. What Ty Cobb became to Detroit on the playing field, Navin was in the front office. He was to baseball in Detroit what Connie Mack is to the game in Philadelphia, Clark Griffith in Washington, Sam Breadon in St. Louis, and what John McGraw was to the sport in New York and Barney Dreyfuss in Pittsburgh.

Frank Navin was one of the real giants of the national game, and when he died in 1935 a few weeks after achieving his life's goal and great ambition—the winning of the World's Championship—he was vice-president of the American League and its outstanding representative. After the retirement of Ban Johnson in 1927, Navin became the junior league's first figure. The voice of Ernest Barnard, Ban's successor, was not as influential in the game's council halls as that of Vice-president Navin, and young Will Harridge had not yet grown to the stature of the Detroiter. All three of the American League presidents, Johnson, Barnard, and Harridge, leaned heavily on Navin for counsel, as did the late commissioner, Judge Landis.

Navin was known as baseball's poker face. He was regarded by many as a cold, dispassionate man. Ball players, and others who had dealings with him, at times have said: "That guy has ice water in

38

his veins." But his poker face was a mask. Underneath was a warm friendly man, exceedingly loyal, who loved life, had a whimsical sense of humor, and was one of the most charitable of club owners.

A former member of his beloved Tigers had to leave a pretty bad record behind him not to have received help from his old boss if the player was in need. In fact, even if he had left the club under strained circumstances, Navin was quick to forgive and carried no grudge. One of the pitchers of his early championship team, Edgar Willett, cast his luck with the Federal League in 1914. The Feds were regarded as an "outlaw" organization, and it cost the major leagues several million dollars to get them out of the field. However, when Willett was in tough straits late in his life, Navin not only gave the pitcher financial help while he was alive, buying him a horse, cows, and a plow, but helped Willett's widow after Edgar's death.

He rarely smiled, seldom laughed, and couldn't have cried if he had wished to. He showed little emotion at a ball game, whether the Tigers were winning with a late-inning rally or were being routed, 11 to 0. He kept all of his emotions well hidden and under the surface. "I wish I could let my feelings out like some other men," he once said, "but I just can't."

At another time, talking with sports writers he said: "I guess I got that set look on my face that you fellows like to kid me about from my long dealings with ball players. You never know what strange propositions they will pop at you, and you have to be ready for any emergency."

2

Navin probably developed that poker face as a young man when he helped augment his earnings by serving as a croupier in a gaming house. He looked on with apparent disinterest as he raked in the losers' chips and paid the comparatively few winners. Who then knew what emotions ran through his being, emotions that he could not afford to show in public?

Next to baseball, his great love in the way of sports was horses and racing. And, despite Judge Landis' strong objection to a baseball man having the slightest association with racing, Frank Navin retained his love of thoroughbreds to the grave. He once owned a stable of race horses, and Mrs. Navin, his widow, ran a stable until a few years ago. One of her pet horses was "Ball Player." Navin had a stock farm near Lexington, Ky., and while he went there for rest and diversion, he invariably left word in Detroit to have his baseball telephone calls transferred to Lexington.

Though he was generally considered a baseball conservative, that really was only one side of his nature. Navin actually loved to gamble, and to take chances. He studied horses, knew them, and was a cool, calculating bettor on the track. He made his own selections, and didn't pay much attention to tips or hunches. One day he had a young horse figured to win, and put a fairly large sum on the beast at 8 to 1. He stood to lose $5,000, and win $40,000 if his judgment was correct. It was the first race of the program; as the barrier went up, it knocked the jockey off the horse and the animal never left the box. With no show of emotion, Frank said: "I wonder what's good in the second."

However, sitting on his emotions through the years wasn't conducive to good health. Friends said: "If Frank let out a good yell once in a while, or enjoyed a hearty laugh, he'd feel better." For the last fifteen years of his life, Navin was under the care of a stomach specialist, who recomemnded a restricted diet and for the club owner to keep away from all emotional excitement except watching his beloved Tigers. He knew if he told Frank to keep away from his Tigers, Navin would have engaged another specialist.

In 1930, five years before his death, his physician gave him a heart-to-heart talk. "Frank, if you want to stick around for a while, you'll have to get out of baseball and live a quiet and peaceful life. I strongly urge you to sell the Detroit ball club."

"I couldn't think of doing that," Navin replied.

Repeating the doctor's dire prediction if he didn't get out of the game, Navin said: "Well, boys, I'll stick around until we win a World's Championship. Then maybe I'll give a little thought to his advice." When that time came there was little time left to heed it.

3

Navin first showed his poker face in Adrian, April 18, 1871, where he was one of a large family, the offspring of Irish-born parents. An older brother, Thomas Navin, preceded him to Detroit, where Tom became a prominent lawyer and a power in Michigan Republican politics. Tom always was particularly fond of and proud of his younger brother, Frank, and helped him in his formative years. The Navins always went in strong for family ties. When Frank was the opulent president-owner of the Tigers in later years, the club's secretary and business manager was nephew Charles F. Navin, and another nephew, Arthur T. Sheahan, was road secretary.

Frank Navin graduated from a business college and later from the Detroit College of Law. He was admitted to the bar, but never followed the legal profession. As a young man he ran for justice of the peace, but despite Tom's influence, there were too many Democrats in his district and he was defeated. Had he won this election, baseball probably never would have heard of Frank Navin, but the defeat at the polls ruined a budding political career and sent Frank looking for opportunity in new fields.

While he was going to business and law schools at night, he worked for a while for the city of Detroit and then took a job with Sam Angus at $40 a month, selling insurance. Frank wasn't too good a salesman, but he could make figures stand up and say "Uncle," so Angus moved him into the inner office. And it wasn't strange that Navin should ask permission to wrestle with the figures of his problem ball club.

During the early struggling days of the Tigers in the American League, Navin was one of the men who had real faith in the future of Detroit baseball. Perhaps he had an Irish psychic sense, and even at the turn of the century visualized what the 20's, 30's, and 40's held in store, not only for the city of Detroit, but for its baseball club. And he never weakened in his faith and vision.

As Navin moved from bookkeeper to the "works" behind the club, he frequently was accused of being tight and operating very close to the vest. When Detroit won its early pennants, they said the Tigers were an underpaid team of champions, much as they said it of Sam Breadon's Cardinal pennant winners of recent years. In his early years he had to fight Bill Yawkey on the matter of salaries, because the money for fatter pay envelopes just didn't come through the turnstiles. Over the years, some players called him "hard-boiled," "a tough guy to deal with," and "a nickel-nurser," but on the whole his players liked and respected him, and he did not have nearly as many salary squabbles as other clubs.

"No business can pay out more than it takes in," he used to say, and if the salaries of some of the early Tiger heroes would dismay ball players and fans of today, so would the salaries paid to Christy Mathewson, Mordecai Brown, Chief Bender, and Eddie Plank forty years ago. There were many times in the early days when Navin operated on a very thin margin, especially after he took over full

41

control of the club, but as he increased the size of his park and his personal fortune, his players shared in his new opulence.

Frequently he would go out of his way for ball players, his own as well as others. Once Frank Isbell, second baseman of the Chicago White Sox, in his fading years, tried to get his release from Charley Comiskey, the owner of the Chicago club, so he could accept a chance to become manager and part owner of his home-town team in Wichita, Kansas. The Old Roman declined to give Frank his release, saying: "I can't get waivers from other clubs in the league, and so long as other clubs think you are American League material, I still can use you."

Navin heard about it, and wrote to all the other club presidents of the American League, asking whether they had held up waivers on Isbell. After all replied in the negative, Frank sent the report to Comiskey. Not long afterward Isbell got his chance as owner-manager of the Wichita club.

"He was one of the most tolerant men I have known," Harry Salsinger, veteran sports editor of the *Detroit News,* once wrote of him. "I never saw him really indignant about anyone or anything. A man whom he considered his true friend and whom he trusted implicitly turned crook and defrauded him of a fortune. 'Well, I guess he was up against it and had to have the money,' was Mr. Navin's only comment."

In discussing the fickleness of fans, who root their heads off for a player one day and jeer him the next, Navin once said: "It's foolish to get mad at the fans. Of course, you can't expect gratitude from them any more than you would from your children for bringing them up decently. The fans are all right, only they've got to do just so much nagging, riding the players, riding the umpires, riding the management. It's all part of their fun. And after all, baseball belongs to them. It is their game, and it is their ball team. And, as a club owner, I know I couldn't live without them."

He rarely found fault with a player. But one thing he wouldn't excuse was stupidity or laziness, and lack of hustle.

Umpires drew most of his wrath, because he felt they should know better. And every now and then, he really would bear down on one of the arbiters. Brick Owens caught it particularly when he called Cochrane out at third base in the sixth game of the 1934 Tiger-Cardinal World's Series. It had much to do with preventing the Detroits from winning in six games; they eventually were defeated in a seventh.

Billy Evans, formerly a great umpire and then general manager of the Cleveland club, called on him the night of the game. He found Navin exhausted, broken-hearted, and bitter at Owens.

Seeking to cheer him up a bit, Evans said: "Yes, you got beat today, Frank, but that means a seventh game and some $50,000 extra for you."

Navin jumped up from the sofa on which he was reclining. "To hell with $50,000," he said with his eyes blazing. "I'd give the $50,000 and five times that much to have won today. I've been waiting thirty-five years to see Detroit win a World's Championship, and here we have one within our grasp, and that umpire blows it for us."

He had some strong favorites among his ball players. He admired and respected Ty Cobb as a ball player, but did not have the same affection for the mighty Tyrus as for some of his other players. He had a high regard for Tommy Bridges, a later-day pitcher, and his aggressive catcher-manager, Mickey Cochrane. One time a writer ventured to remark: "Mr. Navin, don't you regard Charley Gehringer as one of baseball's all-time greatest second basemen?" "He *is* baseball's greatest second baseman," Navin replied.

However, his favorite ball player of his many years in Detroit was "Smiling Bill" Donovan, sometimes also called "Wild Bill." He had two pictures of Donovan in his private office. Sometimes he used to stand before the picture and look at it with real admiration. "There was a pitcher," he would say. "Yes, there was a pitcher. What a heart!"

When George Moriarty, a former Detroit third baseman and manager, was one of the umpires in the third Tiger-Cub World's Series in 1935, he was in one close play after another, and called them as he saw them, in favor of the Tigers. A Cub partisan, seated in a box near Navin, yelled: "Moriarty, you're a thief."

Navin arose in his own box, and called back: "George Moriarty is not a thief. And don't you ever say that again. There isn't a more honest man in the world."

4

In view of the manner in which night ball has spread in baseball, it is interesting now to recall that Frank Navin was dead against it and saw in it the ruination of the great game he loved. "If night baseball ever gets a real foothold in big-league parks, it will be the beginning of the end for the major leagues," Navin remarked a few months before his death.

Perhaps the spirit of Navin still lives in Detroit, for the club was one of the few in the majors at the start of the 1946 season that would not play night games in its park. And the club took pride in the fact that its great attendance of 1945, just under the league record, was compiled with day ball, helped by only seven twilight contests.

"Second division clubs usually are colorless and listless, and don't draw night or day," said Navin in 1935. "First division clubs don't need it. That has been proved time and time again. Night ball wouldn't help Philadelphia and Washington [Connie Mack and Clark Griffith now would dispute that] and I would be against them, or any of our clubs attempting it."

Navin was speaking as his park was sold out for a Sunday game with the Yankees, and he was watching a crew of workmen putting together a huge stage over the home plate at the Tiger park for a night "opera under the stars."

Pointing to the stage, Navin continued: "Why, this night game is baseball's ruination. It changes baseball players from athletes to actors. Its nothing more than a spectacle. Aside from that, night baseball fails to develop young players. The fielding is different, and night pitching is far different from that which prevails in day games. Young players are handicapped by the night style of the game.

"In my honest opinion, night ball has not helped baseball in the minors, and I am sure it hasn't helped much in Cincinnati, the only major-league club which has sponsored it. [Larry MacPhail introduced night ball in the majors in 1935.] I sincerely hope no other major-league clubs will fall for it.

"I am not convinced that it is a paying proposition. The minors have found their Saturday and Sunday crowds have fallen off since they introduced night ball to their fans. When you take everything into consideration—the slump of the day crowds, purchase of lighting equipment and cost of operation, and the fact that few young players are being developed—there is little that can be said for it. I certainly am against it."

All of Navin's dire predictions about night ball ruining big-league baseball have not been fulfilled. Night ball has been especially successful in such cities as St. Louis, Washington, Philadelphia, and Brooklyn, and despite the prevalence of night ball in the minors, good young ball players continue to come up.

Yet, with the two St. Louis clubs and Washington playing 1945 schedules consisting almost entirely of night games and Sunday double headers, week-day games losing their appeal in both leagues, with Saturday just another day, and the game turning from a great sunlight sport to a night spectacle, we wonder whether Navin's words of 1935 do not speak from the grave.

⊗ VI ⊗

THE TIGERS SURVIVE
THE WAR

I

FRANK NAVIN'S PRESENCE WASN'T IMMEDIATELY FELT. IN SAM Angus' first year in the league, 1902, Navin was little more than the bookkeeper. But then the bookkeeper was the business manager, ticket-taker, and general all-around office factotum.

Angus' 1902 manager was Frank Dwyer, a former pitcher-outfielder in the National League with Chicago, St. Louis, and Cincinnati. He had been an American League umpire in 1900, but joined the National League staff in 1901 after Johnson had plucked most of the National's best men. As all American clubs were raiding the National, the Detroit club came up with a National League umpire as its manager.

Dwyer remained only one mediocre season, his 1902 Tiger club winding up a poor seventh with a percentage of .385. Frank served later as a scout for both of the New York clubs, was McGraw's pitching coach for a spell, coached baseball at Cornell, and put in three terms as a New York State boxing commissioner. He served in that capacity with Jim Farley.

It was one of the seasons that saw the Detroit club at its worst. The American League raids on the National League continued unabated. The great Ed Delahanty—brother of Tom, who played for Van Derbeck's Detroit team—jumped to Washington and Elmer Flick to Cleveland. The Milwaukee American League club was shifted to St. Louis, and a whole raft of Cardinal stars, Pitchers Jack Powell, Charley Harper, and Willie Sudhoff, Infielders Rhody Wallace and Dick Padden, and Outfielders Jesse Burkett and Emmet Heidrick, jumped to McAleer's new team and changed their socks from cardinal to brown. Even the bright young star of the New York Nationals, Christy Mathewson, signed an Athletic contract,

46

but jumped back to the Giants before he even put on an Athletic uniform.

Dwyer tried to meet the strengthened competition with the team he inherited from Stallings, most of them survivors of the Detroit Western League club. The club had only one worth-while acquisition, but he was to prove one of the great Tiger pitching stars, George Emmet Mullin. He came from Toledo, and during his later years in Tigerville he commuted between Bennett Park and his Toledo home. He had pitched for Fort Wayne in 1901, and signed with both Brooklyn and Detroit during the following winter. But eventually he selected the club nearer home. George later admitted his first Detroit contract was for $1,200, so the baseball war did little for him. He started in well, too, winning 14 games and losing 15 for a poor club in his freshman year. Many regard him as Detroit's best all-time pitcher—at least up to Newhouser of today. George died at Wabash, Ind., in 1944 at the comparatively early age of 63. He was a red-hot Tiger fan to the end of his days.

Though coaching pitchers supposedly was Dwyer's forte, he had a rather sad parade of pitchers after he got past Mullin, Win Mercer, and Eddie Siever. Roscoe Miller, Yeager, Cronin, Cristall, Egan, McMackin, Kissinger, O'Connell, Fisher, and Terry all pitched at various times. The Egan was the famous Aloysius J. "Wish" Egan, now the club's ace scout, and one of the game's best storytellers.

But the 1902 Detroit fans didn't find Wish or most of his Tiger pitching associates funny. By midseason, the Detroit letter in the July 28 issue of the *Sporting News* carried this head: "TOO MUCH KICKING. Patrons Disgusted at the Tiger Tactics. All Players Could Do to Protect Umpire from Hoodlums at Close of Sunday's Game." B. F. Wright, the Detroit correspondent, lectured Dwyer's snarling Tigers:

I seldom scold the Tigers, but they are due for a warning, if not a warming. They are drifting back into the old kicking rut, and making nuisances of themselves. During the past week I have overheard many grandstand criticisms of their wrangling, and am satisfied that the better class of their patrons desire that they cut it out. Dillon was benched (put out by the umpire) on Friday and Elberfeld on Saturday, the latter act bringing around the umpire nearly all the team—contrary to the rules. One of these unlucky days Ban Johnson will deliver a cuff that will cripple the club beyond the capacity to play a decent game of "four-old-cat." Elberfeld was hit with the ball and painfuly injured, but Johnstone would not allow him a base because he had made no effort to avoid the collision. His kick, resulting in Elberfeld's ejection, possibly cost Detroit the game, for Yeager, who took his place, struck out twice with the winning run on base.

Six days of kicking, with or without cause. . . . In the fourth inning of the Sunday game, Harley (Detroit left fielder) was called out by Johnstone, even though Harley was lying on the plate when touched out by Warner, Washington catcher. Warner, himself, later admitted Cooley was safe. Harley kicked so loud that he was benched, and that made the crowd ugly. But for the Detroit players, Harley among them, clustering around and knocking down three of the hoodlums, Johnstone would have been mobbed and badly mauled at the end of the game.

Before passing up Detroit's 1902 season, it is interesting to recall that it was a fanning bee at the Hotel Ponchatrain between Connie Mack and Umpire Jack Sheridan late that spring which was responsible for the Athletics' coming up with the left-handed wonder, Rube Waddell, and winning their first pennant. Several baseball men were in the group, and Connie was bemoaning his fate; he had a strong team, but an adverse decision by the Pennsylvania Supreme Court had cost him three Philadelphia National-jumpers, Pitchers Bill Bernard, Chick Fraser, and Bill Duggleby. The former moved on to Cleveland; Fraser and Duggleby returned to the Phillies.

"What I wouldn't do for another winning pitcher!" said Mack.

"Why don't you try to get back Rube Waddell, the big left-hander who pitched here in Detroit and was with you in Milwaukee?" responded Sheridan. "He belongs to the Cubs, but is now out in Los Angeles in the Coast League, and some friends tell me he is faster than ever."

"Do you think I could get him?" asked Mack.

"Well, he's sore at Hart of the Chicago club, and won't return there. So there isn't any harm in trying."

Next time the Athletics came to Detroit, Waddell was the big magnet of the Philadelphia club. Announcement that the Rube would pitch always brought them out in droves at Bennett Park. Though Waddell didn't join the Athletics until June 26, he won 23 games out of 30, struck out 210, and pitched Mack into his first of nine championships.

2

Detroit came very near sliding out of the American League after the season of 1902. Carrying the fight to the National League, Ban Johnson moved his Baltimore club into New York, and planned to invade Barney Dreyfuss' Pittsburgh bailiwick. Sensational new raids were made on National League teams, including the seizure of the crack battery of the two Jacks—Chesbro and O'Connor—and Infielder Wid Conroy of the 1902 Pirate champions. The St. Louis Browns signed Christy Mathewson. Angus, owner of the Tigers, signed three of the big stars of the Brooklyns, Willie Keeler, the famous little outfielder, and Pitchers Bill Donovan and Frank Kitson. Angus also signed Sam Crawford, outfielder of the Cincinnati Reds, and Pitcher Vic Willis of the Boston Nationals. However, both Sam and Vic returned $1,000 bonus checks to Angus and signed later contracts with their old National League clubs. Detroit also lost some players who jumped the other way. Kid Elberfeld had been disgruntled and dissatisfied during the latter part of his stay in Detroit, and snapped up the attractive bait which John McGraw offered him to jump to the Giants. McGraw had aroused Johnson's lifelong enmity by leaving the Baltimore Americans in midseason of 1902 to accept the management of the Giants, taking half a dozen of his best players with him. Bill Gleason jumped from the Tigers to the Phillies.

However, there was a fly in the ointment in these big player transactions as far as Tiger fans were concerned. There was a strong suspicion that Angus was acting merely as Johnson's agent prior to the transfer of the club to Pittsburgh. And as the Pirates had won in 1901 and 1902, Ban knew he needed a strong club to buck Barney Dreyfuss in the Steel City.

The proposed transfer of the Tigers to Pittsburgh was more than a rumor. Over a leading story in the *Sporting News,* issue of November 8, 1903, appears this head: "MAY DROP DETROIT. Americans Plan Further Expansion. Strong Indications that Pittsburgh Will Be That City's Successor in the 1903 Circuit."

Writing from Detroit, B. F. Wright felt the shift might be delayed until after the 1903 season, but he was not too optimistic.

In my opinion—and I have been maturing it for more than a month—1903 will be the last of Detroit as an American League city. Perhaps I am overoptimistic or credulous; the bouncing may come at an earlier date, but it does not appear imminent to me at this writing. Before passing on my reasons, I may add that I am not the only doubter in Detroit by a long shot. The belief that Detroit is getting the dinky dink is quite general among the fans, and will doubtless contribute to the fate they deplore.

At the very time this appeared, Ban Johnson was surveying the situation in Pittsburgh. For grounds, he even was contemplating locating at the site of present Forbes Field. The Pirates still were playing at Exposition Park in Allegheny. A Pittsburgh syndicate was formed to back an A. L. club.

Then Frank De Haas Robison, president of the St. Louis Cardinals, helped save Detroit for the American League. At the annual meeting of the National League in New York in early December, 1902, Robison told his colleagues that he had had enough of the war and suggested getting together with Ban Johnson. His declaration in favor of such overtures was backed by Herrmann of Cincinnati, Dreyfuss of Pittsburgh, Hart of Chicago, and Rogers of Philadelphia. A National committee waited on Johnson, Charley Somers, and John Kilfohl in New York, and out of it grew the Cincinnati peace meeting of January 5, 1903.

The National League first proposed a consolidation whereby the old league would return to a twelve-club circuit. In that event Detroit might have returned to the National League. However, Ban Johnson quickly announced that a consolidation would not be considered as a basis for negotiation. The National League then gave in all the way, accepting the American League as a full major to enjoy all the rights and privileges of the National. It further agreed to the American League's placing a club in New York, provided Johnson pledged to stay out of Pittsburgh.

The joint committee then took up the cases of disputed players, men who had jumped from one league to the other since the close of the 1902 season. Most of the wrangling was over sixteen top cases, and the committee's action in awarding these stars was most vital to Detroit and pennants which were not so far ahead. Ban Johnson must have been pretty persuasive, as nine were awarded to the American League—Sam Crawford, Bill Donovan, Norman Elberfeld, Ed Delahanty, Nap Lajoie, Willie Keeler, George Davis, Dave Fultz, and Wid Conroy. The National League got seven, including the great Mathewson. The others were Vic Willis, Tommy Leach, Harry Smith, Rudy Hulswitt, Sam Mertes, and Frank Bowerman.

The treaty wasn't immediately ratified. Charley Ebbets of Brooklyn raised a terrific howl, which could be heard high above the stench of Gowanus Canal. He had lost Donovan, Keeler, and Kitson, got little in return, and was told to like it. Brush of the Giants didn't take kindly to that part of the agreement which permitted the American League to come into New York provided it stayed out of Pittsburgh. "That's all right for Barney, but how about me?" he asked. Ebbets and Brush filed a lengthy minority report. Brush even went to court to try to stop ratification of the pact by the

National League, but on January 21 he withdrew his injunction proceedings, and sweet peace prevailed again in baseball.

The trading of Kid Elberfeld in early June to Clark Griffith's new New York Highlanders almost started the war all over again. The Tabasco Kid was traded for Herman Long, former great shortstop of the old Boston Nationals—but then well past his prime—and Ernie Courtney, a mediocre third baseman. The deal made Brush and McGraw of the Giants furious, inasmuch as they had lost Elberfeld when the peace commissioners distributed players.

"That was just another scheme of Ban Johnson's," said Brush bitterly. "He planned to put Elberfeld in New York, when the peace committee returned him to Detroit. Well, if he can't play with the New York Nationals, we won't stand for his playing with the New York Americans."

Brush and McGraw couldn't get the Elberfeld deal canceled so they signed George Davis, another great shortstop, who had been awarded to the White Sox at the winter peace settlement. Davis even played a few games for the 1903 Giants. There also were charges of McGraw's tampering with other American League players. The old National League Commission then officially approved the Tiger–New York deal involving Elberfeld, and ordered Davis' return to the White Sox. Brush defied the order and again threatened to go to court; there was plenty of talk of a new war, but Brush and McGraw were playing a lone hand and eventually returned Davis to the White Sox.

Even though Detroit had a 1900 population of 285,704—the smallest in the league—and a Cleveland newspaper kept insisting it didn't belong in the big leagues, its position as an American League city never was endangered after it passed through its crisis in the winter of 1902-03.

3

Just about the time that Detroit was sure that its franchise had been saved, Tiger fans received another shock. After Frank Dwyer had been relieved of the management of the club, Sam Angus appointed the club's pitcher, Win Mercer, as playing manager. Perhaps Griff's success in Chicago as a pitcher-manager led to the experiment. However, before Win even took a look at his club he committed suicide by asphyxiation in the Oriental Hotel, San Francisco, January 12, 1903, just about the time that baseball's quarrels were being ironed out in the East.

Winnifred B. Mercer, one of the most handsome players in the game, was on the Coast with two teams of National and American stars, in which he handled some of the money. The Tiger pitcher-manager left letters to his mother and fiancée, both of East Liverpool, Ohio, and to Tip O'Neill, manager of the trip. In his letter to his mother he ascribed his rash act to women. Mercer also was an inveterate gambler, as were many players of his day, and fellow members of the tour said he had experienced an especially bad streak of luck which had made him desperate. However, his letter to O'Neill contained a full statement of his accounts, and everything was in order.

Following Win Mercer's tragic end, Angus, on the recommendation of Ban Johnson, offered the Tiger managerial job to Edward Grant Barrow, afterward for many years the famous business manager and later president of the New York Yankees. Whether the Tigers were high or low, they rarely had a nonentity in the manager's seat. And Ed Barrow truly developed into one of the great figures of baseball. During the time that he held executive posts with the Yankees, the New Yorkers won 14 league pennants and ten World's Championships. However, Barrow had other accomplishments which were equally dear to his heart.

"As manager of the old Paterson club of the Atlantic League, I developed Hans Wagner and sold him to the majors," he once remarked. "As manager of the Red Sox, I took Babe Ruth, a 23-game winning pitcher, and converted him into an outfielder, and as head of the Detroit club I laid the foundation of the club with which Jennings later won pennants."

Barrow has had almost every job in baseball but that of commissioner; he has served as manager of major- and minor-league clubs, owned the club at Paterson, was president of the Atlantic and International Leagues, business manager, president, and chairman of the board of the powerful Yankees. Just to make sure that he knew all elements of the businesses with which baseball is associated, he once was a circulation manager in Des Moines and a hotel manager in Toronto. Once he even tried his hand promoting fights in Philadelphia.

At the time that Barrow came to Detroit, he was a stocky, black-haired, beetle-browed chap of 35, who had just recently shaved off his jet-black handle-bar mustache. He was strong as a bull, and though he had played little ball outside of school, he could lick—and frequently did—most of the players who played for him. When he found a guy who cared to challenge his authority, he locked the doors of the clubhouse, and said: "Let's go to it; the better man goes out first." Hot-tempered and rather hard-boiled, as Toronto manager he once knocked out an International umpire at the home plate in Springfield, Mass., with a powerful right to the jaw. Later as president of the same league, Ed didn't like to be reminded of the incident.

Barrow started out in a blaze of glory and, during the month of May, Detroit fans thought Barrow would be their new miracle man. His club led the race May 1, and still ran second to Chicago May 26. Then came a nose dive and a plunge to sixth June 2. The club rallied, ran fourth most of the year, and eventually finished fifth, winning thirteen more games than Dwyer's 1902 club.

Two of Barrow's leading players that year were the two jumpers awarded to Detroit by the peace commissioners—Sam Crawford and Bill Donovan, Tiger luminaries from the very start. Crawford played left field for Barrow and batted .332, second only to the league leader, Nap Lajoie. Oddly enough Biffing Sam led the two major leagues in triples in succeeding seasons. In 1902, while still playing with the Reds, he hit 23 three-baggers in the National League. In his first season with Detroit, Crawford churned out 25 of these hits, a record at the time. Sam later raised his triple mark to 26 in 1914, and holds the American League record jointly with Joe Jackson. He always had the knack of tearing those terrific drives to right and right center; today most of his triples and many of his caught flies would be homers.

He came from Wahoo, Neb., and before he was sure he had made good as a ball player he learned the barber's trade. Fans and writers of that day called him "the Wahoo barber" and "the slugging tonsorial artist." "Though he wasn't as big as Lou Gehrig, he had power just like Lou," said Barrow. "We paid him $3,500 when I was in Detroit, and what hitting he delivered for that price!"

Some years ago, I visited with Sam out on the Coast. He now lives in Burbank, Calif., and was a defense worker during the war. He refused to speculate on the number of homers he could have hit under present-day conditions. He grinned as he said: "They tell me I hit a ball pretty hard. Conditions are so different. Why, they called Frank Baker 'Home Run' Baker, when he hit from 9 to 12 homers a year." Sam also thinks present-day pitching, even the prewar variety, well below the grade he used to hit against. "We had no soft spots to hit against," he added. "The Athletics and White Sox were our greatest rivals when the old Tigers were going strong. Mack always seemed to have good pitchers when I was in the league. If it wasn't the old staff built around Plank, Waddell, and Bender, it was Coombs, Krause, and good youngsters like Bush, Shawkey, and Pennock. Ed Walsh and Doc White were Chicago's toughest pitchers, but they had others almost as difficult in Altrock, Patterson, Frank Smith, Owen, and later Cicotte."

Bill Donovan, Sam's illustrious teammate, wasn't a soft spot either for any of those early American Leaguers. Though born in Lawrence, Mass., he was brought up in Philadelphia and learned his early baseball on that city's famous Fairmount Park "Park Sparrows." He was a lovable character and as a pitcher and later-day manager, he was one of baseball's most popular figures. Though he liked the night life, he never drank anything stronger than pop or ginger ale. As Bill Slocum, the former New York sports writer, once put it: "There is no credit for you if you like Bill Donovan. Everybody does. But you can take credit if he likes you. Then you must be all right."

His father, Jerry Donovan, was a Civil War veteran, and Bill once took the old gentleman on a Southern training trip. It was the first time Jerry had been in Georgia since he was there with Sherman. As the team moved north through such towns as Columbia, S. C., Charlotte, and Richmond, Jerry would remark: "There ain't so many Rebels out today," or "We surely got a lot of Rebels rooting against us today."

However, old Jerry eventually got tired of basking in Bill Donovan's spotlight. Every place he was introduced as Bill Donovan's old man, and he finally became a rebel himself. "The hell with this business of 'Bill Donovan's old man'; he's Jerry Donovan's son," he roared.

⊖ VII ⊖

BILL YAWKEY COMES
INTO THE PICTURE

I

IN THE WINTER OF 1903-04, SAM ANGUS TIRED OF HIS BASEBALL
venture. Then, too, Ban Johnson wanted stronger ownership in
Detroit. Angus called in both Navin and Barrow, and told them they
could have the club if they could find a backer. Barrow, reminiscing
on his Detroit days, often has said: "I could have had the Tigers
for a song at the time, but few people then had any idea of
Detroit's baseball future. With a little more enterprise and hustle,
I think I could have raised the money."

Johnson first tried to interest a Chicagoan, Fred Postal, in the
franchise. For a while that deal was hot, but Postal cooled off after
he inspected Detroit's poorly built stands. Then Navin helped bring
William Clyman Yawkey, a multimillionaire lumber and ore king,
into the picture. But while Johnson was in Detroit, negotiating with
the elder Yawkey, William Clyman became suddenly ill and died.
After some delay, his picturesque and tempestuous son, William
Hoover Yawkey, then twenty-eight years old, picked up the nego-
tiations and took over most of the club's stock for $50,000. At first
Angus retained an interest in the club, but eventually Yawkey
bought him out. Young Bill immediately made a hit with his young
executives by making them small partners in his business. He gave
Navin $5,000 worth of stock, and Barrow $2,500 worth. Under
the new setup, young Bill Yawkey became president, and Navin
secretary-treasurer. The latter also succeeded Frank Dwyer, the
1902 manager, to the business management of the Tigers. From
his bookkeeper's desk, Frank, the man with a vision, moved into
the front office. It marked Navin's first year as a power in Detroit
baseball. And from the very start, Yawkey considered Frank Navin
his right bower.

When Babe Ruth was in his prime, they used to say: "There

55

couldn't be another Babe Ruth." Baseball just couldn't stand more than one Babe Ruth at one time. That was true of Bill Yawkey, the new Tiger owner and president. There just couldn't be two of them. He was something like Chris Von Der Ahe of the old St. Louis Browns, except that Bill had more money than Chris, had a better education, and was a better businessman. But like Vondy, Bill Yawkey liked to laugh and play his way through life, and his ball club was a plaything—just another way of having fun.

Thomas Austin Yawkey, the present millionaire owner of the Boston Red Sox, was his nephew and foster son; he got the yen to own a big-league ball club because Daddy Yawkey once had owned one. Young Tom, a son of Bill's sister, Augusta, came to live with the Yawkeys when he was just a tot. Bill Yawkey adopted Tom in 1917, after the boy's mother died, and then died himself two years later, March 5, 1919, in Augusta, Ga., the very town in which the Tigers found Ty Cobb. Tom then was a sixteen-year-old prep-school boy at Irving School, Tarrytown, N. Y. Bill was only forty-three when he died, but he crowded a lot of life and excitement into those forty-three years.

The man who started the fortune was the aforementioned William Clyman Yawkey, who sprang from a Pennsylvania family which had migrated from Germany. He was eighteen when the family moved to Flint, Mich., by way of Massilon, O., and the first Bill Yawkey became interested in lumbering. From superintendent of a sawmill in his early twenties, he rapidly became a Michigan lumber king. By the time he was thirty-three, he already was a millionaire, with great pieces of timber and iron-ore lands in Michigan and Canada. He had much of the thrift of his German forbears; he had a reputation for scrupulous honesty, and had a retiring disposition. In many respects his son, Bill, was the exact opposite; he was noisy and a man of few inhibitions, spent money like a drunken sailor and liked to be near the bright lights. During business hours, he was shrewd and capable, even when he had to have a wet towel on his head from the previous evening's joy ride. He could be harsh in business dealings, and despite his playboy proclivities, he was a smart businessman, and could make money faster than he could spend it. And he wasn't a man to talk business over a round of drinks. One of his rules was not to talk business while he was having fun.

Once when a business associate tried to discuss a big transaction at a wrestling match, he boomed: "For cripe's sake, are you here to see these fellows wrestle, or to talk business? If you want to talk business, sit somewhere else."

56

He wasn't only fond of baseball, but liked all sports, prize fighting, wrestling, racing. He would go for roulette, faro, or whatever they had in the house. And he could drink three average drinkers under the table.

He had the Cincinnati idea of a baseball opening in the spring. It was a festive occasion; he always gave a big party on the eve of the season. And when Detroit opened in Cleveland, which often happened, he would take a large party of invited guests to the Ohio city, with usually a wet and noisy session the night before. Other parties were taken to Cleveland during the season. He was aware of Cleveland's contempt of Detroit as a big-league town, and wanted to be sure he'd have some rooters there. Victories over Cleveland always were sweeter than over any other clubs. When he felt particularly pleased with a Tiger victory over the old Blues, or Naps, as Cleveland then was called, he would give Bill Donovan or George Mullin, the winning pitcher, a $100 bill. That dismayed the secretary and business manager, Frank Navin, who said: "That'll spoil them."

At times, when a series of Tiger victories gave him especial pleasure, he would take the entire team on a spree. Once, in an effort to break a losing streak, he got the entire team drunk in New York. And Navin and Hughie Jennings, later his most successful manager, had to sober them up again. But the scheme really worked, and Bill was proud of the efficacy of his treatment. Nevertheless, Navin was constantly scheming to keep him away from the players.

He doted on prize fighters and wrestlers, as well as ball players. He once hired Tommy Ryan, the former middleweight champion, to travel with him and box with him. Bill really was pretty handy with his dukes, and also a fairly good amateur wrestler. However, on one occasion he put a too high valuation on his wrestling ability. It was on one of those opening-of-the-season parties, when Yawkey, in his usual lavish fashion, took several carloads of friends to Cleveland to see the Tigers play their season's inaugural contest.

At a big party at the Hollenden, everyone was feeling high when wrestling became the subject of conversation. One of the gang, Billy Lamb, allowed he was pretty good.

"Pretty good, but not good enough," said Yawkey. "I can throw any man in this room, and that includes you, Billy Lamb, and all your family."

Lamb didn't think so, and the argument grew hotter. "I'll bet you $10,000 I can throw you," said Yawkey.

Now even though he had been imbibing, Lamb knew he himself

didn't have that kind of money. But Yawkey persisted: "If I win, you owe me nothing; but if you win, I owe you $10,000."

Yawkey and Lamb stripped down to the waist; the other men cleared the room; and the two gladiators went to it. The match didn't last long. Lamb was the stronger of the two men, and perhaps in better condition. He got a hammer lock on Yawkey, spun him to the floor, and soon pinned his shoulders to the carpet.

"You *are* pretty good," said Yawkey, breathing hard.

The next day Yawkey sent Lamb a $10,000 check. Bill returned it, saying he hadn't any money up. But Yawkey shot it back and insisted Lamb keep it, saying: "You won it fairly and squarely; it's yours."

While Yawkey was a free spender, in a certain mood he could be penurious and penny-pinching. He never cared much about doctors, said: "They overcharge you" and "go around scaring people." After one of his hard nights in New York, he took a walk down Broadway to clear his throbbing head and saw a doctor's sign on the floor above a saloon. Somehow it struck Bill that this might be an inexpensive fellow, also that a saloon doctor might be just the man for him to consult.

The doctor listened to Yawkey's heart, tapped his chest, and gave him several significant "H'mms" and "A-has."

Bill read the man's mind, that his report wasn't going to be good, but it was far worse than he had anticipated.

"Sir," said the physician, "you are in a dangerous condition. Your heart is quite bad. You may go out any moment like this—" and the man snapped his finger.

Yawkey felt a sick feeling in his stomach, and his knees sagged.

The physician continued: "I can see only one chance for you. You must give up drinking, and give it up entirely. You've got to lead a quiet life, and avoid all excitement. If you don't do that, I see no hope for you. One of these days you'll just take another drink, and drop to the floor. And then they won't call in a doctor, but an undertaker. Two dollars please."

Shaking like a leaf, Yawkey reached into his pocket for the two dollars, paid the man, and staggered down the back stairs. He tried to collect his wits, and then his eyes saw the saloon downstairs. He went in and ordered rye whisky. He gulped it down, waited a bit, but nothing happened.

"More of the same," he told the barkeep.

He actually thought he was feeling better. Then he had three more good hookers. Going out into the corridor again, he leaped up the stairs, two at a time, like an antelope going up a rocky ledge, and burst back into the doctor's office.

"You're a lying blankety-blank quack," said Bill. "I've had five drinks, and I've run up these stairs faster'n you can, and I haven't croaked. In fact, I'm very much alive. Give me back my two bucks."

Without comment, the doctor reached into his drawer, took out two dollar bills, and handed them back.

Despite the way Bill could toss money around, he and his wife, Margaret, brought up their foster son, Tom, to appreciate the value of a dollar. In fact, one dollar was Tom's weekly allowance. It was a carry-over from Old William Clyman Yawkey's thrift.

One day when Tom was about twelve, he remarked to his mother: "I guess some day I'll be about the richest man in the world."

"Tom, before you say that again, come with me to the kitchen," said Mrs. Yawkey. She went to the cupboard, got a bag of beans, and put about half a dozen saucers on the table. She filled five of the saucers with beans, and then placed just one bean in the sixth.

Then pointing to the filled saucers, she said: "These saucers represent the wealth of the Rockefellers, the Morgans, the Fields, the Vanderbilts, etc." Pointing to the one bean, she added: "And this is the wealth of the Yawkeys."

Tom admitted later that kitchen lecture deflated his idea of the Yawkey wealth. But Bill Yawkey did get a lot of fun out of that bean. He made it jump.

2

Shortly after the new deal in Detroit, Clark Griffith, the manager of the new New York Highlanders, came to Tigertown intent on talking business. His quarry was Pitcher George Mullin. Griff had three propositions with which he tried to tempt young Yawkey. He was willing to give $10,000 straight for George, $7,500 and Pitcher Jesse Tannehill, or Tannehill, Infielder Unglaub, and a lesser amount.

"Say, Clark, I'm buying—not selling," said Yawkey. "What have you to sell?" Griffith returned to New York, saying: "That young fellow, Yawkey, is quite unreasonable. He don't know a good deal when he sees one."

Barrow made three deals in 1904, which paved the way for the championship infield of 1907. He got the left side of the infield, Shortstop Charley O'Leary and Third Baseman Bill Coughlin, and the left fielder Matty McIntyre. Coughlin later became captain of the club, and one of Detroit's early American League heroes. However, he was no more popular than the cheerful but aggressive Irishman from Chicago, Charley O'Leary. Charley had played for his home-town team Comiskey's White Sox, in 1900, the year the old Western called itself the American League, but Rube Waddell, then pitching for Mack in Milwaukee, almost ruined the little Irishman's career. He plunked Charley with a fast ball, leaving the right arm mashed and a bone shattered. O'Leary fought to come back in the minors, and a .315 average with Des Moines in 1903 helped bring him back to the American League. Charley didn't hit that well in Bennett Park; in fact, light hitting held him back, but later others on the Tiger roster made up for the shortstop's shortcomings with his shillelagh.

Charley wasn't much for size, only 5 feet, 7 and 155 pounds, but he played marbles—and baseball—for keeps. Billy Evans, the former American League ace umpire, now president of the Southern Association, tells this story on O'Leary:

"In a close game with the White Sox, I called out Fielder Jones, the Chicago playing manager, on one of those hairline decisions at second base," said Billy. "Charley O'Leary had covered the bag. Jones got up yelling: 'He didn't tag me. Charley never touched me.'

"Later in the game, Jones went down to second on another attempted steal, and O'Leary again got the ball to make a play. In making his tag, Charley came up with a sort of uppercut, and whether by accident or design, he tagged Jones right on the chin. No man hit on the button in the ring ever went out colder. But was O'Leary sorry or sympathetic? He leered at me, and said: 'I guess this time, Billy, there is no doubt that he is out.'"

Coughlin also was a real fighter; though in his later years he was the respected and beloved baseball coach at Lafayette College, in his American League playing days he was known as "Rowdy Bill." He could spit tobacco juice with as much venom as any man in the league. He came from Scranton, Hughie Jennings' country, and when he died in 1943 a big delegation of faculty members and students from Lafayette attended his funeral.

In his youth, he had shot off the first finger on his left hand. It didn't hurt his baseball; actually it proved an asset, as it helped him pull the hidden ball trick. He even worked it on Jimmy Slagle of the Cubs in the 1907 World's Series.

"I had to have a special mitt made for that hand, something like the one used by first basemen—only smaller," explained Bill a few years before he died. "I soon found that I could palm the ball in the mitt, so that the base runner and the coach couldn't see it. Then

60

I would tag the base runner as he walked off his bag. I used to work the play beautifully with Germany Schaefer."

Barrow had an interleague deal all cooked up with the Giants whereby he wanted to trade Outfielder Jimmy Barrett to McGraw for Third Baseman Art Devlin and Outfielder Harry McCormick. Barrow still contends it would have been a great deal for Detroit, as Devlin soon became the best third baseman in the National League. But Navin had sufficient influence with Yawkey to block the deal. Barrow also wanted to buy Infielder Harry Arndt from Louisville; Harry then was purchased by the Reds. Ed also got into Navin's hair by wishing to pay $5,000 of Yawkey's money as a bonus to a college pitcher for signing a Detroit contract. Frank was able to veto such extravagance.

Barrow had been trying to get Coughlin from the Washington club ever since he took over the Tigers in 1903. The Senators, with one of their usual tail-enders, were doing badly at the gate, and on July 27 Barrow engineered a deal whereby the Detroit club purchased Coughlin for $8,000, a lot of money for the Tigers, or any other club, to pay for a player at the time. It was Barrow's last deal for the Tigers, and to a certain extent was responsible for Ed's severing his relations with the club.

Probably it was in the cards that there should be friction between Barrow and Navin. Both men were about the same age, ambitious to go to the top in baseball. Both were strong, dominant characters, and neither liked to play second fiddle to the other. Barrow was hot-tempered and blustery; Navin said less but was more resourceful. Actually there developed a fight for supremacy between the two men. Barrow was for spending Yawkey's money; Navin, knowing the club's lean receipts, tried to keep expenses within a budget. He opposed the purchase of Coughlin as being more than the club could afford. When the new third baseman failed for the time to bolster the club, and the Tigers limped into August in seventh place—only one position above Washington—it looked as though Navin was right. There finally was a blowup, in which Barrow tendered his resignation to Yawkey and it was accepted.

There was a touching scene when Barrow made his last visit to the clubhouse to remove his personal belongings. Bill Donovan was spokesman for a players' committee, which presented the departing manager with a diamond-studded locket, and told him of the high esteem in which he was held by the Tiger players.

"I got along fine with Bill Yawkey, though he naturally was disappointed with our poor showing in 1904," said Barrow. "I have only the kindest thoughts for Frank Navin. He was a great baseball man, but as young men in Detroit we just couldn't see eye to eye. I eventually resigned because of differences with Navin, but I think I left them the nucleus of their pennant-winning team. And this perhaps should be worthy of a laugh today. When I resigned, Yawkey paid me $1,400 for my $2,500's worth of stock. Navin held on to his and eventually became one of the wealthiest men in baseball."

For the final weeks of the 1904 season, Bobbie Lowe, the former great National League second baseman, served as manager. The Tigers had procured Bobbie in 1904 from the Chicago Cubs. In Boston, he had been a member of that great infield, Jimmy Collins, Herman Long, Lowe, and Fred Tenney. Bobbie also had the distinction of being one of the four big leaguers to hit four home runs in a game, but that was long before Bobbie wore the striped stockings of a Tiger.

3

Lowe was second baseman of the 1904 Tiger team, but he was getting along in his thirties, wasn't covering his old-time ground, and hit only .255. Before Barrow left Detroit he had arranged for Bobbie's successor. Milwaukee had a hard-hitting shortstop, and a chap who formerly had played second and third base, by the name of Herman "Germany" Schaefer. He had been in the majors before, but Barrow figured he now had gained his needed experience and swung a deal whereby the Detroit club acquired Herman for 1905 delivery. Schaefer, like O'Leary, was a native Chicagoan, who had played for Kansas City in the early American League and later with the Cubs. Herman also was known as the Prince, and with the exception of Ty Cobb, he was the most colorful of all of Detroit's picturesque stars.

Schaefer wasn't a great second baseman in the same sense as Charley Gehringer, Eddie Collins, Rogers Hornsby, or Joe Gordon. Herman was a good defensive second baseman, a fairly good hitter, a splendid base runner, and a "natural" for obtaining publicity. Everybody loved the jovial, droll, pock-marked Chicago Dutchman.

Schaefer legends have come down through the years, and old-timers never get tired of talking of them. Malcolm W. Bingay, one of the editors of the *Detroit Free Press* and Detroit's famous "Iffy, the Dopester" was Schaefer's best publicist. Herman's diamond humor often was coarse, but it was invariably funny, and like Nick Altrock, his later comedy partner in Washington, and Al Schacht, he was a natural comedian. And he could think up a dozen ways to bedevil a pitcher. One of his best ways of vexing the pitcher was to steal bases in reverse. After stealing second base, Herman would turn around and steal first again. Somehow this stealing bases the wrong way had a most disconcerting effect on the pitchers. In fact, it often made a burlesque of the game, and Ban Johnson actually had the rule changed—on Schaefer's account—whereby runners could circle the bases in only one direction, via first base, second base, and third.

Schaefer in a game with Rube Waddell of the Athletics always was a circus. He would address compliments to the Rube from the moment he took up his place at the plate. Frequently Rube would strike out the Prince, but every now and then Schaefer got a hit. When the Athletics played at their old Columbia Park in Philadelphia, home runs over their right-field fence were fairly easy and frequent. But the left-field fence was nearly home-run-proof. Only one or two balls would clear it during the course of a season, and it was a fence supposedly out of Herman's reach.

Waddell had fanned the Dutchman twice in a low-hit pitching duel with George Mullin, with neither club having scored, as the Prince came to bat in the eighth inning. Promptly Waddell shot two strikes over on Herman. Waddell liked to clown on the mound, though he was no wit like Schaefer. However, Rube laughed heartily, and his catcher, Ossie Schreck, asked: "What's the matter, Herman, didn't you see them go by?"

"Well, tell him to pitch another one like that to me, and I'll ride it right out of the park."

"I think we can oblige you. One just like that last one, Rube," called Schreck.

Herman took his bat back and swung as hard as he could, and probably hit the longest ball he ever hit in his life. The ball rode like one of those later-day "jack rabbits" and cleared the distant left-field fence. Herman carried his bat with him as he ambled, happily and leisurely, around the bases. About every five paces, Herman would stop, take his bat to his right shoulder as though it were a gun, point it at the discomfited Rube, and then pull an imaginary trigger. Herman himself supplied the explosion as he repeatedly shot Waddell off the mound.

Like Ruth and Cobb, he had a natural dramatic sense. In another tense game in Chicago, he was out with an injury, but was just about ready to return to the line-up. The Tigers trailed by a run as they came up in the ninth, facing Doc White, the crack White Sox left-hander. Charley O'Leary opened with an infield hit, and Jennings, later Schaefer's manager, called on the Prince to bat for the pitcher.

Now Chicago was Herman's home town, and one place where he wanted to show at his best. And those rooters from the stockyards always enjoyed treating him to a razzberry chorus. It was before the day of official announcers, and the umpire usually blurted out the pinch hitter's name and let it go at that. But that wasn't enough of an introduction for Schaefer. Holding up his hands for silence, he addressed the crowd: "Ladies and gentlemen, presenting to you the world's champion batsman, who now will give you a demonstration of his great hitting skill." The stockyard boys yelled: "Sit down, you clown; Doc will make a monkey out of you."

"You'll see," yelled Herman.

As though he did it every day, Schaefer hit one of the longest home runs seen at the old wooden White Sox park, before the modern improvements. Though the ball was hit out of the park, Schaefer slid into first base. As he picked himself up, he called: "The Prince leads at the quarter." He did the same thing at second and third; at the latter base, he called: "Schaefer now leads by a mile." Then he slid majestically into the home plate. Brushing himself off, he again doffed his cap, bowed to the stands, and announced: "Ladies and gentlemen, this will conclude the great Schaefer's afternoon performance."

On another occasion, when it was raining and Tim Hurst was slow to call the game, Schaefer appeared at the plate in rubber boots and a raincoat. It was quite a time before salty old Tim would forgive him, and anything thrown near Herman was a strike. When Schaefer appeared at bat with a false black mustache over his lip, and the crowd screamed with laughter, Hurst said: "Ye're out of the game, Herman."

"What for?" demanded the clown.

"I don't know what fur," said Tim, "but ye're out," and despite Jennings' spirited protest, he was out.

Schaefer's favorite pal on the Tigers was his fellow Chicagoan, the Irishman Charley O'Leary. Charley was the Prince's straight man. They used to call him "Charley, me b'y," because in one of his many stories he would tell how his mother cautioned him about persons like Schaefer. Schaefer and O'Leary even tried their luck on the stage as a burlesque theater vaudeville team, but their act proved a flop.

Their act went better before a nonpaying audience. Jack Sheridan, the ace American League umpire in the early years of the league, wintered in Chicago, and one of his favorite places of recreation was Hinky Dink's saloon, a rather rowdy spot on the South Side. One evening, after partaking of his liquid refreshment, Jack dozed off with his head resting on his favorite table, right near a drainpipe.

Seeing the umpire asleep, Schaefer and O'Leary went upstairs and knelt on the floor next to the pipe. Herman cupped his hands and moaned as loudly as he could: "Jack Sheridan, your time has come!"

Sheridan half awakened, looked as though he had been dreaming, when that wail came again: "Jack Sheridan, your time has come."

The voice by this time had restored Jack to full consciousness. He blinked his eyes, and tried to collect his wits.

Then it came for a third time: "Jack Sheridan, your time has come." Sheridan didn't wait to hear any more. White as a sheet, he struggled to his feet, and reeled out of the place, a shaken man. It was said that he never patronized Hinky Dink's again, and it was weeks before he took another drink.

All would have gone well, and the culprits might never have been discovered, if Sheridan hadn't called an adverse decision on Schaefer some months later in the following season. There were some words at the plate, and after the umpire had resumed his position, Herman just couldn't resist moaning: "Jack Sheridan, your time has come."

A great light came to Sheridan, and his face flushed with anger. With the crowd failing to understand the umpire's fury, he aimed a punch at Herman's chin, and fortunately for him—and his good standing with Ban Johnson—he missed. "So, it was you, you Dutch so-and-so," yelled Sheridan. "You're out of this ball game, you blankety-blank-blank." Sheridan chased Schaefer all the way to the clubhouse, swinging as he went, and from then on it was as difficult for Herman to get a close one from Jack as from Tim Hurst.

Even in his later years, when failing health and straitened finances took much of the joy out of life, Schaefer still could see the funny side. He was with the Cleveland Indians as a coach in 1918, the last year of World War I, when the club went into reverse. Patronage fell off, and to cut expenses Coach Schaefer was let out. "Now, see what you birds have done," he said half in anger and half in jest. "You've run your losing streak so far you've run me right out of a job." Schaefer died at Saranac Lake a year later at the early age of 49.

Bob Lowe, who finished the 1904 season as Detroit manager, was relegated to a utility infield role in 1905. The Cleveland club had advanced the great second baseman Larry Lajoie to the playing management of the team, and Yawkey and Navin promptly snatched the former Cleveland manager Bill Armour, who had led the early Blues since the American League expanded into a major in 1901. It was considered good business to grab the manager of Detroit's leading rival of the time, and it was quite a feather in Bill's cap when he lifted the Tigers from seventh place to third. It was especially gratifying to Yawkey to have Armour beat out his former team, Lajoie's Naps, who came home in fifth place, and the wealthy young club owner paid Armour a nice bonus at the end of the season.

Armour, one of the last men in baseball to wear a mustache, was a friendly capable chap, who knew and directed a lot of sound baseball. He had been an infielder and outfielder, starting his career in western Pennsylvania with industrial town teams Homestead and Bradford. Later he played for Toledo, Kansas City, Montgomery, and at Paterson, N. J., in 1896, where his manager was Ed Barrow and the great Honus Wagner a teammate. He began his managerial career with Dayton in 1897, and after his Detroit sojourn, Bill became a power in the American Association as president-manager of the Toledo club. He was the owner of a restaurant in Minneapolis when he died in 1922.

Detroit was in the first division for practically all of 1905; the club even led for a day, was in the pennant race for weeks, and *Reach's Guide* for 1906 said: "The 1905 Detroit team showed greater relative improvement than any other club in the league." Armour was given much of the credit for the improvement. We read further:

Mr. Armour's handling of his pitching staff was admirable, and he introduced a new colorful second base combination in O'Leary and Schaefer. Schaefer unquestionably added new strength to the team, as did First Baseman Lindsay and the veteran catcher, Jack Warner, also a young outfielder named Cobb. The team played more "inside ball" than it received credit for. The Tigers had their share of misfortunes through disabilities to Outfielders McIntyre and Barrett, but capable substitutes mitigated these drawbacks considerably.

However, an indication of what the Tigers, especially the young business manager, Frank Navin, were up against was the American League attendance figures for 1905. Despite the leap from seventh to third the Detroit club was a poor last with 193,384, an average of 2,578, and 65,000 under the attendance of the seventh-place Washington club. It didn't bother Yawkey, but those slim crowds gave Navin plenty of sleepless nights.

⊗ VIII ⊗

THE PLAYER OF
THE CENTURY

I

WHEN EDITOR FRANK RICHTER OF *Reach's Guide* CASUALLY MEN-
tioned a young outfielder, Cobb, adding some strength to
the 1905 Detroit club, and no doubt he was one of those who helped
mitigate the injuries of Matty McIntyre and Jimmy Barrett, he
little suspected he was talking of the player of the century.

Yet, there wasn't too much in Ty Cobb's 1905 play really to
warrant Editor Richter's praise. He was only an eighteen-year-old
boy when he joined the club, playing his first game August 30, and
his early play was only average. In the 41 games of the season which
remained, he hit .240, getting one homer and stealing two bases.
But what a barrage of singles, doubles, triples, homers, and stolen
bases were to follow, enough to give him nearly four dozen records
in the book today!

The greatest thing that ever happened to Detroit baseball unquestionably was the acquisition of this rookie, Ty Cobb, in the
late season of 1905. He truly was baseball's superman; Hollywood's
pet adjectives, "stupendous" and "colossal," were understatements
when applied to Ty Cobb.

Tyrus Raymond Cobb was baseball's top man without a shred
of doubt, though there may be a few minority reports. Back in
1942, Taylor Spink, aggressive publisher of the *Sporting News,* tried
to settle once for all who was the greatest player of all time. He
canvassed big-league managers, ex-managers, and the great stars of
this century. Of 102 votes cast, Cobb received 60, with the remaining 42 divided among 14 players. The immortal Hans Wagner ran
second to Cobb with 17; Babe Ruth had 11 votes, and Rogers
Hornsby was the only other player to get more than one vote. The
seven-time National League batting champion was favored by two
of the stars.

68

A few of the comments by men who played against Cobb or tried to manage teams against him should give some estimate of how men in his craft regarded this wonder player of all time. I especially liked the response of Eddie Collins, the former great Athletic and White Sox second baseman, and now general manager of the Red Sox. Eddie's reason for considering Ty the game's No. 1 player was expressed in one word, "Obvious."

George Sisler, one of Cobb's greatest later-day rivals, wrote: "If you played during the years that he was burning up the league, you could never forget the Georgian. I know I never will." Clark Griffith, who managed the New York Yankees the day that Cobb broke in, voted for Cobb "because he was a hitter, a base runner, a great fielder, and possessed the indomitable will to win and the aggressiveness that thrilled those who watched him play."

Walter Johnson, Griffith's great pitcher in Washington, gave as his reason: "Cobb could do everything better than any other player I ever saw. He was always the first one to detect a weakness or mistakes of the opposition and benefit by the same." Tris Speaker, the only player who beat out Cobb for the American League batting crown between the years of 1907 and 1919, picked Cobb because "he could do all that any player should do and had besides great competitive spirit and the willingness to take chances at all times." Connie Mack, his later-day manager, wrote: "He surpassed all the players that I can remember."

Larry Gardner, the great Red Sox and Cleveland third baseman, said: "He had the finest co-ordination I ever saw in a player. Because of his mental and mechanical ability, and his remarkable application of the two, he could do everything exceptionally well."

And even from the National League side of the house came votes and praises for Cobb. Billy Southworth, famous Cardinal manager now in Boston, commented: "Cobb's base running and all-around ability more than matched Ruth's slugging." And Casey Stengel, former crack Dodger outfielder, and manager of the Brooklyn and Boston National League clubs, wrote: "I think he was the most sensational base runner who ever lived. He could get more base hits than any competitor simply by worrying the pitcher to desperation and crossing up the infielder."

Clifford Cravath, former National League home-run champion and ex-Phillie manager, now a judge in California, gave these reasons for naming Cobb baseball's No. 1 man: "He could do everything a little better than the rest of the herd. He had color and the will to win. And he would chase half of the present-day players out

69

of the park with his spikes today. He could dish it out and he could take it."

Hughie Jennings, Cobb's old manager in Detroit, had died long before the poll was taken. Hugh had a little feeling of hurt after Cobb succeeded him as Tiger manager in 1922. Yet, at a fanning bee after Jennings became assistant manager of the Giants, the author recalls Jennings' stressing another feature of Cobb's manifold character, his utter fearlessness.

"Ty had his faults, but he was the most fearless man I have ever known," said Jennings. "He was afraid of nothing. He was a captain in the latter months of the World War, but I always thought what a terrific soldier he would have been under battle conditions. I always felt it was lucky for the North that Cobb wasn't born about 40 years earlier. He would have been a whole Confederate army. When he was in his prime, he had half of the American League players scared stiff."

2

Tyrus Raymond Cobb was born December 18, 1886, on a farm at Narrows, Banks County, Georgia, but the family also had a home in the town of Royston. His father, W. H. Cobb, who at first strongly objected to Ty playing ball, had been a Georgia state senator and was superintendent of the Banks County schools when his eldest son, Tyrus, was launched on his professional baseball career in 1904.

Senator Cobb had his heart set on his eldest son becoming a law-yer; as a boy Ty wanted to become a doctor. "And here is an oddity," Cobb reminisced many years later. "One of the boys I grew up with, who always wanted to be a ball player, now is a famous physician and surgeon in Georgia. I, who wanted to be the doctor, wound up the ball player." However, Cobb still has that hankering for medicine, and to help suffering humanity. Though the great athlete long since has moved from his native Georgia, and now is a resident of Menlo Park, Calif., and Lake Tahoe, Nevada, he announced in the winter of 1945-46 that he would build a memorial hospital in honor of his parents in his old home town of Royston.

Though Cobb had loved to play ball since he was a shaver, it was a big red-haired Southern minister, John Yarborough, known as "Brother John," who really got Ty his start in baseball. In subsequent years, when Cobb returned from successful baseball seasons, he heard himself grilled in the Royston pulpit for wasting his time and unquestionable talents in that worldly pastime, professional baseball.

Brother John was the son of a Methodist minister of Augusta, Ga., and had attended Richmond Academy, where he won considerable fame as a hard-hitting catcher. Following his father's footsteps, John Yarborough was early assigned to a little church in Royston. There he found a group of teen-aged, baseball-minded boys, who weren't too keen about their church attendance. Cobb was one of them. However, the kids knew the young minister could catch and hit, and asked him whether he would manage their team.

Mr. Yarborough prayed for some time on the matter, and then felt he got his answer. If the boys would promise to attend church and Sunday school, he would catch for their team and manage it. The boys readily consented. The club was known as the Royston Rompers, and they wore red uniforms. Speaking of Cobb in later years, the Rev. Yarborough remarked: "Ty, or Tyrus, as he was always called in those days, was a little, skinny, spare-built fellow and I thought he was about the best ball player, naturally, I ever had seen." It was just about this time that Tyrus changed his ambition from becoming a doctor to a ball player, for the Reverend continued: "He told me privately of his ambition to become a ball player and asked me if I would help him get started."

Ty, then only 17, already had written to the Augusta and several other Sally (South Atlantic) League clubs for a trial, but received no response. Yarborough then agreed to write to some people on the Augusta club, with whom he was acquainted, to see that Ty would get a trial.

"Tyrus' father did not like the idea of his son becoming a ball player the least bit," added the Reverend; "so I had to persuade him that it was for the best. I told him: 'Your son is bound to be a player; it is just natural for him, and he is too good to stay out of it. It is better to let him go with your approval than to have him go away without it.' So at last he consented, though he never exactly did approve."

But Yarborough proved a good judge on the length of time Ty would last on the Augusta team. "Tyrus was a very hotheaded young fellow," the minister said. "When he left for Augusta, I said: 'Tyrus, you will get a berth on that team, but you will not stay there.' He turned to me somewhat hurt, and said: 'What makes you say that, Mr. Yarborough? I am just crazy to stay there.' I replied: 'You'll be fined and fired before the season is out, because you are so butt-headed and won't take orders.' "

3

Cobb appeared at Augusta in the spring of 1904, paying his own expenses, and armed with a letter from Yarborough saying he was "a good boy and a good ball player." The Augusta club then was managed by a hard-boiled minor leaguer, Con Strouthers. In Cobb's first game, he hit a homer and a double, but he hit the home run on a ball on which Strouthers instructed him to lay down a bunt. And he showed his inexperience in the outfield. In his second game, Cobb went hitless, and Strouthers fired him, saying: "I want only ball players who do what I tell them to do."

And here is the masterpiece of unconscious baseball humor. After tying the can to Ty, baseball's greatest all-time hitter, Strouthers inserted an ad in *Sporting Life,* the Philadelphia baseball weekly of that period: "The Augusta club is looking for a first-class shortstop and a hard-hitting outfielder. Will pay good money to good men. Con Strouthers, Augusta, Ga., Baseball Club."

As far as the elder Cobb was concerned, he, too, did some wiring. Fired in Augusta, Ty wrote home that he had obtained another outfield berth with Anniston, Ala., in the Southeastern League. Though Ty's father had objected to his boy playing professional ball, he wired his son: DON'T COME HOME A FAILURE. And Tyrus never forgot that wire, and today still says it did a lot in shaping his career.

Cobb hit .370 in 22 games at Anniston, long enough for an enthusiastic Anniston writer to wire Grantland Rice, then sports editor of the *Atlanta Journal,* a 200-word telegram recounting the rare ability and possibilities of the Royston resident. Grant was so impressed that he wouldn't accept the wire unless the Anniston enthusiast paid the charges. He often kids with Cobb about the message.

Cobb was back with the Augusta team later in the season, Strouthers, himself, having moved elsewhere by that time. He hit only .237 in 37 Sally League games, led off for the team, and there were frequent references to his speed and wild base running. It is interesting to note that many of the Dixie public prints of that day referred to him as Cyrus Cobb and Cy Cobb.

The Tiger team trained in Augusta in the spring of 1905, and the Detroit players had their first acquaintance with Cobb, by this time one of the regular Augusta outfielders. Frankly, they believed the young Southerner who barked at everyone and ran all the time was "nuts," and they got a lot of enjoyment out of egging on the brash kid.

On Armour's Detroit squad that spring was a former Detroit semipro pitcher, Eddie Cicotte, who later became one of the foremost pitchers in the game only to be later enmeshed in the unfortunate Black Sox scandal of 1919-20. To recompense the Augusta club for the use of its grounds as a training field, Armour left Cicotte in Augusta, with the stipulation that he could have the pick of the Augusta club later in the season for $500.

In many respects, that 1905 Augusta team was one of the most unusual minor-league outfits in the game, even though it finished only fourth in a six-club league. Before Cobb moved up to the Tigers, he led the league in batting with .326 for 103 games. He stole 40 bases. The averages were compiled by Grant Rice, the league secretary. All three of the club's pitchers, Nap Rucker, Cicotte, and Ducky Holmes, reached the majors, with Rucker and Cicotte climbing the heights with Cobb. Though Rucker spent most of his National League career with second-division Brooklyn teams, he was one of the greatest of the game's left-handers. The club's second baseman, Clyde Engle, later played for the Yankees, Red Sox, and Indians. As a Boston pinch hitter in the 1912 Red Sox-Giant World Series, he hit the fly ball on which Fred Snodgrass, McGraw's old center fielder, made his historic $30,000 muff.

There was a veteran minor leaguer from Phillipsburg, N. Y., George Leidy, on the club, who filled in at first base and helped out in the outfield. Later he became the manager. The New Yorker no doubt recognized the spark of genius in Cobb and perhaps sensed something of his future. He took the hot-tempered Royston boy under his wing, and taught him what he knew, how to wait at bat for good balls, an improved method of sliding, how to judge long outfield flys and to play the difficult low line drives. Interested in Cobb's speed, Leidy had him practice bunting by the hour. Leidy pitched to him, teaching him the hit-and-run, and would make him bunt to a sweater placed on either the right or left side of the infield.

Ed Barrow, by this time manager of the Indianapolis club, tells how he had a chance to buy Cobb and Engle from Augusta early that season for $800. "The Augusta club wanted $800 for Cobb and Engle together, or $500 for one of the pair. Thinking Cobb the less desirable of the two, I offered $300, which Augusta turned down. So I lost this great player for $200."

However, under Leidy's skill, Cobb became more valuable as the season progressed, and some of Grant Rice's Sally League averages reached major-league towns. Suffering from those outfield injuries, Bill Armour sent the Detroit scout, Heinie Youngman, to have a look at "that crazy kid we saw last spring." Arriving in Augusta, Youngman didn't even get to see the boy. The day before he arrived, Ty had a thumb badly spiked and was out of the game. But Youngman heard such glowing reports that he put through the deal for Cobb. Under the terms of the spring deal, he could have had Cobb for $500, but with the permission of Navin, Heinie threw in another $250 and made it $750. And the Detroit club also permitted Augusta to keep Cicotte, who later developed into a $50,000 pitcher. And so the greatest ball player of all time became the property of the Detroit club.

4

Cobb joined the Tigers in Detroit, and played his first of 3,033 games (one of his many records) at Bennett Field, August 30, 1905. The first big-league pitcher he faced was Jack Chesbro, the great New York spitballer, who had won 41 games for Griffith's team the season before. Tyrus Raymond flattened out one of Happy Jack's famous spitters for a double in his first time at bat in the first inning, driving in two Tiger runs. He played center field that day, flanked by McIntyre in left and Sam Crawford in right. The "Infant Prodigy," as Paul H. Bruske, Detroit scribe, quickly dubbed Cobb, proved a good mascot as Detroit, with George Mullin pitching, won from New York that day by a 5 to 3 score. By an odd coincidence, when Cobb called it a career twenty-three years later, serving as a pinch hitter for Jimmy Dykes of the Athletics in Ty's 3,033rd game, at Yankee Stadium, September 11, 1928, he was on the losing side to New York by the same score—5 to 3.

When Ty finally laid aside his cudgel and well-worn spikes, he had a batting average of .367, the highest ever compiled by any hitter, and during the greater part of his career, he batted against the soggy old ball, and pitchers were permitted to use the spitball, the shiner, emery ball and other trick deliveries.

In twelve seasons, bunched within a period of thirteen years, he wore the American League batting crown; along with the ancient Jesse Burkett and the modern Rogers Hornsby, he is one of the three men with three .400 batting averages, and they didn't use the 1887 rules. Cobb scored more runs, made more hits, was oftener at bat than any other player in history. From the time he first hit .300 in 1906, he ran off 23 successive .300 averages; his lowest figure in that time was his fading-out average of .323 in 1928, when he was approaching his forty-second birthday. He stole 892 bases, and holds the modern record for one season, 96 in 1915. It always was a matter of regret to him that he couldn't make it an even 100. That boy never was satisfied.

No player ever made a greater science of hitting than Ty Cobb. He had a remarkable natural ability, a vast amount of nervous energy, the agility and speed of an antelope, but he made himself the hitter and base runner that he was by study and application.

"Batting is a continual problem that you solve in detail, over and over, but never thoroughly master," he once remarked in a reminiscent mood. "The longer I live the more I realize that batting is a mental problem rather than a physical stunt. The ability to grasp the bat, to swing at the proper time, to assume the proper stance, all those things are elementary. Batting rather is a continual study in psychology, a sizing up of the opposing pitcher and the catcher, and observation of a lot of little details that all are of immense importance. It's much like a study of crime, like the work of a detective as he picks up a clue here and there, none of them seemingly important, but all of them adding up to something worth while.

"Every opposing pitcher was an individual problem. When I was in the league, I learned to know them all, their quirks and mental peculiarities, and what they were likely to do under certain circumstances. I learned to study the catchers with equal care. One catcher would call for a certain pitch in a certain spot, while another catcher invariably asked for something entirely different in a similar circumstance. It was my business to learn these quirks and preferences. You stored them up in your brain; they became imbedded in your subconscious, and you had them ready for immediate use when you really needed them."

Cobb was a reckless, daring, crafty base runner. He knew his rights on the base lines; he had the right of way and demanded it. And if an infielder got into his way, and was cut down, it was too bad. Like Hanlon's Baltimore Orioles and McGraw's early New York Giants, he practiced the psychology of filing his spikes to a razor's edge while awaiting his turn at bat. He never thought it did any harm to have those infielders afraid of him. If he made a science of hitting, it was the the same way when he got on the bases. His success there was a combination of speed, daring, and the art of getting the jump and then eluding would-be taggers. His strategy was much like that of General George Patton in World War II; Ty let them know he was coming, scared hell out of them in advance, but they never knew exactly how and where he would strike. He made himself as elusive on the bases as an electric eel. There were so-called "fade-away," "fall-away," and "hook" slides before his day, but few players mastered them as did Ty Cobb. He invariably managed to have the minimum of his person exposed to the catcher or baseman seeking to tag him—usually nothing but a toe with a sharpened spike.

Plays in which Cobb scored from first on singles, from second on sacrifice bunts and outfield flies were of daily occurrence. Sid Keener, sports editor of the *St. Louis Star-Times,* as a young reporter once belabored Paul Krichell, Yankee head scout, and former Brown catcher, for pegging the ball to third as Ty went down to second on a steal. "That probably was the dumbest play I've ever seen," wrote Sid. "Keener was all wrong on that one," recalled Krichell. "I'd call it my smartest play. I saw Cobb had such a lead that I had no chance to throw him out at second, so I pegged to third to be sure we would stop him at that bag if he kept on running."

Paul Krichell knew his Cobb. He is one of the catchers on whom Cobb stole his way around, purloining second, third, and home in succession. Others who suffered this indignity were Ira Thomas, once a Tiger teammate and later Connie Mack's first-string catcher on the Athletics, and Lou Criger, Cy Young's famous old battery partner.

In his early years in the league, Criger was one of the most difficult catchers for Cobb to steal against. In fact, there was an early feud between the Young-Criger battery, then still with the Red Sox, and the young outfielder from Georgia. To use the vernacular of the day, Cy and Lou "hated the brash kid's guts," and Ty returned it in spades.

"There's that so-and-so prima donna up again," Cy would say in apparent disdain. "I passed a good hitter just to get you, you Georgia bum."

Ty would tap his bat on the plate, and reply: "It's a wonder they wouldn't be carting you off to the Old Women's Home. I guess they feel sorry for an old stiff like you, because you fought in the Civil War, and let you stay around." Then Cy would drive Cobb back with a fast one at Ty's head.

"Afraid of that, were you?" Young would add. "All you Southerners are like that. My old man used to chase your pappy over the top of Lookout Mountain. It's too bad Sherman didn't do more to Georgia when he was down your way. He left too many corncobs lying around."

Ty replied in kind, and then would add tauntingly, "Now, let's

76

see your fast one. I could count the stitches on that last one coming in to the plate."

By that time Young had nearly two decades of big-league baseball behind him, but taunted by Cobb's disrespect, he tried to pitch with just a little more speed behind it. Ty would give him that irritating laugh. "D'you call that smoke?" he would mimick. "If you can't do any better than that, I'll drive the next one down your throat, and they can cart you off to the G.A.R. cemetery."

And so it went; Cobb got his share of hits off the veteran's assorted deliveries; Cy got his share of Cobb zeroes in the box score. Criger invariably seconded all of Young's compliments, adding a few of his own. It vexed Cobb that old Lou invariably anticipated his steals and shot him down at second. This was a challenge; so one day when he reached first while Lou was catching, he served notice that he was going to steal second. Accomplishing this mission, he yelled: "And now, you old baboon, I'm on my way to third." Picking himself safely out of the dust at third, he called: "And now I'm coming home, you old ice wagon, and if you're in the way I'll cut the old legs right from under you." He came in with the pitch, and slid safely into the sputtering, swearing Criger. From then on, Lou had no further terrors for him.

Cobb was a real artist. A rash play was always more enjoyable when made against one worthy of his steel. In his first decade in the American League, the player with the quickest wits was Hal Chase, first baseman for the old New York Highlanders. A left-hander, Chase threw with deadly accuracy to the bases. He invariably threw to the bag for which the runner was heading, even though he knew the runner would be safe. He did this so that in the event the runner overran or overslid the bag, he could be tagged out.

"Chase was cute and quick with his hands," recalled Ty, "but one day I decided to cross him up. It was in the ninth inning, with the score a tie. I was on first base, and, getting a good lead, I headed for third on Crawford's infield out. Sure enough Chase pegged the ball over to Jimmy Austin. I was past third, when the throw got there, but instead of trying to return, as they expected, I broke for the plate and scored before Austin could relay the ball there. Scoring from first on an infield out to Chase! I guess that was a play that pleased me more than any other."

Cobb had no angelic disposition. He was self-centered, hot-tempered—butt-headed, as that Georgia clergyman put it. Players who played with and against Cobb have told me that he had a cruel streak in his nature. He was in countless feuds and fights. In his early years in the league, he took his share of beatings, but he later reversed the verdict on most of them with the lone exception of Charley Schmidt, the old Detroit catcher, and one of the strongest men who ever played baseball. He was more or less of a lone wolf during his 22 years with the Tigers, and had few intimates on the Tigers or among the newspapermen who followed the Detroit ball club.

He was heartily disliked, even hated, by many players of his day, even fellow Tigers. Some, not realizing at the start how good Cobb really was, resented his so-called "Southern airs," and his publicity. There even was a story, pretty well confirmed, that one of his early Detroit associates tipped off opposing pitchers to his weakness—if he had one.

Some called Cobb a "dirty ball player." The writer, who wrote major-league baseball in all but Cobb's first six years in the majors, never considered him that. With Cobb, professional baseball was a war, and every game a battle. He was of the type who gave no quarter, and asked for none. Cobb came to Dr. Robert F. Hyland, distinguished club physician to both St. Louis clubs, for a consultation late in his career.

"I knew Cobb was a pretty tough hombre during his stormy career," said Dr. Hyland. "But, when I saw him stripped, my admiration for him increased many fold. His legs from his feet to his hips were a mass of scars and bruises, new ones and old—souvenirs of years of play. In some places, there was a new scar over an old one. I decided then and there that Ty Cobb could take it as well as dish it out. Did anyone ever hear of Ty Cobb crying: 'Joe Blottz spiked me on that play'? If he was spiked, he had his own way of taking care of it."

Cobb was a little touchy if anyone questioned his sportsmanship. When he played ball, he didn't play ball just for fun; he wasn't playing tiddlywinks, nor under tiddlywinks rules. "Baseball is a red-blooded game for red-blooded men," he once remarked, discussing this phase of his career. "It's no pink tea and mollycoddles had better stay out. It's a contest and all that implies; a struggle for supremacy; a survival of the fittest. Every veteran is not only fighting against the other side, but he is trying to hold his own job against some youngster on his own bench or out on some baseball farm. Why deny this? Why minimize it? Why not boldly admit it?

"Some of the writers have accused me of being unfair in my play. Well, that's not my understanding of the word. Where players have stepped on my toes, I have stepped back. I was smacked down plenty when I first broke into the game. If I'd been meek and submissive, and hadn't fought back, the world never would have heard of Ty Cobb.

"When I still was a green kid, gaining my reputation as a hitter, opposing pitchers did everything to stop me. Some weren't too nice. I was their enemy. They didn't hesitate to shy a bean ball at my head now and then to intimidate me. Suppose their efforts had been successful. There's a grapevine through the big leagues, and news spreads rapidly. Other pitchers would have learned that I scared easily, and could be frightened away from the plate. They would have taken similar advantages, and I'd have lasted in the big leagues two years—instead of twenty-four.

"Well, what was I to do? I could turn my back on baseball, and return home, or fight back. I had decided baseball was my game—and business—and it didn't take me long to decide what to do. I fought back. Any time I felt a certain pitcher was deliberately trying to get me, I was ready. A batter knows when a pitcher is wild, or lets one go at his head. I had profited by Leidy's early coaching, and could drag my bunts down the first-base line pretty well. I could do it, so that pitcher would have to cover first base, and I would go into that bag full speed. There usually was a collision, and I didn't come off second best. Pitchers quickly discovered that if they tried any rough stuff on me, I could be just as rough—and tough—as they were.

"Many persons have accused me of deliberately spiking infielders. The Athletics fastened a bad reputation on me in my early career, when during a tense late-season game, I spiked Frank Baker. It is true that I spiked him, but Baker was rather clumsy in covering the bag, and I wasn't the only player who ever spiked him. The fault was his, not mine. I was merely taking what belonged to me, the base paths. The rules gave me that right, and I insisted on it. I always went into a bag at full speed, and I had developed a quick dart at the bag, feet first. I had sharp spikes on my shoes, so if the baseman stood where he had no business to stand, and got hurt, it was his own fault.

"The public likes to see a scrappy, hard-fought game. I tried to give them that kind of baseball, both as a player and as a manager. Above all, they like to see a winner, and if they can't have a pennant winner, they want to see their home team win the game they are playing. In a winner, they idolize spirit, determination, fight. Baseball is governed by broad general rules; there is no biting, gouging, or hitting in the clinches. But there is a wide latitude which permits daring plays and a display of spirit. Maybe it is a sign of good sportsmanship to stand on one side and apologize for defeating an opponent. It may express the superior breed of a gentleman, but it isn't our great game of baseball. And we, as a nation, have done pretty well playing the greater game much as we play our game of baseball."

And Cobb had proper respect for his enemies of the diamond. Talking to Jimmy Powers, sports editor of the *New York News,* early in the war, Cobb laughed at his first experience with the mighty Hans Wagner, his closest rival as baseball's No. 1 player. "I met Honus for the first time in the 1909 Detroit-Pittsburgh World's Series," said Ty. "Wagner, of course, was at short for Clarke's aggressive team. I got on base early, and cupping my hands, yelled down to Wagner: 'Hey, Krauthead, I'm coming down to second on the next pitch.' He didn't say anything, but when I got down to second he had Gibson's throw and was waiting for me with the ball. He slapped it into my mouth and split my lip for three stitches."

6

In Ty Cobb's first complete season with the Tigers, 1906, his presence had no magic effect on the Detroit percentage. The Tigers, who climbed so courageously from seventh to third in 1905, slipped back to sixth a year later, an intense disappointment for Yawkey, Navin, and Armour. In fact, the drop cost Armour his job, for Navin, after some difficulty, hired Hughie Jennings as Bill's successor. It remained a sore subject with Armour, who always felt that had he been retained, he could have won the same pennants which soon were to tumble into Hughie's lap. "The plums were ripe, and ready to fall," Bill used to say.

Armour's 1906 club showed some signs of its future potentiality when in a late September series it kicked Griffith's Highlanders out of the American League pennant by beating them three straight, after the New Yorkers had taken a seemingly crucial series from Chicago. Those three Tiger victories gave the Hitless Wonder White Sox their eventual three-game margin over New York.

The 1906 season also saw the Tigers acquire two valuable players from Minneapolis, Davey Jones, a fleet-footed outfielder and first-class lead-off man, who had formerly played for the Cubs, and Charley "Dutch" Schmidt, a hefty 120-game catching backstop. They never will give Charley a niche in the Hall of Fame for his catching, but he was a horse for work and a fine competitor. He once boxed Jack Johnson, the old heavyweight champion, in an ex-hibition and for amusement he used to drive spikes into the club-house floor with his fists. Another famous Schmidt stunt was to lie on the floor, and defy the whole club to pull him to his feet.

Despite the fact that Cobb showed all the earmarks of being an outstanding hitter and all-around player, it is doubtful if Armour recognized Ty's great possibilities. He had Cobb in and out of his line-up, and though the kid from Georgia hit .320, Armour used him in only 97 games. It was around this time that Detroit almost lost this player of the century to New York.

The late Frank Farrell, New York owner at that time, once told the author that "if Griff [Clark Griffith] had been a little more enterprising in 1906, we would have had Ty Cobb, and the entire history of the New York Americans would have been different. Griff couldn't decide on giving up the necessary players Detroit wanted in the deal."

However, that isn't Griffith's version on it. "I believe I was one of the first people to realize that Cobb would become an eventual star," he told me as this manuscript was being prepared. "Of course, no one could realize that he would reach the height to be the greatest of all times. When I was in New York and Cobb was a youngster with the Detroit club, I did everything to try to make a trade for the player. Both teams were training in the South in the spring of 1906, and Cobb had some trouble with the Detroit management. When I heard of it, I immediately got in touch with him and tried to arrange a trade for Cobb, but Hal Chase was not mentioned in the deal. [This has frequently been reported.] Can't remember the name of the outfielder I had at that time but he and a pitcher were the only ones we ever offered. To tell the truth, we never came any-where close to making the deal."

Cobb had a difficult time trying to fit himself into Armour's team. Players of that era made it tough for kids breaking in, especially if the youngster aspired to a job held by some members of a poker set. At that time, comparatively few players came from the deep South, and Ty was as Southern as Jeff Davis. Most of the other Tigers were from north of the Mason-Dixon line. They used profanity of the sort which made the Virginian say: "When you call me that, smile." Only, when they used it on Cobb, they didn't smile.

They knotted his clothes, broke his bats, and heaped other indignities on him. And Cobb was of the type that didn't take such hazing meekly—or graciously. He constantly fought back; he was cocky, fresh, and belligerent. That only made the hazers increase their tempo. "Ty did a lot of fighting when he first was with Detroit, but he had a lot of guts to stick it out," Bill Donovan once told me. "Those Tigers weren't too nice to him."

He would try to take his turn at bat during hitting practice, but his older teammates shoved him aside. "Go out and chase flies, busher, where you belong," was the taunt they hurled at him.

"Can't I take batting practice with the regulars, Mr. Armour?" Cobb would say to his manager.

"Sure, son, go up and hit," the manager replied. And then Cobb would find that some playful—or spiteful—Jungle Cat had sawed his bats in two. That made him raving mad.

Probably the fact that Cobb had to take all this hazing made him look for a victim of his own. He found him in Dutch Schmidt, the big catcher. Perhaps the fact that Charley came from Coal Hill, Arkansas, should have made them fellow sons of Dixie, but Cobb regarded the catcher more as a Dutchman than as a Southerner. The 1906 training camp was the first for both, and Ty began a calculated campaign of tormenting big Charley. However, goading normally peaceable players was always a Cobb characteristic.

He probably regarded burly Schmidt's pig-iron toughness as a challenge. At any rate he never overlooked an opportunity to goad good-natured Charley. He was indefatigable and relentless about it. He would kick Schmidt's suitcase out of his hand and down the platform. Once he even dumped a glass of toothpicks into Charley's soup in the dining room. In every way the fertile mind could devise he indicated he was spoiling for a fight, and preferably with tough Schmidt.

Schmidt saw through it, but realized that damaging the promising Cobb was the surest way he knew of getting his own ticket back to the bushes. He was berated, shoved around, and tormented by Cobb at every opportunity. Not even the Dutchman's vast good nature and calculated patience could stand up under that indefinitely. Schmidt was restrained by another consideration, which however fanciful, was very real to him. He knew his own overwhelming strength, and was afraid he might do Cobb some serious harm. He had a genuine reluctance to be the victim of a lynching, and as long as they still were south of the Mason and Dixon line, he really thought he might play the leading role in a necktie party if he seriously manhandled the stripling Georgia Peach.

He decided to bide his time and wait until they were north of "the line." Schmidt interceded when Ty had an altercation with a woman who had done his laundry. The two players almost came to blows then, but cooler heads among the coaching staff interceded. Bobbie Lowe, by this time serving as a coach–utility man, had been fully aware of the problem, and had done his best to keep Cobb and Schmidt apart. At the practice field, with Armour's connivance, he had managed to have them work out at different times, or invented schemes to have Cobb in the field while Schmidt was at bat, and another catcher doing the catching when Ty took his batting drill.

But the laundry woman incident and Schmidt's intercession brought the matter to a head. When Schmidt left for the field, Cobb headed for the arena immediately afterward. Lowe saw him start, and tried to warn Schmidt, but there wasn't time. As soon as Cobb reached the field, he jumped Schmidt and Charley unleashed all the pent-up resentment which he had been forced to harbor. Cobb, then still underage, was no match for the muscular Schmidt in a rollicking free-for-all, but he wasn't ready to admit it, even when Schmidt was giving him a beating. And Schmidt, who related the story years later to Bud Shaver, remarked admiringly: "The son-of-a-gun wouldn't yell 'Nuff,' so I was glad when they pulled me off him. I didn't want to hurt him too bad."

They had a return engagement, which Schmidt again won without too much difficulty. He became one of Cobb's greatest admirers, an admiration the Dutchman carried to his dying day. His loyalty and admiration really dated from that first scrap, but Charley never felt fully secure in Cobb's vicinity for several years. He carefully restrained relaxing his grip on beer steins or any other ready weapon of defense when Cobb was within reach of similar weapons. Finally, in Philadelphia, Cobb got in a jam from which Schmidt helped extricate him with his powerful fists and from then on the Dutchman was a willing, if wary, ally of Cobb, and Ty became one of the Arkansas German's best boosters.

"EE-YAH" MAN WINS
FIRST A. L. PENNANT

I

NEXT IN IMPORTANCE TO FRANK NAVIN'S SHIFTING HIS EARLY bookkeeping desk from Sam Angus' insurance office to his baseball business and the coming of young Ty Cobb to the Tigers in 1905, the most important move in the metamorphosis of the Detroit club from a penny-pinching second-division club to baseball riches was the signing of Hugh Jennings, shortstop of the fabulous old Orioles and manager of the Baltimore Eastern League club, as Tiger chieftain after the unhappy season of 1906.

Jennings' enthusiasm, natural ability, and dynamic personality did wonders with the Detroit material Bill Armour turned over to him. While it is true that Hughie's magic eventually deserted him, and fourteen years later he left the Tigers with an aggregation much like the one he took over—in seventh place—his tenure of office, especially the early years, was among the most dramatic and gripping in colorful Detroit baseball history.

And it wasn't easy for Navin to get permission to sign the chattering, red-haired, freckle-faced Pennsylvania Irishman to a Detroit contract. He had a difficult time selling Hughie to Ban Johnson, and without Ban's O.K. no manager or player could come into the American League in 1907. He then was Czar Ban I, at the very height of his power, and one of his pet aversions was Baltimore Orioles.

Winding up his major playing career with the Philadelphia Nationals in 1902, Jennings developed quite a reputation as a picturesque, live-wire manager in Baltimore, the scene of his early triumphs, as a fighting, hard-throwing shortstop. Several National League clubs were angling for his services, and then came a report that Detroit was interested in Jennings. Ban Johnson heard about it and sent for Navin.

The "Ee-Yah" Man, Hugh Jennings

The American League Champions of 1907

Play on Which Cobb Spiked Baker in Hectic 1909 Race

"What's this I hear about you being interested in Hugh Jennings?" Ban asked.

"It's true," said Navin. "I think he would make a good man for us."

"I don't want him in the American League," said Johnson with his usual positiveness.

"Why, what is there against him?" asked Navin.

"He's got that old Oriole stamp on him, and he's too close to John McGraw. We cleaned Oriole rowdyism out of this league, and I won't have it brought back by Jennings," Ban snapped.

Ned Hanlon's Orioles of the National League were a rough and rowdy club of fighters and umpire baiters. As manager of the American League Orioles of 1901 and 1902, McGraw had played pretty much that kind of ball and he was constantly in Ban's doghouse. Then Johnson hated McGraw more than any other man in baseball, for in midseason, 1902, when the baseball war still was on, McGraw accepted an offer to manage the New York Giants and took a half dozen of the best Baltimore players with him. And Jennings was McGraw's crony and intimate. They had played alongside of each other on the old Oriole infield, had gone through St. Bonaventure College, and frequently palled together during the off-season.

Navin wasn't discouraged. "Yawkey will be awfully disappointed if we don't get Jennings," he added. "He likes him, and has seen him work in the East. Thinks he's just the kind of a man we need to put life into our club. And if you don't agree to let us hire Jennings, I think Bill will be so mad that he'll pull his money out of the club, and we'll be as badly off as ever."

"Well, if you feel that strongly about him, go ahead and engage him," said Johnson grudgingly. "But I still don't like him, and he'll have to understand from the start that Oriole tactics will not be tolerated in the American League. I warn you, I'll clamp down on him hard the first time he gets out of order."

Considered from a perspective of forty years, Navin practically stole Jennings from Ned Hanlon, captain of the champion Detroits of 1887, who then ran the Baltimore Eastern League club. Hughie, then only 36, was still signed to a player's contract, and played in 75 games for his 1906 Baltimore team. When Navin expressed a wish to Hanlon that he release Hughie so he could accept a Detroit offer, Ned placed a $5,000 price tag on him. That was more than Frank wanted to pay. So the wily Detroiter drafted Jennings. The Class A draft price then was $1,000 (it was long before the Double A and

Triple A minors) and Navin procured Hughie for this modest sum. It was probably the only time that a big-league club drafted its manager, and a pennant-winning manager to boot.

2

Hugh Ambrose Jennings was one of the real rich personalities of the game. Even though Ban Johnson listed him as one of the rowdy Orioles, Jennings was a warm friendly person. This may be an awful thing to say about an old Oriole, but there was even a certain sweetness about him. Though a close associate of John McGraw, he did not have McGraw's truculence, love of physical encounter, or fiery temper. He had laughing Irish blue eyes, had a fine sense of humor, and could see the ludicrousness of a situation which would have made McGraw fighting mad.

He was a one-man show on the coaching lines, and when Detroit was winning pennants was almost as much of an attraction as Ty Cobb. He pulled up fistfuls of grass from around the coacher's box, raised his left foot, and with clenched fists gave vent to his famous cry of "Ee-yah! Ee-yah." Fans liked to sit in back of him in the third-base bleachers and kid with him, and throughout baseball he was famous as "the Ee-yah man."

Hughie was born April 2, 1870, in Pittston, Pa., in the Pennsylvania hard-coal country, not far from Minooka, the birthplace of Steve O'Neill, the present Tiger manager. He was a catcher in his early days, and caught for the strong independent Lehighton, Pa., club. In his first game in professional ball with Allentown, he almost killed the batter with an intended peg to shoot a base runner down at second. His throw, from a distance of a few feet, caught the unfortunate guy on the back of the head and knocked him cold.

The league in which Allentown was a member blew up in 1891 and Hughie caught for a coal-town team against the Louisville club in an exhibition game. Louisville then was big-league, and Jack Chapman, the manager, was so impressed with the young redhead that he took him along and played Hughie at first base. Jennings later shifted to shortstop, where he was to achieve his greatest fame. Louisville traded him to Baltimore of the old twelve-club National League, where the manager was Ned Hanlon, and Jennings was thrown in contact with such brilliant stars as Willie Keeler, McGraw, Joe Kelley, and Wilbert Robinson. Hughie was a made hitter, as he batted only .232 and .192 in 1892 and 1893. But you learned

86

fast on those Orioles, and if you didn't, you didn't last long in the club.

As Baltimore won its spectacular pennants of 1894-95-96, Jennings improved with the team, as his batting averages for those three seasons skyrocketed to .332, .386, and .397. In 1895 he stole 60 bases, 72 in 1896, and it was back to 60 in 1897. His fielding was on a par with his hitting and base running, and with a great arm he pegged out runners from left field.

Some of the Oriole stars were shifted to Brooklyn in 1899, and Hughie played on two more pennant winners under Hanlon in that city in 1899 and 1900. By this time, Hughie stretched the elastic too far in his strong right arm, and it never regained its old snap. But Hughie could still hit and run, and he moved to first base.

Unlike many of his fellow players of the gay nineties, Jennings didn't spend his winters sitting on his seat and swilling up a lot of beer. He managed to pick up his share of schooling in the coal country, attended St. Bonaventure College, and later matriculated in Cornell's law school. He continued his perusal of Blackstone in a Scranton law office, was admitted to the bar in Pennsylvania, and later entered a Scranton law partnership.

Though Jennings contracted tuberculosis late in life and died of meningitis in 1928 at the comparatively early age of 58, for a time he seemed to have as many lives as a cat. On June 28, 1897, while playing shortstop for the Orioles, he was nearly killed by Amos Rusie of the Giants, the Bob Feller of his day. One of Rusie's fast balls struck him under the left temple, and for several days the "Ee-yah man" hovered between life and death. But Jennings had a hard head. Some years later he was taking a workout in the Cornell gym, and intended to top it off with a swim. The place was poorly lighted, and no one had bothered telling Hughie that an attendant had drained the pool. He dove head first into the concrete lining of the pool, and again it was feared he would die, but Hughie pulled through. During his Detroit days, he was driving with some friends over one of Pennsylvania's slippery roads during the winter off-season. The car went over the side of a mountain; two persons were killed, another was seriously wounded, but Hughie escaped with a few bruises.

This was the man Navin and Yawkey selected to lead their assortment of temperament and hodgepodge of personality. Hughie could be very firm; a determined glare could come into those blue eyes, and he didn't mince words in telling a player of his shortcomings. But he never tried to drive his club as McGraw drove his

Giants; he never bawled out his club vulgarly and though he had a pretty rough bunch rarely used profanity. He was tireless off and on the field, and tried to cultivate team harmony. Rather than cry about the game that was lost, he was more likely to say: "All right, they pinned our ears back today, but tomorrow is another day."

3

Jennings won Detroit's first American League pennant with practically the same club which came home sixth in 1906. The one important acquisition was hard-hitting Claude Rossman, the hefty first baseman. Claude was no Hal Chase around first base; his biggest difficulty was throwing to other bases and that weakness eventually got him out of the league. But he was a cleanup slugger, had a lot of heart and the ability to come through in the pinches. He started the 1907 training season with Cleveland, but Lajoie had both Rossman and George Stovall for first base, and decided to keep the latter. Navin was pleased to purchase Rossman for a nominal figure.

Cobb, not yet 21, won his first batting championship that year, finishing with an average of .350. Sam Crawford was second among the 100 game players with .324, and collected 34 doubles, 17 triples, and 4 homers. From there on, it was a big drop to Rossman's .277. Even so, the Tigers led the league in hitting with .266, ten points better than the Athletics, who trailed the Tigers in hitting as well as in the standing of the clubs. In Detroit's early American League days, victories for Tiger fans were sweetest when won from Cleveland, the club's geographical rival. However, for the next six years the hated enemy became Mack's ever-troublesome Athletics. Later, Detroit's No. 1 rival became the New York Yankees.

Bill Donovan was magnificent that year, and that first pennant never could have been won but for his amazing contribution, 25 victories against only 4 defeats. Ed Killian, the southpaw, was another 25-game winner, but lost 13 games. Siever was Jennings' spot pitcher, and managed to win 19 games, while losing 10. Big George Mullin was the workhorse of the staff, and not too lucky. Even with a champion, he could do no better than .500, winning 20 games and losing as many.

That 1907 American League race still is vivid in the minds of old-time Detroit fans. Nothing but sheer courage and an invincible will to win ever pulled the Tigers through. At one stage Horace Fogel, one of Philadelphia's leading sports writers, counted the

"Detroit upstarts" right out of the race. Horace could work himself into a lather over Jennings' grass-pulling antics. He appealed to Ban Johnson to stop it, saying it was "silly, destructive and an insult to American League fans." Happy to have a real live contender in Detroit, Ban permitted Hughie to go on being his own lawn mower. On the Detroit side, Joe Jackson, Malcolm Bingay, and little Batchelor kept egging on their beloved Tigers in their newspaper columns. Bingay began figuring, "Now, if the Tigers can win three straight in Washington, and if the White Sox can hold the Athletics to an even break," to such an extent that he became "Iffy, the Dopester."

For most of the early season Chicago led, and while the Tigers were in the first division, few took the pennant chances of Hughie's boys seriously. There was quite a thrill in Detroit on July 25, when the Tigers dislodged Cleveland in second place for a day, and an even greater boot, August 2, when the Tigers took the lead for the first time. The frightened Philadelphia White Elephants scrambled back in front, but Detroit gamely recaptured the lead on the road, August 26. Again the Mackmen shot in front and by September 19 increased their lead so substantially that with the Athletics closing at home and the Tigers being obliged to make another eastern trip, the jig seemed up for the Felines. But Chief Bender, the Athletics' right-handed ace, developed a lame arm, and Rube Waddell became undependable; so the Tigers took fresh courage and began hacking away at Philadelphia's seemingly safe margin.

4

By the time the Tigers reached Philadelphia, September 27, they had whittled the A's' lead down to three points. Three games were scheduled at Phillie's old Columbia Park, on Friday, Saturday, and Monday. The Tigers won the first game, 5 to 4, giving them the lead by a whisker. The result was a fine tribute to Tiger guts and tenacity. Bill Donovan, yielding 13 hits, defeated Eddie Plank, giving up 9, and the box score was cluttered up with Athletics left on the bases. And Germany Schaefer stole two bases, all run in the right direction.

With the park all sold out for the Saturday game, September 28, a beautiful fall rain washed out the game. It necessitated a double-header for the Monday, September 30, and that developed into one of the historic days of baseball history. Instead of two games being played, the clubs struggled 17 innings to a 9-9 game, which virtually gave the flag to Detroit.

Ty Cobb, who tied up the game with a two-run homer in the ninth, calls it the thrill game among his 3,033 in the American League. Hughie Jennings, with a mirthful smile lighting up his blue eyes, could fan of this game by hour, right down to his dying day. It was one of the few times in Connie Mack's sixty-three-year baseball career that he really boiled over, and he still claims he was robbed of the American League penannt on that long afternoon. An important decision favorable to Detroit by Silk O'Loughlin brought about a feud between Mack and Silk which was terminated only by the umpire's death, and as the result of Rube Waddell's blowing a six-run lead the contest practically was the big fellow's swan song in Philadelphia. He appeared in only one Athletic contest after that.

It was one of the craziest games ever played. Donovan had two days of rest after his Friday victory, and Jennings sent Bill in to start what was to have been the first game against Jimmy Dygert, Mack's pony spitball pitcher. Maybe Bill got up too early, for in the early innings the Athletics slapped him around as though he were a batting practice pitcher. By the end of five innings, the Mackmen led by a score of 7 to 1, and the great Philadelphia crowd, which packed the little grandstand and bleachers and stood by the thousands in the outfield, began to think it a lark. They hurled jibes at the Tigers for their effrontery in thinking they might be champions.

And then Donovan suddenly settled; he gave up only two more runs, and getting better as the long afternoon wore on, he hurled shutout ball in the last six frames. In addition to the O'Loughlin decision, Connie Mack also blames his failure to win that day to Jennings' sentiment. "We hit Donovan hard enough in those early innings to knock three pitchers out of the box," said Connie. "But if we'd made 18 runs, Hughie wouldn't have taken him out. Bill's father, brothers, and a whole host of Philadelphia relatives and friends used to come out whenever Donovan pitched against us, and Jennings never would have humiliated him in his own home town."

Mack's eyes gleamed and Hughie was depressed as the A's shot up the Tiger ace for three runs in the first. Dygert, the Philadelphia starter, was guilty of two errors in the second and chased Rossman over the plate on a stupid play. After little Jimmy walked Donovan, filling the bases, it looked as though a real Tiger rally was on.

90

But Mack called in Waddell, and the Rube buzzed third strikes over on Davey Jones and Schaefer.

The Rube also was good for the next four innings, and the Elephants apparently made it easy for him by nicking Wild Bill for two runs in the third and another pair in the fifth. Harry Davis homered in the first of these two-run innings, doubled in the other. That's when the Columbia Park crowd started gloating. As for the Tigers, they began muttering: "Why the hell doesn't Hughie get Donovan out of there; sentiment is all right, but this is murder."

Then in the seventh, the fighting Tigers got into the ball game, scoring four runs as they capitalized heavily on a bad muff by Oldring, which nettled Waddell. Two walks and the error filled the bases; Crawford's double into the overflow crowd scored two; Cobb's infield out fetched in a third, and Crawford raced home as Murphy was tossing out Rossman. The A's rallied with one in their half, and Detroit got this back in the eighth, but when they came up for the ninth the Tigers still were two runs in arrears.

It was a never-to-be-forgotten ninth for Mack and Cobb. Crawford opened with a single, after which Cobb, with no reputation as a home-run hitter, smacked a Waddell pitch over the right-field fence. Ty hit only five round-trippers that season. The hit not only tied the score, but it knocked Waddell out of the box and Mack off the bench. As the ball climbed over the high barrier into Twenty-ninth Street, Mack slid off the bench and sprawled among some bats scattered over the ground. Connie quickly called in Plank, who was being held back for the second game, and Eddie got rid of the side without any further Detroit scoring.

Donovan was a different pitcher after Detroit fought its way into the ball game, and became better and better as the long contest proceeded. Each club scored one run in the tenth, but from that point there was no further run-making and the game eventually was called because of darkness at the end of the seventeenth.

However, the day's real excitement came in the fourteenth, when Harry Davis banged a long fly into the center-field crowd for what looked like a ground-rule double. Just as Crawford tried to get in front of the ball, a Philadelphia copper, on duty in the outfield, arose from a box on which he was sitting and passed before Crawford. Jennings, Crawford, and the other Tigers quickly yelled, "Interference." The contention of the Athletics, also that of the flatfoot, was that he got up from his box to get out of Wahoo Samuel's way. For some time, O'Loughlin, the umpire behind the plate, gave no decision, as players from both teams started milling and arguing around him. Mack always claimed that Silk said to Topsy Hartsel, when the Tiger complaints first started: "I saw no interference."

Eventually, Silk asked Tommy Connolly, his associate on the bases: "Was there interference, Tommy?" and the veteran replied: "There was"; so O'Loughlin called Davis out. It was one of the few times Mack had a brain storm; he invaded the umpire's dressing room after the game to bawl out Silk and never spoke to him again until shortly before the umpire's death. What made it even tougher for Mack, and a happier day for the Tiger, is that Danny Murphy, the next hitter, followed with a long single, which would have scored Davis standing up.

While the argument over Davis' hit raged, Rossman and Monte Cross, substitute Athletic infielder, started swapping punches, as players and policemen were tangled all over the place. One version is that it was Bill Donovan who clipped Monte with a blow which almost knocked him down, and that a copper started to lead Bill away. This story has it that Schaefer saved the situation at this point, saying to the officer, "You can't pinch Bill in Philadelphia; he has so many friends and relatives here, they'd take the badge right off of you." The cop was impressed, saw Rossman swinging wildly, and took him along instead of Donovan, who remained to pitch out the game. Jennings wound up the game with Ed Killian, and later Crawford, as his substitute first baseman.

By holding the Athletics to a tie, the Tigers succeeded in leaving Philadelphia a half game ahead. The race had only a week to go, and Jennings' next stop was Washington, where the Tigers won four straight. Mack was playing Cleveland at the time, and his pitching staff practically was reduced to Plank and Dygert, and little Jimmy kept Philadelphia in the running by pitching three shutouts in four days. The Tigers were on their way to St. Louis for their final series when they learned, October 4, that Walter Johnson of the Senators had beaten Plank, 2 to 1. That practically clinched the flag, but the Tigers put the final spike into their first American League pennant pole, October 5, beating the Browns, 10 to 2. After that the entire team went on a beautiful bender, and in their final double-header with the Browns, the new champions were on the losing end of both games, 10 to 4 and 10 to 3. But who cared? The Tigers' final advantage over the Athletics was only six points, .613 to .607, but they had won.

Detroit had eagerly supported its new champion. Not only the little stands at Bennett Field, but the wildcat bleachers on Cherry Street outside of the park, were crowded during the hectic season with shouting, enthusiastic Tiger fans. The town was coming of age, and already was being acclaimed as the center of the new automobile industry. But, when the American League's attendance figures were compiled, Detroit, with its small park and still small relative population, was next to the bottom with 297,079. The new champions outdrew only the tail-end Senators, and only by seventy-five thousand. Navin knew, with the salaries his players were sure to request next spring, that a pennant winner in Detroit might prove an expensive luxury.

⊗ X ⊗

HERMAN ASKS HERRMANN
A QUESTION

I

THE TIGERS WEREN'T AFRAID OF THE FAMOUS CHICAGO CUBS. THE Chicagoans could spread-eagle everything in the National League, but hadn't the "Hitless Wonder" White Sox beaten them, four games to two, in the World's Series of the fall before? "They're not so tough," Hugh Jennings told his men. "If the White Sox could hit their pitching, we can certainly hit it. Cripes, I've got a far better hitting club than Fielder Jones."

"Sure, we'll beat 'em," chimed in Germany Schaefer. "They fired me once. I got to make 'em feel sorry."

"All we got to do is play them like we played the Athletics," said Cobb in his Georgia drawl.

There was an interesting meeting in the Chicago hotel room of Garry Herrmann, chairman of the old National Commission, on the eve of the Series. The other two members of the Commission, Ban Johnson and Harry Pulliam, were there, as were the two managers, Chance and Jennings, and the umpires Jack Sheridan and Hank O'Day. Schaefer was there as a one-man committee, representing the players. Players of both teams had discussed a contingency the afternoon before, and Germany wanted an official decision on it.

As the meeting neared adjournment, Herrmann asked: "Has anybody else a question they vant to ask?"

Germany got up, and said: "Yes, Mr. Herrmann, I've got a very important question I want to ask."

Garry looked a little annoyed, and Ban Johnson scowled. Was the American League's top comedian going to clown right in the midst of a dignified pre-World's Series meeting?

"Vhat is it, Herman?" asked Garry, in his pronounced Teutonic accent. Though born in Cincinnati, Garry always talked as though he came from the banks of the German Rhine.

94

"I wanna know is a tie game a legal game," said Schaefer.

The remark hit most of the meeting as quite funny, and there were some loud guffaws. The three commissioners didn't laugh. So Germany was trying to be funny, they thought.

Garry Herrmann stammered a few minutes, as though trying to get Schaefer's thought. "Vell, a tie game is legal, so far as gate receipts and records are concerned. But you know as vell as I that if we play a tie, due to rain, darkness, or some other act of God, it doesn't constitute a game and must be played over. But why do you take up the Commission's time to ask such idiotic questions?"

"Because the rules say the players share in the first four games," continued the Tiger second baseman. "And I wanna know if in case there is a tie, and it ain't a legal game, whether the players' pool will be the first five attendances."

Schaefer, indeed, had raised a poser. Under the John T. Brush rules put into effect in 1905, the players shared in the receipts of the first four games. No tie had arisen in the 1905 Giant-Athletic and 1906 White Sox–Cub series, but with the World's Series games then started at 2:30, with darkness creeping over the fields at 5, a tie was always possible.

Garry went into a short huddle with his associates, Johnson and Pulliam, and then gave his pronouncement: "There being no precedent, it is the ruling of the Commission that if in any one contest neither side shall be the winner, the players' pool will be on the gate receipts of the first five attendances."

"That's all I wanted to know, Mr. Herrmann. Thanks," said Germany.

It was clear and warm when the Series opened in old West Side Park, Chicago, on a Tuesday, October 8. A great crowd for that period, 24,377 fans, was on hand to give the Cubs encouragement. They overflowed the wooden grandstand and bleacher and sprawled all over the field. Bill Yawkey headed a small but vociferous delegation from Detroit, who could outdrink and outshout any Chicago rooting section four times its size. Judge Landis, later the commissioner of baseball, was an ardent Cub rooter and jawed back at the bellicose Detroiters.

It seemed an interminable time before they got the game under way. Chance and Jennings, the rival managers, and the umpires gassed at the plate as though this were the first time Abner Doubleday's rules had been interpreted. Then a St. Louis jeweler stepped up to the plate, and Ty Cobb, handsome, lithe batting champion of the junior league, was summoned; the players of the two clubs made a horseshoe around the pair, as the jeweler handed the Georgia Peach a diamond-studded gold medal, a suitable reminder to Ty's progeny that Cobb had won the 1907 batting crown.

The jeweler couldn't resist the temptation to orate a few hundred words, and the partisan Chicago crowd became impatient and yelled: "Play ball," and "Give 'im his medal and shut up." A loudmouth offered this congratulation: "Good thing you got that medal now, young fellow, 'cause you ain't going to get no more hits in this series." As an oracle of doom, he wasn't so bad, as Ty was to come out of the Series with a meek .200 average.

Minutes were used up in these preliminaries, and it was 2:42, when big Orvie Overall stepped into the box to pitch his first delivery to Davey Jones, the Tigers' lead-off man. Smiling Bill Donovan warmed up for Jennings. As he left the bench, Hughie said: "All you got to do, Bill, is pitch like you've been pitching all season."

"The arm feels good; I think I'll do all right," replied Bill.

The Cubs scored first, picking up a run in the fourth inning, when Chance walked, took second on Steinfeldt's sacrifice, and came home on Kling's single. Evers also singled, sending Kling to third, but as Johnny stole second, Kling tried to come in, and was nailed at the plate. It was a field day for the base stealers, as the Cubs stole seven bases on Schmidt and the Tigers four on the great Kling.

That fourth-inning run looked big, especially as the game went into the late innings. But the 1907 Tiger club had power, and it played for that big inning. Helped by some sloppy Chicago fielding, they broke through with three runs in the eighth and handed Donovan what looked to be a safe lead.

Jones, who had a good day with three hits, led off with a clean single to right and stole second. Schaefer knocked a stiff one down to Tinker, who in his anxiety to cut off Jones at third fumbled the ball long enough to prevent him from making a play at either third or first. Germany was safe, and he promptly stole second. Crawford came through with a timely single to right, sending Jones and Schaefer home with the runs which made the score read: Detroit, 2; Cubs, 1. Schulte pegged the ball over Kling's head in his effort to cut down Schaefer; the ball bounded away from Kling, and Crawford cantered around to third. Yawkey's delegation was letting out loud war whoops, while Hughie Jennings pulled up grass and yelled "Ee-yah" to his heart's delight.

"Keep it up, Ty! Ee-yah! Ee-yah!" encouraged Hughie, as the young American League batting champion stepped to the plate.

Ty's best was a tap to Overall, on which Crawford was boxed on the third-base line, between the plate and third. In the attempted run-down, Kling's slow and wide throw pulled Steinfeldt off third, and Crawford slid safely back to the bag, while Cobb was safe at first. Jennings chuckled and danced in high glee in his coacher's box. Wahoo Sam scored a moment later after Rossman drove a long fly to Slagle in center. But this was to be the high point for Detroit in that World's Series.

Donovan snuffed out the side in order in the Cub half of the eighth, but his support dug a pit for him in the ninth, enabling the Chicago players to tie the score. It was a heartbreaking inning for Smiling Bill. Chance led off with a single, and for a moment Donovan lived up to his old nickname, "Wild Bill." He plunked Steinfeldt in the ribs. Tinker tried to sacrifice, but bunted a little pop fly to Rossman. Coughlin next messed up Evers' ground ball for a boot, and there was a snarling Cub on every base. But Donovan should have got out of it. Chance scored on Schulte's out at first, Kling taking third. The Cub chief next sent up Del Howard to bat for Tinker, who had struck out three times. Del didn't do so good either. He swung hard and missed two quick strikes. Then came one of the unforgettable catching plays of World's Series history, as famous in its day as Mickey Owen's failure to squeeze a ninth-inning third strike at Ebbets Field in the Yankee-Brooklyn Series of 1941.

Donovan fed Howard another sharp curve, and again Del swung and hit nothing but the lake breeze. For a fraction of a second it looked like the ball game for the Tigers, but the ball plowed through Schmidt for a passed ball, and Kling scored the tying run from third, while Howard made first in safety. Pat Moran batted for Overall, and, feeling they had Schmidt completely demoralized, Evers tried to steal home before Pat completed his turn at bat. But this time Charley held on to Donovan's pitch, and pressed it none too gently on the little Trojan.

In the tenth, the Cubs almost won. Slagle scratched a single and stole second and third. Donovan struck out Sheckard, but Chance walked and also stole second. Slagle then tried to come in on a short passed ball, but O'Day ruled that Howard, standing at the plate, had interfered with Schmidt's throw to Donovan, who covered the plate. The Cubs growled long and loud at the decision, but it stood.

Ed Reulbach came in to pitch for the Cubs in the tenth, and the Tigers couldn't touch him. The collegian's blinding fast ball, in the evening dusk, made the Tigers look like tame kittens. After three overtime innings, O'Day called it at the end of the twelfth because of darkness. But for all that palaver at the plate before the game, it could have gone another inning.

The tie pleased no one, the players, the fans, the old National Commission. There was snarling, swearing, and recriminations in the Tiger clubhouse. Big Schmidt wasn't the most popular player in the place. "God damn, why didn't you hold that pitch, you big Dutch so-and-so," more than one told him. Donovan merely sat down and glowered. He had struck out 12 men, and still couldn't win. Cobb cursed to himself; he had been up five times without getting anything that looked like a hit. Crawford felt somewhat better; the club had done no worse than a tie and he had got three hits out of it.

Chatter downtown in Chicago's Loop was not too complimentary. Those who were quick to smell a rat thought they smelled a big one. It had been printed in the papers that day that the Commission had decided the players should share in a tie game, and here the very first day the Series started with a deadlock. The inference was that Schmidt let that third strike go by, so as to tie up the ball game.

The Commission didn't like it, either. Ban Johnson always hated to lose to the National League, and he especially had no love for Charley Murphy, the Cub president, even though at one time both Ban and Murphy had been Cincinnati baseball writers. All three of the commissioners, Herrmann, Johnson, and Pulliam, remembered only too well Schaefer's apparently innocent question of the night before: "Is a tie game a legal game?"

"I don't like it. I don't like it for a damn," said Ban, pacing up and down in Herrmann's room at the Congress Hotel. "If I thought they were pulling something . . ."

They talked over all phases of the game. The Cubs had taken desperate chances, got away with some, failed in others. Neither team played World's Championship ball, as the two clubs committed eight errors, five by the Cubs. They even discussed the play whereby Howard had interfered with Donovan and prevented Chicago from winning in the tenth. But both clubs had fought hard, and quarreled frequently with the umpires. Eventually, it was the consensus of the Commission that the tie's coming so soon after Schaefer's visit was a coincidence, and no investigation was ordered. However, the Commission decided then and there that while the 1907 players would be permitted to share in the tie, as well as the next four games, in all subsequent Series, the players' pool would be on the first four games actually played, regardless of whether they were played to a decision.

2

When the Series was resumed in Chicago, October 9, Jennings advised his players: "Forget that tie. That's gone, and I don't want to hear any more about it. We didn't win it, but we didn't lose it." But, alas for Hughie, the defeats were to pile up from there on.

Jennings pitched his second ace, George Mullin, in this game, and after Schmidt's erratic catching and throwing in the first game, the Ee-yah man sent in Fred Payne to catch the burly right-hander. Chance called on Jack Pfeister, his left-hander. Each side got nine hits, but Payne could no more stop the Cub base runners than did Schmidt in the first game. They stole five additional bases on Payne. For the Tigers, Cobb got his first World's Series hit, but Crawford was held hitless. Rossman had a big day with a triple and two singles. Claude's three-bagger, linked with Payne's single, gave Detroit a brief one-run lead in the second. It didn't last long, for in the Cub half of the second, Chicago filled the bases with none out on Kling's clean single and two scratch hits. Then big George forced in a run by walking Tinker. Even the partisan West Side crowd gave George a hand when he got out of that deep hole with no further scoring, as he fanned Pfeister and Slagle and enticed Sheckard to hit a grounder to Schaefer.

However, it was only a stay of sentence, as the Cubs got to Mullin for two runs in the fourth, enough to win by 3 to 1. Tinker singled, was sacrificed to second by Pfeister, stole third and came in on Slagle's infield hit, Sheckard's double scored Jimmy. There were a few fielding fireworks on the Detroit side to give Yawkey and Navin a few pleasant moments. In the first inning, when Slagle got around to third, Schaefer pulled the hidden ball trick on him. When Jimmy wandered off third, Germany shot the ball over to Coughlin before the perplexed Slagle could get back. O'Leary came up with several circus stops, and in the third inning Crawford made a leaping one-handed catch of Kling's drive, and doubled Chance off second.

It was more of the same in the third game, played in Chicago on October 10. Jennings was criticized for starting Ed Siever, who was banged for seven hits and four runs in four innings. By the time Ed Killian, Hughie's twenty-five-game winner, came in, the game was lost. Killian held the Cubs to four hits the rest of the way.

However, the Tigers could get only six scattered hits off Ed Reulbach, who had finished the first game so brilliantly. It took Killian, a good-hitting pitcher, to score Detroit's only run in the sixth. Ed singled, moved up to second when Jones walked, to third when Schaefer banged into a double play, and scored on Crawford's single. Schmidt was back of the plate again for Detroit, and for one day the Cubs did no base stealing. However, of their ten hits, five were two-baggers. They didn't have to steal second. The final score was 5 to 1.

The Series moved on to Detroit for the fourth game, October 12. Though the Tigers now trailed by two games, neither Yawkey, Jennings, the team, nor the Detroit fans were down. At the end of three games, the supremacy of the Cubs in hits wasn't much, 29 to 24, and there was a strong hope the Tigers would find use for their bats and tie up the Series at Bennett Park. Cobb, who had only two singles in 12 times at bat, was especially overdue, and was expected to break out before the home fans.

"We're going to win this one; aren't we?" Yawkey said to Jennings.

"You're damn right we are," said Hughie. "Bill Donovan hasn't let us down all year; he can't pitch in that kind of bad luck again," referring to the right-hander's unfortunate first game.

But it wasn't a Bill Donovan day. Wild William was moving into his thirties, and he usually needed warm, sunny days to be at his best. He had a reputation for being a warm-weather pitcher. This day was cold and rainy, and the crowd which attended—11,306—was considered good for Detroit of that period. Bundled in heavy coats, they snugly filled the stands at Bennett Park, with some stragglers standing in the outfield. The crowd included two trainloads of fans from Chicago, who had engaged two specials to come to Detroit and root for their beloved team.

Detroit fans did all they could to encourage the Tigers, and before the game Jennings was presented with a diamond-studded watch by an admirer, and a great floral tiger, the size of a full-grown jungle beast. Unfortunately, it didn't scare the Cubs. "What you going to do with that, Hughie?" scoffed Chance. "Eat it?"

"No, we'll ram it down your throats," snapped Jennings.

"Who, you and Cobb?" taunted the Peerless Leader. "I thought you told me he was a hitter."

"He'll hit plenty before this is over," said the Ee-yah manager.

"That's what you say," shot back Chance.

Chance also came back with his first game pitcher, big Orval

Overall, and the giant Californian thrived better on the cold, rainy day than Donovan, the Philadelphian. The hits were 7 for the Cubs and 5 for the Tigers, with Cobb finally blasting an extra base hit —a triple—but Chicago made a run for nearly every bingle. The game was held up by rain for 15 minutes while the Cubs were at bat in the fifth inning; Donovan further chilled during the delay and wasn't the same pitcher after play was resumed. Bill hit Frank Chance on the left hand in the first inning, and broke a finger. Husk had it tied up, and went on playing, even stealing a base. They were tough hombres in those days, and Chance gave a grunt of pain as he hit the ground. "It didn't hurt; did it, Frank?" sympathized Germany Schaefer, with a sardonic leer.

Donovan did all right until the rain came, only three scattered Cubs reaching base on him in the first four innings, and the Tigers put a run under him in the fourth when Cobb delighted the home crowd with a triple to center and scored on Rossman's single.

In Chicago's half of the fifth, Johnny Evers, first man up, reached base on a wild throw by Charley O'Leary. While Schulte was at bat, the rain which started as a drizzle increased to a steady downpour and Jack Sheridan stopped the game. For a time, it looked as though the game might have to be thrown into the discard, but after 15 minutes the rain suddenly stopped and Sheridan ordered play resumed. Donovan had to resume pitching without warming up and had noticeably stiffened up. He couldn't find the plate for Schulte, who walked, and Tinker pushed along Evers and Wildfire with a neat sacrifice. That Donovan had slipped was apparent a moment later when Overall, his mound opponent, lined out a clean single which was good for two runs.

A combination of a slow, water-sogged infield, slow thinking, and slow fielding by the Tigers gave Detroit fans a distressful seventh as the Cubs put over three more runs on one scratch hit. Schulte opened with a safe bunt to Donovan, and on a sacrifice Tinker also bunted to Bill, who threw too late to second for a force play on Schulte. It was a case of "Everybody's doing it" so Overall also bunted. This time Donovan got Orvie at first, the other two runners advancing. Slagle then hit to O'Leary, whose peg to the plate was wild and Schulte scored. Sheckard then bunted, and was safe when Donovan and Rossman couldn't decide who was to take the ball. By this time the bleacherites arose and gave their Tiger champions the old razzberry, with a French Canadian flavor. Chance forced Sheckard at second, Tinker scoring, and Slagle taking third. The Cubs then rubbed it in by scoring a third run on a half-successful double steal. Chance went down to second on a delayed steal, and Schmidt fired the ball down to Germany at second. As Herman chased Chance back to first before tossing the ball to Rossman, Slagle leisurely trudged in from third base. And so it ended, 6 to 1.

3

By the fifth game, played in Detroit on a Saturday, October 12, Tiger fans no longer were in a World's Series mood. The day was raw and windy; no one then had thought up the idea of selling three-game strip tickets, and recollections of the seventh inning of the Friday game were painful and poignant. Detroit's attitude toward the Series was very much "the hell with it," and the Tiger fans stayed away in large numbers. Only a slim 7,370 crowd saw Detroit go down for the last time, and get shut out in the bargain.

In a way, the 2 to 0 defeat was unexpected—both in Detroit and all over the country. On the following day, Sunday, October 13, the Series was to switch back to Chicago, and Charley Murphy had his West Side Park all sold out for a likely Sunday game. Without actually suspecting larceny or chicanery, the average fan reasoned: "They won't pass up that big Sunday crowd in Chicago, even though they have to give Detroit one."

However, the end of the Series was a fine boost for the game's honesty, even though it was another bitter pill for Detroit. For some reason or other, Frank Chance had held back Mordecai Brown, ace of his staff, until this fifth game and Brownie wasn't fooling when he tossed in that three-fingered delivery, a sort of parent to the present-day fork ball. Mordecai wound it up with whitewash, though the Detroits got as many hits, seven, as the Cubs garnered off Mullin.

"You've got to do it, George, if anyone can," Jennings told the big fellow from Toledo. Discouraged by the inability of Schmidt and Fred Payne to stop Chicago base runners, Hughie even sent weak-hitting Jimmy Archer, later a Cub star, to catch Mullin in the last game. But the Cubs continued running, and wound up with four more stolen bases. Jones, Coughlin, and Rossman each stole a base themselves on Kling, but after getting runners in scoring positions, the Tigers couldn't get them over. Twice young Archer fell down in the clutch.

Mullin pitched well enough to win the average game, but a Cub run in each of the first and second innings beat him and ended the Series. George couldn't find the plate for Slagle, the Cub lead-off man, and Jimmy walked. He followed it with his sixth steal of the Series, and Steinfeldt's sharp single drove him home. An error by Rossman paved the way for Chicago's second run in the second. Rossman spilled Coughlin's throw on Evers' grounder, and Tinker's single sent the little Keystone King to third. Brownie walked, filling the bases, and Evers scored while Schaefer was tossing out Slagle. Chance wasn't such an "ol' Oriole" after all; he sat this one out to nurse his injured digit, and Del Howard played first in his stead.

A rather sick-looking pack of Tigers gathered in their clubhouse lair under the old wooden stands. Defeat was pretty bad, but losing four straight was gall and wormwood. "You did your best," said Hughie. "The pitching did all right; we just weren't hitting the way we can hit."

"Hell, we didn't hit worth a damn," said Schaefer. "And I got to go back to Chicago, and get the pants kidded off of me all winter."

"Me, too," said Charley O'Leary.

The whole team left for Chicago after the game. Though the Series was over, a hastily arranged exhibition game was billed for the following day, the Sunday when Murphy expected a full house, the receipts of which went to the players. Chicago didn't fall for it, and only an additional $1,600 was picked up for the players' pool. For the first time, the winners and losers split on a 60-40 basis, and liberal Bill Yawkey tossed $15,000 into the Detroit players' pot. As a result each of the Tigers entitled to a full share pulled down $1,945.96, a fairly decent bonus for winning Detroit's first American League championship.

Claude Rossman was one of the few Tigers who came out of this Series rout with an unblemished reputation. He thumped Chance's crack pitchers for a .400 batting average. Davey Jones followed with a satisfactory .353, but after opening with three hits Sam Crawford made only two more and closed with .238. And young Cobb had to be satisfied with .200. Schaefer couldn't laugh off his .143, and poor O'Leary was down to .055. The fact that Joe Tinker, the famous Cub shortstop, hit only .154 was small comfort to "Charley, me b'y."

And they read Detroit out of the American League again! In his final resumé of the Series, the late I. E. Sanborn, of the *Chicago Tribune*, then one of the nation's ace baseball reporters, had this to say:

There is one feature to the series which demands comment and that is the showing the Detroit public made in the matter of supporting its team of champions. All reports indicated Jennings and his Tigers had set the whole State of Michigan crazy with excitement and there were fears the Detroit management would not be able to provide one half the accommodations necessary to take care of the mob which would try to attend the World's Series there.

But the whole State of Michigan proved to be prudently crazy. Noise and rejoicing there was in plenty, but when it came to coughing up the substantial rewards for the players it proved lacking to a certain extent. The attendance at the two games in Detroit was a serious reflection on the patriotism of the citizens. Of course, there was the bad weather to take into account, but it did not compare with the freezing conditions which obtained during the first three games in Chicago last fall. Then there were the two defeats the Tigers suffered here [in Chicago], but that should not have cooled a fan's ardor. There was considerable complaint about the disposition of tickets, but there always is that complaint in connection with every World's Series.

There is only one conclusion to be drawn from Detroit's attitude toward its champions, and that is the well-known adage that a city of that size will not stand for a loser, and I look for the disappearance of Detroit from the major-league map within a few years. Even with President Yawkey's strong box and civic pride behind the club there, it will not satisfy the other seven clubs to carry along a city which will not make a losing club profitable nor a great success out of a winner.

If Cy Sanborn's wraith hovered over Briggs Stadium at the fourth Tiger-Cub World's Series in 1945, and saw the streams of humanity pour into the pretty, well-kept Detroit ball park, he must have felt rather silly over his 1907 prophecy.

Cy, if your scorebook still is handy, score yourself a big fat error on that one.

TIGERS REPEAT IN 1908

I

MUCH CRITICISM OF DETROIT AT THIS TIME EMANATED FROM Cleveland and Chicago. It was said that one of Ban Johnson's mistakes was to drop Buffalo or Baltimore, and keep Detroit in the circuit. There was a move on for a "return to Buffalo."

This again went past the rumor stage, but the October 31, 1907, issue of *Sporting News,* a fortnight after the Series, ran a story which carried the happy tidings: "STATUS SETTLED. Detroit Will Not Lose Major Franchise. Possesses Vested Territorial Rights Which Cannot Be Affected by Knocking." B. F. Wright, the Tiger correspondent, again lifted his cudgels in behalf of his beloved Detroit. And Iffy, the Dopester, sputtered at the very thought.

Are these persons aware that the Tigers the past season played to over 100,000 more spectators than in 1906? Wright asked. What Cleveland really wants is not to get rid of Detroit because it isn't bigger, but because Detroit's Tigers are too big. Yes, throw out Detroit, and Philadelphia and Chicago, and take in three really big cities that are on no baseball map, and the Clevelands might win a pennant—perhaps.

One brash soul who had great faith in Detroit's baseball future despite these so-called "knockers" was Frank Navin. The volatile young Bill Yawkey, having won his first pennant, felt satisfied and decided he had had his fill of baseball. Anyway, he was planning to move to New York, and he gave Navin a chance to buy half of the club for $40,000. He even loaned Navin the money for his first payment, remarking: "You've got a good team now, Frank, and you can pay the rest as you go along." Frank accepted with enthusiasm; under the new arrangement he took over the presidency and full control of the club's affairs. He held the post until his death 28 years later. Yawkey remained as a silent half owner.

The young club owner's first winter in office was no bed of roses and one vexing problem came up after another. He ran into the

American Federation of Labor, and it threatened to boycott his park for the 1908 season. In letting out a contract to repair Bennett Park, he unwittingly made it with a nonunion firm, and carpenters with no union cards nailed new shingles on Navin's roof. There was a lot of angry talk, and Navin called some of Detroit's union leaders to his office. They gave out a statement that "they were satisfied that Mr. Navin is not antagonistic to union labor," and called off the boycott.

Navin had labor difficulties of his own, as the champions of 1907 proved quite difficult when the new Tiger president sent them their 1908 contracts. Ty Cobb, the twenty-one-year-old batting champion, was most obdurate, but George Mullin and Claude Rossman were almost as tough. There even were reports that Mullin might be traded to the Browns for Waddell, the St. Louis club having acquired Rube that winter from the Athletics.

That brought a statement from Hughie Jennings on February 20, shortly before the Tigers were to leave for their Little Rock training camp. "I believe that Ty Cobb, Mullin, Rossman and the rest of the holdouts will soon come into the fold," said Hughie. "Cobb's case is a matter for him and the club to settle. If the club made him a reasonable offer, he will come around all right—I think, and the club's latest offers seems most reasonable to me. Ty likes to play ball too well to remain idle long after the season opens. Rossman and Mullin have only trivial differences with the club and undoubtedly will be on hand when the bell rings. Personally, I would not have Rube Waddell for a gift, but he may help McAleer [the Brown manager], although I fail to see how."

Cobb didn't think that "latest offer" reasonable, and treated it with Cobbesque scorn. Ty always was a good businessman. Ban Johnson and other club owners got into it. It was felt that if Navin gave in to this twenty-one-year-old youth, and yielded to his demands, other older players would become dissatisfied, and the entire big-league wage scale would become disorganized. In the National League, Honus Wagner, the veteran Pirate batting king, who rarely caused Barney Dreyfuss any salary trouble and remained loyal to Dreyfuss all through the American League raids, also staged a real holdout struggle. In a way, Cobb was responsible for it. Ty was asking for $5,000, about the same that Dreyfuss offered the Dutchman after Wagner had been 12 years in the league. So Honus, too, wanted to get in on the new prosperity.

The entire country became interested and took sides, much as it did later in Babe Ruth's salary controversies with Col. Ruppert, and during the height of the dispute, Navin tried to put the young Georgian in his place when he gave out a statement, through the Associated Press, that "the creation cannot be greater than the creator—that Cobb is not bigger than baseball." The 1908 training season was almost over before Cobb finally compromised for $4,500 and reported to Jennings in Little Rock. But even this was a raise of over $2,000. He drew $250 a month in 1906 and was paid $400 a month in 1907 for his contribution to the Tiger pennant of 1907. Tyrus worked for his $4,500 in 1908 and 1909, and then hit Navin for another big raise. This kicked up another commotion, and Cobb forced Frank to double the ante; Navin paid his outstanding star $9,000 in each of 1910, 1911 and 1912.

In 1913, Cobb went over $10,000 for the first time, collecting $11,332.55, and in 1914, the first year the Federal League was in the field as a quasi-major, Navin boosted the figure to $15,000. With the Federal League still a strong bidder for stellar major talent the following winter, Cobb won a $20,000 a year contract for 1915 and 1916. Eventually, in post World War I years, as playing manager, he went as high as $40,000.

2

The club had abominable training weather in Arkansas, and not only Cobb, but Crawford, missed most of the training. Wahoo Sam was called home by the serious illness of his wife. The Tigers started in poor condition, and were easy prey to the other better trained teams in the early weeks of the season. When in middle May the club was sixth, Horace Fogel, the Philadelphian, proudly proclaimed: "The Tigers, a one year sensation in 1907, have fallen back to their normal level." But the Detroits leaped from sixth to third, and by May 29, they were tied with New York for first place. Griffith's team then nose-dived from first to last; the Old Fox was dethroned; and the New York team limped home in the cellar under Kid Elberfeld, the former Tiger shortstop.

After the Fourth of July holiday, the Eastern clubs dropped back and the 1908 American League race developed into a remarkable free-for-all between the four clubs of the West, the Tigers, White Sox, Naps (Cleveland), and Browns. While Detroit led most of the time, the Tiger lead rarely was more than a game, and as late as September 27, only 23 points separated the first four teams. St. Louis, which had been strengthened that year by Waddell, finally dropped out, leaving the other three to battle right down to the wire. It was the year that Ed Walsh was the superman of the mound. With the weak-hitting White Sox, who made only three homers all year, behind him, he pitched 464 innings, took part in 66 games, and was credited with 40 victories against 15 defeats. He pitched in seven of Fielder Jones's last nine games, and but for a 1 to 0 defeat by Cleveland, when Addie Joss hurled a perfect game, October 2, he would have pitched the Chicago club into the pennant.

On next to the last day of the season, October 5, Lajoie's Cleve-landers had the flag in their grasp. If they won a double-header from the Browns that day and also won their final from St. Louis, they would win the flag regardless of what Detroit and Chicago did in their remaining two games. However, the best the Naps could do was an even break, losing the opener to Bill Dinneen, 3 to 1. On the same afternoon, with Walsh opposing Mullin, the White Sox won by a 6 to 1 score.

That made the pennant hinge on the final game of the season between the Tigers and the Sox at Chicago's South Side park, October 6. It was a freak situation, as the winner would capture the pennant, and the loser would slip to third place, for Cleveland, in between, could assure itself of second by defeating St. Louis. The game proved one of the saddest ever played in Comiskey's orchard, and one of the most glorious in Detroit's history. With all the chips down and a great partisan Chicago crowd trying to egg on its Hitless Wonders, the Tigers won the important game with almost ridiculous ease, 7 to 0. Wild Bill Donovan hurled one of the classics of his career, giving up only two hits while he struck out ten.

Jones started with Doc White, his left-hander, usually effective against Detroit, but the Felines batted him out in the first inning with a four-run barrage. The hard-worked Walsh was rushed in with only one out, but the ball game already was lost, and Piano Legs Frank Smith finished. The Tigers thumped the trio for 13 hits, with the clean-up pair, Sam and Ty, magnificent, poling seven hits between them. Crawford hit a double and three singles; Cobb a triple and two singles. After the eventful game, the three leaders ranked as follows: Detroit—won 90, lost 63, .588; Cleveland—won 90, lost 64, .584; Chicago—won 88, lost 64, .579.

While Donovan (18-7) and Mullin (17-12) again had fine sea-sons, and Willett and Killian rendered efficient service, the second Tiger American League pennant would not have been possible with-out the masterful hurling of a freshman member of the staff, Edgar

Oren Summers, a sturdy son of Lagoda, Indiana. They called him "Eddie Kickapoo," and he was one of the early knuckle-ballers of the big leagues. Eddie was the Dave Ferriss of 1908, finishing the season with 24 victories against 12 defeats.

Ty Cobb won his second batting championship, but with the reduced average of .324. It was the third lowest average to win the American League hit crown and from 1908 on no one dropped under .324 until Snuffy Stirnweiss of the 1945 Yankees sneaked in with .309. Even so, St. Louis tried to talk Ty out of it. Dode Criss, a pitcher-pinch-hitter on the Browns, hit .341, but appeared in only 64 games. Ban Johnson threw out the claims of Dode's boosters, and decreed Cobb the official champion. Crawford again was second among the 100-game players, with .311, and high up were Matty McIntyre with .295 and Rossman and Donie Bush with .294.

Bush appeared in only 20 games, but he, too, helped save the pennant for Jennings with his great September play. The Tigers had been handicapped much of the season by infield disabilities. O'Leary was injured at a vital stage of the race, and old "Cap" Coughlin broke down at third. Jerry Downs and Wade Killefer did some timely and capable relief work, but Navin really plugged the hole in early September when he purchased the aggressive Indianapolis shortstop, Owen J. Bush. Donie came too late to be eligible for the 1908 World's Series. A fearless, fighting little guy, who covered acres of ground, he quickly developed into the greatest shortstop in Tiger history and remained with the club until 1921, when he moved on to Washington, where Griffith soon promoted him to the management of the Senators. He also led the Pirates, White Sox, and Reds, and now is president of his home-town team, the Indianapolis Indians of the American Association.

Though Bush never hit .300, he was for years one of the outstanding lead-off men and run-getters in the game. A little man, five feet, six inches, he crowded the plate, and had an uncanny knack of drawing bases on balls. And once he got on, it was up to Cobb or Crawford to bring him around.

3

Everybody looked for a better World's Series when the Tigers and Cubs again tangled in 1908. Chance's smooth club only won the National League pennant after its famous postseason play-off game with the Giants on the Polo Grounds, and while Detroit also had to fight to the last day of its season, the Tigers had a chance to rest and recuperate after their flag-clinching day, October 6. The Cubs had to rush to New York for their play-off, October 8, and then tear back to Detroit for the World's Series opener on the tenth. This was expected to tire the National League champs and put them under a strain. Detroit fans also kidded themselves that the 1908 Cub club wasn't as strong as its predecessors. Chicago had won easy pennants in 1906 and 1907 as the Cubs won 116 and 107 games, respectively. In 1908, they dropped to 99 victories, and staggered in ahead of New York and Pittsburgh by a game. And wasn't Detroit a much better ball club? Eddie Summers had given Jennings another winning pitcher, but the sensational young Bush had joined the club too late to be eligible for the Series.

Certainly the tribe of Jennings was keen for revenge, and felt it would get it. The Tigers had shown their stuff and fight in wearing down the Naps and White Sox in that grueling American League race. Cobb hit .368 and stole two bases, but otherwise it was a drab week for the Tigers. The crowds in Detroit again were mediocre, only 29,929 fans attending the three games at Bennett Field, while even in Chicago interest waned as Charley Murphy, the Cub president, offended his cash customers.

Detroit won the toss for the first game, but with the Giant-Chicago play-off on a Thursday, it was decided to start the series on a Saturday in Detroit, and then jump to Chicago for the next two games, so as to be sure of getting in the Sunday game at Murphy's West Side Park.

The first game was played under wretched conditions, which partly explained the crowd of 10,812. As in the fourth game of the 1907 Series in Detroit, it rained throughout the game. The downpour started a half hour before game time, but after talking it over with the three commissioners, Sheridan and O'Day decided to start the game. The rainfall was incessant for six innings and then fell off to a drizzle. Ground attendants were kept busy pouring sacks of sawdust into the pitcher's and batter's boxes. The sloppy going had much to do with the ineffectiveness of the pitchers; Chance used three aces, Reulbach, Overall, and Brown, while Jennings employed Ed Killian and Summers, sticking to the latter as he went through a bruising five-run ninth inning.

The Tigers got off to a one-run lead in the first inning, when McIntyre opened with a single, stole second in the mud, and came home on Cobb's single. Killian got by for two innings, but the left-hander went out in the third as four rain-spattered Cub runs crossed the plate. Schaefer had as bad an inning as Killian. He slipped on the wet grass and sat down on his knickers while trying to field an infield tap by Evers and later let Kling's grounder roll through him. The boys gave Chicago another gift run in the seventh. Big Schmidt slipped on the wet infield and couldn't pick up Evers' little poke, and Johnny got another Santa Claus hit. He got around to third on a sacrifice and Jerry Downs's fumble on Chance. As Chance stole second, Evers ran in from third.

Then with dramatic suddenness the Tigers slugged back, and by the end of the eighth, they had the ball game in their grasp. Bill Yawkey danced in his box like a wild Comanche, Frank Navin's heart pounded like a trip hammer under his poker face, and the rain-soaked crowd went into hysterics. That's what it had been waiting for. It was followed by that awful letdown in the ninth, but it was fun while it lasted.

It started with a three-run rally in the seventh. Cobb and Rossman opened with singles, and Jennings "Ee-yahed" all over the place. The Cubs got the next two, but Jerry Downs drove in Ty and Claude with a double. Summers' fly dropped safe in water-sogged center field, and Jerry rode home. Overall then relieved Reulbach and after hitting McIntyre with the wet ball he retired O'Leary. But big Orvie proceeded to get into trouble of his own in the eighth, when the Felines grabbed the lead by scoring twice. Cobb really did some running in this inning. After Overall walked Crawford, Chance yanked the Californian and called in Brown. Mordecai's first pitch to Cobb was wild, Wahoo Sam taking second. Chance then muffed Brownie's peg on Cobb's sacrifice, as Crawford made third and Ty got a life at first. That 10,812 crowd sounded more like 100,812; what it lacked in numbers, it made up in noise. Rossman clicked off a single, scoring Sam with the tying run, and Cobb sped for third. Evers cut in on the relay, threw wildly to third to cut off the Georgian, and Ty never stopped running, until he, too, had scored. That put Detroit one run to the good.

Jennings personally handed the ball to Summers as the Tigers took the field for the ninth inning, saying: "You can do it, Eddie, just take your time, and know you've got eight men behind you. Just pitch natural, like you've been doing."

But the ball game quickly slipped from Kickapoo Eddie's wet grasp. He got rid of Evers, and on a dry field would have retired Schulte, but Frank beat out his slow dribbler to O'Leary. Then came the play that unquestionably beat Summers. Chance hit a ball at the pitcher, who slipped in going after it, and it got away for another single. The knuckle-baller unquestionably let it annoy him, and Steinfeldt followed with a short single to left field, which filled the bases.

Hofman's single sent in Schulte and Chance and started the rout, as Tinker and Kling followed with other singles for three more runs. While the Chicago cannonading was on, Summers gave up six straight hits, without Jennings ever lifting the young pitcher. Final score, 10 to 6.

4

If Bill Donovan's first game in the 1907 Series—the twelve-inning tie in which Schmidt dropped the fatal third strike pitch in the ninth—was a heartbreaker, so was Smiling Bill's first effort in the 1908 Series. Jennings had pointed him for the Sunday contest at West Side Park, in which his opponent was expected to be Overall. That Sunday, October 11, was an especially turbulent day in Chicago. Charley Murphy, the Cubs' stormy president, upped his prices considerably, and great blocks of tickets got into the hands of speculators. A story was bruited around the Loop that Chubby Charley himself had passed the pasteboards along to the specs. This angered the loyal Cub fans, and instead of an expected crowd of over 25,000, only 17,760 showed up. Ropes were stretched in front of the bleachers, and in the outfield, for an overflow crowd which never came. It was these ropes which precipitated all that rhubarb in the eighth inning.

For seven innings, Donovan and Overall gave that Sunday crowd quite a show, as they mowed down opposing hitters almost as fast as they came to bat. Bill was even a little tighter than Orvie, as a Cub reached base on him only twice, and each time it was his pitching rival, Overall. The Californian got a life in the third when Rossman muffed Donovan's throw on the pitcher's infield tap, and Orvie singled in the sixth, only to be promptly doubled up with Sheckard on the latter's grounder to Downs. In seven innings, only 22 Cubs had faced Donovan.

The Cub eighth started harmlessly enough, when Bill whizzed a third strike over on Steinfeldt. And then came disaster! Hofman scratched an infield single for Chicago's second hit, and then Joe Tinker hit a slow wide pitch for a high fly to right field. For several seconds the ball hung in the air, and it looked as though it was a foul, when the wind took hold of it and blew it into the right field bleachers inside the foul line. The ropes were stretched in front of the open seats, and under a ground rule, hits in back of these ropes were to be ground rule doubles.

Klem, the umpire at the plate, immediately waved both Hofman and Tinker home, ruling it to be a home run.

Jennings sprang off his bench like a tiger leaping down on its prey and led a pack of yelping, snarling Tigers to where Bill Klem was standing. Ty Cobb, giving loud yells of disapproval, stormed in from right field, while Coughlin, Schaefer, and others got into the rumpus.

"That's no homer; that's a ground-rule double," shouted Hughie. "We talked that all over before the game."

"It's still a home run in my book," shot back Klem.

"Why is it a homer?" snarled Cobb. "The ball dropped in the ropes in back of me, and that was to be two bases."

"That ground rule doesn't cover the bleachers, when there is no overflow crowd," said Bill. "Balls hit into that bleacher have been home runs here all season."

"But that wasn't our agreement. You should put those runners back on base," insisted Jennings.

And so it went for nearly a quarter of an hour, as Jennings, Cobb, Coughlin, and Schaefer ran first from Klem to Connolly, the American League man, and then back to Klem again.

Eventually the game was resumed with two runs in for the Cubs. Irritated by the decision and his arm stiffening by the delay, Donovan was a different pitcher when he faced Kling. He seemed to be sticking the ball right through the middle, and the Cubs hammered it back for line drives. Kling cracked out a double, took third on Overall's out, and scored on Sheckard's single. Jimmy stole and came in on Evers' single. Schulte's triple to center brought in the crabby second baseman and Wildfire promptly followed on a Donovan wild pitch. Then Chance walked, and stole second without either Donovan or Schmidt making a play on him.

Ban Johnson turned his head away so he couldn't see any more of it, saying bitterly: "What the hell is going on here, anyway?"

But the agony finally ended for American League sympathizers, when Steinfeldt, up again, flied to McIntyre for the third out.

The Tigers side-stepped a shutout in the ninth, when Jones, batting for O'Leary, walked, took second on Crawford's out, and scored on Ty's single.

5

Monday, October 12, 1908, was a red-letter day for the Tigers and their faithful Detroit fans for many a year. It was the only game in two Series with the Cubs in which Detroit newsboys could carry their extras along Woodward Avenue yelling: "Tigers win. Read all about Ty Cobb getting four hits."

Yes, it was a glorious day while it lasted. With George Mullin pitching fine ball, and Ira Thomas throwing out two of Chicago's would-be base thiefs, the Tigers won most emphatically by a score of 8 to 3. And Cobb had the kind of a World's Series game his admirers had been expecting of him right along. The Georgian hit a double and three singles and stole two bases.

The Tigers finally found a pitcher they could hit in the left-hander Jack Pfeister. Chance let him stay in and take the drubbing, too, as the former Giant-Killer gave up all eight of the Tiger runs in the eight innings he pitched. Though Mullin pitched a grand game, he had no cakewalk, and Tiger bungling gave Chicago three unearned runs in the fourth, giving the Cubs a temporary lead of 3 to 1. With one down in this inning, Evers walked and was caught napping off first, but reached second when Rossman threw wildly to O'Leary. Schulte fouled out for the play which should have retired the side. Then Chance singled Evers home and stole second. Coughlin next threw low on Steinfeldt's grounder, putting Husk on third, and when Rossman pegged wildly again, the Cub manager scored. Hofman's triple counted Steinie, but Mullin got Tinker on an infield grounder. It stopped Cub scoring for the day.

Detroit more than got back these three with a joyous five-run scoring riot in the sixth inning. It was to be twenty-six years before Tiger fans were to enjoy another similar World's Series inning. And there would have been more but for a beautiful Chicago double play, in which Artie Hofman doubled the great Cobb at the plate. The Tigers filled the bases with none out, when Pfeister walked Mullin, McIntyre slashed out a single, and Pfeister threw O'Leary's sacrifice bunt to third too late to force Mullin. By this time the Giant-Killer had a fine kettle of fish on his hands, and he didn't squirm out of it.

Both Crawford and Cobb outfooted infield hits, each letting in a run, and the score was tied. But there was more fun in the offing! Rossman's steaming single drove in O'Leary and Crawford and sent Ty scampering to third. Still, with nobody out! Schaefer then lifted a fly to Hofman in center, and Cobb started home the moment the ball was caught. But Circus Solly threw a strike to the plate, and Kling pressed the ball on Ty for a double play as the Peach slid hard into the catcher. However, a fifth run came over when Thomas poled a double, scoring Rossman.

Just for good measure and to be on the safe side, the Tigers got two more off Pfeister in the eighth on Cobb's double, a perfect bunt by Rossman, an intentional pass to Thomas, Coughlin's sacrifice fly, and a single by that hitting pitcher, Mullin.

6

Jennings held a meeting in the clubhouse before the fourth game, in Detroit, October 13. The Ee-yah man was elated, and gave the boys a real pep talk. "We looked like our real selves for the first time in the two Series," said Hughie. "It made me feel good the way we slapped around that left-hander. With our left-handed batting order, there's no reason why we can't hit their right-handers. Overall and Brown are good, but they're no better than Bender, Joss, and Walsh, and we can beat them."

Detroit was hepped up for the encounter; Mullin's well-pitched game the day before and the tattoo played by the Tiger bats on the West Side fences inspired the entire town. That 8 to 3 score also worked wonders as a tonic at the turnstiles, as a crowd of 12,907 jammed their way into Bennett Park, the best Detroit crowd of the two Series. The fans echoed Jennings' sentiments. "We're hitting now; watch us go from here on," said the expectant fans.

However, those Tiger bats went dead again against the magic of Mordecai Brown. Inning after inning went by, as the fans sat back waiting for the big rally which never came. Hughie pulled up grass and yelled until he was hoarse; Coughlin swore a blue streak; Cobb fumed and raged, but still there were no hits—or mighty few. After a brief hour and 35 minutes game, the Tigers were on the wrong side of a 3 to 0 shutout. The losers made only four hits, divided by O'Leary and Sam Crawford. Mordecai also hit Captain Coughlin. They were the only Felines to reach base, as Brownie walked none and the Cubs made no errors. It was a good day for yawning in the stands.

There was only one real chance for the stands to yelp, and then tidy fielding by that great Cub machine silenced the crowd as though a great gag had been jammed into its collective mouth. With the Tigers trailing 2 to 0, O'Leary opened the sixth inning with a clean single, and Crawford banged another safety to left. And the great Cobb was up! Ty tapped a bunt, which for a moment looked as though it would be safe. But anticipating the play, Steinfeldt, the third sacker, remained on his base. Brownie pounced on it, wheeled around, and his throw to third forced O'Leary. Then, a moment later, Kling shot the ball down to Tinker and nipped Crawford off second base. So, instead of having two on and nobody out, they now had only Cobb on first with two out. Ty went down to second on a steal as Rossman fanned to retire the side.

Making his first start, Eddie Summers pitched well enough in this contest to win the ordinary game, but Brown was no ordinary opponent. Though the Cubs reached Eddie for nine hits in eight innings, they broke through in only the third inning, scoring two runs after two men had been retired. Then Schulte walked and stole second. Chance also walked, and singles by Steinfeldt and Hofman drove in Schulte and Chance. After Davey Jones batted for Summers in the eighth, George Winter pitched the ninth and Cobb's muff gave the Cubs a gift run. Again two were out when trouble started. Then Evers singled and stole second, and Schulte walked. Chance raised a short fly to right, which Cobb muffed after a run, and Evers tore home.

7

The fifth game was almost a carbon copy of the fourth, only this time the Tigers made only three hits while being shut out by Overall, 2 to 0. As in the preceding day, the winning Cubs made ten hits. By an odd coincidence, it was the same score by which the Tigers lost the last game of the 1907 Series, and the crowd dwindled to a poor 6,210.

In his last effort, Jennings played out his string and called on Donovan to keep the Tigers in the Series for another day. But Bill's World's Series luck continued to be bad. No one yet has devised a system whereby a pitcher can win if his side gets him no runs. Smiling William again pitched with his heart and head, and even stole the only base of the game, but he was stymied by Overall's three-hit masterpiece. The three sparse Detroit hits were a double by McIntyre and singles by Crawford and Coughlin. Overall struck out ten Tigers, including four in the first inning, believe it or not.

Much of the action of the game was crowded into the first inning, when Chicago scored a run as Evers, Schulte, and Chance followed each other with singles. This was followed with the crazy Detroit inning, in which Schaefer left a full house. Overall had terrific speed, but with some batters he was losing the corners and got into early difficulty, only to pitch himself out of a yawning abyss. McIntyre walked, and then O'Leary fanned. Crawford singled, and Cobb struck out. Rossman swung at a wild pitch for his third strike, and reached first in safety. That put a Tiger on every sack for Schaefer, but the Prince also fanned.

Stout-Hearted George Mullin

Herman (Germany) Schaefer

George Moriarty

Donie Bush, Famous Shortstop

The Cubs scored their second run off Donovan in the fifth, when Kling walked, was sacrificed to second by Overall, and came home on Evers' double. Evers and Chance each made three hits in this windup game.

It was a disconsolate bunch of Tigers who gathered in their clubhouse and dressed after it was over. Being licked soundly in 1907 was bad enough, but getting it again in 1908, and winding up with a double whitewashing—in which the Tigers got only seven hits—was really galling.

Jennings, one of the mainsprings of the old Orioles, who recognized baseball greatness, took a little sting out of it, when he remarked: "Don't feel too badly about it. We were beaten again by a great team. A great team!"

8

The 1908 Tigers didn't get as rich pickings for their licking as did the 1907 Detroit team. There was no liberal Yawkey to toss $15,000, the club's share, into the Tiger players' pot. Navin now was pulling the purse strings and he pulled them tighter, using his share of the receipts as part of the payment he made Yawkey for his stock. As it was the total receipts of the 1908 Series—$94,975.50 —was the poorest, with one exception, since the modern World's Series first was played under the John T. Brush rules in 1905.

The slice for each individual Tiger was $870, 21 players getting a cut. Despite the excellence of their performance, the winning Cubs got only $1,317 a man. Charley Murphy divided $800 among the players of the two teams for unsold reserved seats at the two games in Chicago. It was a backwash of the ticket scandal. And the two teams again played a post-Series Sunday exhibition game in Chicago on October 18 which netted each player an additional $145. So, it wasn't such a bad winter after all! The 1908 Series also was the first in which four umpires were used But no one thought of having four umpires on the field at the same time. Jack Sheridan and Hank O'Day worked the first game, Tommy Connolly and Bill Klem the second, and from there they alternated.

And the 1908 Tiger-Cub World's Series also gave birth to that well-known organization, the Baseball Writers' Association of America. It was born out of a lot of indignation at the Hotel Ponchartrain, Detroit, October 14, on the morning of the fifth game. Those guys had to be indignant to get up that early.

The writers had taken quite a pushing around, beginning with the Giant-Cub play-off game at the Polo Grounds, October 8, where a troupe of actors, politicians, and barbers early invaded the seats reserved for "gentlemen of the press," and the late Hughie Fullerton, former Chicago scribe, dictated some 5,000 words sitting in the lap of the late Louie Mann, well-known character actor. This was followed by more indignations at the Series.

In Chicago, Charley Murphy had placed the out-of-town writers in the back row of the grandstand, even though he was a former baseball writer. In Detroit, the writers had to climb a rickety ladder to the roof of the first base pavilion and attempt to write in the rain and snow.

Out of the meeting at the Ponchartrain grew a temporary organization which elected Joe Jackson, sports editor of the *Detroit Free Press*, its first president. Apart from the fact that the meeting was held in Detroit and the Tigers were one of the contending teams, there were other good reasons for picking Joe. He could drink most of the other writers of 1908 under the table. Jackson held the post longer than any other man, serving ten years, before he was succeeded in 1918 by I. E. "Cy" Sanborn, the man who in 1907 saw such a poor future for Detroit as a major-league town. Ever since that 1908 meeting, the writers have been in complete control of their press boxes, both during the championship season and the World's Series, have policed them, and had the final say as to who should come in and who should be kept out.

⊜ XII ⊜

THE ATHLETICS ARE
NOSED OUT AGAIN

I

HAVING WON THE 1908 FLAG BY A WHISKER, JENNINGS REPEATED and made it three straight pennants by winning a third close race in 1909. It was back to the 1907 setup, the Tigers and Athletics. Of those strong Western contenders of 1908, all but Detroit fell by the wayside; the White Sox slipped to fourth, while the Indians and Browns plummeted to sixth and seventh, respectively.

Connie Mack had made over his team; such young players as Eddie Collins, Frank Baker, Jack Barry, and Jack Coombs had blossomed into full-fledged stars; with such veteran holdover aces as Bender, Plank, Davis, Oldring, and Danny Murphy, they made up a formidable aggregation, good enough to sweep American League pennants in 1910, 1911, 1913 and 1914, and win the World's Series in the first three of these years. The 1909 A's weren't quite ready, but they let the Tigers know they were in a terrific fight and won the year's series from the Felines, 14 to 8. Connie brought east a sensational college southpaw from California, Harry "Lefty" Krause, who burst into the big leagues with ten successive victories in which only five runs were scored on him. During his great run, he beat the champion Tigers thrice, twice by 3 to 1 and once by 7 to 1, but in a late-season pay-off game, the Tigers ran him dizzy.

Jennings, too, had to make important replacements, and by the late summer, the original championship team of 1907 was scarcely recognizable. The entire infield of Coughlin, O'Leary, Schaefer, and Rossman was gone, though Charley held on as infield utility infielder. During the previous winter, Jennings had traded Ira Thomas to New York for George Moriarty, a fighting third baseman, who became one of Detroit's most popular, aggressive, and fiery players and a later-day manager. He was not only a daring, but skillful, base runner, with a specialty of stealing home. He filched the home dish

12 times in one season. W. J. Cameron, with the *Detroit News* in 1909, whose comments on the Ford radio hour later made his voice known in every American home, wrote an article on Moriarty's steals, "Don't Die on Third," of which hundreds of thousands have been printed in pamphlet form. It first appeared May 19, 1909, and told of how in a deadlocked game with Cleveland, Moriarty got around to third on a single, sacrifice, and outfield fly. Mullin, a pretty good hitting pitcher, was up. But Mory didn't gamble on the chance of Mullin's driving him home; he took matters in his own hands.

Cameron wrote:

Moriarty is crouched like a tiger about to spring—Now! Now! A white streak across the field! A cloud of dust at the home plate! The umpire stands with hands extended, palms downward. A bursting roar of acclaim echoes and re-echoes across the spaces of the park. Again and again it bursts forth in thrilling, electric power. Thirty-six thousand eyes strain toward the man who is slapping the dust from his white uniform. *Moriarity is home.*

"All the world's a baseball diamond," continued Cameron, comparing Moriarty's progress around the bases to the various stages in the greater game of life, and how many persons reach partial success, only to perish at third for want of greater daring and initiative:

Any fool could have led off spectacularly, but only a trained body and an alert mind could have stolen home right under the nose of the catcher whose hands were closing over the ball. Even a game means work. Work itself is a game and has its rules and its sudden openings. So, Don't Die on Third. Bring to third every bit of your honest strength; study conditions; postpone thinking of your luck until you hear the umpire call "Safe." Then you'll score all right.

2

The 1909 team had got off to a fine start, and with the exception of one day, May 22, the Tigers led continually from April 26 to August. At one time they were so far in front it looked like a breeze, but the young Athletics kept getting better and better, and fought their way to the top. They were helped as the Tigers slumped badly through their second eastern trip, and remained in the doldrums at home.

Jennings told Navin in the club's office, "We've got to do something, Frank, or we'll piddle away the pennant."

"Well, what do you want?" asked the club president.

"We plugged up the left side of the infield by getting Moriarty and Bush, but now the right side is falling down," said the "Ee-yah man." "Schaefer isn't coming up with anything at second, and they run on Rossman whenever he gets the ball. It has him worried; he's fretting and it has affected his hitting."

"Have you any suggestions?"

"Yes: I'd like to get Jim Delahanty from Washington, and First Baseman Tom Jones from the Browns. If I got them, I could beat Mack out for the pennant."

Navin promptly got busy on the wire. Both the Senators and Browns were down, and receptive. Jim Delahanty was procured in a swap for Schaefer in early August, and a week later Tom Jones came in a trade for Rossman, Navin sugaring both deals with a little cash. Delahanty was the second best of the five Delahantys, and a younger brother of Tom, who played with the Detroit Western League club in the nineties. Jim was a better hitter than fielder, and had a vocabulary which would have had the Rev. Yarborough put his hands to his ears. But Jim's bark was worse than his bite. Jones was just the reverse, a far better fielder than hitter. He was one of the best defensive first sackers then in the league, and he immediately bolstered up the Tiger infield.

Rossman didn't go to St. Louis when the deal was made, and remained in Detroit for some time. He was aware of his first-base shortcomings, and wanted the promise of an outfield assignment before he went to St. Louis. "If I would not do for Detroit, I cannot possibly help St. Louis," he said knowingly. "I want to quit the infield, and play an outfield position. My arm is strong, and my hitting will come back if they take me off first. All I ask is that McAleer, the Brown manager, play me in the outfield."

The acquisition of Delahanty and Tom Jones promptly worked wonders for the team. They were the two shots in the arm which it needed. The Athletics came to Bennett Park in first place for an important three-game series, August 24, 25, and 26, and the Tigers blew them from the top perch as they swept the series, 7 to 6, 4 to 3, and 6 to 0. Though Donovan had only a mediocre season, he saved the first game for Summers, pitched the second, and Mullin wound up with a four-hit shutout. From then on, the Tigers never let go the lead, but they couldn't shake off the Mackmen until the last few days of the race.

In the game of August 24, Ty Cobb spiked Frank Baker, the young Athletic third baseman, rather badly in the right arm, just below the elbow. There was a gash several inches long, and fairly deep, but the arm was tied up by the trainer, and Baker played out the game and the series. However, the spiking became a national issue, with the fans lining up pro- and anti-Cobb. Outside of Detroit, the antis had a substantial majority.

In an editorial in its issue of September 2, *Sporting News* gave Ty quite a verbal spanking. It started off:

Complaints that Ty Cobb uses his spikes to injure and intimidate infielders are so common that his mere denial will not relieve him of the odium that attaches to a player guilty of this infamous practice. The list of his victims is too long to attribute the injury of all to accident or to the awkwardness of the victim.

However, in the same issue, Joe Jackson, the new Detroit correspondent, rushed to Ty's support. He put a blast on what he termed the "provincialism" of many of his associates in the press box:

Attacks on Ty Cobb, the Detroit star, all season long bring forth these remarks. Cobb is being criticized, right and left, and being pictured as a murderer of his fellows, mostly by men who have not seen the plays on which he is being attacked. The latest onslaught is in connection with the spiking of Baker of the Athletics. That player's right arm was cut by Cobb, on a close play, in the first game of the big series here, August 24. Baker asserted that Cobb went after him; Connie Mack said that he would make a complaint to the league, and diverse Philadelphia newspapers started a new anti-Cobb crusade. As a matter of fact, Cobb was entirely within his rights and merely went into third base in an effort to beat the play.

The race continued hot, and when Detroit came to Philadelphia in middle September for a four-game series, the City of Brotherly Love was a caldron of Cobb hatred. And how those Kensington boys could hate! Cobb received stacks of abusive mail and telegrams, with threats that a bullet would be drilled through his middle if he attempted to play right field at Shibe Park. Feeling ran high, and Jennings, knowing his Philadelphians, actually feared Cobb might meet with bodily harm. He showed some of the most violent letters to Connie Mack, and though the veteran Philadelphian was quite angry with Cobb, he got in touch with friends on the Philadelphia Police Department, and no president ever was more carefully guarded than was Cobb in that Series. A motorcycle escort guarded Ty to and from the ball park; a solid wall of bluecoats stood between Cobb and the crowd herded behind the right-field ropes, and fifteen plain-clothes cops were scattered through the stands to keep anyone from taking a pot shot at the Georgian.

Detroit came to Philadelphia leading by three and a half games, and if the A's swept the four games, they would recapture the lead by a half game. They almost succeeded, winning three of the four games, but the one victory which the Tigers won in the second game from Lefty Krause, their early season jinx, practically won the marbles. The Series, filled with rancor and acrimony, proved a gold mine for both clubs, as over 120,000 fans, a record for a four-game league series at that time, crammed Mack's new park and shouted indignities at Jennings' athletes. Cobb was booed throughout; Shortstop Barry of the A's was slightly spiked, and Bush collided sharply with Collins in the first game, Eddie getting out of it with a badly swollen ankle, which added to the fireworks.

Plank won the first game from Summers, 2 to 1, but Mullin won over Krause in the second, 5 to 3, a game the Tigers just had to win. The Felines ran the Coast collegian ragged, as Cobb beat out an important bunt to the young lefty, and the Tigers stole seven bases purloined by as many different players—Cobb, Crawford, Delahanty, Moriarty, Tom Jones, McIntyre, and Bush.

In a Saturday game played before a shouting, demonstrative crowd of 35,409—12,000 of them massed behind outfield ropes—Chief Bender vanquished Donovan, 2 to 0, in a classic pitching duel, the famous Indian giving up only three hits and Wild Bill four. The Tigers also lost the fourth game, when Summers again was nosed out by Plank, 4 to 3, but Jennings got out of town with a lead of one and a half games, and eventually won the flag by practically that margin, Detroit winding up with 98 victories and 54 defeats for a percentage of .645, against the Athletics' 95 wins, 58 defeats, and .621 percentage.

4

Where Donovan carried the pitching load in 1907 and young Summers in 1908, it was George Mullin's heroic pitching which put over Hughie's three-time winner. It was the year of years for the big right-hander, as he won 29 games and lost only 8 for the magnificent percentage of .784. While young Krause was running off his early ten-straight streak for Mack, Mullin bunched eleven successive victories for Jennings.

Donovan, the former ace, had an off season, for while Bill enjoyed his old knack against his home-town team, the Athletics, his arm ailed a good part of the season, and he won only 8 games against 7 defeats. Fortunately Willett, who had shown much promise in 1907 and 1908, took up the slack, and came through with 22 victories, with only 9 defeats on his debit side. Summers helped again, with a 19-9 showing, and Jennings found spots for Killian, who won 11 and lost 9.

Cobb boosted his league-winning batting average to .377, and for the first time scored over 100 runs, carrying in 116. He beat out Eddie Collins in stolen bases, 76 to 67. And for the only time in his career he was the league's home-run leader with nine. While Ty and Crawford often didn't speak off the field, they remained the greatest "One-Two" punch in baseball. Wahoo Sam belted the ball for .314, and Davey Jones was third on the Tiger hit parade with .279. In his first complete season in the league, Donie Bush hit .273, and scored 114 runs, only two less than the Georgia Peach.

An important Tiger acquisition that season was a burly catcher, Oscar Stanage, who came from the Newark Internationals; he caught seventy-seven games that year, then developed fast and for a decade served as Detroit's first-string catcher.

⊗ XIII ⊗

BABE ADAMS PROVES
A STUMBLING BLOCK

I

BY 1909, THE WORLD'S SERIES HAD GROWN INTO SOMETHING REALLY substantial, and after total receipts of $101,728 and $94,975 in 1907 and 1908 respectively, the figures jumped to $188,302 when the Tigers battled the Pittsburgh Pirates to a seventh game in the fall classic. Crowds were considerably bigger, with three turnouts in Pittsburgh averaging 27,400, with a top crowd of 31,114 for the second game. Barney Dreyfuss had opened his splendid new park at Forbes Field that very year, and immediately celebrated with a winner. National interest in the Series was greater than in any up to that time. Detroit also had become much more World's Series-conscious—at least at the gate. Tigertown always had been demonstrative, met its teams at the depot, wined and dined its baseball boys, but this time the fans really marched to the ticket sellers with their ducats. With Navin having enlarged his stands since 1908, the Tigers played to 63,410 in four games at Bennett Field, with only one Detroit crowd dropping under 17,000.

Ban Johnson once, in his cups, said bitterly: "We do all right in World's Series, except when the Detroit club, with that damn National Leaguer, Jennings, gets into it. Then we get hell beaten out of us." There wasn't any intimation that Jennings, with his old Oriole contacts, wasn't trying, but Hughie's lifelong friendship for John McGraw put a National League curse on him as far as Ban was concerned.

Yet Jennings' teams always had a tough World's Series row to hoe. And looking at Jennings' Series campaigns from a perspective of three and a half decades, we now are in a better position to realize what Hughie was up against. In losing twice to Chance's Cubs, he lost to one of the greatest teams of all time. And in 1909, he faced a Pittsburgh club which was so strong that it breezed by a Cub club which won 104 games in an effort to make it four straight. Clarke's 1909 Pirates won 110 games, excelled only once in the majors, and matched by that great Yankee team of 1927.

It was the Tigers' luck to run up against a freshman pitcher, Babe Adams, used sparingly during the league season by Clarke (he won 12 games and lost 3), but who rose to the heights in the Series. His name became a household word, and whenever a young first-year pitcher shows unusual promise he still is referred to as a second Babe Adams. Pittsburgh's big pitching three that season were Howard Camnitz, Vic Willis, and Lefty Leifield; between them they won 66 games and lost 25. Yet not one of this famous trio could twist the Tiger's tail; the only Pirate victory which Adams didn't bring in was won by a right-hander, Nick Maddox, with a 13-8 record.

The then young National League president, John Heydler, always felt he was entitled to an assist in Detroit's discomfort and Adams' opportunity. Heydler, former secretary, had become acting president of his league after Harry Pulliam's midseason suicide. The pre-World's Series meeting was held in Washington, and after the session the commissioners, Herrmann, Johnson, and Heydler, went out to the ball game, where the Tigers were playing the tail-end Senators. A young Washington pitcher, Dolly Gray, made Hughie's boys throw their bats away for eight innings, but eventually was beaten by Willett, 3 to 1, when Detroit scored twice in the ninth.

Heydler, a former National League umpire, a pretty good sand-lot player and a lifelong baseball student, observed that there was a striking resemblance between Gray's delivery and that of young Adams, of his Pittsburgh club.

He looked up Fred Clarke before the first game in Pittsburgh, and remarked: "I don't know who you intend to start in the first game, Fred, but I saw that fellow Gray, with the Washington club, pitch against Detroit in a late September game. They couldn't touch him. Gray is a side-arm pitcher with a delivery very similar to that of Babe Adams. I think Babe is faster, and could give the Tigers a lot of trouble."

Clarke played the hunch.

The 1909 Series was the only one in which the batting champions of the two leagues opposed each other, as the nation's spotlight shone on young Ty and the National League immortal, Honus Wagner. The Georgian came off a rather poor second best, as the big Dutchman led his team with a .333 average, while Cobb was a hundred points behind with .231. Jim Delahanty not only led the

Tigers, but both clubs, with an average of .346, getting nine hits in the seven games.

2

The Series started in Pittsburgh on a Friday, October 8, before a crowd of 29,577, the greatest that had attended a World's Series game up to that time. Pirate fans looked on in amazement when they saw young Adams warm up against the formidable Mullin. It was expected Clarke would oppose George with his No. 1 pitcher, Howard Camnitz, but the Kentucky Rosebud was just recovering from an attack of quinsy and Fred took Heydler's tip and gave Adams the nod. It developed into a low-hitting affair with the Pirates getting only five hits against six for Detroit, but the Pirates averaged nearly a run per hit and won by a score of 4 to 1.

Detroit had a chance to get to young Adams for a bunch of runs in the first inning, but the kid remained cool under fire, and the Tigers could squeeze only one run out of it, all they scored that day against Babe. Davey Jones drew four balls, and was pushed to second on Bush's sacrifice. Cobb also walked, and Jennings and the Tiger rooters who made the trip to Pittsburgh were all expectant when Crawford came to bat. "Ee-yah! Ee-yah! You can do it, Sam," encouraged Hughie. But the best the clouting Nebraskan could do was to slap the ball back at Adams, whose throw to third forced Jones. Delahanty, however, came through with a clean single to left, driving in Cobb, and on Clarke's futile peg to the plate to head off Ty, Del made second. But the rally died a quick death when Jim was hit on the foot by Moriarty's grounder, a technical hit for George, but also the third out.

Spectacular outfielding by Tommy Leach prevented any Detroit scores after that, especially in the fifth inning, when with Jones on base Tommy made a miracle catch in deepest center on Cobb's bid for a homer.

Fred Clarke, who was to get only four hits out of the seven games, tied the score for the Pirates with a fourth-inning homer into the left-field bleachers. After that fumbling claws by the Tigers put the hard-working Mullin in one jam after another. In the fifth, Delahanty let Abstein's grounder roll through his legs. There must have been grease on it, as Cobb also fumbled the ball in right field, and the Pirate first baseman made third. After Wilson struck out, Gibson's double scored Abstein and Bush wrestled Adams' grounder all around the infield. That put the Pirate catcher on third, from where he scored on Leach's sacrifice fly.

127

The fourth Pirate run came in the sixth, when Wagner doubled. The Dutchman took a big lead, and Schmidt threw down to Bush to catch him napping, but Charley's peg was wild and rolled out to center field, Wagner going to third, from where he romped home on Abstein's infield out.

3

There was action galore in the second game played on a Saturday, October 9, with the attendance going up to a new high of 31,114. It was one of the most pleasant World's Series recollections for old Tiger fans, as their ball club really looked the part of champions. It was a warm day for early October, a good Bill Donovan day, and Bill performed nobly in Pittsburgh's smoky sunshine. Camnitz' quinsy was sufficiently improved for Clarke to start his ace right-hander, but Tiger bats had the Rosebud hanging on the ropes after three innings, and there was no letup after Vic Willis, another pitching headliner, took over.

Wild Bill gave up only five hits, two of them doubles by Leach and Dots Miller in the first inning, and the second two-bagger was one of the historic hits of World's Series play. It resulted in four umpires being assigned to subsequent blue ribbon games.

Donovan was in a quick hole when he passed Bobbie Byrne, the first Pittsburgh hitter, and Leach followed with a double, the fast Byrne scoring. Clarke sacrificed Tommy to third, but Donovan whizzed a third strike across on Wagner. Miller then hit a long stinging liner to a low bleacher in deep right field almost at the foul line. Part of the stand was in foul territory, part was on fair soil, and as the bleacherites stood up just as the ball was nearing some temporary stands, no one, including the umpires, knew exactly what had happened.

Both of the umpires, Evans and Klem, later among the greatest arbiters of all time, were then comparative youngsters. The American Leaguer was behind the plate and Klem was calling 'em on the bases. "Did you see it, Bill?" Evans asked Klem. "No, I was hoping you saw it," Klem replied. "Well, what'll we do?" he asked.

Billy was thinking hard and walked slowly out to where the ball had hit, Klem a few paces behind him. As they approached, the loyal Pittsburgh crowd yelled: "It was a homer! It was a homer!"

"Let's ask them where the ball landed?" Evans suggested to Klem, and the National League Bill acquiesced.

Evans put up his hands for silence, and yelled at the crowd: "Just where did the ball land?"

Several men in the front row pointed to a spot on the ground, just inside fair territory, and said: "It hit there, and then bounced into the stands and landed there." (The spot where it eventually rested.)

"That's just what I wanted to know," said Evans. "It is a ground-rule double." Leach was permitted to score, but with Clarke and the Pirates growling, Miller was returned to second base. Dots was left when Abstein vexed Dreyfuss and Pirate fans with his first of three strike-outs.

After that the Tigers and their loyal legion had all the fun. They tied it after two were out in the second on singles by Moriarty and Tom Jones and a double by Schmidt. More fun in the second, when the Jungle Cats rolled over three runs to give Donovan a substantial lead. Abstein gave Davey Jones a life when he muffed Byrne's throw; a single by Bush and a pass to Ty filled the bases with none out. Crawford again fell down in the pinch, lifting a short fly to Clarke, but Del again came through, tearing a hot single to left on which Jones and Bush ran home and Cobb scurried to third. Clarke yanked Camnitz at this stage and substituted the veteran Vic Willis. While Vic was pitching to Moriarty, Cobb showed the National League a little of his stuff with a clean steal of home. Schmidt drove in two more Tiger runs in the fifth with a crashing single, scoring Crawford, who had doubled, and Tom Jones, who drew a pass. The final score, 7 to 2.

After the game, the National Commission summoned the two umpires to their room at the Schenley, and Ban Johnson asked: "Will you men tell us exactly what happened on that hit by Miller into the bleachers in the first inning?"

Evans explained what had happened, and how the play actually had been called by the right-field bleacherites, Billy then was only twenty-five, but he had the temerity to offer a sensible bit of advice to baseball's governing triumvirate. "Gentlemen, may I be permitted to make a suggestion?" asked Billy. "You have two umpires in the game, and two seated in field boxes. Why do you not make use of the two extra men, by stationing them at the foul lines?"

Billy Evans' suggestion was adopted, and the following year all four umpires were employed, two called foul-line patrols. The two extra men later were assigned to the bases, but they now run out with long drives to be sure to see where the ball lands.

With no Sunday ball in either Pittsburgh or Detroit, the third game was played at Bennett Field on a cold blustery Monday, October 11, and this time Detroit fans really went to town for a World's Series contest. Encouraged by the Saturday second-game victory, a crowd of 18,277, far above anything in Tigerville in 1907 and 1908, came out for the game. They packed the stands like sardines, and were massed behind ropes all around the field. And in order to keep the wildcat bleacherites from seeing what was going on, there were big canvas strips tacked to scaffolding outside the park. They flapped noisily when the lake winds took hold of them.

The Buccaneers shot up the place early, getting off to a six-run lead with five runs in the first and another in the second. The Tigers looked like dead ducks when they went to bat in the seventh, with the scoreboard still reading: Pittsburgh, 6; Detroit, 0. But the Tigers made it a ball game by pouring four hot runs over the plate in that inning, and each club wound up with a pair of runs in a frenzied ninth, the final score being 8 to 6. Detroit fans were almost worn out when Delahanty went out on a long fly to Clarke for the last out. It was a tough day for Sam Crawford as he came up with five "horse collars," while Delahanty and Bush swung the big bats for Detroit, each polling three hits. Though poked for ten hits, Nick Maddox, the Pirate right-hander, staggered through, as Jennings called on Summers, Willett, and Works. This was Hans Wagner's day, the big Dutchman's top in fifteen World's Series games; he drove out three solid hits, was mixed up in most of the scoring, stole three bases, and was brilliant in the field.

The Pirates' five-run broadside in the first was hard to take, and Pittsburgh runs came streaking over the plate so fast there seemed no end to the parade. While Summers was knocked out after he gave up three hits and a walk and wild-pitched a run over the plate, he was only partly to blame. Bush tossed in a damaging fumble on Wagner, and Crawford and Schmidt were guilty of hideous wild throws. Another muff at the plate by Willett gave Pittsburgh a sixth run in the second.

Maddox had the Tigers tamed for six innings, but they broke out with that frantic four-run rally in the seventh. Delahanty opened with a double, and there was a fine can of peas when Moriarty hit to Miller and Abstein dropped Dots's high throw. Johnstone at first called George out and immediately had Jennings and the whole Tiger team swarming around him. Johnstone then reversed himself, claiming he thought he had got the advice from O'Loughlin, the man behind the plate, that there had been interference. Now the umpires had the whole Pirate gang yipping at them. Eventually order was restored with Del on third and Mory on first. The argument didn't seem to help Maddox, as Tom Jones, Davey Jones, Bush, and Cobb punched out singles. But with four runs in and the tying runs on base, Wahoo Sam popped to Abstein for the third out.

Willett went out for a pinch hitter, and Ralph Works was slammed for those two runs in the ninth, the runs which finally licked the Tigers. Byrne singled and Leach doubled. Clarke's long fly sent Bobbie home and Wagner's single drove in Tommy.

The Tigers had a rally left, and despite the cold afternoon Detroit fans were sweating when it was over. Mullin struck out, batting for Works, but a pair of Pittsburgh errors started things. Abstein, who had a bad day, muffed Wagner's throw on Davey Jones, and Byrne's wild throw saved Bush. Cobb then belted a savage drive to right, which under ordinary conditions would have been a homer, but it landed in the overflow crowd, and was ruled a ground-rule double, Jones and Bush scoring. With the crowd yelling itself hoarse, Crawford and Delahanty couldn't help. Wagner tossed out Sam, and Delahanty sent that final long fly to Clarke. A moment later, leaden clouds which had hovered over the ball park all day broke in a heavy rainstorm and the big crowd was drenched as it left the grounds.

5

The fourth game was played on one of the coldest days in which a World's Series tussle ever has been waged. At game time, the thermometer read 32° and a strong biting wind blew across the field. However, the wind didn't cool off the Pirates any more than George Mullin's superb pitching. This time Clarke started his left-handed ace, Leifield, and Lefty gave way to a pinch hitter after the Tigers had scored all of their runs on him.

The usually mild-mannered Bill Donovan got into Bill Klem's hair in this game, and the crowd gave the young National League umpire an awful razzing when he tossed the popular pitcher off the field. In the second inning, Donovan joined the Tiger coach at third base to give him some advice from the bench, but lingered so long that Klem walked down and ordered him to the bench. Donovan wouldn't budge. "I'm talking to this man; you go on and do your umpiring," said Donovan. "Well, you can't talk to him all afternoon; you've said enough. Back to your bench," roared Klem. "What are you doing, trying to make yourself look important?" countered Wild Bill. They continued to exchange compliments, with Klem giving his final order: "And now, Donovan, it's not the bench for you, but out of the ball game." Still Donovan refused to go, as the crowd yelled its encouragement to him.

Finally Klem pulled his watch on Jennings, and said: "I'll give you just thirty seconds to get Donovan off the field. And if he's not gone by that time I'll forfeit the game to Pittsburgh. And if I've got to forfeit, I wouldn't like to be in your shoes when you're standing before Ban Johnson."

"You better go, Bill," Jennings said to Donovan, and with a few more snappy remarks Wild Bill departed.

Despite the freezing weather, another fine Detroit crowd of 17,036 was on hand, and they really ate it up. It was the first time in Jennings' three pennant years that the fans left Bennett Field with the fond satisfaction of having rooted home a winner. After the early innings, there was nothing to do but sit back and relax and enjoy Mullin pitching a five-hitter.

Two Tiger runs poured over the plate in the second inning. Leifield hit Delahanty with a pitched ball, and Moriarty drove a hefty single to center. On Tom Jones's tap to Leifield, Del was trapped between home and third, but he delayed his demise long enough for Mory to reach third and Tom second. Both scored when Stanage rammed a solid single to right.

Leifield got by the third, but three more Detroit runs were rung up at the plate in a busy fourth inning. And Lefty got into all his trouble after Honus Wagner had smoothed things for him with a brilliant double play. After Tom Jones scratched an infield single, Wagner snapped up Stanage's hot shot, tagged second for a force on Tom, and then threw to first for a double play on Oscar. Leifield then walked Mullin; Davey Jones cracked out a single; and both Bush and Cobb pulled outside pitches down the left-field foul line for doubles, Mullin, Jones, and Bush scoring. It was Detroit's game all the way, 5 to 0.

6

It just didn't seem to be in the cards for the Tigers to get out in front. The scene shifted back to Pittsburgh on the thirteenth, and the cold windy weather accompanied the baseball caravan.

Babe Adams won again for the Pirates, but this time he wasn't as tough as in the opener, even though he held the Tigers to six hits. Sam Crawford finally broke out with a homer, double, single, two runs, and a steal; Davey Jones also drove a homer, and Wagner helped the Navin-Jennings cause with two errors. It was a game which Detroit could have won with any kind of pitching, but Kickapoo Summers' knuckler failed to mystify the Pirates as the cold afternoon drew to a close. As had happened in Eddie's other World's Series starts, Jennings had to yank him as a barrage of base hits exploded around his ears. Fred Clarke, who hadn't made a hit since he homered off Mullin in the first game, cracked out two bingles in this game, including a three-run home run which rocked Summers in the eighth.

Detroit started off well, when Davey Jones, first batter up, crashed a homer into the center-field bleachers. It seemed an augury of good things to come, but the Tigers quickly lost the lead as the Pirates pecked away for single runs in the first, second, and third innings. Detroit tied it up in the sixth, when the Cobb-Crawford combination functioned in American League fashion. Cobb slapped a single to right, and came all the way home on Wahoo Sam's steaming double to center. Then Honus Wagner threw Delahanty's grounder to the grandstand, and the barber galloped home with the tying run.

"That's the break; we're back in the game," said Hughie, happily, after the Dutchman's error. "From here on, we ought to go places."

But it was Summers who faded in the very next inning, as the Pirates salted away the game with four juicy runs. After Adams fanned, Byrne singled, and on the hit-and-run play Leach knocked another single through the space vacated by Bush. Clarke then floored the Tigers with one of his rare hits, a round-tripper into the center-field bleachers, Byrne and Leach prancing in ahead of him. For good measure, the Dutchman stole another run. Wagner was hit by a pitched ball, stole second and third bases, and came home when Schmidt threw wild to third.

In the first half of the eighth, Sam Crawford hit the longest ball of the Series, a terrific home-run clout deep into the center-field bleachers. It was almost amusing how Hughie locked the old stable door after the horse was stolen. After Pittsburgh picked up another run, with none out, in its half of the eighth on Wilson's double and Gibson's single, Jennings chased Summers, and Willett, his successor, quickly retired the side.

In many ways, the sixth game proved the best and most exciting of the Series. With the possible exception of the sixth game of the Tiger-Cub Series twenty-six years later, in which Tommy Bridges won his memorable game from Larry French, it probably was the most keenly enjoyed Series victory ever scored on the Detroit grounds. Unfortunately the crowd, fearing the worst, dwindled to 10,535, but that loyal legion saw a real ball game. What made it so enjoyable was that after the Pirates bashed out three runs off Mullin in the first inning, the Felines came from behind to pull out the ball game.

With only one day's rest since hurling his fourth-game shutout, Mullin pitched another classic. "How do you feel?" Hughie asked him the morning of the game. "I want to start you, if you are right, but if you're not I want you to tell me. In that case, I'll pitch Willett." The players all wanted Mullin; George knew they were depending on him, and the big right-hander replied: "The arm feels fine; I think I can tie that Series up for you."

Clarke gave his twenty-two-game winner, Vic Willis, a chance to bring in the clinching game for Pittsburgh, but it was a poor Series for the Pirate aces. After Vic blew an early lead, Camnitz tried it again, and old Deacon Phillippe finished up.

It looked as though Jennings had made a poor pitching choice, and had expected too much of Mullin, when the first four Pirates to go to bat reached base and three of them scored. By that time, Detroit's chances of winning the game didn't look worth a plugged nickel, and the only regret of many of the faithful 10,535 was that they hadn't stayed away.

Byrne opened with a sharp single to left, and Tom Jones couldn't handle Leach's hot grounder and it went for an error. Clarke lined a long single to right, scoring Byrne, and Wagner doubled into deep left, scoring Tommy and Fred. Honus took third on the throw-in. Three runs in, and still no one out! It looked like a slaughter. Then, it seemed almost by magic, Mullin got the next three, leaving the Dutchman on third. With the infield playing in, Delahanty threw out Miller, Abstein struck out, and Mullin tossed Wilson's easy tap to first. From then on, George was invincible until Pittsburgh scored a final run in the ninth.

It was fun for the fans as the Tigers started to get those runs back. Bush carried one over in the first inning when he walked and ran all the way home on Crawford's double. The Felines tied it up amid great excitement in the fourth inning. Crawford walked and took third on the biffing Delahanty's long single. On a hit-and-run play, Crawford scored, but Chief Wilson nailed Del at third with one of his rifle throws. He threw what baseball men termed a perfect strike to Byrne. Undaunted Tom Jones stung a single to left, and when Manager Clarke let the ball roll through him, Mory brought in the run which deadlocked the game at 3-3.

Detroit took a one-run lead by notching another marker in the fifth, the inning which finished Willis. Bush led off with a single, and reached second on Cobb's out. Crawford's hard smash went right into the Dutchman's big hands, but Wagner dropped it. He saved himself an error by hastily recovering the ball and throwing Sam out at first. But it would have been a double play had he held the ball, as Bush was well off second base at the time. It cost Pittsburgh a run, as Delahanty followed with a double, scoring Donie.

Detroit tallied a fifth run off Camnitz in the sixth, and it took almost all the ingredients in Jennings' cook book to score it. Schmidt opened with a single and took an extra base on Wilson's fumble, only to be shot down at third base on Mullin's tap to Camnitz. Davey Jones forced the big pitcher and stole second. Then Bush walked, and Cobb rose to the emergency by slapping a double to left, scoring Davey. It proved a valuable run as the Pirates made a belated attack on Mullin in the ninth.

That Pittsburgh ninth was another classic round in Detroit history. Conversation on both sides was sulphuric, and spikes rode high. Miller and Abstein opened with singles, and Wilson tapped a sacrifice bunt in front of the plate. Schmidt fielded the ball to first, but the ball, the runner, and Tom Jones all reached the base around the same time. Wilson collided heavily with Jones and knocked him out, and as the ball rolled away Miller scored. After a ten-minute delay, Tom was carried off the field, though he wasn't hurt as badly as was reported. Crawford moved in to first, and McIntyre to the outfield.

Again Mullin was in a mighty tough spot. The Pirates had runners on third and second, with none out, and only one run needed to tie. Gibson hit to Crawford, and despite his coach's advice, Abstein set out for the plate. The Tigers had been riding him hard over his many strike-outs. Schmidt had the plate well blocked, but Bill came in with his spikes high in the air. Charley was badly spiked in retiring the first baseman, and they almost tangled at the plate. Abbaticchio then batted for Phillippe, and Mullin, giving it everything he had, blazed a third strike over on him. On the third strike, Wilson tried to steal third, but was out on a close play, in which Moriarty was spiked. The end of the game was almost a Donnybrook fair.

8

Detroit won the toss for the seventh and deciding game, played on a Saturday, October 16, at Bennett Park. But the Tigers stopped with the winning of the toss. Babe Adams again rode high for Pittsburgh, and his parting 8 to 0 shutout was bitter medicine for the 17,562 fans who braved a cold and windy day to overflow the stands and give the home gang vocal encouragement. For loyal Detroit, the final crushing defeat proved a drab finish for what had been a dramatic rip-snorting Series.

Jennings knew the blustery afternoon was no day for Donovan, but he felt he had to sink or swim with Wild Bill. He had won that brilliant second game, and he was Hughie's money pitcher. And though Bill's arm failed to limber up in the 40° temperature, he would have felt hurt had Hughie entrusted the assignment to anyone else. Donovan really lived up to his old nickname of Wild Bill, walking six and hitting a seventh in three innings, and when George Mullin took over in the fourth, he felt the strain of over-work and gave up the last six Pittsburgh runs.

The Pirates outhit the Tigers by only eight to seven, but ten bases on balls by the Detroit pitchers tell the story. A tip-off on the kind of game it was could be found in the box score, where Fred Clarke had no official times at bat, despite the fact that he went to the plate five times. He drew four walks—and tapped a sacrifice, scored twice, and stole two bases.

There was a violent outbreak in the first inning, and the Series almost wound up in a battle royal. Bobbie Byrne, the very first batsman of the game, was hit by one of Wild Bill's wild inshoots, advanced to second on a sacrifice, and ran down to third on a hit-and-run play on which Clarke swung and missed a Donovan curve. Schmidt's good throw to Moriarty had the runner shot down at third, but they weren't playing for marbles, and Bobbie went into the base hard. Mory had the bag blocked off, and in the mix-up, Byrne's ankle was badly sprained and it was necessary to carry him off the field. Moriarty also was pretty well bunged up; he tried to keep on playing, but after running out a double in the second inning, his foot became so swollen that George, too, had to call it a day.

While the Tigers felt keenly the loss of their third straight World's Series, individual checks for $1,274.76 took away a lot of the sting. As far as Navin was concerned, he reaped a rich harvest. At that time there were no league shares, and Frank pulled down $51,273.67 for his end. It enabled him to pay off all of his obligations to Bill Yawkey, and he owned his half of the club free and clear. The dreamer who had seen something in Detroit's baseball future was getting quick returns.

⊗ XIV ⊗

TY GETS HIMSELF
AN AUTOMOBILE

I

WITH THE EXCEPTION OF THE ST. LOUIS BROWNS OF THE ORIGINAL major American Association, no big-league club ever had won four straight pennants, and the big question in the spring of 1910 was whether Jennings' Tigers could hogtie the jinx which had thrown other great clubs of the past. They couldn't. Hughie yelled "Ee-yah" with no avail, Ty raved, Bush and Moriarty sputtered, but it wasn't in the cards. Mack's young Athletics spread-eagled the field and breezed in by fourteen and a half games. The Tigers had a May flash, when they looked like the old champs by running off an eleven-straight winning streak, but that merely inspired Mack's brash kids to another with thirteen links. A wretched midseason streak, in which the Detroits lost five out of seven games to the tail-end Browns, was the blow which just about slew the Tiger. The club couldn't even take the runner-up position, which went to New York, managed by Stallings, the early Tiger chief, as Detroit just nosed out the Red Sox for third place.

Even though Donovan came back and won 18 out of 25 games, and Mullin won 21 out of 33, Jennings' club suffered from a general pitching letdown. It is interesting to note that Wild Bill wasn't taken out of a single game, and Mullin out of only one. Two youngsters, both named Ralph—Stroud and Works—showed pitching promise. The latter later became a sports writer. Injuries to Delahanty, who missed 50 games at second, Moriarty, and Tom Jones also held back the club; Crawford tumbled under .300, and we read in *Reach's 1911 Guide,* "Factional troubles existed and frequent rows helped make the days more unpleasant for Hugh Jennings, manager of the fallen champions." Cobb knocked down a colored waiter in Cleveland, who hadn't shown sufficient respect for a white gentleman from Georgia, which got Ty into difficulty with the Cleveland authorities and brought reams of front-page notoriety. And he had a memorable fist fight with Billy Evans under the Detroit stands.

Cobb also won the most historic batting race in the American League in a hairline finish with King Larry Lajoie of Cleveland, .385 to .384.

The Chalmers Automobile Co. offered cars that year to the batting champions of the two major leagues. Horning in on Hans Wagner, Sherry Magee of the Phillies won his car easily in the National League; but the junior league struggle was a humdinger between Cobb, the young batting king, and Lajoie, the early monarch, who had led the American League in 1901, 1903, and 1904. It was no secret that most of the players, even a number of Cobb's mates on the Tigers, were pulling for the Cleveland second baseman.

The two stars were nip and tuck all season, and with nothing at stake but the batting title, the Tigers closed the season in Chicago and the Indians in St. Louis. After getting four hits in seven times at bat in the first two games of the series, Cobb knocked off in the final Saturday and Sunday games, October 8 and 9, the two pitchers, Mullin and Willett, playing his outfield patch in those games.

Lajoie got only one hit out of four times up in the Saturday game, and dropped several points in back of Cobb. Cleveland then played a Sunday double-header with the Browns, fairly well pitched games, which the old Naps won by scores of 4 to 3 and 3 to 0. Though the games weren't slugging matches, Lajoie made eight hits in as many times at bat, four in each game. One of the hits was a triple, another a clean single, and six others were bunts.

The St. Louis pitchers were Albert Nelson in the first game and Herman Malloy in the second, while Johnny "Red" Corriden, then a rookie just brought up from Omaha—and now a Dodger coach —played third base for the Browns. At the direction of Manager O'Connor, who caught the second game, Corriden played far back on the grass for Lajoie. Although a great all-around player and hitter, Larry never was a particularly fast base runner and by this time he was completing his thirteenth season in the majors. After Lajoie beat out all of those bunts, there was a smell to the high heavens, and Detroit was especially indignant. Everyone called for justice for Ty.

It was known that the finish would be very close, with most of the country's newspapers giving the verdict to Lajoie by a fraction of a point. These figures were compiled from unofficial averages;

Lajoie had played in 159 games and Cobb in only 140. The *Chicago Tribune* had Larry leading by three points, .385 to .382; the *Cleveland Leader* gave it to their home-town idol, .382 to .381, and the *St. Louis Republic* by .38111 to .38067. Detroit papers took heart when *Sporting News,* the baseball bible, gave it to Cobb by the margin of a gnat's eyelash, .38415 to .38411. They proved nearest right, as the official returns gave the title to the Georgian by one point. However, the Chalmers company reached a happy solution by giving a car to both Cobb and Lajoie.

Ban Johnson was much displeased with the entire business, and began an investigation immediately after the 1910 World's Series, to which he summoned O'Connor, Corriden, Harry Howell, a Brown pitcher-coach, and other players. Johnson's finding revealed that Cobb was not too well liked by other players, and several Browns wanted—very much—to see Lajoie win the batting championship and the Chalmers car. An anonymous note had been sent to the St. Louis official scorer, promising him a suit of clothes if he gave Lajoie the benefit of the doubt on all close plays. Howell had made several trips to the press box to inquire whether the Lajoie bunts were being scored as hits.

Corriden was absolved from any blame, for as a recruit player, he was merely following Manager O'Connor's orders. At Ban's insistence, both O'Connor and Howell were dropped by the St. Louis club. O'Connor, who had a contract for 1911, sued the Browns for back salary and collected $5,000. Howell became an umpire in the minors.

Serving notice on Cobb that he would be tough in the future, Joe Jackson, a young South Carolina slugger, finished the 1910 season with an average of .387 for 20 games, two points above Ty. Originally the property of the Athletics, Cleveland acquired title to Shoeless Joe in a 1910 midseason trade, and the Indians brought him up in the fall from New Orleans. Cobb saw him in a few September games, and remarked: "That fellow is going to be one of the greatest hitters in baseball. He can't miss."

2

Frank Navin put in Sunday ball in 1910, not the bootleg variety at Burns Park, outside of the city limit, but right out in the open at Bennett Park. Michigan hadn't yet legalized Sunday baseball, but Detroit rapidly was becoming more industrialized, and the workers wanted recreation on their day of rest. Some of the older residents opposed Frank's bold move, but most of the city's employers favored it. It was Sunday ball which helped change Detroit from an American League filler-in to one of the big breadwinners of the league. At the time only Chicago, St. Louis, and Cincinnati had Sunday ball in the majors.

While Sunday ball still was a live issue in Detroit, there was a tumultuous and disorderly scene in a Tiger–Red Sox Sabbath game. It came at a time when Navin was particularly anxious for his Sunday games to be conducted with utmost decorum. The score was tied in the ninth, when Moriarty, having reached third base, suddenly set sail for the home plate, guarded by Bill Carrigan. George slid in safely, and the game was over.

As Mory was still stretched out on the ground, the irate Carrigan, a tough collegian, sent a squirt of tobacco juice in his general direction, which landed in George's eye. From a half-crouching position, Moriarty swung a hard right to Holy Cross Bill's jaw. Players on both sides jumped into the melee, with Tiger fans doing their best to keep it from being a private fight.

As the battling ball players fought down to the dressing rooms, the mob of riotous fans tried to follow in their wake. Navin, fearing this might be the end of Sunday ball, climbed on top of the Tiger dugout, extended both hands for silence, and exhorted the crowd to leave the park quietly. Carrigan eventually escaped from the park in a pair of overalls loaned to him by a groundkeeper.

Overnight, Ban Johnson slapped a $100 fine on Moriarty, and the next day George was summoned to Navin's office. "George, that was quite a mess you stirred up out there yesterday," began Navin, "and on a Sunday, too."

"I'm very sorry, Mr. Navin," said George, "but under the circumstances, I couldn't do anything else."

"Well, George, we'll take care of Ban Johnson's fine, but don't let it happen again."

"No, Mr. Navin; I won't," said George, happy to escape so easily.

As Moriarty had the door half opened to leave, Navin called after him: "I mean don't ever let any of those fellows spit in your eye again."

3

Veteran Tiger fans will never forget the season of 1911, a razzle-dazzle year, in which the Tigers threatened to wreck the American League in the spring, winning 21 of their first 23 games; on May

8 they had a "believe-it-or-not" lead of .409 over the second place club. With the exception of one day, July 4, they were continuously in first place until August 4, and then, collapsing in the final month of the race, limped home a poor second, thirteen and a half games in arrears of the winning Athletics.

There were some winter reverberations of the feuds of the former season, in which Crawford and Bush didn't speak to Cobb and there was talk of Navin's trading Wahoo Sam to Washington for Clyde Milan, the speed boy. Sam didn't ease the situation when, in a Detroit interview, he said that Cobb was the "club favorite" and could get away with murder. He said that Ty could miss morning practice, report just before game time, and break other club rules, whereas some ordinary Tiger would catch hell for such transgressions.

Ty also reported late for 1911 training, showing up in early April for an exhibition in New Orleans, after skipping the early training at Hot Springs and Monroe, La. He reported pounds overweight. In fact, F. A. Beasley, the *Sporting News's* new Detroit correspondent, wrote: "It may be that Ty is undergoing a steady, though gradual transition, and that he will eventually lose his great speed and become a slugger, as he is sure to grow more on the lines of Sam Crawford." A rather amusing prediction when Ty was only twenty-four years old!

Despite his scanty training and the fact that he looked like a fat cherub when he reported, Cobb started in where he left off in 1910, and burst open the 1911 campaign with a rush of base hits and stolen bases. Realizing the club's pitching had faltered in 1910, Navin had his scouts bring in a raft of young flingers, and it was largely rookies—Jack Lively, Jean Lafitte, Tex Covington, along with Ralph Works—who carried the pitching load during the great spring drive. "Jack Lively is the best of the Jungleers' corps of young pitchers, and he'll be in the big leagues for years to come," wrote one enthusiastic scribe.

In fact, by the end of May, Detroit writers and fans were asking for more of a battle. A Beasley column is headed: "TRUE TIGER FORM. Fans Do Not Believe They Are Going beyond Speed—Actually Keen for Something to Show up in Detroit That Will Give Jennings a Hard Fight."

"Some of the enthusiastic boys have about concluded the Tigers can't lose and that the rest of 'em might as well quit the race," the column follows . . . "The town is daft over Del Gainer, the new first baseman. Cobb for the time is forgotten and will only share the glory with the Central League recruit, so long as the latter holds up to his present stride."

Del, a lean, tall, talented, right-handed-hitting first baseman, was the early spark plug of the club, but when Jack Coombs, the big Athletic right-hander, broke Gainer's wrist with an inside pitch on the Tigers' first eastern trip, he really pricked the Tigers' pennant bubble. Hughie moved Delahanty over to first base, and played Charley O'Leary and Paddy Bauman at second, and the club kept pounding away in the lead until early August, but it never had the same drive after Gainer's injury.

Even though the club slumped badly in August and September, Cobb finished on high and had the greatest season of his spectacular career. In a way, it was partly due to that fellow Southerner from South Carolina, Joe Jackson, that Ty was driven up to the amazing average of .420. Joe was even tougher than Cobb thought he would be. Always a great competitor, Ty was spurred to his greatest effort when he saw this crude, illiterate former cotton-mill hand lash pitchers to all fields and finish with an average of .408.

Coming east in 1945 for the *Esquire*-sponsored East-West Boys' All-Star game at the Polo Grounds, New York, Cobb reminisced with the lads about his great batting struggle of 34 years before.

"With only twelve games left for the season Jackson had a nine-point lead over me and the advantage of a six-game series between us in his own park in Cleveland," Cobb told his youthful listeners. "Joe and I were good friends. But I refused to talk to him, even refusing to answer when he tried to talk to me. While he was trying to figure out what it was all about I beat him out. If he had been relaxed and hitting naturally, I would never have overcome that nine-point lead, for he was truly a great hitter."

But, even had Jackson relaxed, to beat out Cobb that year the Carolinian would have had to go over .420, and that hasn't been done in the American League in this century.

Despite Beasley's fears that spring that Ty was losing his speed, the Peach scored 147 runs that season, the high for his career, and drove in 144 more, while he regained the stolen-base leadership from Eddie Collins by filching 83 bases. And he won another Chalmers car in the league's first most valuable player contest, getting 64 votes out of a possible 64.

Sam Crawford also had a remarkable batting resurgence. Sam couldn't exactly muscle in on the batting race between Cobb and Jackson, but he finished a good third with a healthy .378, tops for his career, and an improvement of 89 points over his heckled season of 1910. And to show he could run as well as slug, Sam stole 37 bases. Navin sold Matty McIntyre to the White Sox that year, and a newcomer, Delos Drake, alternated with Davey Jones in the third outfield post.

4

With increased business, Navin had patched up his old wooden stands in 1911, added bleachers and grandstand seats, and brought the capacity of Bennett Field up to 14,000. But that wasn't nearly enough. The crowds continued swarming into the park during the high spots of 1911; Cobb was drawing them in and Detroit started moving up rapidly in the turnstile standings.

Navin, always with an eye on the future, started a big building project after the 1911 season. He ripped down the old wooden stands, and built a large single-deck concrete stand, seating 23,000. He moved the entire field around, and the batter now hit from the southwest corner of the field in contrast to hitting from the old home plate in what now is right field. The old wildcat bleachers were completely blotted out.

During the rebuilding, the name of Bennett Field went by the boards. "That field is your monument, and your name belongs on it," friends told Navin; Bill Yawkey argued the same way; and the new structure was dedicated as Navin Field.

The park was scheduled to be formally opened April 18, 1912, but Frank ran into a lot of foul weather. It rained that day, one of those pitchfork spring rains, and by the nineteenth it still was too wet for play. So the opening frills were staged on the twentieth, two days late, but it had a happy ending as the Tigers smacked down their old Cleveland enemies in a furious ball game, 6 to 5. Mullin defeated Vean Gregg, as the three Detroit outfielders, Vitt, Crawford, and Cobb, made 10 of the 12 Tiger hits. Ty also stole two bases.

There was a big baseball banquet at the Hotel Pontchartrain to celebrate the event; the Detroit Board of Commerce threw the party for Navin and Bill Yawkey. Garry Herrmann, Ban Johnson, and Jennings were the leading orators.

5

Jennings' magic, which had lifted a sixth-place club up to the pennant in 1907, kept it there the next two years, and gave Detroit five years of fighting first-division baseball, suddenly ran out in 1912. Despite an influx of new and promising talent, the 1912 club plunged all the way from second to sixth. The Tigers never were in the race, getting no higher than fourth, and they even had to fight off the Browns to finish sixth. It was an inauspicious beginning for the new concrete park. One of the few high spots was a Fourth of July no-hit game pitched by George Mullin against the Browns. And in another exhilarating batting race, Ty Cobb went over .400 for the second successive year, winding up with .410. He again had to pursue a terrific pace to finish ahead of Jackson, as Shoeless Joe came in a good second with .395. "Ah hit .408 and .395, and Ah cain't win," moaned Joe. "That's a mighty tough league." It surely was; Ty Cobb was in it.

Cobb continued to be a stormy petrel, and got much publicity apart from his spectacular batting. His first explosion occurred in Chicago in April, before the club even had its home opening. The management had given Ty a noisy room in the hostelry which housed the Felines. A railroad yard was outside of his window, and coughing switch locomotives, playing leapfrog, were interfering with his slumber. He said he wasn't feeling well, and called on the clerk to change his room. No war conditions prevailed at the time, but the clerk, his dander up at Ty's demanding tones, was strangely disinterested. Cobb then telephoned Jennings' room, and told Hughie: "I've got to have this room changed. I can't hit unless I get some sleep. Those engines are driving me nuts."

Hugh tried to calm his star's wrath. "I don't know what I can do this time of the night," he said, "but I'll see what I can do tomorrow."

By tomorrow, it was too late, as Jennings' ace bird had flown home. Learning he could get a late night train for Detroit, Cobb packed his trunk and took it. The Tigers played the last two games of their White Sox series without their star performer.

However, this was but a minor revolt to the incident which provoked the famous Detroit players' strike a month later. While the Tigers were on their first eastern trip and playing in New York, Cobb jumped over the rail of the old wooden stands at Highlander Park, and took several punches at a fan who had been berating him. The fellow's name was Lueker; he was a press man and a minor politician. Some pretty sharp language had passed between Cobb and the fan before Ty leaped into the stand and started punching. Lueker later testified that others seated near by had hurled the epithet which had heated Cobb's Dixie blood to the boiling point. Westervelt and Silk O'Loughlin were the umpires, and Cobb was tossed out of the game, a rookie, Perry, going to center field. Receiving the umpires' account of the incident, league president Ban Johnson suspended Cobb indefinitely.

The "rhubarb" took place on a Wednesday, May 15; Thursday was an open date; and on Friday the Tigers defeated the Athletics, 6 to 3, at Shibe Park. In the meantime, the Detroit players had held an indignation meeting; they were a snarling pack of Tigers, and decided they wouldn't take the field for the Saturday game with the Athletics, May 18, unless Ty Cobb was reinstated. A telegram to that effect, signed by all the active players, was sent to Ban Johnson in Chicago. As has been pointed out before, Cobb wasn't personally popular with many of his fellow players, but they respected him as the No. 1 craftsman of baseball. And they thought he was in the right in taking things into his own hands when he had been abused from the stands.

Hughie Jennings knew the players weren't fooling; they meant it, and he advised Navin to that effect over long-distance telephone. "Well, it will cost us $5,000 for every game in which we can't put a club on the field; you've got to get together a team somehow— somewhere," said Frank.

Hughie and his coaches, Jim McGuire and Joe Sugden, hastily recruited a team of Philadelphia semipros and a few boys from St. Joseph's College. One of them was Pitcher Al Travers, now Rev. Albert Joseph Travers, S. J., professor of Spanish at Philadelphia's St. Joseph High School. McGuire caught; Sugden played first base, and Jennings got into the game as a pinch hitter. All the rest were semipros. Travers was paid $25; and Jennings later gave him an extra $25 for sticking the nine innings; the other May 18 "Tigers" were rewarded with $10 bills.

No odder assortment ever appeared in big-league uniforms in the long history of the game, but a curious crowd of 20,000 Philadelphians came out to see the fun. And they saw plenty of it. The Athletics slapped the priest of the future for 25 hits and won by a score of 24 to 2, as Jack Coombs, Carrol Brown, and Herb Pennock each hurled three innings for Mack. The A's certainly took advantage of the opportunity to fatten their batting averages, as Eddie Collins, Strunk, and McInnis each churned out four hits, and Eddie stole five bases.

Johnson, indignant at the burlesque, frothed in Chicago, and breathed vengeance at the strikers. He jumped a train for Philadelphia to read the riot act. In Detroit, Navin gave out a statement: "I am heart and soul in sympathy with the strikers. As a matter of business, I had to see to it that there were strike-breakers to take the places of the players who walked out, or make myself liable to a fine of $5,000 a day for every day the Tigers failed to appear. I do think, however, that there were wiser ways of settling the matter than by striking."

The following day, a Sunday, was a cooling-off period, and Ban called off the Monday Tiger-Athletic game at Shibe Park. He called the striking Tigers into his room and told them he would drive them all out of baseball unless they took the field for Detroit's next scheduled game, in Washington, May 21. Ban, then all powerful in the American League, put the fear of God into most of the men; there were a few hotheads who urged keeping up the battle, but Cobb himself advised the players to call off the strike. They played the game on the twenty-first, a curious contest, in which Mullin won a 2 to 0 pitching duel from Walter Johnson, in which each team made only two hits.

By a fickle twist of fate, the striking Tigers suffered heavier fines than Cobb. Each of the players who had their signatures on the telegram to Ban were fined $100; Cobb got off with a $50 fine and a ten-day suspension. At a special meeting of the American League in Philadelphia, May 21, the league sustained the fines and gave its official approval to Ban's handling of the case.

Later in that season, while Cobb was driving with his wife to a railroad station in Detroit, he was attacked by three thugs. The men jumped on his running board, and one of them slashed away at the slugger with a knife. Though Ty suffered several cuts, and bled profusely, he stopped the car and singlehandedly fought off the attackers. Cobb reported the incident to the police, but his assailants never were run down. The motive for the assault was not known, but one supposition was that it was to avenge the beating he had given the New York fan.

Even though the 1912 Tigers finished nowhere, Navin's scout dug up a quartet of interesting and valuable players, Pitchers Jean Dubuc and George Dauss, Infielder-Outfielder Oscar Vitt, and Outfielder Bobbie Veach. Dubuc and Dauss both pitched some excellent ball for Detroit, though the latter was destined to become Babe Ruth's favorite home-run victim. Vitt, a doughty San Franciscan, was drafted from the San Francisco club at the end of the 1911 season; though listed as an infielder, Jennings used him during most of 1912 in left field. A scrappy, truculent player, he later became manager of the so-called Cleveland "Cry Babies," when a Detroit club nosed him out of a pennant.

Veach came in August from Indianapolis with a $3,500 price tag on him, another of Detroit's outfield bargains. He quickly pushed Vitt out of left field, and by hitting .342 in 23 games served notice on American League pitchers that a new siege gun was in the Detroit outfield. Though a phlegmatic chap who lacked Cobb's inspirational qualities, he packed a terrific punch for his size, and was one of Detroit's batting headliners for the next decade. Like Cobb and Crawford, he batted left-handed. Ty, by this time had been moved to center, because of his greater speed, and the outfield of Veach, Cobb, and Crawford, and later Veach, Cobb, and Heilmann, became the most explosive in the history of the game.

Two distinguished members of the three-time champions, Charley O'Leary and Bill Donovan, severed relations with the Tigers that year. Navin gave "Charley, me b'y" his pink slip after the 1912 training season and Donovan left in August to take over the management of the Providence Internationals, a club in which Navin then was interested. Wild Bill later went to New York as manager in the early years of the Ruppert-Huston ownership. O'Leary later caught on with little Miller Huggins, Cardinal manager in St. Louis, and accompanied Hug to New York as his coach when the mite manager succeeded Donovan in 1918. It was the path to new riches for the popular Charley, as he tacked six rich Yankee World's Series purses to the three that he previously had pulled down with the Tigers.

6

The season of 1913 was pretty much a duplicate of 1912, another sixth-placer, with the percentage dipping from .451 to .431. It was a bad year, both for Navin and his new park and Jennings on the field. The spring was a record-breaker for cold, wet, and dismal weather, and the wretched climate prevailed during most of the season. It hit the lake cities especially hard. Moreover, when the Tigers played there was little to stir the red blood of the enthusiasts. The Jungleers were most ineffective against their old rivals, the champion Athletics, losing the year's series to Mack, 15 to 7. *Reach's Guide* made the observation: "Detroit had little in the way of artistic success to commend the Tigers to their loyal constituents."

Cobb again provided such artistic success as there was. He won the batting crown for the seventh successive season. Again it was a tussle with Joe Jackson, and at the finish Ty led by the usual margin. This time Joe didn't drive the Georgia Peach over .400, and Cobb wound up with .390 to the shoeless one's .373. While Cobb and Eddie Collins were nip and tuck in stolen bases with 52 and 54, respectively, Clyde Milan of the Washington club rushed easily to the fore with 74.

Crawford was slowing down perceptibly in the outfield, but his big black bat still played a lively .316 tune. Chattering Ossie Vitt, the 1912 left fielder, moved friskily around the infield, playing second and third base, but we read further in *Reach's Guide*: "Manager Jennings' experimental moves, started in 1912, were slow in bearing fruit." Jennings picked up Rondeau, a young catcher, Sea Lion Charley Hall, a fog horn-voiced pitcher formerly with the Red Sox, and Hughie High, pint-sized utility outfielder.

Pitching was the millstone around Hughie's neck. Jean Dubuc was his only better-than-.500 twirler with 16 victories and 14 defeats; Willett had a fair 13-14 year, but from there down the staff was most mediocre. The line of the old champions rapidly was thinning. In that cold rainy season, George Mullin never could thaw out. The smoke disappeared from his fast ball, and many Detroiters felt badly when they read in "Sal" Salsinger's column that the old World Series hero had been waived to Washington. Between the two clubs, stout-hearted George won only 4 games and lost 11.

7

Baseball conditions were badly upset in 1914, with the advent of the quasi-major Federal League, which for two years was a painful thorn in the sides of the National and American Leagues. Of their better players, Navin and Jennings lost only Pitcher Edgar Willett to the independents. Eddie jumped to the St. Louis Feds, while Louden, a former part-time Tiger third baseman, cast his lot with Buffalo.

However, both Cobb and Crawford were difficult to sign, with the Feds promising to double the salaries of outstanding stars. Both outfield aces skipped the Gulfport, Miss., training season, but eventually signed in New Orleans shortly before the Tigers moved north. Cobb got into big brackets, and for the first time went over $20,000. Navin offered him two contracts, one for one year at a higher sum, and another two-year contract for a somewhat lesser figure. Ty took the one-year document.

Crawford, usually easy to sign, was tough this spring. He was 35, knew he was getting close to the end of his trail, and took advantage of his opportunity. Sam was a member of the Comiskey-McGraw "Round-the-World" tour of the winter of 1913-14. Federal League promoters met the ball players at the dock in New York; they snatched Knabe and Doolan of the Phillies; got Tris Speaker a 100 per cent raise, and big salary boosts for Weaver, Doyle, Merkle, and other headliners. Wahoo Sam was offered heavy sugar to go over to the independents. Navin eventually induced the former Nebraska barber to put a signature on a contract by virtually insuring his big-league future; Sam signed a four-year contract.

Navin quickly got back this additional salary outlay when the 1914 Tigers got off to a thrilling start. The Tigers showed the rest of the pack nothing but their striped heels as they tore through May. By May 21, Jennings' flying Felines had won 19 games and lost only 9, putting them 3 games ahead of the Athletic World's Champions. Detroit suffered as the Mackmen caught the Tigers around Memorial Day, but as late as July 22, the Tigers still were in second place, only a game behind Philadelphia. When Moriarty was side-lined with an injury, it seemed to throw the entire club off its stride; George Burns and Marty Kavanagh, two young infielders, slumped in their hitting, and the Detroit club slid to fourth, its eventual resting place. But, after two years in sixth place, this improvement was welcome enough. The 1914 Tigers also suffered from Cobb's protracted absences from the line-up, first with a broken rib and later with a broken thumb. He suffered the latter hurt while scrapping with a husky Detroit butcher boy. The Peach played in only 97 games, but again was awarded the batting championship with a .368 average. This time Eddie Collins was second with .344 for 152 games. Under present American League rules, requiring the batting champion to appear at bat 400 times, Ty would have missed out that year. He was at bat only 345 times.

Jennings continued with his experimentation, and the inspired play of Burns and Kavanagh in the spring and early summer made possible Detroit's return to a contender role. Burns, a hard-hitting right-handed hitter, was acquired from Ottumwa in 1912 but was farmed to Sioux City in 1913. He pushed Del Gainer off first base. The latter never was the same player after Coombs broke his wrist in 1911, and was sold to Boston. Kavanagh was a red-headed jolly Irishman from Harrison, N.J., eligible for baseball's "most homeliest" team. "Marty's not so handsome to look at, but he surely is a pretty boy down there at second base," laughed Jennings.

However, Hughie's greatest 1914 pickup was a big Polish left-hander from his own northeastern corner of Pennsylvania's hard-coal country, Harry Coveleskie of Shamokin. Harry acquired fame as far back as 1908, when as a rookie pitching for the Phillies he beat Hughie's pal McGraw out of the National League pennant by defeating the Giants three times in the last week of the season. McGraw and his coaches later "rode" Covey out of the National League by imitating trombone players on the coaching lines, and singing "Sweet Adeline," a tune with which Harry allegedly had serenaded his Shamokin sweetheart. He was 27 when Hughie brought him up from Chattanooga, and he paid rich dividends on a $3,500 investment, winning 21 games and losing 13 that season. Dauss came fast that year, winning 23 and losing 12. Covey and George carried the staff, ably assisted by Dubuc, George Boehler, and three newcomers, Teller "Pug" Cavet, Ross Reynolds, and Miles Main. Navin had drafted the latter from Buffalo the previous fall; Miles had one promising year in Detroit and then jumped to the Kansas City Federals.

⊗ XV ⊗

A HUNDRED VICTORIES
AND STILL NO PENNANT

I

Hughie Jennings in later years called his season of 1915 his "biggest disappointment in Detroit." The Tigers came home second with 100 victories, 54 defeats, and a percentage of .649, higher than any of Detroit's seven pennant-winning percentages with the exception of .656 in 1934. But Carrigan's Red Sox won 101 games and lost 50 for a percentage of .669. The 1915 Detroits were the only American League 100-game winners ever nosed out for a flag. The National League has had two such clubs, the 1909 Cubs and 1942 Dodgers. Yet Jennings' 1915 club, as well as the Tiger fans, knew exactly where they blew the flag—in competition with their nearest rival, Boston. The swaggering Red Sox won the year's series from Detroit most emphatically, 14 games to 8.

It was another season of Federal League confusion and unsettlement. After Plank and Bender jumped to the Feds, and other Athletic stars pointed Federal-League-loaded salary pistols at Mack's head, Connie broke up the great team which had dominated the American League ever since the Tigers had held sway. With Mack's team out of it, it was felt the scramble would be between the second-place Red Sox of 1914 and the Tigers and Senators, the other first-division clubs. The prediction proved correct, except that the sixth-place White Sox, under the direction of the so-called "bush-league manager," Clarence Rowland, and strengthened by Eddie Collins, horned into the pennant fighting instead of the Senators. In fact, Chicago led the race for such a stretch that they called the new manager "Svengali" Rowland; there even were rumors he was hypnotizing his players.

Cobb's seasons were so uniformly brilliant that it is difficult to point the finger at one, and say: "This was Cobb's greatest," but

1915 certainly was one of his very best. This time he didn't scuffle with any butcher boys, played the full season of 156 games, led the batting race again with a .370 average—38 points ahead of second-man Eddie Collins—scored 144 runs, and established a modern record with 96 stolen bases.

"I've always regretted I didn't make it a hundred steals that year," said Cobb, some years later. "With a little greater effort, I believe I could have gotten those four additional bases. It also was a great disappointment not to get into the World's Series that year. I was little more than a youngster in my three Series; by this time I had matured, and think I could have shown those National Leaguers something."

The Tiger 1915 outfield really was a punishing affair. Veach came fast that year, hit .313 in 152 games, and bombarded the fences with 40 doubles and 10 triples. And Crawford still had plenty of dynamite in his cudgel; he just missed .300—finishing with .299 —but, like Cobb, he played out the full 156-game string and was second to Ty in number of hits. Jennings came up with a new second baseman, Ralph "Pep" Young, a former Philadelphia high-school player, a chattery chap and smart lead-off man. Kavanagh hadn't followed up his fine promise of 1914, but filled in for Burns in some 50 games at first. Vitt displaced Moriarty, the steal-home man, at third. George was released to the White Sox at the end of the season. Bush hit only .228, but still could make himself troublesome at the plate, and with the pounding outfielders behind him scored 99 runs.

As in 1914, the big southpaw Coveleskie and the sturdy right-hander Dauss carried the staff. The pitching of the pair produced identical marks in the records; each pitcher won 23 games and lost 13. Bernie Boland, a new acquisition from Nashville, made a strong start with 13 victories against 6 defeats. Detroit gave up a promising young outfielder, "Babe Doll" Bill Jacobson, to the Browns to get a pair of pitchers. It was a trade of giants, as Jennings obtained two six-foot-four-inch right-handers, Big Bill James and Grover Lowdermilk, for Jacobson, a six-foot, three-inch fly chaser. James, a husky son of Ann Arbor, had a 13-13 record that season.

Those near pennant winners of 1915 started off splendidly; the Tigers sat in the No. 1 seat from April 19 to May 1, and again from May 5 to 14. After that the Felines held first place only one day, June 7, but for most of the season they ran second, never more than a short mashie pitch from the top. In July, Harry Salsinger suggested to Navin that he buy Carl Weilman, the tall Brown left-hander, just to remove him from circulation. "Weilman is the same old poison for the Tigers, and will beat them out of the pennant yet," lamented "Sal." No wonder Harry urged anything short of kidnaping. In a five-game series, the lanky St. Louisan licked the Tigers three times. In the first game, he edged out Dauss, 1 to 0. In the second game, the Tigers, by a superhuman effort, overcame a seven-run deficit to tie the Browns in the ninth, 7-7; then Weilman took over for St. Louis and Coveleskie for Detroit, and the Browns won in the fifteenth, 8 to 7. Then Carl won the last game of the series easily, 7 to 2.

However, the big series which cost the Tigers the pennant was fought in Fenway Park in middle September. It was termed a "little World's Series," and proved all of that, with packed stands and frenzied excitement at all four games. Jennings' team came into Boston gnashing at the heels of the Red Sox, and there was general jubilation in the Tiger camp when Dauss got away with the first game, September 16, winning handily over Foster, Collins and Mays by 6 to 1. But that was the high tide of the Tiger advance, the Red Sox sweeping the remaining three games.

Leonard won the second tussle, 7 to 2, from James, Boland, and Oldham. It made the Saturday game on September 18 the crucial contest, and Coveleskie and Ernie Shore dueled 12 innings before the tall North Carolina right-hander was a 1 to 0 victor. Ruth, then an American League freshman, defeated Dauss in the Monday game, 3 to 2, and Boston picked up two full games in the standings. It was a deficit Detroit couldn't overcome in the remaining fortnight of the season. Relieving Stanage behind the plate in the second and third games was a young catcher from Oregon, Del Baker, later manager of the Tigers.

Ty Cobb saw to it that the series was played in the usual Tiger tempo. The venerable Tim Murnane, former player and then one of Boston's crack writers, wrote that the Tigers had been particularly rough with the Red Sox in the Carrigan team's August visit to Detroit, and that "the Boston newspapers took up the cue, and made rather much of it.... The result was that the big crowd was ready for the visitors when they came here Thursday, and the Tigers got a warm reception. Ty Cobb was the recipient of a little special 'attention' and the fans rode him hard until he lost his temper and threw his bat at Pitcher Mays. That was a bad break, considering the temper the fans were in, and it was considered necessary for a squad of policemen to escort the famous

Georgian off the field for fear that he might be roughly handled. ... Boston is willing to concede Cobb to be a great ball player and gave him full credit for what he does as a player, but there is a limit beyond which even he can't go."

Of course, Tim, writing from Boston, failed to say that Mays and his left-handed teammate Leonard were notorious in that day for "dusting off" hitters, and when they dusted off Ty, bats, or fists, were almost sure to fly.

2

The season of 1916 was another "might-have-been" year for Detroit. The Tigers were hot contenders in another stiff race, and with their 1915 percentage they would have won easily. Despite the loss of their greatest star, Tris Speaker—sold to Cleveland— the Red Sox repeated in the American League, but with ten fewer victories than they posted in 1915. The Tigers, however, fell thirteen under their 1915 victory total, and wound up in third place, four games behind Boston, and two in back of the runner-up White Sox.

Detroit's big thrill came on August 25, when, after running second to the Red Sox for weeks, the Tigers bolted into first place for the first time. "From here on watch our smoke," was the Tiger war cry, but the smoke quickly faded. The Felines held the lead only two days, when the pace became too severe; on the September home stretch, the Tigers fell back to second and then to third.

The 1916 season also made history in that it saw Cobb finally dethroned as American League batting champion, after he had wielded the scepter nine successive years. Ty had his usual bright season, hitting .371—two points higher than in 1915—but Speaker, Cleveland's new expensive acquisition, shot by the Georgian and finished with .386. If Cobb had to lose the title, he probably rather would have lost it to "Spoke" than to any other man in the league. Ty was an out-and-out individualist, who made few close friends among players, and Speaker probably came closer to being an intimate of Cobb than any other player.

Although Cobb lost his batting crown that year, Detroit came up with another batting champion of the future in Harry Heilmann, a handsome, pleasant-faced Irish-Dutchman from San Francisco, who next to Tyrus Raymond was destined to become Detroit's greatest hitter. He was acquired in another of Navin's strokes of good fortune. Heilmann was with Portland, Oregon, of the old Northwestern League, in 1913, and Fielder Jones, manager of the old Hitless Wonder White Sox, was president of the circuit. He recommended the young slugger to Navin, and the price tag supposedly was only $1,500. Harry played a little with the 1914 Tigers, and then was optioned to San Francisco in 1915. He got into 136 Detroit games in 1916, as Hughie tried to see where he fitted best, playing him at first base, second, and in the outfield. The young Californian hit .282.

On the Tigers, he was known as "Slug" and "Harry, the Horse." A former Golden Gate Park player, he attended Sacred Heart College in his native city and then St. Mary's. His mother was of Irish extraction, and his father of German origin, and the good Heilmanns were much concerned in the early days of Harry's ball playing. When he brought home some of his early baseball pay, they feared Harry was doing something which wasn't honest. "Nobody pays such kind of money to a boy for just playing a game," said Papa Heilmann.

A big 200-pounder, six feet, one inch tall, Harry batted right-handed. And without the famous Tyrus' speed, he beat out comparatively few infield hits. He had to line 'em out. Harry had 15 fine seasons with the Tigers, 18 in the majors, and when he finally called it quits in 1932, he had a robust lifetime average of .342. Slug now is Detroit's favorite sportscaster over Station WXYZ, and one of the best in all the land. A gifted, versatile talker, he is as popular in his present field as he was as a top-ranking ball player.

Another valuable addition that season was the tall hurler Howard Ehmke, former Buffalo Federal Leaguer, who joined the Tigers in the fall after a spectacular record with Syracuse, where he won 31 games and lost only 7. He won 3 out of 4 for Jennings in September. Jennings also engaged the popular St. Louisan Jimmy Burke as coach. And by handling 593 chances at the hot corner, Ossie Vitt hung up a third-base fielding record which stood up for 21 years. Harland Clift, formerly of the Browns, excelled it with 603 in 1937.

3

With Uncle Sam jumping into World War I while the Tigers were on their 1917 training trip, baseball flourished in the first war season. The war hadn't yet hit home; comparatively few players were in, and the crowds remained good, but it wasn't a good season for Detroit. After the Tigers had been warm contenders in 1915 and 1916, the 1917 team literally was left at the post. The Tigers floundered in the second division for the first half of the season, and only finished fourth when Bill Donovan's New York team went to pieces at the finish. The 1917 Tigers won only three more games than they lost, winding up with a percentage of .510, and finishing 22 games behind the new champion Chicago White Sox.

Even so, the Tigers retained their old sock, finishing well in front in team batting as Ty Cobb had little difficulty in regaining his crown with an average of .383. This time young Sisler of the Browns was his leading rival, coming in 30 points behind Ty.

The team trained that spring in Waxahachie, Texas, and Harry Salsinger wrote, "It's Rain! Rain! And more rain! We might as well have trained in Detroit." They might as well have stood in bed. Wishing to capitalize on all those fielding chances the season before, Ossie Vitt was the club's lone holdout and stayed in California; it seemed to give the Detroit scribes more merriment than concern. Ty Cobb did his early training in South Carolina, and he joined the club just as Hughie's Tigers and McGraw's Giants were starting a barnstorming trip. And immediately the fur began to fly!

One of the early games of the trip was in Dallas, where Ty spiked Charley Herzog in going into second base. It resulted in a hot verbal tiff on the field between Ty on one hand and McGraw and Herzog on the other. That night Cobb and Herzog had their historic fist fight in Cobb's room at the Oriental Hotel. There have been numerous accounts of this fight, but as all the Detroit and New York writers were guests at a party thrown by Joe Gardner, former Dallas club owner, Oswin K. "Uncle Jake" King, publisher of *Uncle Jake's Sport News,* and former Dallas sports writer, has the best version. Uncle Jake had a ringside seat.

That night Cobb approached Herzy in the Oriental lobby, and said: "If you didn't get enough this afternoon, see me any time in my room. It's 404. I'll be there all evening."

Benny Kauff came over and asked Herzog what Cobb had said. Charley told him, and added: "I can't take that."

So Herzog, Kauff, and Uncle Jake, an acquaintance of Herzog's in Baltimore, went up to Cobb's room. The door was open and Cobb was in his shirt sleeves. Herzog went right on in, and immediately started throwing punches at Cobb, as Kauff and King stood just inside the door.

"They exchanged a few blows and clinched," reported King. "Cobb pushed Herzog against the foot of the bed and had him

157

bending backward over the footboard and at his mercy. Tyrus asked Herzog if he had enough and Buck said, 'I guess so.'

" 'If anyone else wants anything, tell 'em to come right up,' said Cobb, as we left the room."

Jake said it was ridiculous to say the fight ended in a draw. He said Herzog left the room limping, and holding his hands to the small of his back.

4

The Tigers toppled to seventh in the second World War I season of 1918. It was a season of uncertainty for baseball, and a worse one for baseball in Detroit. The Tigers were back to where they were under Barrow and Lowe in 1904. Only 35 points stood between them and the tail-end Athletics. The German spring advance which carried them to Château-Thierry chilled baseball enthusiasm early. There was no President Roosevelt to give the game a war "green light"; in fact, President Wilson's secretary of war stunned baseball with his "work or fight" order, which terminated the big-league races on Labor Day. But by that time Detroit had seen about enough of its war Tigers.

Navin sold George Burns to the Athletics before the start of the season, and Jennings' parade of first basemen furnishes a pretty good tip-off on what Detroit fans endured that season. Lee Dressen played 30 games at the bag; Heilmann, 37; Griggs, 25; Kavanagh, 24; and even Cobb helped out in 13. Vitt and Bobby Jones played third base; Young and Jack Coffey took a crack at second; and only Donie Bush stuck it out all season, at shortstop.

And, where the club had led in team hitting for years, it even slumped in that department—to sixth. Only Ty Cobb kept the old batting eye aflame, and in a year of generally reduced batting averages, due to a low-quality baseball, Cobb was up there as usual, easily leading the league with an average of .382. His closest contender was George Burns, the former Tiger, who hit .352 for Connie Mack. Had Burns remained with the team, there would have been no such nose dive.

If 1918 was a dismal season for Detroit, the Tigers at least rang down the curtain in a blaze of glory, winning their final Labor Day double-header at Navin Field from the fading World's Champion White Sox by scores of 11 to 5 and 7 to 2. Cobb set off a few skyrockets with three hits in each game; Bill Donovan was the winning pitcher in the second contest, and Hughie Jennings finished the contest at first base. Good old Wild Bill, let out as New York manager the season before, pitched several games for his old friend Hughie late in the season.

With baseball over for the duration, Cobb entered the Army in the new chemical warfare section, and, always quick to go places, soon wore a captain's bars. Hughie Jennings enrolled as a Knights of Columbus war worker and got over to France just before the Armistice. A good raconteur and entertainer, the Ee-yah man entertained the boys overseas with tales of the old Orioles and of Schaefer, O'Leary, and Schmidt of his champion Tigers. Bill James, Howard Ehmke, Bernie Boland, George Cunningham, Red Oldham and Del Baker were among Detroit's service players. Like Cobb, Heilmann got in after the Labor Day closing.

5

With the nation wishing to find release from the tension of war years, baseball enjoyed a tremendous boom in the first year of peace, 1919. All sports enjoyed a sensational revival, but the national game more than any of them. The shortsighted club owners were entirely unprepared for this new outburst of prosperity; they reduced their 1919 schedule from the customary 154 to 140 games, and even trimmed salaries. The latter action helped bring on the game's worst scandal, the sellout of the 1919 World's Series by eight stars of the White Sox in October.

The game came back with a great bang in Detroit, and Navin enjoyed a lush season. His new park wasn't big enough to take care of his baseball-hungry crowds. And the Tigers leaped from their 1918 seventh place to another good spot in the first division. It sounds crazy now, but the Tigers had to wait until February, 1920, to learn whether the team finished third or fourth, and whether the individual players were to get a cut out of the World's Series. At that time, only the second- and third-place clubs were cut in.

It was the year Owner Harry Frazee of the Boston club sold Carl Mays to the Yankees after the submarine hurler stalked angrily out of a Red Sox game in Chicago. Ban Johnson ruled out the deal, and declared Mays ineligible to pitch for New York, but the Yankee colonels, Ruppert and Huston, checkmated Ban's moves with injunctions and other court action. With the games Mays pitched for New York, the Yankees had a five-point, third-place lead on Detroit, .576 to .571. The White Sox were pennant winners, and the Indians the runners-up. In Ban's book, the games pitched by Mays for New York were thrown out, and Detroit was third. The old National Commission, of which Johnson was a member, held up third-place money, pending a settlement of the dispute.

The league was split wide open in an internal feud; Navin was one of the leaders of the so-called "Loyal Five" supporting Johnson—the others being Mack of Philadelphia, Griffith of Washington, Dunn of Cleveland, and Ball of St. Louis. The "Insurrectionists" were the Yankee colonels Ruppert and Huston, Comiskey of Chicago, and Frazee of Boston. After a succession of suits, countersuits, and general acrimony, the "Loyal Five" gave in at the February, 1920, league meeting, when Mays's transfer to New York was approved and the Yankees awarded the third-place purse.

Nevertheless, 1919 was an interesting year for the loyal legion of Tiger rooters; after an indifferent start, the Felines advanced to within four games of the top in a fine August rally, but lost their gains on a final disastrous eastern trip. Previous to the season's opening, Navin swapped Vitt to Boston for Catcher Eddie Ainsmith, who caught 106 games that year, Outfielder Chick Shorten, and Pitcher Slim Love, a six-foot, seven-inch Texan. The Red Sox had sold Dutch Leonard, one of their former World's Series pitching stars, to New York, but Ruppert went into a high dudgeon when after a holdout Dutch wanted some of his salary deposited in a savings bank. Navin caught him on the rebound for $7,500, but Dutch later proved an expensive bargain for the Detroit club.

Jennings' postwar team lined up with Bobbie Jones, Bush, Young, and Heilmann on the infield. Cobb and Veach were outfield regulars, with Ira Flagstead, a hard-hitting newcomer, and Shorten dividing the right-field post. Ainsmith did most of the catching, but Stanage still was around, and caught 36 games. The elastic ran out of Harry Coveleskie's arm during the war, but young Ehmke, back from a year in the Army, took up the slack, winning 17 games and losing 10. Dauss, as usual, was the pitching leader with 21 victories and only 7 defeats. Leonard and Boland hovered around the .500 mark with records of 14-13 and 14-16 respectively.

Ty Cobb, approaching his thirty-third birthday, won his twelfth and last batting championship with an average of .384, and the player who gave him most competition was his young fellow-outfield slugger, Bob Veach, who was second with .355. Oddly enough, Ty and Bobbie finished with the same number of hits—191. Flagstead hit .331; young Heilmann now was getting the range with .320; and the entire team moved up to second place in club batting.

The 1920 season saw the Tigers plunge back to seventh, and it ended Hughie Jennings' twelve-year sojourn as keeper of the Tiger cage. Maybe it wasn't Hughie's fault, but somehow he didn't seem to have the knack of developing pitchers. His staff never was the same after Donovan and Mullin, the two headliners he inherited from Armour in 1907, burned out their arms in the Detroit club's service.

It was, indeed, a doleful season for Navin, the team, and the Detroit fans. It was the year Babe Ruth, playing his first season in New York, electrified all baseball by hitting 54 home runs, nearly doubling his former record of 29. Tiger pitchers fed Ruth ten of these "home-run balls." Georgie Dauss, Ruth's pet, was slapped for four, Ehmke for three.

The team made a terrible start, which chilled the enthusiasm of Tiger fans at the very outset; the club lost its first 13 games. It was well in May before Dutch Leonard produced the first victory, a 5 to 1 decision over Morton of the Indians. The wretched start was blamed on a long barnstorming trip, which the Tigers and Boston Braves made through the deepest sticks of the South. The clubs ran into rain, floods, hail, and some mere apologies for ball fields.

During the trip, Eddie Ainsmith wrote a parody on a favorite Southern refrain:

> Away down South in the land of cotton,
> Where the sky is high,
> And the grounds are rotten.
> Stay away! Stay away!
> Stay away! Stay away!

Of course, all the trouble couldn't be blamed on that training jaunt. Cobb had his worst season up to that time, and people were predicting it was the beginning of the end. Sisler was the new batting champion with .407, and Ty was tenth among the hundred-game players with .334. He was in only 112 games, being out of the line-up twice for protracted periods. On June 7, he had an outfield collision with Ira Flagstead, and suffered several torn ligaments in his left knee. He did not regain his speed for the balance of the season. Donie Bush also bogged down at short. Heilmann, still playing first base most of the season, and Veach hit .310 and .307, respectively, but the whole club deteriorated as badly at bat as in other departments. At the finish the club had the same position in the batting tables as in the league standing—only the Athletics were below them.

Feeling that Jennings wasn't helping young pitchers enough, Navin engaged Jack Coombs, the former Athletic and Brooklyn pitcher, as pitching coach. Jack had been manager of the Phillies for half a season, and as early as May 6, during that frightful getaway, it was rumored that Coombs would succeed Jennings as manager. Jack since has become one of the best instructors in baseball as the successful coach at Duke, but either his plentiful 1920 material was poor or he didn't have time to work on it. A batch of pitching fledgelings, Ayres, Baumgartner, Alten, Wilson, and Okrie, were brought up, but there wasn't a jewel in the carload. Two young third basemen, Sam "Bad News" Hale and Ralph "Babe" Pinelli, were tried out, and did fairly. Sam later developed into a pretty good player with the Athletics, while Pinelli became a regular third baseman with the Cincinnati Reds and is the present-day National League umpire.

7

And for about three days in November, 1920, Detroit found itself back in the National League. It was around the time that the National League and those three old Insurrectionist clubs, the Yankees, White Sox, and Red Sox, got behind the so-called "Lasker plan" and dictated the appointment of a single civilian commissioner for baseball. Ban Johnson, supported by his old Loyal Five of the Mays feud, was in favor of retaining the old three-man National Commission government and castigated the Lasker plan.

The majority, however, weren't fooling and meant to have their way. At a meeting in Chicago, November 8, they voted to form a twelve-club "New National League." John A. Heydler was elected president-secretary-treasurer. It took in the eight National League clubs and the three anti-Johnson American League clubs, which would have meant two clubs each in New York, Chicago, and Boston, and awarded the twelfth franchise to Detroit. Backers in this now fruitful territory were to be procured later.

This was a real squeeze play on Frank Navin. Frank was one of the first to realize that Johnson was fighting a losing cause and that the jig of the old regime in baseball was up. He had informal talks with Colonel Ruppert of the rival American League faction, and out of it grew a plan for a conference of all the sixteen club owners in Chicago, November 12. The New National League quickly disbanded, and when the meeting was held, with both major-league presidents excluded, Judge Kenesaw Mountain Landis of Chicago was named as the commissioner-dictator of baseball.

⊖ XVI ⊖

TY COBB BECOMES
THE BOSS MAN

I

FRANK NAVIN WAS RELUCTANT TO LET JENNINGS GO; HE NOT only appreciated what Hughie had done for the club, but he had a strong personal liking for the Scranton Irishman. But the crowds were beginning to get impatient for a change, and the collapse of the 1920 team was a sorry disappointment. Frank then made one of the most important decisions of his life: he offered the post to his hot-tempered Georgia star of stars, Ty Cobb. The Peach held the reins in six highly publicized seasons and it still is a moot question whether Ty was a managerial success or failure.

There also still is some question as to whether Cobb really wanted the job. I know Jennings thought so, and Hughie had no feeling of resentment about it. When he came to the Giants, he remarked one day during a fanning bee, "Cobb wanted his managerial chance, and deserved it. He was getting along as a player, and he had done much for baseball in Detroit. Tris Speaker, his great rival, had won the pennant and World's Series for Cleveland in 1920, while directing the Indians from center field. I think that impressed both Cobb and Navin, and whetted Cobb's ambition."

Ty himself says he wasn't overly interested, and E. A. Batchelor, Sr., crack Detroit sports writer of that period, more or less confirms it. "In December, 1920, I went to New Orleans with the University of Detroit football team," recalled Batch, "and Ty Cobb happened to be in town and staying at the same hotel. He had just been offered the job of successor to Hughie Jennings and he asked me what I thought of it.

"Frankly, he was afraid to take it; he didn't know whether he wanted to add the managerial responsibility while he still was playing regularly and he also wasn't sure his talents ran in that direction. He could take a pretty good inventory of himself. I talked

164

with him for hours on the subject, and told him I thought he possessed all the necessary qualifications. I think I sounded pretty convincing and believe I may deserve an assist in Ty's accepting that post.

"Maybe I was wrong in 1920, as it was proved that Cobb lacked the patience to make allowances for men who didn't think as fast as he did, nor had his mechanical ability to play ball. Like so many other great performers, he was impatient with stupidity, lack of ambition, and lack of what he considered normal baseball ability. The result was that he proved to be a poor teacher and that he never could get his team imbued with real team spirit. He couldn't understand why anybody who had a good enough physique to be in the major leagues couldn't do approximately the things he did. He found that some of the fellows who could hit, field, and run the bases almost as well as he could didn't have the 'will to win' nor the interest in the game which made him great."

Ty Cobb didn't need to add the managerial worries for financial reasons. He already was the wealthiest of any of the players. He had the knack of employing money to make more money. For years, he played the cotton market with astuteness and skill. In the early days of the automobile industry in Detroit, he got in on many good things, and he got in at the bottom in Coca-Cola, a Georgia enterprise, and laid the foundation for a fortune estimated at well over a million. And Ty was willing to share his good things with friends.

Henry Edwards, former head of the American League's service bureau and before that baseball writer on the *Cleveland Plain Dealer,* relates the following story of how Cobb passed around hot investment tips at this time: "In 1921, the Cleveland Indians trained at Dallas. The rodeo was on at Fort Worth and Tris Speaker was a featured participant. As a result, he left Joe Wood and myself to act as host in his suite of rooms. One day when I was serving in such capacity, the late Tiny Maxwell and Jim Crusinberry, prominent sports writers of that day, dropped in. Then came Ty Cobb from his camp in San Antonio. After chatting a while Ty said: 'I want to give you three friends of mine a tip that will make you all rich. Each of you buy a few hundred shares of Coca-Cola. [It then was selling for $1.18 a share.] And after you buy, don't sell for a little profit, forget about it for a few years, and live off it when you want to retire.'

"Of course, none of us took this well-intended advice. Had we done so, each could have made between $250,000 and $300,000 by

1929, as Coca Cola declared three big stock dividends and now is selling for $181 a share.

"The last time I saw Ty was at the dedication of the National Baseball Museum at Cooperstown, New York, in 1939 and he greeted me with: 'Henry, don't you wish you had taken my tip down in Fort Worth?' My reply was: 'Ty, this was a mighty fine day for me until you brought that up.'"

The incident which finally resulted in Cobb's accepting Navin's managerial offer was the presence of Clarence Rowland, former White Sox manager, in Detroit the winter after Jennings was let out. With no big-league playing or managerial experience, Rowland, now president of the Pacific Coast League, was put in charge of the White Sox in 1915. He won the pennant and World's Series in 1917, but was released when the club slumped to sixth in 1918. Big-league players then called him "the bush-league manager." Rowland had had several talks with Navin. Some Detroit fans tipped off Cobb, and said: "You wouldn't want to play for that guy, would you?" Ty replied: "I surely wouldn't; I guess I better take the job myself."

2

Once Cobb made his decision to take over the management, he threw himself wholeheartedly into the new work. Ty wanted to do everything well, and he hoped to be as successful as a manager as he still was a player. Writing from Detroit's San Antonio training camp that spring, Harry Salsinger told something of the new manager's contagious enthusiasm. His story was headed: "Cobb's Tigers to give fans something different from cut-and-dried stuff of other teams," and went on to say: "It is a pleasure to be with the Tigers this spring. More than a pleasure; it is an education....We get baseball on the field and off. Baseball until midnight and baseball before breakfast."

McGraw's Giants, with Jennings serving as assistant manager, trained at San Antonio the same spring, but there still were reverberations of the Cobb-Herzog feud of 1917, and the two teams played no practice games with each other.

Cobb worked magic with the club's batting figures, but didn't help much in the 1921 standing of the clubs. From seventh in batting in Jennings' last year, the club soared to first with a hefty team average of .316, eight points higher than Cleveland, the next club. It was a year of sock; the Tigers scored 883 runs, but had

852 scored against them. And while the club was in the first division a good part of the year, it eventually receded to sixth. And the new champion Yankees beat them, 17 games to 5.

Cobb made over the team; he took Heilmann off first base and stationed him permanently in right field. It proved a good tonic for Harry, as he led the league with an average of .394, five points ahead of Ty, second with .389. It was the beginning of Heilmann's odd trick of winning batting championships in odd-numbered years; Harry also was the first right-handed American League batting champion since Nap Lajoie in 1904.

At first base, Cobb played Luzerne Atwood "Lu" Blue, who soon became a Detroit favorite. Jennings had had him since 1919, but twice farmed him out. Lu threw left, and was a change-about hitter. No doubt liking the name of Bobbie Jones, Ty told him he was the regular third baseman. And he came up with two fine catchers that season, both of whom became Detroit stand-bys—Johnny Bassler, who hit .306 in 115 games, and Larry Woodall, who batted .363 in 46.

The club seemingly started out with a pretty good corps of pitchers, with "Sal" remarking: "Tyrus Raymond Cobb is like the old woman in the shoe. Tyrus has so many good pitchers, he doesn't know what to do."

But, they didn't work so well in league competition, partly as the result of the yawning abyss between first base and third. The territory around second base was just a swamp of despondency and defeat in which to lose ball games. Pep Young had an erratic season at second base, and Donie Bush bogged down entirely at shortstop, and was sold to Washington on waivers. After that two rookies, Sargent and Merritt, tried their luck at the difficult position, and even Ira Flagstead, the outfielder, played 55 games at short.

3

After the 1921 season, there were frequent reports that Bobbie Veach, who had hit .338, couldn't get along with Cobb and wanted to be sent elsewhere. Trying to put more fire into Bobbie had long been one of Ty's problems. When Veach first appeared in the Tiger outfield, he was a happy-go-lucky guy, not too brilliant above the ears. His general attitude was that by a stroke of good fortune he was elevated above his station and his cue was to mollify his associates rather than compete with them. As a result he was as friendly as a Newfoundland pup with opponents as well as teammates. Since that was the exact opposite of Cobb's attitude and method of playing baseball, it irked the Georgian no end, and while he was a high-salaried private under Jennings he often put the spurs to Bobbie.

As Detroit manager, Cobb decided on a more drastic method of prodding Veach. I've got to thank Bud Shaver, former *Detroit Times* sports editor, very close to the 1921 Tigers, for this interesting anecdote. Ty cooked up a plot to get more hits out of Veach and drafted Heilmann as fellow-conspirator.

Cobb outlined the deal in a conversation with Heilmann, something like this: "That Veach up there at the plate giggles and chatters like a schoolgirl. He'll never get base hits when we need 'em unless we find some way to get him mad and keep him mad. That's your job. You bat after him. Get on him. Accuse him of being a yellow belly, a quitter, and everything else in the book. I don't care how you ride him, but I want you to get him mad and keep him mad."

When Heilmann demurred on the grounds that he didn't want to lose Veach's friendship, Cobb reassured him, "Don't worry, when the season ends I'll explain to Bobbie that I put you up to it and for his own good."

Heilmann consented and whenever waiting his turn to bat, roundly abused Veach as a yellow-bellied busher, who fell all over himself making friends with enemy pitchers because he was afraid of them.

This abuse, of course, infuriated Veach and he relieved his feelings in the only way he could, and the way Cobb anticipated—by whaling the cover off the ball. It also made him a competitor with Heilmann, whom by this time he hated almost to a frenzy. At the end of the first season of this "noble experiment," Veach had contributed heavily to the Tigers' victories and swelled his own batting average, but Cobb didn't stay around to explain as he had promised. He took off for Georgia and his hunting dogs. Heilmann then tried to explain to Veach unaided, but it was no go. Bobbie greeted Harry's friendly overture with snarls.

"Don't come sucking around me, with that phony line," he exploded. "You think you're a wise guy, but I'll show you."

And so the feud which started as a gag grew into a genuine one that lasted season after season. So Heilmann reflects today, with genuine remorse, that while he helped to make Veach a great ball player, he lost him as a friend in the process.

In an effort to bolster Cobb's 1922 pitching staff, Navin swung the biggest minor-league player deal he had made up to that time.

He acquired Herman Pillette and Sylvester Johnson, the two crack pitchers of the Portland Pacific Coast League club, for $40,000, though he paid some of it in players, Pitchers Middleton, Parks, and Crumpler and Infielders Hale and Sargent. Both expensive right-handers lasted with the Tigers only four seasons. Pillette had a brilliant freshman year, winning 19 games, but subsided to a 12-19 season in 1923. Then he showed up with a two-year lame arm, which came back later in the Coast League. He still pitched for Sacramento in 1945, and has been around so long that his nickname now is "Old Folks." Syl Johnson bounced in and out of the majors until 1940, when he pitched for the Phillies. He still was a wartime pitcher in 1945 with Seattle, and signed for 1946 as manager-pitcher of the Vancouver club.

Navin made other additions to the club and furnished Cobb with a new second-base combination, Shortstop Emory Elmo Rigney and Second Baseman George Cutshaw. Rigney, a former Texas A. and M. boy, was acquired from Fort Worth. He jumped right in, played the full 155 games and hit an even .300. A better hitter than Donie Bush, but not quite as nimble in covering ground, Rigney ranks with Donie as the two best of Detroit's all-time shortstops. Cutshaw, a veteran with the Brooklyn and Pittsburgh National League clubs, was purchased from the Pirates.

And during the course of the 1922 season, the Tigers brought up another of their famous clouting outfielders, Robert Roy "Fat" Fothergill, a colorful roly-poly fellow. The Tigers first acquired him from Bloomington in the Three-I league in 1921, but Bob was sent to Rochester for seasoning. He came from Massillon, O., had an Elmer-the-Great appetite, and when he landed in Detroit his measurements were 185 pounds and five feet, ten and a half inches. But the longer he was in the league, the shorter and wider he became until he was well over 200 pounds and looked like a bouncing ball.

Once when Fat Fothergill was batting, Goofy Gomez, the quaint Yankee left-hander, stopped a game to inquire of the umpire: "I thought the rules stipulated, only one man could go to bat at one time." The "ump" said, "That's right," whereupon Lefty inquired, "Well, who's that guy up there with Fothergill?"

But Fothergill was surprisingly spry on his feet, especially in his earlier years in the league. Mickey Cochrane tells this one on him. "I still was with the Athletics, and catching George Earnshaw. George pitched one in close, and Bob got the idea it was aimed at his head. He was very sore. He took a terrific swipe at the next pitch, and hit perhaps the longest homer of his career. As he went around the bases, he was yelling at Earnshaw, and just before he reached the plate, he turned a complete somersault in the air without using his hands, landing on the plate on his feet."

Fat Bob came to an early end, dying in St. Joseph's Mercy Hospital, Detroit, March 20, 1938, after a stroke at the age of 39 years.

The 1922 Tigers trained in Augusta, where Cobb by this time had a fine Southern home, and despite the horrible start of 1920 were bamboozled into another "Seeing Georgia and the Carolinas" training jaunt by Walter Hapgood, business manager of the Boston Braves. After this expedition, Ty proclaimed: "No more Hapgood trips for me." However, his Tigers got out of it with no worse casualties than a sprained wrist for Sylvester Johnson, the new pitcher, and several charley horses.

The club again got off to a woeful start, but picked up momentum as it went along, and though the race was entirely between the Yanks and St. Louis Browns, Detroit nosed out the Indians and White Sox for third place in a photo finish. The Tigers had a percentage of .513; Cleveland, .507; and Chicago, .500.

Cobb spearheaded the advance to the show position with the third .400 batting average of his career, .401, which was second to Sisler's magic figure of .420. Heilmann ran fourth with .356, and the third Detroit outfielder, Veach, connected for .327. Fothergill, the newcomer, bounced the ball for .322 in 42 games.

Prior to Cobb, only one other major-league hitter had collected three .400 averages, Jesse Burkett, of the old Cleveland Spiders and St. Louis Cardinals. Since Ty, Rogers Hornsby, modern National League slugger, turned the feat. A lot of brickbats were thrown around Cobb's .401 average, and I was right in the middle of them. In a rainy midsummer game at the Polo Grounds, New York (the Yankees still were playing there), John "Information Please" Kieran, then baseball writer for the *New York Tribune*, scored an error for Scott on a grounder which Cobb hit to the Yankee shortstop. The rain had chased me out of the press stand into the covered grandstand, and I put it in my scorebook as an infield hit for Cobb. I then sent the daily Associated Press box scores out of New York, and the play appeared as a Cobb hit as it was flashed around the country.

The unofficial batting averages at the end of the season, compiled from these A.P. box scores, had Cobb hitting .401. All probably would have been well if the late Irwin Howe, American League statistician, hadn't been so darn honest. In giving out the official batting averages, he announced that in the Detroit–New York game in question he had accepted my unofficial A.P. score in preference to Kieran's official score sheet. This gave Cobb the .401 finish; if Howe accepted Jack's score, it left Ty just under .400 with .399. Howe gave as his reason my superior scoring experience. Had he offered no explanation, no one would have known anything about it.

It raised merry hell for a while, especially as Ban Johnson upheld Howe in the subsequent controversy. Some felt the league had gone to some length to give Cobb this third .400 average, and the decision was especially unpopular in New York. It was brought before the Baseball Writers' Association, of which I then was president. It put me in the paradoxical position of having to argue for Kieran's official hit against my own scoring. By a close vote, the Association voted not to accept the .401 average, but it appeared in the Reach and Spalding *Guides* of 1923 and is accepted in all records today.

4

Prior to the start of the 1923 season, Cobb and Navin pulled one of the Detroit club's worst deals, when they traded away Howard Ehmke, the long angular lad from Silver Creek, N. Y. Howard had been a good pitcher at Navin Field, but Cobb always felt he should have been a better one, and they had some heated discussion on the subject. So Ty swapped Ehmke, Hollings, a fair second-string pitcher, and Floyd "Babe" Herman, a rookie first baseman, to the Boston Red Sox for Second Baseman Del Pratt and Pitcher Warren "Rip" Collins. Navin even sweetened the deal with a few cash sugar plums for Harry Frazee. The Herman involved was the famous Babe Herman of Ebbets Field, the daffiest of the Daffiness Boys, but not so daffy that he couldn't hit .393 and bash out 35 homers in his 1930 season in the National League.

However, the two principals of the deal, Pratt and Collins, flopped badly. Pratt, a former hard-hitting second baseman with the Browns and Yankees, had slowed down to a walk, and Ty had to get him out of there after Del played 60 games. He put Cutshaw back, whereupon George required an appendectomy. Fred Haney, a scrappy Californian, later manager of the Browns, finished up at second. As for "Two-Gun" Collins, later an officer in the Texas Rangers, that was sorry business. Out repeatedly with injuries, he won only 3 games and lost 7. And the temperamental Rip and the tempestuous Ty didn't hit it off at all. To make it even more painful, Ehmke enjoyed an amazingly good year in Boston, winning 20 games and losing 17 for the Red Sox tail-ender.

Even though the Pratt-Collins deal went sour, Cobb finished in his highest spot in his six managerial years, second to the famous Yankees. Of course, the Tigers were 16 games behind New York, and just nosed out Cleveland, .539 to .536, but the runner-up position was quite a feather in Ty's cap. Heilmann provided a lot of the dynamite, winning his second batting crown and reaching his peak of .403. He beat out Babe Ruth by ten points. Cobb dipped from .401 to .340; Veach hit .321; and Rigney and Fothergill, both .315. And with the Tigers still coming up with those outfield sluggers, Heinie Manush broke in that year with a .334 average for 109 games. He was a bargain pickup from Omaha, and did so well that Flagstead was passed along to Boston. Babe Ruth continued to plaster Dauss for historic homers, but George had his best season since 1919, winning 21 games and losing 13. Pillette was unlucky, but Syl Johnson started to show with a 12-7 record, while Bert "King" Cole, a left-hander from San Francisco, won 13 games and lost 5.

5

Navin and Cobb were pleased with the way things were going. Ty hadn't won any pennants, but he was making good progress and the club was making good money. Navin, the former bookkeeper, who had bought the club for a shoestring, and had had tough sledding for his first five years, now was a rich man. Not only was he doing well in baseball, but other investments were turning out most profitable. He still liked the ponies, and was a regular at the Windsor Jockey Club across the river when the Tigers were on the road. It now was his habit to stuff seven or eight $1,000 bills in his pocket, depending on the number of races. He would bet one on each race. Once he had a losing streak of 18 straight, but old Poker Face never batted an eyelash. "I'll start winning again," he said, and did.

But Navin continued sticking the money he made in baseball back into the club. By now Detroit was shooting up so fast that it almost suffered from growing pains. After advancing in population from 465,766 in 1910 to 993,678 in 1920, the City-on-the-Straits now was in the midst of its climb to 1,568,662 in 1930. Henry Ford started it all with that foolish old "horseless carriage," and his rival automotive tycoons now were helping him to carry the ball. With Chicago losing its old position as an American League breadwinner after the White Sox scandal, Detroit now ran second to only New York, with its great Ruth magnet, in American League gate receipts. Who was that Cleveland editor who wanted to drive Detroit out of the league?

Bill Yawkey, who had retained half of the stock after he let Navin run the property, died on March 5, 1919, and in 1920 William O. Briggs, Sr., the automobile body builder, and John Kelsey, another opulent Detroiter, acquired the stock from the Yawkey estate, each taking a quarter interest in the club.

Navin conferred with his partners after the 1923 season about new alterations at Navin Field to give the park a still greater capacity. "Detroit really is going places," said Frank. "We've got to make this park big enough to get some people into it on our big days," he said. Frank always was a good enough businessman to hate to turn any crowds away.

"Make it as big as you like. We're behind you," said Briggs. From the start of his association with the Tigers, Briggs, too, was a strong advocate of plowing profits back into the club. So, they pushed back the walls at Navin Field, and added 6,000 additional seats by double-decking the grandstand from first base to third. The new grandstand seating capacity now was 29,000. The press coop was installed on the roof, and an elevator put in so that "Iffy," "Sal," "Batch," Bud Shaver, Sam Greene, Bert Walker, and Harry Bullion wouldn't be too winded by the time they reached their lofty perch. And on August 3, 1924, Frank and his nephew, Charles Navin, really packed them in as a crowd of 42,712 was clocked at the turnstiles. Of course, it was a Sunday game with the now hated Yankees, and Earl Whitehill turned back Herb Pennock, 5 to 2.

The Yankees had won the pennant in 1921, 1922, and 1923, and an impressive World's Series victory in the latter year. But Cobb felt he was going up; maybe Huggins' Yankees were coming down. "The Yankees are world beaters in the full sense of the word, and every man in Huggins' regular line-up is a star," said Ty early in 1924. "But we are a coming club. We may not win the American League pennant this year, but the club that wins will have to beat Detroit. I am absolutely certain that we will be in the running this year."

Ty was only partly correct, for the team that beat out Detroit didn't win the pennant. In the best Tiger race since 1915, the Tigers finished four games behind the second-place Yankees, who in turn came in two games in arrears to the surprising Washington Senators, led by the then boy manager, Stanley "Bucky" Harris, who later was to try his managerial magic on the Tigers. Yet Ty's Tigers gave the town plenty of thrills and excitement. Up to the end of July, Detroit bobbed in and out of first place, and as late as middle August the Jungleers enjoyed three days in the front seat. Almost to Labor Day, Ty thought New York was the club to beat, but while he was fighting off the Yankees, Harris' inspired lads swept on to win Washington's first pennant.

It was the high point in Cobb's managerial career; he was in the race until the last week of the season, and it was a race which he conceivably could have won. The Washington champions finished with only 92 victories. Cobb had the satisfaction of beating the Yankees on the year's series, 13 to 9, but lost to Washington by the same margin. As usual his club set the pace in hitting, but the top hitters weren't as high as usual. Veach had been sold to Boston, and Heilmann, suffering from sinusitis, was down from his .403 of 1923 to .346, while Cobb, missing only one of his 156 games, hit .338.

But what a magnificent spring the old-timer had, hitting .450 for the first month of the season! In May, the *Sporting News* said proudly:

Poor old Ty Cobb! Leaning toward his thirty-eighth milestone, and going into his twentieth season, he's hitting only .450. When he steals a base nowadays he does it because he figures it more strategical to be perched on second or third than on first. When he pilfered home last week he did so simply because his team needed the run to win. Tyrus certainly is a dilapidated old man. It is to smile!... Long live the king!

Second base again proved a soft spot for the club, and Pratt, playing 63 games, was at the foot of the second-base class in individual fielding. A youngster, Leslie Burke, and a veteran minorleaguer, Frank O'Rourke, did their best to fill in. However, help was on the way, and it appeared in the form of Charley Gehringer, the Mechanical Man, and Detroit's greatest all-time infielder. Charley had the easy grace of a panther and developed into a sweet hitter. Bobbie Veach always has been credited with being his discoverer. While on a postseason Michigan barnstorming jaunt, Bob ran into Gehringer at Fowlerville, and was an immediate convert. With much eloquence he told Frank Navin of the find. "You better get a scout up to Fowlerville, and get a string on a kid second baseman they've got up there, before somebody else beats you to him," said Bob. "This boy can't miss." Frank took the tip, and acquired Detroit's prize infielder for a song.

Charley came down to Detroit in the spring of 1924, and was farmed to London, Ontario. Back with the Tigers in the fall, he played his first game against Boston, September 22, and proceeded to hit .545 in five games. Gehringer was given another year's seasoning at Toronto in 1925, hit only .167 in eight Tiger games that fall, but became the regular Detroit second baseman in 1926, Cobb's last season in command.

Cobb also came up in that hectic 1924 season with a valuable left-handed pitching acquisition, handsome Earl Whitehill, a Cedar Rapids boy, who was acquired from Birmingham. Earl won 17 games and lost only 9 that season, and became one of Detroit's better pitchers. However, Cobb often vexed Ban Johnson, as well as fans around the league, by trudging in from center field to give young Whitehill instructions on how to pitch to certain batters. Ban eventually gave specific orders against these walks by Cobb to the center of the diamond.

And 1924 was the season of the most turbulent game ever played at Navin Field, on a Friday, June 13, a contest which Billy Evans forfeited to the hated Yankees, 9 to o. There was little love between the Tigers and Yankees as Huggins won his early pennants, and even less in 1924, when Detroit became a hot challenger. Though Babe Ruth had passed Cobb as the game's top drawing card, Ty never worshiped at the feet of the new Sultan of Swat. He nettled Ruth at every opportunity. As Cobb would pass Ruth as the teams changed positions, he would remark to a near-by fellow player: "Do you smell something? Something around here really stinks— like a polecat."

The Yanks were leading the league at the time of this June series, but the Tigers were clawing at their heels. The June 13 game was a slugging match, and after eight innings, New York led by 10 to 6. The Yanks had knocked out Lil Stoner, and Bert Cole was pitching for Detroit. Bob Meusel, one of the strong silent men on the Yankees, was first up in the ninth, and Cole hit him in the back with a pitched ball. The King always said it was accidental, but Bob got the idea that it was the pitcher's kidney punch. With an oath, he flung his bat at Cole's head and then charged out to the mound like an enraged bull. Bob and Cole mixed for a while before Billy Evans could break it up. And before anyone could say, "Chuck Hostetler," every player on both sides became involved. Cobb came charging in from the outfield, and Ruth met him at the plate like two football players colliding. Meusel challenged the whole Detroit club, and Fred Haney started swinging his busy fists at any Yankee within reach.

As a player fight, it would have been a pretty good brawl, but the spectators declared themselves in. Some 1,000 rooters rushed out of the stands on to the field, and started swinging, at any Yankees within reach, at each other, at Detroit coppers, who tried vainly to preserve the peace. Some husky customers even uprooted seats from their concrete moorings to toss them into the arena. The riot lasted nearly half of an hour, and there were quite a few battle casualties among the fans. Unable to clear the field, Evans forfeited the game to the Yanks.

Ban Johnson indefinitely suspended Cole and Meusel, and requested written reports, not only from Evans and the other umpires, but from Cole, Meusel, Ruth, and Haney. After admonishing all the culprits, Ban kept the King and Meusel out for ten days, fined Bob $100, and Cole and Ruth each $50. The day after the brawl, a Saturday, the whole town turned up at Navin Field, expecting to see a repetition, but nothing happened other than another New York victory. But the returns from a 40,000 crowd helped Navin defray the expense of putting in new chairs. The Detroit home attendance for the full year was 1,015,136, the first time it reached a million.

6

After coming within five games of the pennant in his fourth year as manager, Cobb started slipping back again. His club fell back to fourth in 1925, 15 games out of the running, and by 1926 he was down in sixth, or practically where he started when he succeeded Jennings in 1921. It was a heartbreaking experience for Navin, who thought the club was ready for new pennants. In the privacy of his office, he would let his hair down to Wish Egan, his confidant among the scouts. Standing wistfully before pictures of Donovan, Mullin, Schaefer, Crawford, and the old gang, he would ask sadly: "Are those days never to return? Is Detroit never to have another winner?"

Cobb again had a strong .302-hitting club in 1925; Harry Heilmann, in a third odd-numbered year, won a dramatic batting championship from Tris Speaker; Ty hit .378 himself; and Absolom "Red" Wingo, one of Cobb's fellow Georgians, was right behind him with .370. Absolom, a former outfield rookie with the Yankees, was procured the year before from Toronto for $50,000 to fill Veach's shoes in left.

176

Ty had his usual infield difficulties, as O'Rourke and Burke played second, Jackie Tavener and Rigney shortstop, and Haney and Bob Jones third. Tavener was a newcomer from Fort Worth, a club with which Navin had a working agreement. He covered more ground than Rigney. In September, while "Rig" was playing short, he was badly beaned by Howard Ehmke, the former Tiger. It put him out for the season and helped shorten his career. The pitching again slipped back, with only Dauss standing out by winning 16 out of 27 games. Whitehill experienced that second-year jinx, only breaking even in 22 games, while Rip Collins, the pitcher who came in the ill-fated Ehmke trade, won only 6 and lost 11.

Heilmann's successful batting race of 1925 saw one of the epic finishes of major-league history. 'Tris Speaker apparently had an unbeatable lead as the clubs reached the last month of the season. The great Spoke's legs bothered him in September; he sat out most of the month, playing only a few innings or appearing as a pinch hitter. He was hitting around .390. On Labor Day, Heilmann was some 50 points behind, but he put on a whirlwind September batting campaign.

But Speaker's lead kept him in front up to the very last day of the season, October 4. Oddly enough the Tigers closed the season with a double-header with the Browns at Sportsman's Park, the scene of the O'Connor shenanigans of 1910. While Tris sat on the bench in the final Cleveland–White Sox game, Harry the Horse galloped to the batting championship in St. Louis with six hits in nine times at bat. He had three singles in six times up in the first game, and "three for three" in the second, one of them being a homer. The final figures gave him .393 for 150 games; Speaker .389 for 117 games. Incidentally the Browns that year were no pushover, but a third-place club.

After Harry made three hits in the first game, several of his teammates figured he had passed Speaker by the width of a hair. They suggested: "Why don't you lay off in the second game? You've got the title won."

"Not me," said Harry. "I'll win it fairly, or not at all. I'll be in there swinging.'

7

Cobb's last season in Detroit, 1926, was another of those might-have-been years for the Tigers. It was a rather crazy race, as six clubs had percentages ranging between .591 for the pennant-winning Yankees and .513 for the sixth-place Tigers. It was the year the

Yanks, seventh-placers of the preceding year, made their sensational leap to the pennant. A sixteen-straight spring winning streak gave them the big jump; they led practically all the way, fighting off Cleveland's September challenge. Ty's Tigers were within gunshot of first place most of the season, but never could put on a concentrated drive.

Although they were sixth in the league standing, 1926 was another great year for the Tigers in the batting tables; they grabbed three of the four top positions. They bobbed up with a new batting champion in Heinie Manush, who hit .377. Ruth followed with .372, and the two other Tiger fly-chasers, Heilmann and Fothergill, were tied at .367. Cobb's eyes bothered him, and he was out with other injuries; he took part in only 79 games and hit .339. In his first season as regular second baseman, Charley Gehringer hit .277. Johnny Neun, now a Yankee coach, was pushing Lu Blue off first base; and Ty tried Jack Warner, an Evansville boy, at third base.

Mediocre pitching, as usual, was the source of the team's weakness. Dauss started to pitch that home-run ball to other hitters in addition to Babe Ruth. Two newcomers, Sam Gibson and Ed Wells, a left-hander, did pretty well. The Detroit club outbid half of the major-league teams to induce Owen Carroll, Holy Cross's wonder pitcher, to ink a Tiger contract. Ownie was with Toronto most of that year on option, and never earned his big bonus. Another Tiger pitching fledgeling farmed to Toronto that season was Carl Hubbell, later great Giant left-hander, procured a year before from Oklahoma City.

The red-letter day of the year was Harry Heilmann Day, August 9. A 40,000 crowd of Heilmann fans crammed into Navin Field to pay homage to Harry the Horse. Larry Fisher, the automobile king, came across with a new car, the Knights of Columbus with a diamond stickpin, and Paddy Pexton with a hunting dog with a huge green ribbon around his neck. And they put the usual jinx on their hero. Harry went hitless in a free-hitting game which Detroit lost to the old Yankee foe, 9 to 8. But Slug whacked out plenty on days when he was not the special guest of honor.

What are Cobb's own views on his six-year managerial career? Even today, he is irked when anyone intimates that he was a managerial failure. Some half a dozen years after he ended his managerial career, I had dinner with him in San Francisco. "Maybe I was not a managerial success, but just as surely I was not a managerial failure," he said with his usual positiveness. "I took

178

over a seventh-place club in 1921, and with the exception of that year, all of my clubs won more games than they lost. Four were in the first division. We played interesting, exciting ball, drew well at home, and next to the Yankees were the best attraction on the road. I was continually handicapped by inadequate pitching, but Whitehill and several other good prospects were developed. Heilmann developed into a full-fledged star under my management; he was a natural hitter, and I taught him everything I had learned in my long career. We always had hitting clubs, so I must have imparted some of my own hitting knowledge to my players."

☙ XVII ☙

GEORGE MORIARTY
TAKES OVER

I

TY COBB'S LONG AND HONORED CAREER IN DETROIT ENDED WITH an unhappy chapter, and one which all lovers of the game and admirers of this "player of the century" must sincerely regret. Shortly after the 1926 World's Series, rumors came over the baseball grapevine that the two great playing managers of the American League, Ty Cobb of Detroit and Tris Speaker of Cleveland, would not be back in 1927. While Ty's 1926 team limped home sixth, Speaker's Indians had their best year since 1921, and finished second—only three games behind the Yankees. Everyone conceded Tris had done a magnificent managerial job, and had played 150 games.

Rumor became a reality, when late in October, Frank Navin announced that Cobb would not be re-engaged as manager. He gave as his reason that "the Detroit club of 1926 was badly demoralized and that it did not get the results I thought it capable of attaining." At the same time it was said that Ty Cobb would retire from baseball. A week later Navin announced that the club's old third baseman, George Moriarty, then an American League umpire, would be Cobb's successor. When the announcement was made, George was hunting in Minnesota with two of the players he was to take over—Outfielders Harry Heilmann and Heinie Manush.

In late November, baseball was in for another shock. This time the dateline was Cleveland, where it was said that Tris Speaker would not continue as playing manager of the Indians but that the old Gray Eagle would retire to private business.

Naturally, the fans of Detroit and Cleveland and the great American public were aghast. What was behind all this? The story finally blew wide open in the closing days of 1926 when Judge Landis gave out the stenographic notes of a hearing he had held

Bobby Veach

"Old Slug" Harry Heilmann

"Old Bobo" Louis (Buck) Newsom

Hank Greenberg

in Chicago, November 29, to which Cobb, Speaker, Joe Wood and Dutch Leonard had been summoned. Wood was the old Red Sox and Cleveland player and then baseball coach at Yale. Though Landis repeatedly urged Leonard to come to Chicago for interrogation, the left-hander refused to leave California.

The hearing dealt with rather unpleasant business, and concerned a Tiger-Cleveland ball game in Detroit on September 25, 1919, a few days before the end of that season. The Tigers won the game, 9 to 5, apparently without too much trouble. There was evidence that some bets were made for some of the contending players—on both sides, and placed through a Detroit park attendant. Cobb and Wood had written to Leonard in October, 1919, about these bets, and the pitcher had turned the letters over to Ban Johnson, who allegedly paid $15,000 for them. Leonard supposedly had become angry with Cobb when Ty released him to the Vernon club in midseason of 1925.

Johnson considered the letters so damaging that at a secret special meeting of the American League's board of directors in September, 1926, it was decided to ease Ty and Tris out of baseball by permitting them to retire and save their families from any scandal.

At first the two stars gave their consent to this arrangement, believing it was best for their families. They also wanted to save Wood from any embarrassment at his college job at Yale. Later the players decided to fight, and engaged counsel. Then Landis got into it, feeling the ugly rumors were worse than having the thing brought into the open. He took personal charge of the case, going over the head of Ban Johnson, who thought it strictly an American League matter and that he had settled it. And against the wishes of Ban, Landis made the matter public, December 30, 1926.

In mid-January, while Landis was considering the evidence, Johnson came out with a vitriolic outburst, in which he said: "The American League is a business. When our directors found two employees who they didn't think were serving them right, they had to let them go. Now isn't that enough? As long as I am president of the American League, neither one of them will manage or play on our teams."

Then, half contradicting himself, Ban added: "I don't believe Ty Cobb ever played a dishonest game in his life. If that is the exoneration he seeks, I gladly give it to him. But it is from Landis, Cobb should demand an explanation. The American League ousted Cobb, but it was Landis who broadcast the story of his mistakes.

"I love Ty Cobb. I never knew a finer player. I don't think he has been a good manager and I have had to strap him as a father straps an unruly boy. But I know Ty Cobb is not a crooked ball player. We let him go because he had written a peculiar letter about a betting deal that he couldn't explain and because I felt that he had violated a position of trust."

Among other things, Johnson intimated that Landis was holding back something. That had quick reverberations, and in a stiff statement Landis called Johnson and his club owners to a showdown meeting, January 23, 1927. It never was held, for in a special meeting the American League club owners repudiated Johnson's action, commended Landis' handling of the case, expressed the conviction he was holding back nothing, and gave Johnson an enforced vacation, while Frank Navin "took over" the league's affairs, pending a reorganization.

Landis weighed the evidence for two months before giving his decision, and when he gave it, January 27, it was a clear acquittal. After reviewing the entire case, and stressing Leonard's repeated failure to come east to face Ty and Tris, he summed it up as follows: "This is the Cobb-Speaker case. These players have not been, nor are they now, found guilty of fixing a game. By no decent system of justice could such a finding be made. Therefore, they were not placed on the ineligible list.

"As they desire to rescind their withdrawal from baseball, the releases which the Detroit and Cleveland clubs granted at their request, in the circumstances detailed above, are cancelled and the players' names are restored to the reserve lists of those clubs."

The reaction of the general public was most favorable. Some of the country's leading citizens, including Hoke Smith, Cobb's senator from Georgia, vigorously had gone to bat for the two great stars. Few wanted to see such great luminaries leave the game under a cloud. Though Ban said Cobb wouldn't play any more in his league, Tyrus joined the Athletics and enjoyed two more .300-hitting seasons in Philadelphia. Speaker went to Washington, but later joined Ty on the A's. And between Ty's 1927 salary with the Athletics, his bonus for signing, and a percentage of the gate, he made around $70,000 that year.

In the interval between the Cobb-Speaker hearing and Landis' decision, another scandal involving the Tigers was accorded columns of newspaper space. While the papers were full of the Cobb-Speaker case, Charles "Swede" Risberg, one of the expelled "Black Sox" of 1920, decided this was a fitting moment to explode a bomb of his own. He charged that in 1917, when the White Sox were battling the Boston Red Sox for the pennant, the Detroit players "sloughed off" a series to Chicago. Detroit batterymen were paid some small amounts at the time, but the White Sox supposedly tried to return the favor even more fully by endeavoring to assist Detroit in finishing third in 1919 after the Chicago team had clinched its pennant. With the *Chicago Tribune* defraying the expenses, Chick Gandil, the banned White Sox first baseman, came to Chicago and corroborated Risberg's charges.

Landis had to drop the earlier case to hold court on this new one. He kept this one right out in the open, and over one hundred reporters crowded into his Chicago office to take in the two-day circus. The final score seemed to stand 35 to 2, with the Tigers and "lily white" White Sox all testifying that the "sloughing" story was fiction and Risberg and Gandil alone supporting it. Cobb, Stanage, Dauss, Willie Mitchell, Bill James, Bernie Boland, Howard Ehmke, Ben Dyer and a lot of other 1917 Tigers all testified. While on the witness stand, Donie Bush, by this time manager of the Pirates, yelled at Risberg, "You're still a pig." "I'm *not* a pig," was the Swede's snappy comeback.

The case finally boiled down to the fact that the 1917 White Sox had got up a purse to reward Tiger pitchers for winning late-season games from the Red Sox, and Stanage, then the first-string Detroit catcher, also was declared in. Chick Gandil was the collector on the White Sox, and Bill James dispensed the gifts to deserving Tigers. Eddie Collins admitted Gandil collected $45 a man, but he didn't chip in his share until the World's Series. That was not an uncommon practice at the time, and not particularly reprehensible.

However, the Cobb-Speaker and Risberg-Gandil cases had an important bearing on subsequent baseball legislation. Inasmuch as Swede and Chick brought up something which had happened nearly nine years before, Judge Landis put in a statute of limitation for baseball. The Judge also clamped down hard on baseball bettors. In new rules for conduct which he dictated, he provided for permanent expulsion for any culprit "betting any sum whatsoever upon any ball game in connection with which the bettor has any duty to perform." It also provided for ineligibility for one year for betting on any game in which the player has no duty to perform, and the same penalty for offering or giving any reward by the players of one club to those of another "for services rendered, or supposed to have been rendered, in defeating a competing club."

Would Cobb have remained Tiger manager if it hadn't been for that unfortunate action by the American League directors? I once asked Frank Navin, and he replied simply: "No; I had decided on a change."

Moriarty, despite his spunk and spirit, proved little improvement over Cobb. He lifted the club to fourth in 1927, but dropped back to sixth in 1928, and by 1929 he was back at umpiring.

Mory's 1927 Tigers were a presentable aggregation, finishing with a percentage of .536, with 11 more victories than defeats. However, it was the year the Yankees had a super-team, spread-eagling the field with 110 victories and a .714 percentage. The Felines finished 28 games behind this great New York team, but did manage to win 8 from Huggins' powerful World's Champions.

As in the past, George had a strong hitting club, but even in hitting the Tigers trailed the formidable Yankees by 18 points. However, Harry Heilmann again was batting champion, marking the fourth time Slug won the crown in an uneven year. Harry beat out Al Simmons on the last day of the season in another hectic batting battle, .398 to .392. Fat Fothergill was fourth with .359, just nosing out Cobb, who hit .357 in his first year in Philadelphia. Gehringer moved up to .317 in his second year as a regular, and people started raving about his second base play.

Before the season started, Moriarty swung a seven-player deal with the Browns whereby the Tigers obtained Marty McManus, former St. Louis second baseman, Catcher Bill "Pinkie" Hargrave, and Infielder LaMotte for Infielders Frank O'Rourke, Mullin, Miller, and Stuffy Stewart, a young left-handed pitcher. Stuffy was another of those good pitchers who got away from Detroit. McManus was busier than a bird dog catching fleas that season, playing 39 games at shortstop, 35 at second base, and 22 at third.

Moriarty's pitchers were all around the .500 mark, with White-hill and Gibson right on it with 16-16 and 11-11, respectively. Holloway was 11-12 and Stoner 10-13. Carroll, the expensive collegian, started to show promise by winning 10 out of 16. Moriarty had Carl Hubbell at his San Antonio training camp, but the left-hander was farmed to Decatur. "I belonged to the Detroit club for three years, and never saw Navin Field," Carl once remarked.

There were two red-letter days for Detroit fans that season, Ty Cobb's first appearance at Navin Field in an Athletic uniform, May 10, and the final Sunday double-header of the campaign,

184

October 2, when Heilmann staged his blitzkrieg against Cleveland.

For weeks Detroit had planned to give Tyrus Raymond a royal welcome when he first came to his old habitat in Connie Mack's toggery. The reserved seats were sold out, and then Cobb, Umpire Red Ormsby, Al Simmons, and Ban Johnson almost wrecked the home-coming party.

Five days before Cobb was due in Detroit, he had been a principal in the most riotous American League game in Philadelphia since that seventeen-inning tie in September, 1907. Coming up in the ninth inning of a May 5 Athletic–Red Sox game, Ty apparently tied the score for the A's with a home run near the foul line. The ball was fair when it left the park, but Ormsby, the plate umpire, said it curved foul when he last saw it, and called Cobb back. Ty jostled the umpire, while Simmons, the next batter, really pushed him around. Bottles and debris flew, and there was general hell for fifteen minutes. And in Chicago, Ban Johnson immediately slapped indefinite suspensions on Ty and Simmons.

That was bad news for the reception committee in Detroit. It immediately got busy with a petition, to which thousands of Tiger fans signed their autographs, asking that Cobb be reinstated for the May 10 game in Detroit. Ban consented, saying in his finding that Cobb hadn't been as rough on the umpire as Simmons, and made both Ty and Al eligible to play on the eventful day.

Detroit did itself proud, and showed it hadn't forgotten those twenty-two brilliant years which Cobb had spent at Trumbull and Michigan Avenues. He was lionized everywhere, and a Tuesday crowd of 35,000 gave him a heartwarming welcome. They cheered his every move. Ty isn't an emotional fellow, but he was visibly pleased. The crowd overflowed behind ropes strung across right field. He went out to his old friends the bleacherites and the boys behind the ropes, shook hands with many and thanked them for their loyalty and support. With Grove pitching against Whitehill, the Athletics won by a score of 6 to 3, Ty giving his new team a good start by doubling into the right-field crowd in the first inning to drive in two runs. Sam Green closed his account of Ty Cobb Day with this paragraph: "For daring and strategy on the bases, for the knack of taking advantage of every slip—mental and mechanical—by his opponents, for skill with the bat, Cobb is still Cobb."

Harry Heilmann's last-day batting finish is equally unforgettable. Before the final Sunday, he trailed Al Simmons by two points. Al closed the season with a single game in Washington, while

Slug had a chance to win or lose in two games with the Indians. Simmons bagged two hits in five attempts, giving him a closing average of .392. Due to the difference of time, Harry knew almost before he started what he had to beat. Jack McCallister of Cleveland used two right-handers, George Grant in the opener, and big Garland Buckeye in the second game.

In his first two times up, Harry smacked doubles. In his third time at bat, he rolled to third base and was out. The next time up, he pulled a Lajoie—he bunted, caught the third baseman flat-footed, and beat it out. It gave him three out of four. Some of the fans implored him to retire. "You've got Simmons beat; call it a day, Harry," they yelled. But not Slug; he knocked the next one out of the lot for a home run.

Would he come back for the second game and risk the championship which now was his? There need be no doubt of the answer. Every man, woman, and child in the park cheered him as he went out to right field at the start of the game. His bat churned out a homer, a double, and a single this time in four tries. What an exhibition of guts when the chips really were down! He beat Simmons by six points, and was every inch a champion.

3

There was an interesting sequel to Bob Fothergill's .359 average of 1927 during the following winter. "The Mandarin," as Navin frequently was called, was getting more liberal with his ball players as the crowds increased in Navin Field. But Bob felt Frank hadn't sufficiently rewarded his .359. A lovable chap, Fothergill had a solid conviction that there was no higher estate in life than being a ball player. He was genuinely sorry for all the rest of mankind who had to work at something less congenial. He would walk into a hotel with his cigar atilt at an angle of 45 degrees and a blissful expression in his eyes. Then those thick steaks, washed down with a case of brew, helped make life even more livable—and made him look more and more like a Navy blimp. In New York, the bleacherites had yelled: "Hey, Bob, when does the balloon go up?"

Fothergill's waistline and his annual salary had a definite relationship, regardless of .359 batting averages. Bob knew this, of course, and when he called to do his winter bargaining he had his heavy coat well draped around his rotund form. It was an unseasonably warm winter day, and Bob was fairly well used up when he climbed the stairway leading to the throne room.

Navin knew the purpose of the fat boy's visit and "The Mandarin" was not above using a little Chinese guile in driving bargains with his players. He had taken the precaution to turn on all his steam radiators and tightly closed all the windows when he spotted Fothergill's approach.

Navin was unusually garrulous. He talked to Bob about everything, including the weather, new cars, the fate of the nation—everything except Bob's salary and his .359 batting average. He even suggested that Bob remove his coat, make himself at home, and have a nice enjoyable chat.

Bob tried to make some excuses, and stood him off for an hour at great cost to his physical comfort, and eventually his finances. When Navin finally pulled a contract out of a desk drawer, Bob, sweating like a stoker, put pen to it in a mixture of ink and Fothergill sweat. It was for several thousand less than he intended to demand, but anything to get out of there! After his departure, the Mandarin's inscrutable pan not only parted in a genuine smile, but there are those who declare it could only be described as a grin of great glee. At any rate it was so unusual and noteworthy that clerks in the upper office dated events from it for several years.

However, there was little glee in the 1928 season for the Detroit owner. During the winter, he traded Heinie Manush and Lu Blue to the Browns for Pitcher Elam Vangilder, Outfielder Harry Rice, and Shortstop Clarence Galloway. The deal was made particularly with the idea of strengthening Moriarty's pitching department, but was no howling success. Vangilder won 11 games and lost 10. Rice, though faster than Manush, hit .302, while Manush wound up with .378, only one point behind Goslin, the league leader.

As Moriarty's team slid back to sixth, they even lost the old Tiger punch, finishing fifth in batting with .279. Heilmann was down to .328, and Fothergill's average tumbled 40 points to .317. Gehringer was one of Moriarty's few rays of sunshine as he hit .327, while Paul Easterling, a new catcher, batted .325. Carroll, the Holy Cross ace, had his only really good season in Detroit, winning 16 and losing 10, while the Beaumont club, in which the Tigers then were interested, sold Carl Hubbell to the Giants for $40,000. Carl had developed a screwball and was now ripe for picking. It was history repeating itself, for back in 1911 Jennings passed up a big Missouri right-hander, Jeff Tesreau, because of his wildness, and "Big Jeff" developed into a pennant-winning pitcher under McGraw in New York.

⊛ XVIII ⊛

FIVE DREARY YEARS
UNDER BUCKY

IN SCOUTING AROUND FOR A NEW MANAGER, NAVIN THOUGHT THE answer to his prayer might be Stanley "Bucky" Harris, who led Washington to spectacular pennants in 1924 and 1925. Bucky had retired as playing manager in 1928, but some of the glamour of his Washington pennants still remained. While the Yankees took over the business of pennant winning, Harris' club had remained in the first division, winding up third in 1927 and fourth in 1926 and 1928. Griffith permitted Harris to leave Washington to accept a better contract under Navin, while Walter Johnson succeeded the former boy wonder as headman of the Senators.

Though born in Port Jervis, N. Y., just across from the Pennsylvania line, Bucky grew up in the same corner of the Keystone State which produced Hughie Jennings. His early career was in the coal mines—just as it was with Jennings. In fact, it was Hughie who gave the black-haired Stanley his first start in baseball. In 1916, Harris played for the professional basketball team representing Jennings' home town of Pittston, Pa., and the then Detroit manager was much impressed with the youth's performance. Hearing the kid also was a baseball player, he invited Harris to his 1916 training camp. The Tiger front office sent Harris to Muskogee without keeping much of a string on him, and after several seasons of minor-league ball he came up with Washington in 1919.

Harris was personable, had the ability to hold and make friends. Among managers he was considered one of the smartest in the game, a fellow who played sound—and often daring—baseball. Yet Bucky's five-year term at the head of the Tigers was one of the most dreary in Detroit history.

It was a difficult period for Navin, and now he scarcely ever smiled. He lost much of his personal fortune in the market crash, and a friend whom he had trusted let him down badly. When asked whether he would prosecute the man, he asked: "What would I gain by sending him to jail?" He shook up his scouting system, invested in farm clubs, put the enterprising Jack Zeller in charge. "What do we do wrong here?" he would ask his confidant, Wish Egan. "Don't we live right?" Those pennants of 1907, '08, and '09 were becoming only a faint memory.

In 1929, Connie Mack made his famous comeback, winning his first pennant in 15 years, as the change in Tiger managers brought an improvement of only 13 points. Mory's sixth-place percentage was .442; Harris was in the same slot with .455. And the Philadelphia White Elephants fairly feasted on the Tigers, winning 18 games. The Felines got only 1 out of 11 at Shibe Park. "Mack comes back, and we are worse off than ever," Navin commented sadly.

Stanley had the boys hitting again, and they were back at the top of the parade in club batting. And while they led the league in scoring with 926, the pitchers and infielders could give them back even faster. The '29 Tigers had 928 runs scored against them. Fat Fothergill was high Tiger with .350 for 115 games, and Slug Heilmann and Dale Alexander, a new first baseman, came in neck and neck, .344 to .343. Alexander was a big 225-pound farmer from Greenville, Tenn., who was another of those "Good-hit-no-field" guys. The reported price paid the Toronto club for Alex and Johnny Prudhomme, a pitcher, was $100,000. A pretty good check also went to San Francisco for Outfielder Roy Johnson, a part Oklahoma Cherokee and a brother of Bob Johnson. He clipped out 201 hits, batted .314 in his freshman year, but wasn't too easy to handle. What a sparring partner he would have made for Ty Cobb!

And there was a stunner for Detroit fans, especially the Heilmann worshipers, when shortly after the close of the season— October 14—there came an announcement from Frank Navin's office that Harry the Horse had been sold to the Cincinnati Reds of the rival league for a sum well over the waiver price. Harry had slowed perceptibly that season, and there already were signs of the arthritis which in 1932 side-lined the famous hitter in Cincinnati. He had had some difficulty with Harris, ran into one suspension, and on another occasion was lifted from the regular line-up. Of the three powerful Detroit outfield sluggers—Veach, Cobb, and Heilmann—all now were gone. Though Heilmann had only one good season with the Reds, many Tiger fans never forgave Harris for selling the popular Californian down the river.

2

Even though 1930 saw the Felines move up only one notch, it was an eventful year for the Jungleers, as two of the greatest players ever to wear Tiger stripes, First Baseman Hank Greenberg and Pitcher Tommy Bridges, got their names into their first Detroit box scores, though Hank appeared only once as a pinch hitter.

Harry Bullion, former *Detroit Free Press* baseball writer, first tipped the author off to Greenberg in Florida in the spring of 1930. The Tigers trained that year in Tampa, and Harry raved about a young Jewish high-school player from New York. "You ought to know him; he comes from your town," said Harry. "Comes from the Bronx. He hit a ball, and I'll swear it went a mile. We train in the middle of a race track without any fence, and that ball just kept a-rollin' and a-rollin'."

Hank was to send many other balls a-rolling in his Tiger clothes, though that season he was farmed to Raleigh and Hartford. Scout Jean Dubuc literally snatched Greenberg, who was to draw a higher Tiger salary than Ty Cobb, from the doorsteps of the Greater New York clubs. A son of Rumanian-born parents, Hank was a hitting star for James Monroe of New York's Bronx. His father has a textile business and is fairly well to do. As a kid, Hank was a Giant fan and invested his two bits for a distant seat in the center-field bleachers. He played a little semipro ball around New York, and the Yankees showed some interest in him. But, with Gehrig doing his "Iron Horse" act, Hank figured he could have whiskers to his knees before ever getting a chance at first base in the Stadium, and signed with Dubuc.

Greenberg was paid a $9,000 bonus for signing, and the Detroit club's permission to go to college. However, the tall Bronxonian attended New York University only one season. Hank later said he could have collected a $7,000 bonus for signing with the Yankees.

Bridges, who was to slay the World's Series jinx which had fastened itself on Tiger pitchers, was signed after graduating from the University of Tennessee in 1929. He was farmed to Wheeling, where he had a fine record. In 1930, the Tennessean was sent to Bob Coleman's Evansville club, where Tommy, a curve ball pitcher, had a lot of control trouble. It was a summer in which it was insufferably hot on the plains of Indiana. In reporting on Tommy's progress to Navin, Wish Egan spoke of the little right-hander's wildness. "And he looks pretty frail," added Wish.

"Hasn't it been terribly hot down there?" asked Frank. "He needs a cooler climate. The lake breezes ought to do him good. Bring him right up here." Tommy finished that season with three Tiger victories against two defeats, and except for his period in the Army during the war has been in Detroit ever since.

Navin and Harris celebrated Memorial Day, 1930, with a not particularly memorable deal with New York for a pair of former Yankee stars. The Tigers acquired Waite Hoyt, right-hander ace of the World's Champions of 1927-28, and Shortstop Mark Koenig for Pitcher Owen Carroll, Outfielder Harry Rice, and Infielder George "Yatz" Wuestling. However, Hoyt didn't fit into the Detroit scheme of things, and by the next season he was passed on to the Athletics. The old hop also had faded from his fast ball. Koenig's eyes already had bothered him before he left New York, and he came to Detroit wearing glasses. By the end of that season, Harris tried to make a pitcher out of him. It again was a terrible year at shortstop as Akers, Wuestling, Koenig, and Rogell all took a crack at it. Billy Rogell, now a Detroit councilman, was acquired in midseason from Toronto, and plugged the hole for the next eight seasons. And Fat Fothergill, getting bigger by the minute, was waived to the White Sox.

3

From sixth to fifth was a little improvement, and by 1931 Navin thought the upward trend might continue. Somehow everything went wrong, and the unhappy Tigers bogged down in all departments. Even in hitting, with Slug and Fat gone, they dropped off 31 points and cascaded from first to sixth. One of the few bright spots was the substantial improvement of Outfielder Jonathon Stone, who was living up to the Detroit outfield tradition, and led the club with an average of .327. Dale Alexander was two points below him, but every day he was showing he wasn't a big-league first baseman.

Charley Gehringer was out for over 50 games with injuries, and this time there was a third-base parade of Marty McManus, Nolen Richardson, and Marvin Owen. Marv, a Santa Clara University star, was acquired from Seattle and given a prep course in Toronto; he later became one of Detroit's better players. The entire catching staff was remade. Ray Hayworth, a second stringer in 1929 and

'30, now did the bulk of the catching. That gallant little veteran, Muddy Ruel, was purchased from the Red Sox, and the Tigers outbid half a dozen clubs for Gene Desautels of Holy Cross.

The club had three sixteen-game pitching losers, young Bridges, Whitehill, and Uhle, a pickup from Cleveland. Tommy won only eight games in his first season as a regular. His curve ball fanned 105, but he walked 108. Detroit was a cellar dweller 36 days, and finished in seventh place only four and a half games out. The Tigers won only one season's series, and again were sandbagged by the A's, 18 games to 4. There was little joy in Gilead!

4

Things did go a little better in 1932 and 1933, the club finishing fifth with percentages of .503 and .487. The former club won 15 more games than the misfits of 1931. The 1932 team had one-half of a batting champion, as Dale Alexander nosed out Jimmy Foxx by three points. The behemoth was sold to the Red Sox in midseason, playing 34 games for the Tigers and 101 for Boston. His first-base successor in Navin Field was Harry Davis, an agile fielder, but rather light with the bat.

There still was no old-time Tiger punch in the 1932 line-up, as the club remained sixth in batting, but Bucky did recruit some kind of a hitting outfield with Stone in left, Gerry "Gee" Walker in center, and Earl Webb in right. The trio hit .297, .323, and .285, respectively, fair hitting, but a far cry from the days when Veach, Cobb, and Heilmann averaged .390 between them. Webb was a pickup from the Red Sox, and Gee and his brother, Hub, had been snared a few years before by Scout Eddie Goosetree when the brothers were attending the University of Mississippi. In 1931, Hub had played center field for the Tigers against right-handers, Gee only against the southpaws. By 1932, Hub was gone, and Gerald had the center field patch to himself. Picturesque and colorful, he became one of Detroit's most popular players. Joyner "Jo-Jo" White was another promising 1932 outfield acquisition.

The improvement of the 1932 team was largely due to steadier pitching. Whitehill, in his last season in Detroit, won 16 and lost 13; Vic Sorrell, a spectacled right-hander, broke even in 28 games; Tommy Bridges won 14 and lost 12, while Chief Hogsett, an Indian left-hander, won 11 and lost 9. Whitlow Wyatt, later a star in Brooklyn, won 9 and lost 13.

Tommy Bridges was like the little girl with the curl; when he was good, he was very, very good, and when he was bad, well, he was pretty bad. He could make monkeys out of the third-place Senators, defeating them 5 times, while the World's Champion Yanks tripped him on 6 occasions. And Tommy missed the toughest perfect no-hitter of all baseball history to his Washington victims, August 5, 1932.

Going into the ninth inning of a game in Washington, the Tigers led 13 to 0. For eight innings, no Senator player reached base. Tommy's control was perfect, and the Senators looked pitiable trying to hit his elusive curve. He quickly blotted out Ossie Bluege, later Washington manager, and Maple, a rookie catcher, in the ninth, and it was the turn of Bob Burke, the pitcher, to go to bat.

Now, the chance of Washington's winning that game under such conditions was about 10,000 to one, but Walter Johnson, the Senator manager, played out his string and sent in Dave Harris, a pinch hitter. Harris stood between the Tennessean and baseball immortality, to be one of six big-league pitchers to hurl a perfect game. It might have made Tommy, rather than Cordell Hull, the most famous citizen of Smith County. Then bang! Harris lined the first pitch to left field for a clean single, and the perfect game became a dream. Bridges acted as though nothing had happened, and pitched his curve to Sam Rice, the twenty-eighth batter. He tapped a grounder down to Harry Davis; Tommy ran over to first base to take the throw, and it was all over.

Walter Johnson was extensively criticized at the time. It was felt that as a former great pitcher, he should have permitted Burke to go to bat so long as Washington's cause was well-nigh hopeless. Walter replied: "I had to play out the game. There's an old baseball saying: 'You're never beaten until that last out is entered in the box score.'" Bridges never criticized Johnson, but Detroit fans wished Walter hadn't been so darned conscientious.

Within a period of two years, Bridges missed a no-hitter three times by that one hit margin. He hurled a one-hit game against the Browns, and on May 24, 1933, he worked on another perfect game against Washington when Joe Kuhel inserted the only hit of the game, a homer in the seventh. Oddly enough, Kuhel was the only Washingtonian to reach base until the·pitcher's turn to bat in the ninth. Then Joe Cronin, by this time Washington manager, again sent Dave Harris to bat, and Dave walked, making 29 Senators to face Tommy against 28 in the earlier game.

5

The season of 1933, Harris' last in Detroit, had several interesting developments. During the previous winter, Bucky traded his crack pitcher, Earl Whitehill, to the Senators for Fred Marberry, the Boy Manager's crack relief pitcher on the Washington champions of 1924 and 1925, and Carl Fischer, a southpaw. Hank Greenberg, who had been farmed out to Raleigh, Evansville, and Beaumont, finally won his Detroit "D," replacing Harris Davis at first base in June. Hank hit .301 and smacked 12 home runs in 117 games and it took a world war to get him out of the regular line-up. Ervin "Pete" Fox also was brought up from Beaumont, and *Reach's Guide* for 1934 had this observation: "The Detroit team had a powerful pitching staff and wideawake infield, but seemed to lack outfield batting power." Imagine that, a Tiger team with good pitching, and no power in the outfield! That was something!

It's likely that Navin didn't consider that pitching as hot as Editor Jimmy Isaminger seemed to think. While Whitehill enjoyed his best season with the 1933 Washington champions, winning 22 and losing 8, Marberry won 16 games for Harris and lost 11. Fischer, the other pitcher obtained in the Whitehill swap, didn't do so well, 11 wins and 15 defeats. That also was Sorrell's record, and by a curious freak Tommy Bridges hit his 1932 14-12 showing right on the nose. And Detroit came up with a tall, handsome youngster, a six-foot, four and a half inch Arkansas high-school boy, Lynwood Thomas Rowe, but known ever since as "Schoolboy" Rowe. At Eldorado, Arkansas, High, he won every athletic letter they had in the book. He won 7 games that season for the Felines and lost 4. A .269 team batting average, sixth in what still was an era of slugging, weighed down the team.

In Bucky's last two seasons with the Tigers he had a part-time outfielder named Frank Doljack, who would have been a character in any league. Doljack was all extrovert, but of a curious kind. Superbly equipped to be a slugging, rangy outfielder, he had little spirit or ambition. Frequently in those days, he was in the company of Shortstop Billy Rogell, who was his exact opposite. Councilman Billy, as a ball player, was an introvert, inclined to be dour and morose. Probably the fact that Rogell had been up with the Red Sox, and then was shuffled back to the minors, tended to make him that way. While Doljack had the voice of a gangster, he was as friendly as a toy spaniel. Billy was aloof, and if he did any chatting it usually was with a sympathetic bellhop or elevator boy in the hotel lobby.

Anyway, late in the season, by dint of an almost superhuman effort, Tommy Bridges succeeded in winning a tough game from the Athletics, still a strong team, at Shibe Park. It was gloomy Rogell, who had been in a protracted slump, who won the game with a drive off the scoreboard, which Ed Coleman, then the Athletic right fielder, managed to kick into a home run.

When the Tigers reached Washington, their next stop, Rogell and Doljack soon were draped around the cigar counter where the chief attraction was the pretty cigarette girl. The gangster-voiced Doljack was as affable as always. "You sure put the wood to that round-tripper in Philly," he said approvingly to Rogell. But Bill was not to be roused from his contemplation of man's inhumanity to Rogell by such overtures.

"Aw," he grumbled, "I just thought it was another can o' corn that Cramer would eat up, the lucky stiff!"

Doljack snuggled closer to the glum Rogell and took a confidential stance. Then in the tone and diction with which Edward G. Robinson whips his movie gangsters into line, he said out of the far corner of his mouth: "Listen, Rogell. Don't start thinkin'; you'll weaken the ball club."

During the Harris administration, there also was a young Tiger player whose name will be omitted but who would have made Ring Lardner's "Alibi Ike" look like a busher. One spring he introduced a personable young creature as "the missus." So later on, it was somewhat disconcerting to have an entirely different female show up at the Tigers' Chicago hotel, inquiring for her husband, who was the same "Alibi Ike."

Manager Harris engineered a wary reconnaissance of the situation and summoned the player to his room for a conference. He seemed completely unruffled by the disclosure that there was a strange woman in the lobby claiming to be his wife.

"She is my wife," grinned Alibi Ike. "I married her right here in Chicago last June."

Harris rolled with that punch and pressed the inquiry further. "But what about the young lady you introduced to us as your wife at the training camp?" he asked.

"Oh, her?" grinned the player airily. "She's my first wife; don't you see?"

Harris relaxed; that seemed to ease the situation. "Oh, I didn't know you got a divorce. When did it happen?"

"I didn't," chuckled the athlete. "We're still married."

Bucky looked like a man who needed a stiff drink, but managed to remonstrate reprovingly: "Good God, boy; that's bigamy; don't you realize that?"

Alibi Ike set him right gleefully. "Oh, no, it ain't," he chortled. "Y' see, I married 'em in different states."

6

Harris tendered his resignation to Navin a fortnight before the end of the 1933 season, and left the club for his Washington home, September 27, four days before the Tigers rang down their final curtain.

Discussing his resignation with Detroit sports writers, Harris said: "I made up my mind definitely to quit while we were in Philadelphia on the last eastern trip, when it became certain that we would not finish in the money. I wrote Mr. Navin of my intention from there. Then when I got back to Detroit, I went into his office and we talked things over. He said he would like to have me back another year, but I feel that if a manager cannot deliver in five years, he should resign." Harris quickly landed another job with Bill Yawkey's foster son, Tom, on the Red Sox.

And all Detroit was pretty well fed up with that sixth straight second-division club. Even usually loyal Malcolm W. Bingay, Iffy the Dopester—by now editor of the *Detroit Free Press*—had had his fill and wrote his own Declaration of Independence. The *Free Press* ran his two-column editorial, in 12-point Roman type, big enough to smack Frank Navin and any one else interested, right in the face. It didn't pull punches, and was headed:

WE WANT TIGERS—NOT TAME KITTENS

Twenty-four years ago the Detroit Tigers won their last pennant.

Detroit has not had a winning baseball team since Hughie Jennings was dropped with scant ceremony to make way for Ty Cobb as manager.

Cobb was a flop.

Moriarty, who followed, was worse.

And Bucky Harris has shown himself no better.

Detroit, long one of the best baseball towns in America, has been steadily losing interest in the sport because of lifeless teams under a lifeless management.

If baseball is a sport, then Frank Navin should bestir himself to present to the paying public some form of competition.

If baseball is merely a vaudeville performance with the gate as the index of a team's success, then the sport fans are entitled to know it.

Professional baseball is naturally a business, a money making proposition. But there must be behind it a sporting instinct, a desire to win, in order to give the public its money's worth in thrills.

Bucky Harris is a nice young man. But he is not an inspirational leader. He has had five years of trial here and has done absolutely nothing.

If he had been as good as he has been touted to be, Foxy Clark Griffith would not have dropped him.

Washington, the team that canned him as manager, is at the top of the league. Detroit is doomed, as usual, to the second division.

It's up to Mr. Navin to show some sporting blood, take a gambler's chance, spend some money, get an aggressive leadership.

Yes, professional baseball is a business.

But it must also be a sport in order to survive.

The Tigers have not shown the old fighting spirit since Bill Yawkey died and Hughie Jennings was given the gate.

Detroit baseball needs the enthusiasm behind the ownership that Jim Norris gave us in hockey.

⊗ XIX ⊗

COCHRANE WORKS
A MIRACLE

I

WHO TO GET TO SUCCEED BUCKY, WAS THE NEXT QUESTION. Navin went over a number of names in his mind. Babe Ruth, approaching 39, was slowing up to a walk, and was disgruntled in New York because Jake Ruppert wouldn't fire McCarthy and give Babe a crack at managing the Yankees. Ruth had the managerial bug badly at the time. He still was the biggest figure in baseball, and a terrific draw at the gate. Would getting Babe be the sporting chance Iffy spoke of? Navin got permission from Ruppert to talk to Ruth, and getting the big slugger on the long-distance telephone asked him to come to Detroit for a conference.

"But, I'm just catching a train for San Francisco to take a boat for Honolulu," said the Babe. "I got some exhibition games to play in Hawaii. Can't it wait until I get back?"

"No, it can't wait," snapped Navin. "I would like to get this matter settled."

Ruppert always claimed Ruth booted his managerial chance by not seeing Navin and closing then and there. "Navin told me he wanted Ruth for manager, and the job was in Babe's lap," Jake once told me. However, Ruth was in a spot. Christy Walsh, his business manager, had signed contracts for Hawaii appearances and had to deliver his star. There was later correspondence between Frank and the Sultan of Swat, and Ruth, no doubt advised by Walsh, asked for a stiff straight salary and a cagey percentage of the gate. As this was likely to run into big money in Detroit, Navin cooled off in his overtures.

He then got the idea that if he could get an inspirational catcher, as well as a manager, he might kill two birds with one stone, and solve his problem. He began toying in his mind with the idea of getting Gordon Stanley "Mickey" Cochrane, the great catcher of the Athletics. At the close of the 1932 season, Connie Mack had sold Al Simmons, Mule Haas, and Jimmy Dykes to the White Sox, but otherwise he still retained the great players who had won the pennants of 1929, '30 and '31. Navin knew that the depression had hit Mack hard and that he needed ready money. He sounded Connie on Cochrane, and Mack said: "I'll sell you the battery, Grove and Cochrane, for $200,000." When Navin showed no interest in the left-hander, Connie submitted another proposition, Catcher Hayworth and $100,000 for Cochrane.

If Mack was broke, Navin was also badly bent by the market crashes. He had to borrow $25,000 the spring before for training expenses. He went to see Walter Briggs, who had taken over John Kelsey's stock at the latter's death, and now was half owner, though few Detroiters knew the extent of his holdings. Navin showed Briggs a list of four managerial possibilities, including Cochrane.

"Get Mickey; he is the man we want," said Briggs.

"Mack wants a lot of money for him—$100,000," countered Frank.

"That's all right with me; if he's a success here, he may be a bargain at that price. I'll furnish the money. Go and get him."

At the American League annual meeting in December, 1933, Navin finally closed the deal with Mack for the great Mickey. Frank refused to give up Hayworth, but tossed in a young catcher, John Pasek, with the $100,000. He immediately announced that the black-haired Cochrane would be playing manager of the club.

Mickey was one of baseball's most dynamic characters, a ball player who drove himself at a terrific pace. Among catchers of the last generation, he is classed with Bill Dickey of the Yankees, and he unquestionably deserves a niche among the great catchers of all time. At Boston University, he was considered a better football player than a ball player. It was years before he really liked to catch. Mickey spent his early minor-league experience in Dover, Del., of the Eastern Shore League, where he played under the name of Frank King. Cochrane then wanted to play the outfield. Jiggs Donohue, the old White Sox first baseman, was Dover's manager, and he told the young collegian: "I got outfielders. You catch— or it's off the pay roll." Mickey caught.

He quickly moved up to the Portland club of the Pacific Coast League, and Mack says the Athletics purchased the Portland club just to get Cochrane, paying $50,000 to the affiliate club for the catcher. Cochrane still was a crude catcher when he came into the American League in 1925, but he was so aggressive and such a great all-around ball player that he quickly pushed his new buddy, Cy Perkins, former first-string "A" catcher, to the side lines. Mickey got into 134 games and hit .331. Three years later he was voted the most valuable player in the league.

2

Cochrane's acquisition was one of the greatest strokes of good fortune ever to come to the Detroit club. Though his Tiger managerial career lasted only four and a half seasons, he was the right man for the right job, at the right time. However, there were many factors in Detroit's change of fortune in '34. For one thing, Joe Cronin's 1933 Washington pennant winner, helped matters by flopping ingloriously, tumbling to seventh place. Two days after Navin put over the Cochrane transaction, he completed another sweet deal with Clark Griffith, acquiring Outfielder Leon "Goose" Goslin from Washington for Jonathon Stone. Frank must have hypnotized old Griff to put that one over. The Goose was 32 when he came to Tigertown, but he had three more good years under his feathers.

The three Tiger G-men, Gehringer, Greenberg, and Goslin, became the toughest trio in baseball. In 1934, Charley hit second only to Gehrig, the league leader, with .356 and played second better than ever. Greenberg was now coming fast with a .339 average, 139 runs batted in and an extra base collection, which included 63 doubles (four under the record), 7 triples, and 26 homers. Goslin raised a lot of hell with a .305 average and 13 round-trippers. Cochrane, of course, was a daily inspiration, both as manager and catcher; he took part in 129 games, hit .320, and pulled down his second most-valuable-player trophy. And at third base, Marv Owen enjoyed the best season of his career, and hit .317. Rogell had a fine year at short.

Oddly enough a feud developed between Pete Fox and Goose Goslin, something similar to that between Heilmann and Veach of an earlier Tiger edition. The two players did not speak throughout the 1934 and 1935 seasons, though Goslin played only a passive role in it. It was Pete who refrained from speaking. The Goose was one who found it difficult to keep his lip buttoned. The feud grew out of a slighting remark which Goslin made about Fox's ability as an outfielder, particularly his mental equipment. Fox, who came from a poor family and had to work hard even as a lad, did have a limited education and was sensitive about it. He also was, and is, a grim little fellow, game as a pebble, and his feud with Goslin improved rather than diminished his value to the Tigers. He was Goslin's implacable competitor and the Goose was no push-over in any competition.

And Bud Shaver of the *Detroit Times* deserves his assist. The club experienced a mediocre May, winning 15 games and losing 14; Mickey made several shifts in his batting orders but still was unable to shake up a winning combination. "Say, why don't you have Jo-Jo White lead off, and you bat second?" Bud said to Cochrane. "That ought to be a great hit-and-run combination, and then let the G-guys drive you around." Cochrane took the hunch and that was the line-up which rode on to the flag.

Of course, the pitching braced tremendously, and Schoolboy Rowe, with blazing smoke on his fast ball, was the big winner with 24 victories tucked under his belt against only 8 defeats. It was while he was blowing them down at the plate that he called up to his young Arkansas bride in the stands, "How'm I doin', Edna?" He heard that as long as he remained in the loop.

The Schoolboy won 16 straight games, tying a league mark held jointly by those three great American League masters, Walter Johnson, Joe Wood, and Bob Grove. A paid crowd of 33,318, said to be the largest in Shibe Park up to that time, came out on August 29 to see whether Rowe could establish a new record, but he was bombed out in six innings by the Athletic shock troops, as the Tigers lost the game, 13 to 5.

Tommy Bridges also was magnificent with 22 victories and 11 defeats, and Cochrane got some good pitching out of Harris' old work horse, Marberry, who won 15 and lost 6. Eldon Auker, a rookie with an underhanded delivery in 1933, improved overnight and had a 15-7 rating. Luke "Hot Potato" Hamlin, recalled from Toronto, got in a few winners, and General Crowder, picked up from the fallen Washington champs, won five out of six games after being purchased by Detroit in August.

And Detroit went absolutely daft over its first pennant winner in a quarter of a century. The depression had smacked industrial Detroit a hard right to the kisser, but people were having money again, and they spent it at Navin's ball orchard. Iffy the Dopester stepped down from his editorial stool, took the road again, and told Detroit, "If we take this series from the Red Sox, and if we can get that expected help from Chicago, the Tigers will be in first place by Monday." Not only editor Iffy, Charley Ward, the regular baseball writer, but two other *Detroit Free Press* staff men, made the trips with the team. After Iffy had read that riot act the preceding fall, nobody was going to scoop him and his sheet if Detroit was to get into Pennantland again.

That 1934 pennant came, after an almost interminable wait with almost ridiculous ease. The club won 101 games, the only one of Detroit's seven American League pennant winners to reach the century in victories. With much the same team as Harris had in 1933, it won 26 more games. It won the pennant by a margin of 7 games over the second-place Yankees. It was in first place 97 days, in second for 36, and after snatching the lead, August 1, the Tigers never again were headed. They won the year's series from every other club and were almost as effective on the road as at home. In Navin Field, they won 54 games and lost 26; on the road, it was 47 wins and 27 defeats. And they even clinched their flag sitting down. While they were idle, September 24, John Merena, a Red Sox left-handed rookie, did the job for them, blanking the Yankees, 5 to 0.

⊗ XX ⊗

THE DEANS DO THINGS
TO THE TIGERS

I

HAVING WON THAT FIRST PRECIOUS AMERICAN LEAGUE FLAG IN 25 years, the next big question was whether the Tigers could win the World's Championship for Detroit. Tigertown still remembered how National League champions had manhandled Jennings' clubs in the old days. Other American League clubs, the Red Sox, Yankees, and Athletics, could kick the National League around, but not Detroit. This time, were the boys to square accounts?

The National League champions were the Gas-House Cardinals, with the two Deans, Ducky Medwick, Rip Collins, Pepper Martin, Lippy Durocher, and led by the live-wire second baseman, Frankie Frisch. With the help of the Braves, Phillies, and Dodgers, who knocked the Giants off in six of their last seven 1934 games, the Cardinals blinked their surprised eyes and found themselves in possession of their fifth pennant. A combination of Brooklyn's defeat of the Giants and Dizzy Dean's shutout of the Reds clinched the flag for St. Louis on the last day of the season. All along Cochrane and his players had counted on playing the Giants, as Bill Terry's New Yorkers had a seemingly fool-proof September lead. Tiger sympathies were all with New York; Terry was finishing the season with a jaded team, and the Polo Grounds promised a richer players' purse than Sportsman's Park, St. Louis. And Hank Greenberg, the boy who used to sit in McGraw's bleachers and dream of becoming a Giant, looked forward with anticipation to New York's home-run paradise.

"You could bunt 'em into that Polo Grounds stand," Hank's teammates informed him.

The Detroit club had to change its psychology, when almost overnight the National League situation changed and Cochrane's players learned that instead of playing a tired stumbling New York outfit, they would meet a red-hot St. Louis aggregation, which was closing the season in high. The Dean brothers especially were in fine fettle; in a September double-header with Brooklyn, Dizz pitched a three-hitter in the first game and Paul followed with a no-hit game in the nightcap. "Now, why in the hell didn't that Paul tell me he was goin' to pitch a no-hit game," said Dizzy. "I'd bore down and pitched one, too." In the last week of the season, the two Deans worked in every game for Frisch but one. Dizzy finished the season with 30 victories and only 7 defeats; Paul with a 19-11 record.

Everyone in the Tiger camp knew the Cardinals would be tough, but they could see only victory ahead. Frank Navin was hopeful, but Iffy could find a dozen reasons why the Tigers couldn't lose. Harry Salsinger, Bud Shaver, and Sam Greene all figured the 1934 Tigers were one of those teams of destiny, who could take this final hurdle.

Cochrane was confident, without being cocky. He had good reason to remember the Cardinals, for in the 1931 Athletic-St. Louis Series the irrepressible Pepper Martin almost stole his shin pads, and the Redbirds committed other transgressions in defeating one of Connie Mack's greatest Athletic teams. Everyone wanted to win, but Cochrane had a few extra reasons. He had a few issues to settle with Martin, also with Frisch, his rival manager.

The 1934 World's Series schedule called for two games at Navin Field, three in St. Louis, and then two more in Detroit provided sixth and seventh games were necessary. Cochrane was pleased that his club would open at home.

Despite the fact that Dizzy Dean had pitched the Cardinals' pennant-clinching game on the final Sunday of the season, September 30, Frisch had him ready to start the series on Wednesday, October 3. Cochrane debated in his mind whether to oppose Dizzy with his ace, Rowe, or hold back the Arkansas schoolboy for the second game. Eventually he decided to start his late season pickup, the former Washington veteran, Alvin Crowder. It wasn't an overly popular choice for the noisy assemblage of 42,505 fans, 95 per cent of them rabid Detroit rooters. "What's the matter with Rowe? Where's the schoolboy?" were mutterings in the stands, as the General went out to warm up.

Crowder didn't do so badly, but the Tiger defense wobbled badly behind him. This especially was true of that iron-man infield, which booted five chances, most of them damaging errors in the early innings. Dean, Frisch, and Durocher didn't make the situation any happier with their wisecracks: "Can't you pick 'em up, boys? Can't you find the handle?"

All in all, it wasn't a very jolly afternoon for Detroit. With Dizzy Dean laughing and clowning his way through the game, the Cardinals easily drew first blood by a score of 8 to 3. The Redbirds hammered Crowder, Marberry, and Hogsett for 13 hits, Joe Medwick, who was to become a storm center of the Series, leading the charge with a homer and 3 singles. The Jersey man also ripped up Cochrane's right thigh in a slide to the plate. Tiger fans had little to cheer them but the liquid refreshment they brought into the ball park. By the time that Hank Greenberg boomed a homer into temporary seats in left field in the eighth, Detroit was trailing by six runs, and in an earlier inning Hank had fanned with runners on third and second, his first of nine strike-outs during the Series.

St. Louis started its scoring merry-go-round early. One was down in the second, when Orsatti singled to left, and Durocher's fly to White provided the second put-out. Dean rolled to Rogell for what should have been the third out, but the Mechanical Man, Gehringer, muffed Billy's toss for a force play at second on Orsatti. Martin followed with a grounder to Owen, whose throw to first was wide, and filled the bases. Rothrock, the former Red Soxer, pumped a single to left for two runs before Gehringer threw out Frisch.

Tigers bobbled their way to another St. Louis gift run in the third, and Durocher taunted in his grating voice: "You guys are being too good to us." Medwick banged a single to left and was forced by Rip Collins. In trying for a double play, Rogell threw wildly to first and the Ripper galloped to second. He scored when Bill DeLancey's grounder rolled through Greenberg. The Tigers scored their first run in their half of the same inning. After Dizzy got the first two, Jo-Jo White walked and singles by Cochrane and Gehringer sent him over.

After Ducky Medwick brought further grief to Detroit fans with a fifth inning homer, Mickey sent Doljack to bat for Crowder in the second half. Marberry took over the Detroit pitching chores in the sixth, and the Gas-House Gang feasted on Fred like a gang of hungry boys turned loose in a candy shop. Dizzy started it with a double to center. "What was that you throwed me?" he yelled at Marberry after sliding into second. He didn't tarry there long, tearing home as Martin clipped another single to center. Rothrock sacrificed Pepper to second, and there was a moment of relief as Frisch fouled to Owen. But the irrepressible Medwick still was full of hits, and his single to right sent Martin galloping home. Collins kept it up with another single to right. By this time Cochrane had had enough of Marberry; he shooed the big Texan away and called in the Indian, Hogsett, from the bull pen. Orsatti immediately greeted him with a smoking two-bagger to left, and Medwick and Collins scored the third and fourth runs of the inning.

2

It was a different story in the second game when Schoolboy tied it up for Navin, Cochrane, and 43,451 Tiger fans with one of the greatest World's Series efforts ever pitched into the records. Over the years, Rowe was not a successful World's Series pitcher, but this day he really blew them down 'with his fast one. He well could call up to the stands and get Edna's approbation. It was the day Dizzy Dean said Lynwood was nearly as fast as Dizz's brother Paul. Even so, though Rowe retired 22 Cardinals in order at one stage of the game, he just managed to bring victory home in the twelfth, 3 to 2. And Detroit needed a break to tie in the ninth and save Rowe from defeat.

Frisch opposed Rowe with his veteran left-hander, Wild Bill Hallahan. The Irish boy had had only a fair season, but he had been a hellcat in the Cardinals' World's Series of 1930 and 1931. Wild Bill always had guts spelled with a capital G. And for eight innings, he was plenty tough.

Rowe's start was not spectacular and didn't indicate the game he was going to pitch, as the Cardinals reached him for two quick runs. In the second inning, Delancey beat out an infield single to Gehringer and came home when Orsatti exploded a triple to left. A second St. Louis run trickled over in the third, when Martin led off with a single, was sacrificed to second by Rothrock, and driven in by the always dangerous Medwick. But from the time Ducky singled, St. Louis never put another man on base until Pepper Martin doubled in the twelfth. By retiring those 22 straight Redbirds, Rowe tied a record which Herb Pennock, Yankee southpaw, hung up against the Pirates in 1927. Pennock, however, started with the first batter of the game, and Pittsburgh didn't break through until the eighth inning.

The Tigers got one run back for Rowe in the fourth when Rogell and Fox bunched doubles, but Hallahan also pitched hitless ball in the next four innings and it looked as though Rowe's great pitching would avail him naught. But Dame Fortune smiled on the Tigers in the ninth. Fox started off a rally with a single to right, and Rowe cleverly sacrificed Pete to second.

Jo-Jo White started to go to bat, when Cochrane got a hunch. He called him back and yelled to Gerald Walker: "Go up there, and bring him in, Gee."

There were curses and mutters of dismay on the Tiger bench when Gee raised a foul between the plate and first base. Either Delancey or Ripper Collins could have caught it, but each expected the other to handle it. The ball fell safe. Remembering how Fred Merkle and Chief Meyers had let a similar foul by Tris Speaker escape them in the crucial game of the Giant-Red Sox World's Series of 1912, John Heydler, the National League president, yelled: "Why do these plays always have to happen to us?"

In the Boston game 22 years before, Speaker had followed the break with a clean single tying the score, and now Walker did the same. Like a streak of white lightning a single streaked into left field, scoring Fox with the run which deadlocked the score at 2-2. And the roar of that crowd almost blew the roof off Navin Field. Frisch yanked Hallahan at this stage and substituted another left-hander, Bill Walker. He promptly caught Gee napping, but the popular Mississippi boy was forgiven. Walker had enabled School-boy to carry the game into extra innings, and the crowd sensed victory was in the offing.

The St. Louis Walker gave up only one hit after relieving Hallahan, but that one bingle beat him. The Tigers couldn't touch him in the tenth or eleventh, but after Durocher tossed out Cochrane in the twelfth, the left-hander suddenly lost control. He walked both Gehringer and Greenberg, and that put him in a hole. He tried to pitch carefully to Goslin, but the Goose smacked a resounding single to right, and the happy Gehringer sped home with the winning run. It was the first time that Detroit had seen a World's Series victory at the Michigan and Trumbull Avenue grounds since George Mullin won the sixth game of the 1909 Series from Pittsburgh.

3

"That's just the one we needed," said Cochrane happily, as he led his charges to their special for St. Louis, where the next three games were scheduled. "Some of the boys were nervous in that first game, but getting this one under their belts will make them feel all right," he confided to Cy Perkins, his coach. "Tommy ought to take care of tomorrow's game. I told him he would pitch."

But Frisch had another of his troublesome Deans ready. It was a game which had Cochrane raving. Tommy Bridges was knocked out by the Redbirds in the fifth, and the Tigers had 13 men left on base. Dean gave up eight hits and walked five men, but it wasn't until the ninth inning that the Tigers side-stepped a shutout. "You guys are a great team," snapped Mickey. "You are in a pig's eye."

After Bridges gave up a run in each of the first two innings, he seemed to hit his stride in the next two frames; then the Gas-House Gang put that charge of TNT under him in the fifth. It had St. Louis burghers yelling like Comanches while the rally was on. Martin opened with a double to right, and Rothrock fetched him in with a triple to left. Frisch lined a single to right, sending Rothrock home. Cochrane sadly dismissed Tommy, and again called in Hogsett. And it didn't make Mickey feel much better when the Indian left-hander stopped the Cardinals cold, yielding only one hit for the remainder of the game. The scoreboard read: Cardinals, 4; Tigers, 1.

4

Cochrane's tongue-lashing aroused his players for the fourth game, October 6. Like a college coach goading his young football charges with sarcasm and ridicule, Mickey got his players fighting mad, and they ripped into five of Frisch's pitchers—Carleton, Vance, Walker, Haines, and Mooney, for 13 hits. There wasn't an unlucky one in the lot, as the Tigers evened up the Series at two-all with a 10-4 victory. The 37,492 St. Louis crowd was amazed with this display of Tiger power. Big Hank Greenberg was the real big gun of this attack, as he banged out a homer, two doubles, and a single.

Eldon Auker coasted in on this one on his submarine ball, but the game actually was closer than it looked in the box score. It was 4-4 as late as the seventh inning, when the Tigers scored a run, a gift by Martin. This old American League nemesis had a terrible day, bobbling three chances. Gehringer singled and took second on the Goose's sacrifice. Rogell rolled to Durocher, whose throw to third headed off the Mechanical Man, but Pepper muffed it for his third error and Gehringer was safe. Orsatti made a hard try for Greenberg's line fly, but couldn't squeeze it. It fell safe for a double, scoring Charley. The bottom then dropped out of the game, when the Tigers put on a five-run-scoring merry-go-round in the eighth.

Not only did Detroit defeat the Cardinals decisively in that game, but they also nearly put Dizzy Dean out of the Series. During a Cardinal rally in the fourth inning, big Spud Davis, the catcher, batted for Vance and lined out a single. Using a little psychology, Frisch employed Dizzy Dean as a pinch runner. Dizz was such a competitor that Frankie figured his winning spirit would be contagious once he was in the game. And the St. Louis crowd yelled with delight. A few minutes later they were changing their tune and calling Frisch all kinds of a damn fool, for risking his ace pitcher on a foolhardy base-running job.

With Dean on first, Martin grounded to Gehringer, whose toss to Rogell forced Dizz. In trying to complete a double play, Bill hit Dean smack on the head with his throw. Dizz went down cold; the ball bounded feet away, and during the excitement, Durocher slipped in with the tying run. There was consternation. After some moments, the Great One still was out. Three sturdy Redbirds, two at his feet and one at his head, carried him like a sack of meal to the clubhouse, where Dr. Bob Hyland, the St. Louis club physician, started working on him. And the first thing he asked when he recovered consciousness was: "Say, did I break up that double play?"

5

Then came a Detroit victory which had the entire club in the seventh heaven. They had felt if they could win it, they were in. If they lost it, well, with the sixth and seventh games to be played at friendly Navin Field, they still would have a good chance. Dr. Hyland quickly discovered during the fourth game that there was nothing seriously wrong with Dean's head; he had a robin's egg on his armor-plate skull, but there was no concussion or fracture. Frisch announced he would go through with his plan to pitch Dizzy in the fifth game, October 7, and that the elder Dean would put the Cardinals back in the lead.

Cochrane talked it over with Bridges, and said: "Tommy, I am going to send you back at them, and we never needed a game more than this one. You had your stuff the other day, but maybe you were working too fast. You can beat those fellows; I know you can. And maybe Dean won't be quite as good after that bump on the head."

Tommy gave one of his lionhearted exhibitions, and stunned St. Louis before a Sunday crowd, which jammed all the aisles and runways at Sportsman's Park with a 38,536 attendance. The Tigers had beaten St. Louis' No. 1 man, and had that big three-to-two edge. Each side made seven hits, but Detroit bunched theirs on Dean sufficiently to win by 3 to 1. The Tigers picked up a first run as early as the second when Greenberg walked and came home on Pete Fox's long double to center. The Detroits got two more valuable runs for Bridges in the sixth. After Gehringer lashed a home run to the roof of the right field pavilion, Rogell singled to center and ran all the way to third when the ball rolled through Chick Fullis, who was substituting for Orsatti. Greenberg's long line drive to Rothrock enabled Billy to score. St. Louis' only tally resulted from Bill Delancey's home run in the seventh.

In his other three times, the young Cardinal catcher struck out, the last time with Frisch on third and Collins on first in the ninth. Delancey then called Brick Owens, the American League umpire, about every name there was in the Gas-House Gang's bad boy book. Owens reported the breach of discipline to Judge Landis, who called Delancey to his hotel room the next morning.

The Judge thought it was excruciatingly funny when he repeated the result of his examination to reporters who were in his good graces. "I asked Bill what he had said to Brick," began the Judge. "He told me this: 'When Owens called that first strike on me, I called him a dirty so and so. When he called the second on me, I said he was a dirty ——— ——— so and so, and believe me, Judge, when he called the third one, I just had to say he was a dirty ——— ——— ——— so and so.' "

And after Landis got through laughing, he said: "You know that boy was so honest, I just had to let him off with a $50 fine."

They were a happy pack of Tigers who returned to Detroit after the fifth game. Everybody said it was in the bag. Cochrane had to warn some of his happy players against overconfidence. "This isn't over yet," Mickey cautioned. "We got to keep bearing down."

"But, we licked the big guy; we can't lose now," Goslin, Gee Walker, and other effervescent spirits on the club replied.

Detroit felt the same way about it, and a great crowd waited at the Fort Street Station when the Tigers pulled in the next morning. The town was World's Series-conscious as never before. With Schoolboy Rowe, brilliant victor of the second game, primed for the home-coming contest, who could stop the Felines? The greatest turnout of the Series, 44,551, with thousands of standees, crowded Navin Field to be in on the kill.

On the morning of the sixth game, October 8, Goose Goslin, while visiting out-of-town friends, encountered the veteran National League umpire, Bill Klem, in the hotel elevator at the Detroit Leland. The previous day, when Klem had been calling them at first base, Goslin had disagreed with the umpire on a play at first and there were a few sharp words. The argument was resumed in the elevator car, with the "Old Arbitrator" giving the Goose more than a verbal spanking. He even borrowed a few niceties from Bill Delancey's vocabulary. Some other baseball big shots were in the elevator; they didn't appreciate Bill's choice of words and the matter got back to Landis. This time it was Klem, the umpire, who was hauled into Kenesaw Mountain's docket. The Judge slapped a $50 fine on him, and for some time after the Series, Klem refused to accept the Commissioner's Series check with the deduction.

No other umpire has approached Klem in officiating in World's Series, as the colorful National League veteran handled the indicator in 18 of them. Klem used to get a Series check at least every other year, but from the time he had the dispute with Landis over the $50 Goslin deduction, the Judge never appointed him again until 1940, and then only because of the special plea of Ford Frick, National League president. Klem was ending his career as an active umpire that season, and Frick asked that he be permitted to finish up in one of baseball's great autumn classics. Oddly enough, the American League team in that Series again was the Detroit Tigers.

Paul Dean and Rowe faced each other in the sixth.

Rowe pitched a satisfactory game, but he wasn't nearly as effective as in his early victory. While he walked none, the Gas-House Boys climbed on him for ten hits, and St. Louis' winning run was driven in by Rowe's pitching rival, Paul Dean. Particularly painful to the Tigers and their admirers was the strong hitting by Leo Durocher, the anemic eighth-place hitter of the National League champions. Though Leo had fielded superbly at shortstop, the Lip had lived up beautifully to his old American League sobriquet of the "All-American Out" in the first five games. He had hit only two singles, and prior to the sixth game was hitting a magnificent .110. And did the Tigers rub it in? "What you carrying that bat to the plate for, Leo?" they asked. "You ain't goin' nowhere." Then for one day, he became a hitting fool, smacking out two singles and a double, scoring two runs, and figuring heavily in the Cardinal scoring.

Paul Dean gave up only seven hits, three to Cochrane, but the Tigers actually had plenty of scoring chances, and missed chances to tie or win in the late innings. Paul was too good in the pinches, and several tough decisions were called against the Tigers. The toughest came when Brick Owens, an American League umpire, called Mickey out at third base during a sixth inning rally. Every one on that 1934 Tiger team still insists the catcher-manager was safe. None was out at the time and the decision unquestionably saved Paul Dean from being knocked out.

Cochrane was rather badly cut up in the third inning, but stayed gamely with his front-line troops. He beat out a slow dribbler to Jim Collins, but stumbled over Paul Dean, running over to cover, just as he reached the bag. The manager went down with another bad gash in his leg, just below the kneecap. Considerable time was taken out, as he was patched up, and the crowd gave him a great cheer when he remained in the game. However, he spent much of the following night in the hospital, getting treatment for his two spike wounds and a pulled ligament.

The Gas-House Gang scored first, picking up a run in the first inning on Rothrock's double and a single by that poison guy for Tiger fans—Ducky Medwick. The Tigers tied it in the third on the play on which Mickey met with his injury. With two out, White walked, stole second, and scampered to third when Frisch messed up Delancey's throw. Cochrane then beat out his infield hit to Collins, permitting Jo-Jo to score.

Rowe ran into a nasty squall in the fifth, when the Cardinals pushed over two runs. The Lip started it by beating out a hit to Gehringer, and Dean's sacrifice advanced the peppery shortstop to second. Martin rammed a single to left, on which Leo flew home, and when Goslin made a wild throw-in, the Wild Horse of the Osage never stopped running until he galloped into third base. Pepper hit scoring dirt as Rogell threw out Rothrock.

The Tigers remained full of fight, and created pandemonium when they came back with two runs in the sixth. White walked again, and sped to third on Cochrane's single. In his anxiety to pick up Gehringer's infield tap, Paul Dean couldn't find the handle. Charley was safe, and Jo-Jo streaked home. Delancey grabbed Goslin's bunt, and threw to Martin to force Cochrane at third on a close decision, a most vital play for St. Louis. Gehringer took third on Rogell's long fly to Rothrock, and scored the tying run on Greenberg's single.

St. Louis broke the deadlock in the very next inning, the seventh,

Gordon (Mickey) Cochrane, Dynamic Manager-Catcher

The Club Which Thrilled Detroit in 1935

with a run which hurt like an aching tooth. With one out, the pestiferous Durocher selected this moment for his first extra-base hit of the Series, a slashing double out of White's reach to center. Many stomachs in the crowd sagged as Dean went a long way toward winning his own game with a solid single to right, scoring Leo.

The Tigers tried hard to get this run back, pushed runners to third in both the seventh and eighth, with only one down, but it was no soap. Fox dropped a Texas League double to left to start the former inning, and Rowe sacrificed him to third. White smacked one down to Durocher, but Leo's peg to Delancey shot down Pete at the plate, and then Jo-Jo went out stealing. In the next frame, Gehringer and Goslin bunched singles with one out, Charley getting to third. But Rogell's fly to Orsatti wasn't quite long enough for Gehringer to try to come in, and the rally blew up when Greenberg popped a foul to Collins. The game ended, 4 to 3.

7

The Cardinals, by tying the Series, put Frisch in the driver's seat for the seventh and deciding game. There was no layoff between the sixth and seventh games—as now is the case, but every one knew the old Fordham Flash would come back with his No. 1 pitching man, Dizzy Dean, who hurled 312 National League innings and thought nothing of pitching after one day's rest. He did it all through September, and thrived on it.

Cochrane had nothing to match the big Oklahoman. Mickey had used up Bridges and Rowe, and had to come back with Auker, who had won the fourth game, while giving up ten hits and four runs. He would have to pitch better than that to beat the truculent Dizz.

The nation at large, as well as many of the Detroit fans, felt the Tigers had blown their big chance when Rowe failed to bring in the sixth game. But unlike 1907 and 1908, Tigertown didn't give the team the absent treatment as the Series ended. Despite the short time to get rid of tickets, 40,902 were out to see the windup, and they had as much fun as one has at a dear friend's bier. As in each of Jennings' three World's Series, the 1934 event passed into history with the Tigers on the wrong end of a shutout. But this was more than an ordinary whitewashing; the Cardinals rubbed in salt with the whitewash as they trampled down the Felines, 11 to 0.

The St. Louisans were tough and in aggravatingly good humor—even before the game. Even though knowing he was going to pitch, Dizzy Dean got hold of a Tiger rug, which Al Schacht, the baseball clown, used in a comedy act, and paraded around the field, grinning at the Tigers and their fans. "I got that tiger skin already," chided Dizz. The Tigers yelled: "We'll send you back to Tobacco Road, you bigmouth," but Dean only wisecracked about tame kittens.

For two innings, Auker held off Dean, and then came one of the most unhappy half hours in Detroit baseball history. Seven big St. Louis runs went up on the scoreboard after the Gang batted in the third. Dean contributed a double and single to the fat inning, as Cochrane vainly rushed in Rowe, Hogsett, and Bridges.

Auker retired Durocher, first man up, but the fireworks started when Dean lined a double to left. Martin beat out a bunt, and a pass to Rothrock filled the bases. Frisch brought grief to the stands with a long double to right, which cleaned the bases. Cochrane wigwagged to the bull pen for Rowe, but the Schoolboy couldn't stop the carnage. He did retire Medwick, but Collins singled and Delancey doubled. Sadly Cochrane stopped the game again, and summoned Hogsett. But the rout was on. The left-hander walked Orsatti, and Durocher up for the second time, singled, as did Dizzy Dean. The latter's hit scored Delancey and left the bases still filled. Dizz did a few handsprings, removed his cap and bowed to the crowd. A pass to Martin forced in the seventh run of the inning, when the desperate Cochrane called in Bridges. There was a welcome sigh of relief as Tommy induced Rothrock to hit into a force play, ending the inning. Before the game was over, Cochrane also called in Pitchers Marberry and Crowder, as the Redbirds picked up four additional runs.

A big rhubarb, unique in World's Series play, marred the game in the sixth inning, but for most Tiger fans the game already was past redemption. In this turbulent inning Ducky Wucky Medwick belted a triple with much gusto, scoring Martin, and slid hard into third base as the bag was covered by Marvin Owen. The Tiger infielder was slightly spiked on the play.

"You Hunky —— ——, who you trying to cut down?" demanded Marvin.

"I'll ram that ball down your throat if you try to tag me like that again," replied Medwick.

Both players got up jawing and swinging, but before any blows were struck, the umpires and other players got between the battlers. Neither player was put out of the game for fighting, for in the Washington-Giant Series the year before Judge Landis disapproved of Charley Moran's giving Heinie Manush of the Senators the heave-ho. He wanted to be consulted on future oustings. Collins' single then scored Medwick as the crowd chorused a loud boo.

Delancey fanned for the third out, and as the Tigers went on the field for the Tiger half, Medwick ran out to his position in left field. The left-field bleacherites saw him coming, let out a spontaneous boo, and greeted the Cardinal left fielder with a shower of apples, oranges, rolled up papers, and score cards, and any other litter they could get their hands on. Ducky retreated out of range, and a gang of attendants came out to clean up the debris. But the lads in the stands weren't out of ammunition. They were letting out all of their pent-up feeling, and the disappointment of having the coveted baseball blue ribbon snatched out of their grasp, on the person of Medwick. As soon as Joe again neared the stands, the shower was repeated.

"Get out of there, you louse; we've seen too much of you already," were among the mildest compliments tossed at Ducky Joe.

While the first shower was on, and while the ground keepers were cleaning the field, Landis moved back from his front-row box to an aisle about five rows back, where he soon was engaged in earnest conversation with a friend, the Judge's guest at the game.

The Commissioner now returned to his seat, summoned the two culprits, Medwick and Owens, and the four umpires, Geisel, Reardon, Owens, and Klem, to his box and held court. Klem was the third base umpire that day. After firing a volley of rapid-fire questions, the Judge made a quick decision. He asked Manager Frisch to take Medwick out of the game and send another player to left field.

"Why should I take him out?" groused Frankie.

"Because I say so," shot back the Judge. "We want to go on with this game, and it wouldn't look so good if a World's Series game had to be forfeited. So get it over with."

Frisch sent Chick Fullis to left field; the crowd was satisfied, and the game was played out to its unhappy end. Landis was severely criticized by some of the press for the manner in which he settled this difficult situation. They felt he had permitted the unruly bleacherites to win Detroit's only victory of that sad October 9. Secretly the Judge admitted he couldn't have made such a decision if it had been a close game, but felt with St. Louis leading, 9 to 0, and only three and a half innings to go, it was the sensible thing to do.

Warren Brown of the *Chicago Sun*, then of the *Herald-Examiner*, knew the man with whom Landis had that apparently serious conversation while the storm was at its height. Thinking to get a scoop, he asked this chap what Landis was talking about at the time.

"Well, I'll tell you," confided the man. "The Judge really was quite proud. He told me for years he had been trying to spit tobacco juice the way Pepper Martin lets it squirt from his lips and teeth, and had just acquired the knack."

St. Louis scored two more runs, and the final humiliating score was 11 to 0. Brokenhearted, Navin said dejectedly: "Are we destined never to win one of these things?"

It was a sad aggregation of Tigers who slumped into the clubhouse after Dizzy Dean, laughing and clowning on the mound, turned them back scoreless for the ninth inning. There were snarls, and curses, but few recriminations. "It's over," said Cochrane, "and they surely pinned our ears back today." He went to the joy-crazed Cardinal clubhouse and extended his hand to his fellow tourist of the Orient three years before, Frankie Frisch. "Congratulations, Frank," he said. "You've got a great club. It's a good thing for the National League that you don't have more than two Deans."

For the Tigers, Charley Gehringer and Bridges came out with highest honors, the Mechanical Man for hitting .379 and Tommy for winning that great game from the elder Dean which had given Detroit the three-to-two edge. Pete Fox and Rogell did well with averages of .286 and .276, respectively. Rowe's failure to win that all-important sixth game took some of the stardust off his pitching classic in the second, and while Greenberg hit .321 and led his team in runs batted in with seven, on the negative side were those nine whiffs, many of them in the pinch. In fact, after three games Cochrane dropped Hank from the fourth-place cleanup slot in the batting order to sixth.

But it wasn't such a bad winter for the boys, as each Tiger took home with him a Landis-autographed check for $3,354.67 for his week's work, and though Navin was sorely disappointed at the failure to win the Series, the Detroit club's take, $144,000, didn't look so bad in the ledger, especially when contrasted with the chicken feed picked up in the early Jennings Series.

⊗ XXI ⊗

THE YEAR WHEN
DREAMS CAME TRUE

I

AFTER MAKING DETROIT FANS WAIT 25 YEARS FOR A FOURTH AMERI-
can League pennant, Cochrane's Tigers gave them a second
successive flag in 1935. Though the Jungleers came in only three
games ahead of the Yankees, Ruth-less for the first time since 1919,
the finish wasn't as close as it looks in the record books. Nine games
ahead of New York after the Labor Day games, the Tigers loafed
and stumbled through September, but the McCarthy clan never
quite could catch up.

It was a rather odd kind of a race, and attracted Detroit's second
million attendance gate as Tiger fortunes started down and finished
up. After a rather hoop-la training trip to Lakeland, Fla., in which
Mickey hurt Goslin's feelings by benching him in several exhibition
games, and Izzy Goldstein, a pitcher from Greenberg's Bronx,
walked out on the club, the Tigers got off to a rocky start and for
several days in April saw seven clubs sitting on top of them in the
league standing.

They clicked on only four cylinders through most of May and as
late as May 28, they still were no higher than sixth. Iffy began
iffing like nobody's business. But there was a determined advance
through June, and over the July 4 holiday, Cochrane's brave lads
thrust their whiskers into second place. The White Sox were the
early pace-setters, but New York took the lead in June and the
Tiger kept snapping at the Yankees' heels all through July.

They finally landed at the Stadium for a double-header, July 23,
when a remarkable Tuesday crowd of 62,516 came out to see the
Yanks dispose of this Detroit menace for good and all. The Yanks
were rough on Rowe all right, knocking him out in a few frames as
Allen won, 7 to 5. But in the second game, Sorrell, usually effective
against New York, defeated Gomez, 3 to 1. Crowder served up a

beautiful game, July 24, winning a 4-0 shutout from Red Ruffing. That reduced the Yankee lead to the width of a spider web, .6071 to .6067.

Both contenders were rained out on the twenty-fifth, and the Tigers again were idle on the twenty-sixth, as Washington mowed the Yankees down, 9 to 3. That hoisted Detroit into first place, and the boys never let go. The pennant-hungry Tigers had to be satisfied with dividing their season's games with New York and Chicago, but they knew the trick of fattening on the lowly. They feasted on the seventh-place Browns, 17 to 5 and on the tail-end A's, 14 to 5.

Mickey had another slugging array; his team led easily in team batting with .290 and smacked out 106 round-trippers, second in home-run production. Hank Greenberg, the league's new most-valuable-player winner, contributed 36 of these four-base thumps, tying Jimmy Foxx for the league lead. Gehringer and Greenberg, two of the big G's, finished almost neck and neck in the batting parade, .330 to .328. Mickey was up there with .319, and Fox showed that Goose something, outhitting him .321 to .292. White slipped down to .240, and Gee Walker, whose color early captured the fancy of the Detroit crowds, worked into more games in the outfield, hitting .301.

Rowe wasn't quite as terrific as in the previous year, winning 19 games and losing 13. Tommy Bridges was the staff leader with 21 wins and 10 defeats; Auker had another fine 18-7 record, and Navin cashed a big dividend on his Crowder investment. The General became one of the regular four, winning 16 games, while losing 10.

2

With that fifth precious pennant tucked away, the Tigers faced the Cubs in the World's Series, the team which had mauled the Tigers so severely in 1907 and 1908. However, Frank Chance, the old Peerless Leader, long since had gone to baseball's Valhalla, and this year the Cubs were led by the effervescent and jovial Charley Grimm, a former St. Louis score-card boy, who in 1916 had come to Detroit as a young first baseman on Mack's Athletics. Jolly Cholly had stolen the 1935 National League pennant from the Cardinals and Giants on the home stretch with a spectacular September twenty-one-game winning streak which carried almost to the final game of the season.

Those 1935 Cubs closed in high; they were hotter than a gang of bank robbers with the F.B.I. closing in, and the sports-writing fraternity—outside of Detroit—said their momentum couldn't help but carry them to fresh World's Series triumphs. But Cochrane's gladiators had different ideas. Unfortunately, Cochrane lost his big gun, Greenberg, in the second game and had to fight his war with two soft spots in his batting order, Marv Owen and Flea Clifton. Owen had only 1 hit in 20 times at bat, the Flea none in 16. It was like having three pitchers in your line-up, and put a difficult load on the rest of the gang.

Detroit again staged the opener, and as in the past the first game, October 2, brought no joy for an assemblage of 47,391. Not much fun sitting there watching your team blanked with four hits. It was a battle between two tall pitching sons of Arkansas, Lon Warneke of Mount Ida and Lynwood Rowe of El Dorado, and with the Cubs backing Lonnie with errorless support, there was little chance for the Tiger fans to let off steam. Two of the four Tiger hits went to Pete Fox.

Rowe also was good, yielding seven hits, but he wasn't good enough. He didn't walk a man, and fanned eight Cubs, against only one strike-out for Warneke—Jo-Jo White, Detroit's opening hitter. The game was lost by Detroit before it was ten minutes old, the Cubs scoring two runs with only one out in the first inning. Augie Galan, Grimm's lead-off man, clipped Rowe for a double to center, and Billy Herman dumped a sacrifice bunt in front of the plate. Realizing the play at first would be close, the Schoolboy tried to hurry his throw and pegged into right field. Galan scored and Herman pulled up at second. Lindstrom sacrificed Billy to third, and big Gabby Hartnett brought in the crack second baseman with a solid single to right. The Cubs closed with a final run in the ninth when Frank Demaree reached the left-field seats with a home run.

3

With that opening shutout behind them, the Tigers came back strongly, winning not only the second game in Detroit, October 3, but the next two in Chicago. Rallying behind Tommy Bridges' six-hit effort, the Tigers made good use of their bats, routing first Charley Root, an old Cub stand-by, and then Roy Henshaw, pony left-hander, winning by a score of 8 to 3. Oddly enough that was the same score by which Detroit had won its only game from the Cubs in the two Series of 1907 and 1908, Mullin's victory in the third game of the latter Series.

The Tigers didn't make the fans wait long before setting off the fireworks. It was a case of Biff! Bing! Bang! Bang!! as they had four runs in before the Cubs retired a man. They gave Root an awful going over. White opened with a single to left, and Cochrane brought him home with a double to right. Mickey galloped over the plate when Gehringer lined a single to center, and to top the rally Greenberg pumped a homer into the left-field seats.

Henshaw came in and eventually got the side out with the aid of a double play, but he became wilder by the minute in the fourth, when Grimm also dragged him out, and the Tigers scored three additional runs. It all started with two out, when Henshaw plunked the weak-hitting Owen with a pitched ball. Bridges scratched an infield hit off Henshaw's glove, and a pass to White filled the bases. A wild pitch scored Owen, and then Henshaw filled 'em up again by walking Cochrane. Gehringer smacked in two more runs with a single, when Kowalik, a Cub third-striker, finally spiked the Detroit guns.

With a lead of 7 to 0, Tommy Bridges had a breeze. He gave up only one hit in the first four innings, and when the Cubs scored their first run in the fifth, it was built around two errors by Greenberg.

4

Greenberg had a collision at the plate with the bulky Hartnett in the seventh inning of the second game. He felt a sharp twinge in his left wrist as he picked himself off the ground, but ball players shake off these things in the heat of play, and Hank gamely finished the game. But, on the train ride to Chicago that night, the wrist became exceedingly painful and the big first baseman spent a sleepless night. Calling up Cochrane the next morning, he said: "Mickey, that wrist doesn't feel so good." The wrist was X-rayed, and the verdict was bad enough—two broken bones. It meant that Greenberg, the club's clean-up man and big home-run threat, had to sit out the remainder of the Series.

It left the club in somewhat of a panic. At first, it was Cochrane's intention to go to first base himself, and let Ray Hayworth catch. Then Schoolboy Rowe volunteered for first-base duty, and several other combinations were suggested.

After listening to the conversation of the players, Navin said to Cochrane: "Why not move Owen over to first, and play Clifton at third? Owen has played first base in the Coast League, and Clifton is a good defensive third baseman." Mickey was not overly enthusiastic, when Navin said: "I order it. Please make the change."

The players mumbled and were dissatisfied with the new combination, and Goose Goslin went to see Navin, and asked whether he had ordered the shift of Owen to first, with Clifton going to third.

"Yes, Goose, I did," said Navin. "And it will be done; it was my decision, and if we lose the Series, it will be on my head."

It probably was the only time that a club owner dictated such an important move in a World's Series line-up. Clifton was a dead weight in the batting order, but with that combination, the Tigers won their first Series.

The third game of the Series played in Wrigley Field, October 4, was one of the toughest, most riotous of all Detroit's World's Series battles, with the Tigers eventually pulling it out in the eleventh inning, 6 to 5. A smoldering feud between Umpire George Moriarty, the former Tiger third baseman, and the Cubs broke out in the open. The Cubs had ridden Greenberg rather brutally in the first two games, and Moriarty cautioned Grimm that he and his players were going too far. It then was necessary for Moriarty to call a succession of close plays against the Cubs. In the sixth inning, he waved out Cavarretta on a hair-line decision when Phil tried to steal second. It had the whole Cub team on his neck, and he tossed Grimm, Woody English, Chicago's non-playing captain, and Tuck Stainback out of the park. Earlier in the fray, Ernie Quigley, one of the National League umpires, chased Del Baker, the Tiger coach, off the coaching lines.

The feeling between the Cubs and Moriarty grew worse as the Series progressed, and for strife and bitterness—even vulgarity and profanity on both sides—it seldom has been equaled. At the end of the Series, Judge Landis fined not only four offending Cubs—Grimm, English, Stainback and Herman—but also Moriarty, sums of $200.

The third was a game of many pitchers, Cochrane employing Auker, Hogsett, and Rowe, while Grimm called in Big Bill Lee, Warneke, and French. The Tigers outhit Chicago, 12 hits to 10, with the Goose and Billy Rogell each getting three. The Cubs were leading, 3 to 1, and Lee seemed on his way to victory when the Tigers hit one of those four-run jack pots in the eighth.

White walked and there was a slight lull as Mickey popped out, but Gehringer's double sent Jo-Jo to third, and Goslin banged in the pair with a single down the right-field line. That tied the score at 3-3, chased Lee, and brought in Warneke, the first game shutout winner. He wasn't an immediate success, as Fox and Rogell followed with singles, Goslin scoring. Rogell was trapped between second and first and run down, but it was a good martyr play, as Fox sneaked in from third while the chase was on.

Hogsett had pitched the seventh, but with his team two runs to the good, Cochrane summoned Rowe from the bull pen. Handing him the ball, he said: "You've got to protect that lead, Schoolboy." Rowe nodded his head, and blotted out Lindstrom. Hartnett, and Demaree in order in the eighth. However, the Cubs had a kick left and tied the score in the ninth when two pinch hitters, Chuck Klein and Kenny O'Dea, came through for Grimm.

In the eleventh the Tigers scored the winning run at the expense of Left-hander Larry French. Rogell opened with a single past Hack. Owen tried to sacrifice, but only succeeded in forcing Billy at second. Detroit then got a break when Freddy Lindstrom, who had moved in from center field to third, fumbled on Clifton. Rowe fanned, but White came through with a line single to center which scored Owen.

5

The Tigers took that big three-to-one lead when they nosed out the Cubs, 2 to 1, in a tight fourth game played in Chicago, October 5. Cochrane was a little uncertain about his pitcher, but finally picked Alvin Crowder, who vainly had been gunning for a World's Series victory for the past two years, with the 1933 Washington Senators and the 1934 Tigers. But the General was due, and gave Navin and Cochrane a beautiful game. He held the Cubs to five hits, and their only run resulted from Hartnett's homer in the second inning. Tex Carleton, who had pitched against the Tigers in a Cardinal uniform a year before, opened for Chicago and was succeeded by Bill Lee. It was a game which had Cochrane snapping at everybody and frothing at the mouth. His club had opportunities to score a dozen runs, and had 13 men left on base.

The third inning was a sample, when Detroit cooked only one run out of a double, two singles, and two walks. Crowder opened with a single, and White sent him to third with another one-base knock, but Jo-Jo was out trying for a double. After Cochrane walked, Gehringer poled a double to right center, scoring Crowder. This was followed by an intentional pass to the Goose, filling the bases. It was good Grimm strategy, as Fox forced Mickey at the plate and Rogell fanned.

The Tigers had to sweat out their first run, but the second in the sixth was an out-and-out gift. With two down, Galan muffed Clifton's long fly for a two-base error. Then Billy Jurges let Crowder's grounder trickle through his legs, and the Flea jumped home. Carleton's balk advanced the General to second and White walked. This time it was Cochrane who left two runners when he lifted to Galan. But the one run was just enough.

6

Cochrane wanted badly to end the Series in Chicago by taking the Sunday game, October 6, but it wasn't quite in the cards. He put it up to Rowe, but again the big boy couldn't quite make it. The game started as a Chicago repeat performance of the all-Arkansas pitching duel of the first game, Rowe and Warneke. Lon pitched as well as he did in the opener, giving up three hits and no runs in six innings, when to the surprise of the crowd he walked off the field. Pitching on a cold, windy day, he wrenched some muscles in his right shoulder and couldn't continue. "This is the break," Mickey yelled at his players, but Bill Lee came in and pitched three strong innings. Chicago won by a score of 3 to 1; it was the first Cub World's Series victory on their home grounds since the 1918 Series.

In some respects, it was almost a duplicate of Rowe's 3 to 0 defeat in the Detroit opener. Only this time, instead of being cuffed for two runs in the first inning, the two Chicago markers came in the third. They came like two quick flashes of lightning. Herman, first batter up, tripled to right center, and Chuck Klein, the next hitter, homered into the right-field stands. The Schoolboy then held the Cubs at bay until the seventh, when they picked up a third run on a single by Jurges and Herman's double.

The Tigers gave Grimm and the Chicago stands an awful scare, when the first three Felines up in the ninth—Gehringer, Goslin, and Fox, lashed out singles, Charley scoring. However, the rally flickered quickly as Lee got the next three men, Clifton popping a weak foul to Cavarretta for the final out with the tying runs on third and second.

7

The Series swung back to Detroit for the sixth game. A throng of 48,420, the best of the three games in Detroit, saw the deciding game. It was the game of Tommy Bridges' heroic ninth-inning stand, and the dramatic Tiger rally which immediately followed it. Bridges opposed Larry French, the California left-hander, who was making his first start of the series. Both teams hit briskly, each side winding up with 12 hits, and oddly enough both of the No. 2 hitters—Cochrane and Herman—poled three hits. Both pitchers also had the same number of strike-outs—seven.

It was seesaw and nip and tuck all the way. The Tigers drew first blood, scratching French for a run in the first, and they had a grand opportunity to stow away the game then and there. With Clifton down, Cochrane and Gehringer banged out singles; Goslin popped out, but Fox doubled over third, scoring Mickey. The Cubs then intentionally passed Gee Walker, a right-handed hitter. Cochrane had Gee in center in place of White. With the bases full, Rogell slapped a roller back at French, whose throw to Hartnett forced Gehringer at the plate.

The Cubs tied in the third on singles by Jurges, Galan, and Herman, but Detroit got its one-run lead back with a marker in the fourth. Gee Walker opened with a blow to right, and Rogell sent him to second by duplicating the whack to left. Owen's bunt forced Rogell at second, but Gee made third and scored when Bridges, in turn, forced Owen. It then was Chicago's turn to take the lead with two runs in the fifth, Tommy's poorest round. French singled, but after Galan took a third strike, Billy Herman raised lumps in Tiger throats with a home run over the left-field fence. That made the score: Chicago, 3; Detroit, 2. Klein followed with another blazing single, but Bridges got Harnett on a fly to the Goose.

Grimm's lead was short-lived, as the Tigers scored in the sixth, and the two teams were back exactly where they started. This time it started with two out, when Rogell hit a ground-rule double to the left-center-field corner. And then Owen, who had gone hitless for six games, saved his only blow of the series for this crucial spot. He lined a stanch single to left, which fetched in Billy.

Hack opened the Cub ninth with a long drive over Gee Walker's head for three bases, and the crowd sat frozen in their seats. Except for the shouts of several hundred National Leaguers, the big stadium was as silent as a tomb. But plucky, game Tommy was equal to the occasion. Putting every ounce of energy behind his tantalizing curves, he blew down Bill Jurges on strikes. Bridges took care of French's infield tap himself, tossing out the pitcher, and holding Hack on third. He still had a tough customer in Augie Galan, but the California Frenchman went out on a fly to Goslin, and the grandstand became a bedlam.

Yet even the noise which followed Galan's retirement was only a murmur to the shouts which roared out of Navin Feld within the next ten minutes. The Tiger half started inauspiciously enough, when Clifton struck out again, but Cochrane hit a single just outside of Herman's reach. Billy got a glove on it, but couldn't field the ball. Gehringer went out on a grounder to Cavarretta, but Mickey scampered down to second on the play, putting it up to Goslin. Goose soon saw a pitch he liked, rammed it solidly to right field, and the grinning, joy-crazed Cochrane scored the big winning run standing up. Mickey jumped up and down on the plate several times to make sure that he hadn't missed the dish, and then joined the crowd of happy Tigers and Detroit fans who fought for the chance to hug Goslin and Bridges. The crowd finally rode the Goose into the clubhouse on its shoulders.

Even Frank Navin, Mr. Poker Face, made no effort to hide his emotion. "It was great! It was wonderful!" he kept on repeating. "I have waited thirty years for this day." Judge Landis, Will Harridge, Charley Grimm came into the clubhouse, offering congratulations. Cochrane was radiantly happy as he embraced Bridges and Goslin.

Detroit's first modern World's Championship set off the greatest celebration ever seen in baseball. Washington went berserk when the Senators defeated the Giants in 1924, and Cincinnati put on a wild shindig when the Reds licked the Tigers in 1940, but none of them approached Detroit's spontaneous outburst on that night of October 7, 1935. The whole town went batty, as the screeching fans swept down Woodward Avenue deliriously happy.

It started in Navin Field, almost with the last play. They yelled themselves hoarse in the ball park, and after forty-five minutes most of those who saw the game still were milling around. Repeatedly they yelled for Cochrane. Eventually somebody got the loudspeaker in the club house, and Mickey said: "This is the happiest day of my life. It was the most sensational series I ever played in. My greatest thrill in baseball was scoring that winning run." He ended up with a tribute to that "little giant, Tommy Bridges."

Crowds still were tooting, banging on dishpans, and ringing gongs as they snake-danced through Cadillac Square and Grand Circus Park well past midnight, while the bars at the Book-Cadillac, Detroit A. C., Fort Shelby, Detroit Leland, Statler, and other spots kept open house until the sun rose out of the east the next morning. Detroit had a terrible hang-over, but, gosh, it was worth it.

As for the Tigers, they really could sit down to a feast. The victor's melon was split into 25½ shares, and each player's take was $6,544.76, which still stands as the all-time high as an individual winning share.

⊛ XXII ⊛

TYCOON BRIGGS TAKES
FULL POSSESSION

I

THE DETROIT CLUB'S SHARE FROM THE RICH 1935 WORLD'S SERIES was $150,000, and Frank Navin immediately announced that the sum, as well as much of the profit of the season's million gate, would be spaded back into the ball park, and he was consulting with architects to see what could be done about putting more seats in Navin Field. He was jovial at a big Tiger victory celebration, in which he said joshingly: "I better not make Mickey Cochrane too wonderful. I've got to sign him for next year." But actually he loved and admired the aggressive Cochrane. Before Mickey came, it was his custom to change seats after a losing streak. After Cochrane came, he stuck religiously to the same seat.

Then, on November 13, a little more than a month after the winning of the World's Championship, Detroiters read sad and shocking news. Frank Navin was dead at the age of 64. While riding his favorite Irish jumper, Masquerader, at the Detroit Riding and Hunt Club, the Tiger owner apparently suffered a heart attack. Mrs. Navin had been jogging along the bridle path ahead of her husband, and her first intimation that something was wrong came when she saw Masquerader galloping by without a rider. A searching party was organized after she followed her husband's riderless horse to the stable and hysterically appealed for help.

Navin was found unconscious near the bridle path on the hunt club's property. He was rushed to the Detroit Osteopathic Hospital at Highland Park, but died an hour later.

The entire Motor City went into mourning for this great baseball figure, the man who had entertained dreams for Detroit's baseball future and saw them realized. Expressions of sympathy and tributes to the dead man's splendid character came from national figures and baseball men from all over the country. In a way, Frank was a victim to his love of and loyalty to baseball. He could have gotten out with nearly $2,000,000 for his holdings, and perhaps lived an·· other five or ten years. But he died with a smile on his lips. Didn't he go out as the owner of baseball's World's Championship club?

With Navin dead, Walter O. Briggs, the big automobile body builder, moved more actively into Detroit's baseball picture. During Frank's successful presidency, he was satisfied to remain quietly in the background, but he now purchased the Navin interests from Frank's widow and became full owner. Taking considerable pleasure in the part he had played in bringing Cochrane to Detroit, h€ expanded Mickey's duties and made him vice-president as well as manager. It was Mickey's job to run the whole shebang. Walter O. Briggs, Jr., better known as "Spike," a major in the last war, came actively into the organization as treasurer-assistant secretary. Frank Navin's two nephews, Secretary Charles F. Navin and Road Secretary Arthur T. Sheahan, stayed on for a while, but within a two-year period the Navin name faded from the club's stationery.

Briggs, a self-made man, was a Tiger fan from 'way back. "I used to go to Detroit games every Sunday when the Tigers played at the Sunday park out in Springwells—when Sunday ball wasn't permitted in Detroit," Briggs remarked shortly after taking over. "Those were the days! That's when Jim Burns and Stallings owned the club, and George was manager. Why, you used to see more fights there on a Sunday afternoon than you see now in the big leagues in five years. The players fought each other and the fans; the fans fought the gate tenders; and the tenders fought the ground keeper. The customers would come out all ginned up; fights started before a ball was pitched, lasted throughout the game, and continued long afterwards."

He laughed as he continued: "You know I like aggressive baseball myself. I used to be a bad loser when the home team lost."

2

Anyone who believes in astrology would say that Mickey Cochrane was under a lucky star in 1934 and 1935, but shortly after the '35 World's Series, the planets began to do him dirt. Maybe the start was the death of Navin. Things never were exactly the same thereafter. As vice-president, Cochrane recommended the purchase of Al Simmons, his old Athletic fellow slugger, from the Chicago White Sox for $75,000. He told Briggs that with Al as a regular outfielder, the club couldn't miss in 1936 and the deal was consummated at the December, 1935, winter meeting. But Al and Cochrane were fellow stars on Athletic champions; now Mickey was the big Polack's boss, and the catcher, fighting for ball games, could be rather cutting. Though Simmons hit .327 for the 1936 Tigers, he lasted under Cochrane only one season. By 1937, he was passed along to Washington.

The 1936 season was only a fortnight gone when Hank Greenberg suffered an injury which put him out for the season. Jake Powell, Washington's peppery outfielder, ran into him in a first base collision at Griffith Stadium, and the left wrist which Greenberg injured in the 1935 World's Series was hurt all over again. X-rays showed the left wrist fractured; it was put in a cast, and the prediction was that Greenberg would be able to play in June. But week after week, and then month after month passed by with the slugging Hank still on the shelf. He played only those 12 spring games, hitting .348. After Greenberg's injury, Mickey sidetracked an idea of recalling a big part-Indian first base slugger, Rudy York, from the Milwaukee club. Instead he put through a deal with the St. Louis Browns for Jack Irving Burns, a pretty good fielding first baseman.

As if Hank's disability and several early unpleasantries with Simmons weren't enough, the pitching staff bogged down before the race was six weeks old. Schoolboy Rowe suffered from an acute misery in his long right arm; he stayed home from one eastern trip to have the arm and his teeth X-rayed. Though Lynwood won 19 games while losing 10, he had to be taken out 16 times, and the arm kicked up all season. Auker lost the knack of winning, while General Crowder, a strong competitor in '35, suffered from stomach trouble, pitched only 44 innings and retired in July. Only Bridges held up magnificently, winning 23 games and losing 11.

Poor Mickey, the vice-president and manager, took all these troubles on himself. He worried and fretted, and was plagued with one bad break after another. In the very first series, he had a finger mashed; then he was painfully hurt on the foot by a foul tip. Next came trouble with his eyes and stomach, and a general breakdown in mid-June. After treatment at the Henry Ford Hospital, he was sent to a ranch in Wyoming, told to do a lot of riding and shooting and forget baseball. The team was turned over to Del Baker, a Tiger catcher in the late Jennings period and Detroit coach since 1933. In the fourth All-Star Game in Boston, July 7, 1936, Joe McCarthy pinch-managed the American League team for Cochrane and suffered the first A. L. defeat in that competition.

Cochrane, much refreshed, came back from the west in time to see the raising of Detroit's first modern World's Championship flag on July 24. He didn't get into uniform, but took the cheers of the crowd while seated in a box with Judge Landis, Will Harridge, Walter Briggs, and Tom Yawkey. Shortly afterwards, he again took charge, but did little catching, and appeared in only 44 games. Most every one caught that season, Hayworth, Reiber, Glenn Myatt, and a noisy peppery little guy who caught ten games in the fall, George "Birdie" Tebbetts, who was to become one of Detroit's best catchers.

With all of Cochrane's bad breaks, it is surprising that he finished second, but it was a runner-up position much like that of Ty's Tigers of 1923. Mickey's club could scarcely see the dust of the winning Yankees from their position 19½ games behind, but they nosed out the White Sox and Senators in a last-day battle for the money positions. Detroit had a percentage of .539; Chicago, .536; and Washington, .535.

3

Cochrane's cycle of ill fortune continued unabated in 1937. The season was only a little more than a month old when Mickey met with a tragic accident at Yankee Stadium, which terminated his great playing career at the age of thirty-four. The Tigers had gotten off to a good start, and were battling the Yankees for the lead, despite the fact that Schoolboy Rowe's arm was ailing all spring. The club had an idea much of it was in the tall Arkansan's head, and Lynwood was suspended for ten days for not being in condition to pitch.

The suspension was lifted May 25, and the Schoolboy was making his first start of the season. Cochrane caught him, and tried his best to coach and inspire him. In the third inning, he endeavored to give Schoolboy additional encouragement by hitting a home run. Irving "Bump" Hadley, stocky right-hander, former Brown collegian, and present-day Boston sportscaster, was pitching for the Yankees.

In the fifth inning, he let go a high inside pitch to Cochrane. Mickey tried to duck, and frantically put up his hands to protect his head. The 15,000 New York fans heard the dull thud as the ball hit him, and many thought the ball had struck Mickey's wrist. But Cochrane was out cold at the plate from a blow over the left temple, and didn't regain consciousness until several of his players carried him tenderly to the clubhouse. He was rushed to New York's St. Elizabeth's Hospital; an early cursory examination showed the catcher was in critical condition, and X-rays revealed a triple fracture. An entire nation watched the bulletins from St. Elizabeth's, where for three days the stricken catcher hovered between life and death. Specialists came from as far away as Rochester, Minn., to join in the fight for the great player's life. It wasn't until the fourth day that the physicians were able to report that Cochrane's condition had taken a turn for the better.

As for Hadley, he was terribly upset. He came from Lynn, Mass., not so far from Mickey's home town of Bridgewater. "The ball sailed—I don't know why—it just did," said the unhappy pitcher. As the count was three balls and one strike at the time, it obviously was not a duster, as a bean ball would have been the fourth ball and put Cochrane on base.

Baker again was drafted as emergency manager, and after Mickey was out of danger, Del said: "We'll keep hustling for Mike. It was a cruel break, losing Cochrane that way, but it might have been worse. We'll miss his leadership and his aggressiveness, which fired the whole gang. But we'll do the best we can until he returns."

After leaving St. Elizabeth's, Cochrane was hospitalized for another six weeks at the Henry Ford Hospital in Detroit, where he followed the progress of his team through a bedside radio. It was July 25, two months and a day after the near-fatal injury, that he returned to his bench and picked up the reins, but he announced that baseball had seen the last of Mickey Cochrane as a catcher. He had been warned against returning to active duty by his medical advisers.

The 1937 Tigers followed pretty much the same pattern as the team of the year before. They finished second, but after midseason couldn't give the Yankees much of a race, the New Yorkers winning this year by 13 games. Detroit's fight again was to pull down second money, and Mickey beat his old Athletic pal, Jimmy Dykes, manager of the White Sox, by three games.

The season saw many interesting developments. True to Baker's words, the boys battled gamely while Cochrane fought first for his life and then for health. Gehringer was fairly inspired that year; he led the league in batting with .371, and took his turn in winning the most-valuable-player prize. Greenberg hit .337, brought up his home-run production to 40, and drove in 183 runs, only one short of Lou Gehrig's American League record. Gee Walker was only two points behind Hank with .335, and had a pretty hefty extra-base collection himself, 42 doubles, 4 triples, and 18 homers. The one G-man who didn't thrive that season was Goslin; Father Time gradually was cooking the Goose, as he faded to .238, while Pete Fox was up with the big boys with .331.

And Cochrane returned just in time to be in on Rudy York's magnificent August home-run spree. Rudy, a terrific right-handed hitter, had been in the Tiger organization since 1933, and was developed at Fort Worth, Beaumont, and Milwaukee. Though he played everything in the minors, he eventually settled at first base. But the Tigers had the slugging Greenberg, so Mickey experimented with Rudy at third base, the outfield, and behind the plate. It was while catching in August that York cracked out 18 homers, the major-league record for a month. In 104 games, he hit 35 round-trippers, which still is his big-league high.

Rowe's failure prevented the club from making more of a pennant fight; he was in only ten games, was credited with only one victory and charged with four defeats. The game in which Cochrane met his near-fatal injury, which Rowe lost 4 to 3, was the Schoolboy's only complete game. Bridges wasn't quite up to his usual form, winning 15 and losing 12. Auker snapped back to a 17-9 showing, and despite an earned-run record of 5.27, Roxy Lawson managed to win 18 games out of 25. With all his other troubles, Cochrane tried to manage a picturesque, thirsty Pennsylvania Dutchman, Cletus Elwood Poffenberger, of Conococheague Street, Williamsport, Maryland, and Mickey knew what his mentor, Connie Mack, had been up against when he tried to manage Rube Waddell. Even so, Cletus could pitch, and turned in a Woolworth record—10 wins and 5 losses.

4

After Navin died in November, 1935, Walter Briggs carried out the late owner's plans for further enlargement of the park. He double-decked the right field pavilion and bleachers to bring the new seating capacity up to 36,000. However, the new owner quickly realized that this still was inadequate to take care of the thousands of Detroiters who wanted to see the Tigers play ball—whether they were good or bad. In 1938, he took steps to enlarge further the stand to its present capacity of 56,000. This new capacity is exceeded only by Yankee Stadium in New York. What a change from those old 8,500 rickety wooden stands at Bennett Park!

The park now is an immense bowl. Two-story stands were erected in left and center field; this was made possible by the city council's officially closing Cherry Street, which heretofore had been the northern boundary of the park.

In recognition of Briggs's importance in this development, the new park was called Briggs Stadium, though some of Navin's old American League friends regretted to see Frank's name removed from the ball yard in which he had spent most of his adult life. Not only has Detroit one of the grandest parks in the nation, but one of the easiest to get in and out of.

Mickey Cochrane's misfortunes continued into 1938. On August 6, the popular former catcher, who had won two pennants and finished second twice in his four full years in charge, was summarily fired by Owner Briggs. Not only Tiger fans but Detroit writers rubbed their eyes with stunned surprise when the following statement was issued by Walter Briggs, Sr.

Mickey Cochrane and I had a conference today at which it was agreed that he would no longer continue his connection with the Detroit Baseball Club. He will be paid until the end of the 1938 season.

I regret exceedingly the termination of our baseball relationship both from a personal standpoint and because of the contribution which Mickey Cochrane made to Detroit and to the club when he came here as manager and catcher five years ago, but it seems apparent to both of us that for the good of the club and in justice to the supporting fans, a change should be made.

My son, Walter O. Briggs, Jr., treasurer of the Tigers, and I wish him every success in his future plans and we pledge to the Tiger team and to the baseball fans the best efforts of the club management to procure for the team satisfactory leadership always.

With Cochrane removed from the director's seat, Del Baker, who so frequently had been called upon to pinch-manage for Mickey, was appointed manager on his own.

At the time that Mickey was fired, the club was in fifth place, despite another Tiger hitting carnival, in which Hank Greenberg came within two homers of tying Babe Ruth's record, finishing with 58. Trouble brewed between Cochrane and the elder Briggs a good part of the season, and Mickey had several flare-ups with young Spike. Cochrane was nervous, fidgety, and still under high tension from his 1936 illness and that terrible blow on the head in 1937. The team was floundering around the .500 mark, and Briggs admitted he didn't like to lose.

The final breakup had come in early August. The club had been in a bad slump, and on August 5, the Tigers lost a game to the

Red Sox which could drive any owner or manager nuts. Boston tied the game by scoring five runs in the ninth, and then won in the tenth, 9 to 8. The next day, the Tigers were beaten, 14 to 8. That was the final straw! Because of a physical disability, Briggs couldn't go to the clubhouse after games, but he insisted that the manager come to see him to talk things over after home contests.

"Well, what is the alibi for today?" asked Briggs in the way of greeting.

"To tell you the plain truth, Mr. Briggs, you haven't got the players to win," replied Cochrane.

"That's not what you said in the spring," shot back Briggs. "Maybe it isn't the players; maybe you are the cause and it would help matters if you quit."

"That's all right with me, if you'll pay me for the season," spouted Cochrane. Briggs told him that could be arranged, and it ended the conference.

Cochrane later made a good business connection in Detroit, served with distinction in the Navy during the war, coming out with the three stripes of a full Commander. He coached a near-unbeatable team at Great Lakes, and then saw plenty of sea duty on the broad Pacific. But the Cochrane ill luck had not entirely run its course. When he returned, there was a gold star in the window for his only son, Gordon, Jr.

Much of Cochrane's 1938 trouble with the Tigers sprang from an ill-fated deal he had made the winter before with his old Athletic associate, Jimmy Dykes, skipper of the White Sox. Feeling weak pitching held back his club in 1937, Mickey made big sacrifices to get Vern Kennedy, a 21-game winner with Chicago in 1936. Cochrane gave up Outfielder Gee Walker, Third Baseman Owen, and Mike Tresh, a young Detroit-bred catcher, for Kennedy, Outfielder Fred "Dixie" Walker, and Infielder Tony Piet.

The deal was the most unpopular ever made in Detroit and had an immediate kickback. The trading of Gerald Walker, who had a firmer grip on Detroit fandom than any other player of the previous decade, raised merry hell for weeks. Bootblacks, butchers, bakers, and bankers joined in denouncing the deal. Newspapers were flooded with letters from indignant fans; petitions were circulated which got thousands of signatures, threatening to boycott the club unless the deal was rescinded.

Cochrane's words at the time proved most prophetic: "I hated to let Walker go. I didn't like the idea of giving up Owen, but we had to make some sacrifices. If this business does not turn out to benefit the Tigers, I'll take the rap."

He took the rap all right. There seemed some justification for the deal when Vern Kennedy won his first nine games, but then he stopped short like a bronco with a lasso around his neck. The Athletics threw him for his first loss June 9 in Philadelphia, and shortly thereafter threw him again in Detroit. That took the charm off Vern; for the rest of the season he won only three more ball games, finishing with 12 wins and 9 defeats. Dixie Walker, now the "people's cherce" in Brooklyn, failed to win the hearts of Tiger fans, while the trading of Marv Owen left a big hole at third, as Piet, Mark Christman, now of the Browns, and Don Ross all tried to fill it without much success.

The 1938 club eventually came in fourth under Baker, with Greenberg's home-run rampage holding the attention of the fans to the last game of the season.

York pounded out 33 more homers in 135 games, 116 of them as first-string catcher, but his catching still was mediocre. The 1938 Tigers came up with two fine home-bred prospects, Outfielder Barney McCoy, fleet-footed lad of Irish-Lithuanian stock, and Second Baseman Benny McCoy, from Jenison, Mich. And Schoolboy Rowe, his arm still aching, pitched in only 4 games in the spring. On June 2, he was sent to Beaumont to take advantage of the Texas sun. There he won 12 out of 14 games, and was recalled in the fall.

5

Following the dismissal of Mickey Cochrane as manager and vice-president, John A. "Jack" Zeller, another of the picturesque men of baseball, was advanced from his post of director of minor-league clubs to general manager. He ran the club during the next seven and a half years, and under his direction the Tigers climbed to fresh heights, especially in the important turnstile department. Walter Briggs's joy on winning the 1945 World's Championship was somewhat dampened by Zeller's resignation, which took effect January 1, 1946.

Bald as Frank Navin, Zeller is taller and chunkier than was the former ascetic-looking Tiger owner; in fact Jack was a pretty husky athlete in his day. His career in organized baseball was as varied as that of Ed Barrow, the early Detroit manager and later Yankee president. Jack has been a pitcher, manager, owner of a minor-league club at twenty-five, a lieutenant in World War I, a government auditor, an oil man, scout, minor-league chain director, and then head of baseball's biggest money-maker.

Shrewd, substantial, with a thorough knowledge of all the intricacies of baseball, he proved a valuable right bower for owner Briggs, even though Zeller's manipulation of Tiger material in the minors got him very much into the tousled hair of Judge Landis and cost the Detroit club around a hundred ball players. Though Zeller sold Frank Navin on a modified farm system, and felt it made the Tiger pennant winners of 1934 and 1935 possible, he later turned against it, and recommended its complete abolishment to baseball's Postwar Planning Committee.

Zeller was born in St. Louis, a town long famous for turning out good ball players. His father owned a bookstore there, and as a kid Jack used to browse through his dad's books and magazines. This early experience in the Zeller Book Shop was the foundation for his taste for substantial reading, and there have been few better-informed men in baseball than Jack Zeller.

However, Jack wasn't a bookworm when the baseball season was on. He was a left-handed pitcher and good enough to make the strong semi-pro clubs around St. Louis. On the strength of his showing in that company he was offered a contract by the Joplin, Mo., club in the old Missouri Valley League. That was in 1903, and Zeller still gets a chuckle out of his inaugural game. He shut out Sedalia by a score of 2 to 0.

After several innings, his catcher, a veteran named Lou Stoner, walked briskly to the mound and stormed: "I've been giving you signals, and you pay no attention to them. What the hell's the matter with you; don't you believe in signs?"

"The reason Stoner thought I didn't believe in signs was that I had only one delivery, a fast ball," laughed Jack, relating the incident. "I couldn't throw a curve."

Jack didn't follow up the shutout, for after several wild exhibitions the fast ball wasn't enough for him to get by and he was released. He next hooked on with Sedalia. But later he was forced out again when Sedalia signed Ed Reulbach, later the famous Cub star, under the name of Lawson. It was the same Reulbach who pitched against the Tigers in those early World's Series of 1907 and 1908.

Zeller next was employed by Leavenworth, Kansas, and he got a lot of satisfaction out of his next game against Sedalia. "Reulbach, alias Lawson, was pitching against me," he recalled, "and we had a furious ten-inning battle, and I was lucky to win it by a score of 6 to 5. The Leavenworth fans were so pleased that they showered me with nickels, dimes, and quarters. I raked in about $5 in small change; it came in handy, too, as the league blew up after another few weeks."

Jack turned east, and in 1904 pitched for Providence and Schenectady. He had a wealth of speed and still thinks he might have made his niche as a pitcher if he hadn't ruined his arm early in the season of 1905. "I was then with Haverhill in the New England League, and we had a mid-April exhibition game with Jersey City. The game was played in freezing temperature with snow flurries falling all afternoon. It lasted 12 innings, and finally was called on account of darkness with the score tied at 4-4. It looked like quite a feather in my cap holding off a strong International League club that long, but for the next month my arm was so sore I couldn't lift it over my shoulder. It practically killed my pitching."

Zeller then went into business in New York, and kept up the baseball touch by playing first base for the resort team at Bath Beach, L. I. But the real professional game was in his blood, and in 1908 he purchased half interest in the Springfield, Mass., club in the New England League. It made him the youngest club owner in the nation. Later, he was president, secretary, manager, and ticket taker of Pittsfield in the same league.

In World War I he failed to pass his final examinations at the Officers' Training Camp at Fort Benjamin Harrison, at Indianapolis, so he earned his shoulder bars the hard way. He enlisted as a buck private in the regular army and when the war ended he was a second lieutenant and instructor in musketry and bayonet work at Camp Lee, Va.

After the war, the young St. Louisan became interested in the oil game of the southwest. But he still liked to keep that feel for baseball. Paul LaGrave, the business manager of the Fort Worth club, told him: "While you're going around signing up oil leases, if you see any players that are worth bringing in, we'd like to know about it." It wasn't long before Jack was a full-time scout. And apparently Zeller brought something in that was worth while, as Fort Worth had amazing success in the postwar years, winning seven straight Texas League championships from 1919 to 1926.

The Detroit club then had a working agreement with Fort Worth;

that brought Jack in early contact with Frank Navin, and Navin liked the way Zeller did business. "I like Zeller because he can say no, and mean no," Navin once said. "You can find so many yes men in this business."

Navin suspected some of his scouts weren't entirely disinterested in their recommendations. He made no direct accusations, but felt several of his men were recommending players, often so-called "humpty-dumpties," and were getting a cut of the purchase money. So in 1926, he reorganized his scout machinery and put Jack Zeller in charge. From there on, Jack's stock rose steadily in the Tigers organization until he ran the whole works for Briggs.

6

In 1939, Baker's first year at the helm, the Tigers fell back to fifth, though with a respectable percentage of .526. But it was the first second-division season since the five years of Harris. Gehringer was out of the line-up a good part of the time with injuries, playing in only 118 games, but that gave young McCoy a chance to show off his stuff. Greenberg also missed 17 games, and fell off 25 in his home-run production—from 58 to 33. Barney McCosky was coming fast in center field and as lead-off man; he hit .311 and scored 120 runs.

The club still was trying to find a place for Rudy York, as Birdie Tebbetts, catching 100 games and improving by the game, pushed the big fellow from behind the plate. Still Rudy got into 102 games and hit .307. The club propped up the 1938 third-base hole by obtaining Pinky Higgins from the Red Sox. Zeller swapped Pitcher Auker and Jake Wade and Outfielder Chet Morgan to Boston for Higgins and Southpaw Pitcher Archie McKain. But, with the third-base gap plugged, a new weakness developed next door at short, where Billy Rogell no longer was showing his former skill. Baker staged a season-long parade of shortstops, Rogell, Mark Christman, Don Heffner, Ralph Kress, Frank Croucher, and Ben McCoy.

Still anxious to get that extra winning pitcher, the Tigers started feelers for the colorful and conversational Louis Norman "Buck" Newsom, then of the Browns, during the winter meetings of 1938-39. The picturesque pitcher, a resident of Hartsville, S. C., usually referred to himself as "ol' Bobo." Newsom already had been with the Dodgers, Cubs, Senators, Red Sox, and had put in an earlier term in St. Louis.

The Browns didn't want to get rid of Bobo at the time, but he ran into a spring disagreement with his manager, Fred Haney—the former Tiger third baseman. In a game with the Yankees on May 11, the Yankees were giving the Browns quite a shellacking, but St. Louis staged a rally and brought the score up to 9 to 8. Bill Trotter was in the bull pen, but with the game almost tied, Bobo marched out to the pen on his own, took off his windbreaker, and began limbering up his powerful right arm.

Needing a new pitcher because he had used a pinch hitter, Haney motioned to the bull pen and called in Trotter. This annoyed the crowd. A bunch of knotholers took up the cry: "We want Newsom," and the older fans joined in. St. Louis lost the game, and the fans pitched into Haney.

"Who told you to go to the bull pen to warm up?" Haney demanded of Newsom. "Nobody," said Bobo; "I went myself, in case you would need me."

"Well, I'm giving orders around here," snapped Haney. "When I want you to go to the bull pen after this, I'll tell you."

Now, Buck isn't a timid, backward soul. He talked back in kind, and soon a barrage of blistering adjectives passed between the Browns' pitching ace and his manager. Reports then circulated in St. Louis that Bobo's Brown days were numbered. The story got to Detroit, and two days later—on a Saturday morning—Jack Zeller was closeted with Bill DeWitt, the Browns' general manager, at Sportsman's Park. They sparred all morning, all through the afternoon game in which Newsom beat Vern Kennedy, 5 to 3, for his third 1939 victory, and well into the night. When the session finally broke up, the pair announced one of the biggest player deals of all time, involving ten men. Jack gave up six players, Pitchers Vern Kennedy, Bob Harris, Roxy Lawson, and George Gill, Infielder Mark Christman, and Outfielder Chet Laabs for Pitchers Buck Newsom and Jim Walkup, Outfielder Roy Bell, and Shortstop Ralph Kress. Old Bobo, enjoying a fine season, won 20 games and lost 11, while the unlucky Kennedy won only 9 between the two clubs and lost 20.

Tommy Bridges had another fine season, winning 17 games and losing 7; Rowe, back from Beaumont, staggered through to 10 victories while losing 12, and Al Benton, an Athletic discard, won 6 games and lost 8 as a relief man. Another character, Paul "Dizzy" Trout, who had been a bear cat with Beaumont in '38, won 9 games and lost 10, and in September, Del Baker took the blanket off a tall young left-hander, Harold Newhouser, a product of Detroit's own Wilbur Wright Prep School. He was brought in by Wish Egan. At the age of 18, this remarkable lad pitched for Alexandria in the class D Evangeline League, Beaumont in the Class A-1 Texas League, and Detroit in the majors, all in one season.

⊗ XXIII ⊗

THE UNKNOWN GIEBELL
BEATS FELLER

I

O N JANUARY 14, 1940, THE TIGERS RECEIVED THE STIFFEST FI-
nancial wallop in their history. It would have ruined Navin's
early club. In 1938, Judge Landis had socked Branch Rickey, former
Cardinal farm operator, hard, freeing some 80 of his players, including Skeeter Webb and Pete Reiser. Now, he bore down with
even greater severity on the Tigers in a lengthy decision involving
106 players. He made free agents of 91 of them, and ordered the
Tiger treasury to pay 15 others sums totaling $47,250.

Toledo, Fort Worth, Beaumont, and nine other minor-league
clubs were involved. The Judge slapped fines of $500 each on the
Cubs and Browns for dickering with Ben McCoy and Roy Cullenbine, respectively, before they were officially freed. The Detroit
club was not otherwise punished, but there were continuous references to illegal operations (according to Organized Baseball law)
by Jack Zeller and Cecil Coombs, business manager of the Fort
Worth club. The Judge said Zeller had failed to heed repeated
warnings, that "ineligible penalties would not be imposed in this
instance," but he served an emphatic warning that similar leniency
would not be given in the future. Zeller supposedly was guilty of
wholesale "cover-ups," "fake" transfers of contracts, and "gentlemen's agreements."

In a statement in Detroit, Jack Zeller absolved Owner Briggs of
any blame or responsibility, and took it all on his broad shoulders,
saying "the handling of all minor-league affiliations was my job and
Mr. Briggs did not attempt to familiarize himself in any way with
those operations." A spokesman for the club said Landis' decision
gave the club a terrific jolt and that it would take five years again
to build up its farm organization.

The top players set free were McCoy and Outfielder Cullenbine,

241

the latter a former Detroit sand-lotter. The previous December, Zeller had traded McCoy and Pitcher George Coffman to the Athletics for Outfielder Wally Moses. This deal was canceled by Landis. McCoy then sold his services to Connie Mack for $45,000, and Cullenbine got a $25,000 check from Larry MacPhail, then head man in Brooklyn. However, the Tigers did get a break as Landis did not include Pitcher Dizzy Trout, admittedly a border-line case, and Rudy York, who had been through a lot of minor league machinations.

With the Yankees winning their fourth straight World's Championship in 1939, and good enough to go through the Series of 1938 and '39 without defeat, McCarthy's powerful Bronx Bombers were pretty much the proud cocks of the baseball walk. After Landis handed the Detroit club that January clip to the chin, who then would have had the audacity to believe the 1940 Tigers would be the American League representatives, rather than the Yankees, in the World's Series that fall? But strange things happen in baseball, and many happened that year. In a red-hot finish, the Tigers finished a game ahead of the second-place Indians, and Cleveland, in turn, came in a game in front of New York. The Tigers' winning percentage of .584 was a new low for the American League; Baker's team suffered one more defeat than Jennings' champions of 1908.

Many factors contributed to that pennant, but perhaps the most important was the noble experiment of converting Hank Greenberg into a left fielder so that a place could be made for Rudy York at first base. Greenberg was called to Detroit for a winter conference, and Zeller asked: "How would you like to try the outfield next season, Hank?"

"Do you want to get me killed?" asked the New Yorker.

"No, and I think you'll like it out there," continued Jack. "What's more we'll make it worth your while. We'll make it $10,000 more, if you agree to try the outfield." That jacked Greenberg's salary from $40,000 to $50,000, and it was an argument worth while. He became the left fielder, and the move worked beautifully. Hank, who batted .340 and hit 41 homers, was high man in the league for driving in runs with 150, and big Rudy was runner-up with 134. He hit .316 and bagged 33 homers.

Then Zeller made an interleague deal with the Cubs whereby he traded away Billy Rogell for the veteran National League shortstop, Dick Bartell. Rowdy Richard, a most emphatic person and a ball player of the Jennings-McGraw school, stepped on a few Tiger corns but helped inspire the Jungleers for that one season.

There were other brilliant contributions to the 1940 pennant. Barney McCosky, the local pride, hit .340 and was a standout center fielder. Birdie Tebbetts, with his squeaky voice, moved into the front ranks of the game's catchers and hit .296. Gehringer already was having attacks of lumbago, but had his last .300 batting year. After Landis nixed the Wally Moses deal, Zeller procured another outfielder, the courageous Bruce Campbell, in a deal with Cleveland for Roy Bell. Campbell is the lad who fought back after two attacks of meningitis. Bruce enjoyed a fine season, and was especially good in the 1940 World's Series.

However, Baker couldn't have won but for the fine work of his pitching staff, especially Newsom. Buck was magnificent that year; it was his season of seasons. Even though he was out for three weeks with a broken thumb, he won 21 games and lost only 5. He led the league's regular pitchers in winning percentage and trailed only Feller in earned runs. After losing his opening game to the Browns, Newsom ran off 13 in a row before the Athletics tripped him in 11 innings, July 28.

Schoolboy Rowe staged a spectacular one-year comeback, winning 16 games and losing only three, and Tommy Bridges had a commendable 12-9 season. Both Benton and the left-hander McKain did swell jobs in relief; the latter was credited with five victories and no defeats. Newhouser, now 19, broke even in 18 games; Gorsica divided 14, while big Trout had difficulty, winning only 3, while losing 7. A disappointment was Freddy Hutchinson, a big 210-pound former schoolboy from Seattle. After "Hutch" won 25 out of 32 games for the 1938 Seattle club, the Tigers went up to $50,000 to outbid the Yankees and other clubs for the Coast's "wonder boy." In 1939, Zeller had Freddy in Toledo. Baker tried to use him as a Tiger regular, but after he won only 3 games out of 10, he was sent to O'Neill in Buffalo to see whether Steve could straighten him out. And in late September, Steve sent the Tigers a young right-hander, Floyd Giebell, who soon was to write history.

For a good part of the season, it looked like Cleveland's pennant. However, it was the year of the famous "Cry Baby" revolt in the Ohio wigwam, when the Indians petitioned their boss, Alva Bradley, to fire their manager, Ossie Vitt, the old Tiger third baseman. That happened in June, and contributed as much to Detroit's pennant as Greenberg's homers and Bobo's pitching.

The Indians were pacemakers most of the season, but the Tigers never were far away and grabbed the top rung September 19, to hold it to the end. The Tigers went a long way toward clinching their sixth flag by winning two out of three in a hectic series with Cleveland at Briggs Stadium, September 20, 21, and 22. After Detroit took a nip-and-tuck opener, 6 to 5, Rowe pitched a 5-0 shutout. Before a capacity Sunday crowd, the Indians then shot hell out of almost Baker's entire staff to win, 10 to 5.

The Yankees, after a lame start, threatened to put on a Garrison finish; they had taken the lead for a few hours, September 12, and were right on the necks of the two western clubs.

The race finally hinged on the final three-game series between the Tigers and Indians in Cleveland, September 27, 28, and 29. But Baker was in the driver's seat; he was two games ahead, and if he won one of the three he was in. And who was picked to face the great Bobbie Feller in the first game of this crucial series? None other than young Floyd Giebell, the rookie from Buffalo. O'Neill had suggested it to Baker. "That kid's hot, and I think he can beat those fellows," Steve said. Del talked it over with Greenberg and Gehringer; they approved, and Baker decided on the spectacular gamble.

The Cleveland fans could scarcely believe their eyes when they saw Giebell start warming up against Bobbie. A sports-writing contingent which attended the game in World's Series numbers also blinked, and asked: "What goes?" It was like the time Connie Mack sprang Howard Ehmke, who had pitched only 55 innings all year, for the opening game of the 1929 Athletic-Cub World's Series. And Baker's noble experiment worked as beautifully as did Connie's. Feller held the Tigers to only three hits, but one was Rudy York's thirty-third home run with Gehringer on base in the fourth inning. And that was all that was necessary; Giebell was prodded for six hits, but gave up no runs, and Detroit won, 2 to 0.

That was the pennant, and the Tigers celebrated so lavishly with champagne that they lost the remaining two games of the series, Gorsica losing 2 to 1, and Trout, Newhouser, and Hutchinson dropping the season's final game, 3 to 2, in 14 innings. That displeased the Yankees, and deprived them of second money. But no one in Detroit cared a rap, and to the Tigers they were just ball games; everybody was pennant-slap-happy, and bothered little about the New York peeve. And Detroit's attendance that season reached a new high—1,112,693.

2

The club which the Tigers met in the 1940 World's Series was the Cincinnati Reds, manhandled four straight by the Yankees the

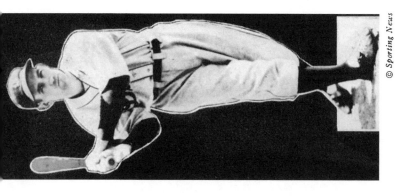

Charlie Gehringer

Tommy Bridges

Mrs. Walter O. Briggs, Sr., Walter O. (Spike) Briggs, Jr., and Walter O. Briggs, S

autumn before. The Tigers, and their fans, looked for no such cleanup, but everyone in Detroit was confident of victory. Perhaps there was an inclination to underrate McKechnie's National Leaguers. "It's the same team that couldn't win one from the Yankees; we beat out McCarthy; so how can we lose to the Reds?" was typical of the reasoning in the Tiger lair. Baker did his best to discourage it. "You don't win games on what the Yankees did in 1939; you've got to win those games out there on the ball field," was his caustic observation.

McKechnie had a more experienced club in 1940 than he had the year before; he had two pitching aces in Bucky Walters and Paul Derringer, and while the Reds didn't have the wallop of the Tigers, they knew the trick of scoring runs.

Greenberg, Bruce Campbell, Pinky Higgins, and Barney McCosky carried the Tiger punch; all hit over .300. Bruce rose to unexpected heights, and was a Detroit threat all through the Series. Gehringer, who wasn't in good physical condition, hit only .214. And where Jimmy Wilson, drafted from a semi-coaching role to do most of McKechnie's catching, was the Cincinnati star, Baker suffered from an anemic punch in his catching position. Birdie Tebbetts failed to get 1 safety in 11 tries; Billy Sullivan produced only 2 singles in 13 times at bat. A dangerous guy on the Reds was the former American Leaguer, Third Baseman Billy Werber, who was the batting leader of both teams and tied Greenberg for most hits, ten.

"You'll take the first one, Bobo," Baker told Newsom on the eve of the first game, which was scheduled for Cincinnati, October 2.

"Who else but me would start?" was Buck's modest observation.

That first game in Cincinnati left a stunned and saddened 31,793 crowd in Redland Park, but it sounded awfully good as it came in over the ether waves to Tiger fans in Michigan. In fact, it was the only time in seven Series that the Tigers drew first blood. It was a picnic for Bobo; the boys got him five runs in the second inning and he coasted home to an easy 7 to 2 win.

Paul Derringer, Newsom's opponent, started the game with a poor World's Series record behind him, no victories and three defeats, and by the second inning a fourth defeat was tacked on the escutcheon of the six-foot four-inch Kentuckian. "Ain't we got fun" was the Tiger battle cry of that happy round. Almost every one was hitting Oom Paul's first pitch, and they were going safe.

Greenberg plunked a first pitch over Werber's head for a single, and York singled solidly to right center. Campbell tapped a sacrifice bunt down to Werber, and the Tiger had a full house with nobody out when Billy's hurried throw pulled Joost, covering the bag, off first base. The merry-go-round continued when Higgins slapped the first pitch to center, scoring Hank and Rudy. Then Sullivan walked, filling 'em up again, and still with none out! Newsom bounced to McCormick, and they finally got Campbell on a force play at the plate. But that was merely a lull in the storm as Bartell stabbed a hot single to center, bringing in Higgins and Sullivan, and a whistling single by McCosky fetched in old Bobo. By this time McKechnie concluded he had seen enough of Derringer's pitching for one afternoon; he summoned blond Lloyd Moore, who got rid of Gehringer on an infield fly, and Greenberg, who started it all, rolled to Werber for the third out.

The joyful celebration which followed Bobo's victory was followed with quick tragedy. His father, Henry Louis Newsom, and other members of the family, had come up from Hartsville, S. C., to see Buck in his first World's Series. The excitement was too much for the father, who died of a heart attack at Cincinnati's Netherlands Plaza the night after the game.

3

From 10 robust hits for 15 bases in the first game, the Tigers subsided to 3 for 5 bases in the second game, played in Cincinnati, October 3. After the first inning, Bucky Walters, the converted infielder, shackled the Tigers. Back in 1933-34, Walters was a second-string infielder on the Red Sox and was permitted to pass out of the American League for the waiver price.

Bucky got off to a jittery start, and the Tigers put over two easy runs in the first. But that wasn't enough, and Detroit lost by a score of 5 to 3. Perhaps having a little attack of World's Series buck fever, Walters walked the first two men who faced him, Bartell and McCosky, and Gehringer followed with a single which scored Dick and sent Barney to third. Greenberg slapped into a double play, on which McCosky scored, but then Detroit's attack fizzled out to two doubles. One by Greenberg in the sixth drove in Gehringer with the third Tiger run, giving the Felines three counters for as many hits.

Schoolboy Rowe's 1940 rejuvenation in the American League did not follow him into the World's Series, and his two failures contributed much to Detroit's ultimate defeat. The Arkansan was the pitcher Baker picked to oppose Walters, and the Schoolboy quickly frittered away his early lead, the Reds reaching him for a pair of runs in each the second and third innings and driving him out with a fifth run in the fourth. And then what hurt especially was Johnny Gorsica's relief pitching. In four and two-thirds innings, the Jersey Pole gave up only one hit. Every one in the Tiger camp was asking: "What if Johnny had started?"

If that game was sad radio music for the fans•back in Detroit, it was like a gift from the gods for Ford Frick and his National League cohorts. For them the sun shone again. It was the first victory for the old league since Carl Hubbell, the one time Tiger farm hand, won the lone Giant victory from the Yankees in the 1937 Series.

The parade moved to Detroit for the third game, October 4, and it was a joyful afternoon for an assembled crowd of 52,877. It was the first time a World's Series crowd went over 50,000 in any town other than New York, but the Briggs Stadium turnstiles hit 55,189 before the Series was over. Tommy Bridges, the little hero of former Tiger World's Series wars, took care of this one. The Reds bit into his curve for 10 hits, but the Tigers, too, wore their hitting clothes and clipped three of McKechnie's hurlers for 13 robust blows, including socks into the stands by York and Higgins. Tommy's starting opponent was a fellow Tennessean, Jim Turner, the milkman from Antioch, and in recent years relief pitcher for the Yankees. The two Tennessee veterans really had quite a battle for six innings, as the score was 1-1 before the Tigers exploded a four-run bomb in the seventh and a smaller one of two tallies in the eighth, winning by 7 to 4.

When the Tigers suddenly snapped out of their lethargy, and attacked° the milkman in the seventh, that was something to see. They certainly gave him the old One! Two!!! punch. Greenberg opened the frame by smashing a hard single to center. York followed by whistling a homer deep into the lower left-field stands. The fans seemed so pleased with this demonstration of power that the next two batsmen, Campbell and Higgins, put on an encore. Bruce lined a single to left, and then Pinky went Rudy a little better, he sent the first pitch into the upstairs left-field stands for a second homer.

Lloyd Moore then came in and put out the fire. He quickly retired for a pinch hitter, and the Tigers staged a two-run scoring bee at the expense of Joe Beggs. Greenberg greeted him with a triple to deep center. This time Rudy watch a third strike go by, but Campbell singled home Greenberg, and Bruce scored when Pinky dropped a double just inside the left-field foul line.

With a two to one edge, Del Baker decided to take a big gamble and pitch Dizzy Trout in the fourth game, October 5, despite the garrulous Hoosier's lowly 3-7 record in the league season. No doubt Del tried to pull another one out of the hat as he had when he pitched Floyd Giebell against Feller in the pennant-clinching game. Floyd would have worked that day, but he was ineligible, having joined in September, just as Donie Bush was kept out of the 1908 Series.

Many thought that Baker should have pitched Newsom, and tried to get that big three-to-one jump, a margin which only one club, the 1925 Pirates, had ever overcome in a seven-game Series. Buck was willing; he said he would pitch that next one for his father, and everyone knew his next game would be a classic. "But, if I had lost with Newsom, where would I have been?" Del said after the game. "Trout showed me stuff in a late-season game that could have beaten any team in baseball."

Besides, up to that time, Derringer was not regarded highly by American Leaguers as a World's Series opponent. The attitude was: "That's one guy we always can lick." However, there is a turning in every lane, and there was a turning in big Oom Paul's lane of World's Series defeats. Encouraged by his team getting to Trout for two first-inning runs, he held the Tigers to five hits, and posted his first blue-ribbon victory, 5 to 2.

Trout suffered a wobbly first inning. He walked Werber, who was always getting on, and Mike McCormick, who forced Billy, scored when Goodman hit the first pitch to the left-field corner for a long double. Ival reached third on an out, and scampered home when Ripple's grounder went through Higgins like a greased pig. Singles by Goodman and Frank McCormick, and a double by Ripple produced another Cincinnati run in the third and knocked out the dizzy one, with the Reds picking up additional markers in the fourth and eighth innings.

With the Series tied at two-all, Baker, of course, pitched Newsom in the fifth game, and Bobo's "game for his dad" was all that he said it would be. Detroit's greatest crowd up to that time was out, and it enjoyed a great show. Bobo's mates soon made it easy for him, but he never ceased bearing down and pitched a three-hit shutout as the Tigers won easily, 8 to 0.

McKechnie threw in four pitchers, Thompson, Moore, Vander Meer, and Hutchings, and for Tiger fans most of the fun was wrapped into the third and fourth innings, when seven of the Jungleers dug their claws into the plate. McCosky opened the third with a single to center, and Gehringer lined another to right. With this setting Hank Greenberg lined a tremendous homer deep into the upper left-field stands.

Thompson got the next three men, and McKechnie permitted Junior to start the fourth. But the Tiger run appetite still was ravenous, and they scored four more in this inning, helped by the wildness of the Red pitchers, who almost gave away their club's pass book. Sullivan walked, moved up a peg on Bobo's sacrifice, and scored when Bartell doubled down the left-field foul line. Dick took third on a passed ball, and then the generous Thompson issued a pass to McCosky. McKechnie chased Thompson, and brought in Moore, whose first act was to keep up the base-on-balls parade by walking Gehringer. Mike McCormick pulled down another terrific drive by Hank in deep center, Bartell scoring. A pass to York loaded the bags again, and Campbell's single through the box brought in McCosky and Gehringer.

5

Following Newsom's second victory in Briggs Stadium, the scene shifted back to Redland Field for a sixth game, October 7. The situation was exactly the same as when the Tigers had the Cardinals three games to two, in 1934 and Cochrane sent in Schoolboy Rowe to put the clincher on the old Gas-House Gang. Again the Schoolboy was sent after this vital game, but this time lasted only a third of an inning. For a second time Gorsica did a fine rescue job, and many wondered why he hadn't started, but it didn't really matter as Bucky Walters threw a five-hit shutout to tie the Series for the Reds for a third time.

For such an important game, Rowe's effort was sad. He pitched a nothing ball, and the Reds were quick to learn it. He faced five batters; four hit him safely, and his only out was in fielding a sacrifice bunt. Werber's opening blast was a double off the left-field wall, and Mike McCormick's sacrifice shoved Billy along to third. Goodman then followed with a bouncer to York, which went for an infield hit when the confused Rowe neglected to cover first base. That tallied Werber. Sharp singles by Frank McCormick and Ripple scored Goodman. Gorsica took over at this stage and checked the Reds when he fanned Jimmy Wilson and Higgins made a fine one-handed stop of Joost's hard smash. But, with the game Walters had under his belt, the Tigers already were dead ducks.

6

When the Tigers went down to seventh-game defeats in 1909 and 1934, they were routed by top-heavy scores of 8 to 0 and 11 to 0. This time they were eliminated in an epic 2-to-1 struggle, a defeat which stuck like a burr in the throats of the Baker men and their loyal fan contingent. It made a gala holiday for Cincinnati, but that was only additional wormwood for the rooters back in Michigan.

There was no day off to sell tickets, and the seventh game was played in Redland, October 8, giving Buck Newsom only one full day of rest after pitching the fifth-game shutout. But the players would have shot Del had he pitched any one else. Bobo was as good as ever, but Derringer, encouraged by his victory over Trout, also served up a classic. Each pitcher yielded only seven hits, but where Newsom struck out six and walked only one, Derringer fanned only one Tiger and walked three. But the breaks were with the big Kentuckian.

Most of the action of the vital game was crowded into the two scoring innings. The Tigers drew first blood, scoring their run in the third without getting a ball out of the infield. Billy Sullivan opened with an infield hit to McCormick. Frank knocked it down, but got the ball too late to Derringer, covering first base. Newsom cleverly sacrificed Billy to second, but Bartell expired on a high infield fly. McCosky drew a pass. Gehringer followed with a hot sizzler to Werber, who knocked it down, but his low throw bounced about ten feet away from McCormick. Sullivan never stopped running, and slid safely into the plate before Frank could get the ball to Wilson. In the meantime, McCosky pulled up at third and Charley at second. It was a wonderful opportunity for big Hank, who singled twice in this game. But this time he churned the Ohio atmosphere for Derringer's only strike-out.

It looked as though this run might stand up, especially as Bobo permitted only four Reds to reach base in the first six innings. Then the Cincinnati burghers stood up for their seventh-inning stretch, and it was, indeed, the "Lucky Seventh" for the McKechnie band. The Reds scored two runs, for the ball game, and the Series.

Frank McCormick led off with a double to the left-field wall, and Jim Ripple followed with another two-bagger to the top of the right-field screen, which became the most discussed play of the Series.

McCormick wasn't sure whether Campbell would make the catch and hesitated between third and second. As a consequence, he was considerably delayed on his journey to the plate. Shortstop Bartell took the throw from the outfield behind second base, and had his back to the plate. Despite the fact that there was a fairly good chance of cutting down McCormick at the plate, Dickie never let go of the ball, and the big Red first sacker scored the tying run unmolested. With the noise of the partisan crowd deafening him, Bartell didn't hear the yells of his fellow players to throw home. Somehow something else also got jumbled up, as Gehringer should have handled the cut-off for a play at the plate. Motion pictures of the game didn't make Dickie look any better. He had a real chance to shoot down McCormick had he pegged home the moment he got the ball.

However, the worst was still to come. Wilson's sacrifice advanced Ripple to third. McKechnie sent up Lombardi, who had a bad leg, to hit for Joost, and Baker, fearing a long fly, ordered a walk for the big California Italian. That brought up Billy Myers, a .130 hitter in the Series. And then the Red shortstop did just what Baker feared Lombardi might do, hit that long fly to the outfield. The count was three balls and one strike on Myers, when Bobo looked over to the Tiger bench for instructions. Baker gave none, and Bobo was on his own. He tried a fast ball, but Myers met it solidly and chased McCosky back to the center-field fence for his long hoist. Ripple jogged home after the catch with the all-important run.

There was little fight in the Tigers after that. Gehringer opened the Tiger eighth with a sharp single, but never left first, and in the ninth Derringer blew down Higgins, Sullivan, and pinch hitter Averill in order. The individual Tiger checks were $3,531.81, but no unhappier bunch of players ever trudged wearily into a clubhouse than did the Felines after McCormick snatched up Earl's grounder.

The spoils of that series, even though four games were played in one of the smallest parks in the majors, set a new record of $1,322,-328.21. The big dough came from those three games at Briggs Stadium—$665,056. Quite a difference from the $94,975, the total receipts of the five game Tiger-Cub Series of 1908!

⊜ XXIV ⊜

BRIGGS WINS A POKER GAME
FOR ROOKIE WAKEFIELD

I

THE FINISHES OF THE THREE SEASONS WHICH FOLLOWED THE PEN-
nant of 1940 were as similar as three peas in a pod. In 1941,
the Tigers were fifth in Cleveland and fourth in Detroit. The two
clubs finished in a tie, with 75 victories and 79 defeats. In 1942, the
Felines were fifth everywhere; they won 73 games and lost 81, the
team winding up two games behind the fourth-place Indians. And
even though the '43 club won two more games than it lost for a .506
percentage, it again was fifth, the Indians and White Sox beating out
the Tigers for spots in the lower rungs of the first division.

The period saw three years of player losses to the services, and
the efforts of Jack Zeller to replace his stars and present some kind
of a worthy Detroit front. Even before the nation officially went to
war, the Tigers lost their big Greenberg home-run gun in 1941. Being
a healthy thirty-year-old bachelor when Congress put in the prewar draft, tall Hank was one of the first big-leaguers drafted by
Uncle Sam. After playing only 19 early Tiger games, his Uncle
beckoned May 7, and asked Hank to give up his $55,000 Tiger
salary for a $50 a month job. Greenberg was discharged, December
5, under a law releasing men over 28, but Pearl Harbor came two
days afterwards and he was in again.

However, the 1941 prewar season was eventful for several most
interesting events. Owner Briggs played a stiff poker game, table
stakes, with the other opulent big-league owners, and won Dick
Wakefield, then an undergraduate at Michigan. Dick had reported
to Coach Ray Fisher, the former Yankee, as a catcher, but Ray soon
switched him to the outfield. The boy's father, the late Howard J.
Wakefield, was a journeyman catcher with Washington and Cleveland, but scouts recognized the son as the best college prospect since
George Sisler attended Michigan. Eleven scouts were on his trail at

one time, and once Cy Slapnicka of Cleveland almost snared him for $40,000, but Detroit matched that offer. Then it went up to $45,000 and finally Briggs won the prize for $52,000, throwing in a custom-made automobile, with all trimmings, to bind the bargain. Mrs. Howard Wakefield, the boy's mother, conducted most of the negotiations, and signed a contract with the elder Briggs in late June. The boy wasn't quite ready, needed brushing up on his fielding, and was sent to Winston-Salem.

Del Baker managed no World's Series club that year, but he had the distinction of leading the American League Stars to the most dramatic victory in the 12 All-Star games. And did it right in his own Detroit orchard, July 8, before a capacity Briggs Stadium crowd of 54,674 rabid partisan American League rooters. Thanks to a pair of homers by the then Pirate, Arky Vaughan, the National League went into the ninth inning leading by 5 to 3. With one run in, two out in the ninth, and the Yankee Joes—DiMaggio and Gordon—on base, the clubbing Red Sox slugger, Ted Williams, toted his piece of lumber to the plate. The National League pitcher was Claude Passeau, who was to give Detroit fans an awful headache four years later. Ted promptly saw a pitch he liked and a shining white streak sped on its way to the upper right-field stand. It was a homer from the moment it left the bat, and left Detroit as happy as after a World's Series victory.

After Dick Bartell had played only five spring games in 1941, he was unconditionally released. "Bartell rode his fellow players pretty hard in 1940, but we were winning then and they didn't mind," said Jack Zeller. "But in 1941, they resented it, and his nagging got under their skins. Baker never cared much for Dick, so we let him go." Frank Croucher played most of the season at shortstop. It also was a season in which Gehringer, tied up with lumbago, dropped to .220 in his hitting. Steve O'Neill was Tiger coach that year, and another Irisher, Pat Mullin, an outfielder, showed unquestionable promise, hitting .345 for 54 games before he met with a serious injury. It was the old story of putting that Tiger uniform on an outfielder and coming up with a .300 hitter.

The winter before Buck Newsom had been given a substantial raise, and owners Briggs and Bradley of Cleveland had a friendly hot-stove controversy whether Bobo or Bob Feller of the Indians was the highest-salaried pitcher in baseball. Buck's stipend was over $30,000. But he now suffered a bad season, winning only 12 games while losing 20, while he had a terrible earned run record of 4.61. Benton had the best record on the staff (15-6), Rowe's arm went bad again, while Trout and Newhouser remained around .500. Giebell proved a flop after that brilliant 1940 finish, but in the fall Baker came up with a new pitching sensation, Virgil "Fire" Trucks, who in 1938 had been termed the minor-leaguer of the year for striking out 418 batsmen in 38 games while pitching for Andalusia in the Alabama-Florida League.

2

After the nation went to war, Walter Briggs was in doubt for a spell whether baseball could continue. Realizing the tremendous job which the automobile industry would have to get out war vehicles, he announced he would give his full time to his bigger business. The same went for son, Spike, who later went into the Army. Practically the full business of the ball club was turned over to Jack Zeller.

Recognizing the need of a new second baseman for the 1942 season, he traded Shortstop Croucher and Outfielder Bruce Campbell to the Senators for Second Baseman Jimmy Bloodworth and Outfielder Roger "Doc" Cramer, a good swap for Detroit. That season Zeller had Steve O'Neill in Beaumont, where he could supervise the development of young Wakefield.

Pitchers Buck Newsom and Gorsica were determined holdouts that spring, the latter even taking his troubles with Zeller to Judge Landis. Bobo, however, was more vociferous; he had been cut around $20,000, and that really was an amputation. He yelled bloody murder in his home in Hartsville, and asked to be traded. Eventually he bobbed up at the Tigers' Lakeland camp late in March, supposedly ready to sign. But the holdout war broke out all over again, and on March 31, just before the club broke camp, Zeller sold him to Clark Griffith of Washington.

After Schoolboy Rowe pitched in two ineffective April games, the club finally gave up on the tall Arkansan and sold him to the Brooklyn Nationals. Al Benton pitched five brilliant innings in the All-Star game in New York, giving up one run and four hits, but then couldn't win in the American League, winning only 7 games and losing 13, but big Virgil Trucks was an immediate success, winning 12 games and losing 8 in his first complete year.

In 1943 there was another managerial shift, and Steve O'Neill was in charge of the Tigers. Baker had done a good job as Cochrane's successor, was a handy man around pitchers, but lacked fire. Steve, formerly a great catcher with the Indians and an ex-Cleveland manager, was the third Tiger manager from the Pennsylvania anthracite country. He came from the same northeastern corner which produced Jennings and Harris. He was born in the little coal town of Minooka, Pa., which produced five big-leaguers, the four O'Neills—Jack, Mike, Steve, and Jim—and Mike McNally. As Tiger coach and farm-club manager, Steve had been groomed for the post by Zeller for several years. O'Neill was another interesting, aggressive, colorful baseball personality, and a shrewd baseball tactician.

By the 1943 season, the war had cut fairly heavily into the Tiger ranks. In addition to Greenberg, the services took Barney McCosky, Pat Mullin, Birdie Tebbetts, Charley Gehringer, Al Benton, Freddy Hutchinson, Johnny Lipon and some lesser lights. Cramer now filled in for McCosky in center field, and Zeller made a smart transaction when he obtained the veteran minor-league catcher-manager, Paul Richards, from the Atlanta club. He formerly had caught with the Giants and Athletics, and, though slowed by a leg injury, he proved a grand war replacement for Tebbetts, catching 100 games that year.

For Detroit fans the season was high-lighted by the grand battle waged by Dick Wakefield, brought up from Beaumont with O'Neill, to win the batting championship in his first complete season in the league. The major loops used a synthetic war pumpkin for a ball that year, and averages were down all along the line. After battling Luke Appling all season, Wakefield's last-week slump gave the veteran Chicago shortstop top honors, .328 to .316. However, Catcher Howie Wakefield's kid had the distinction of being the only American Leaguer with 200 hits. That was bustin' in like a Ty Cobb!

Hal Newhouser, the lanky left-hander, getting taller and faster, had a season much like Al Benton in 1942. Picked for the All-Star squad, he was McCarthy's "middle pitcher," and hurled three scoreless innings as the American Leaguers won, 5 to 3, in Shibe Park, Philadelphia. And then on top of that great showing, Hal proceeded to lose 9 straight immediately after the All-Star Game to finish with 17 defeats against only 8 wins.

However, Dizzy Trout came fast that year and more than took over Buck Newsom's old place on the staff as right-hand anchor man. Dizzy had a little of Dizzy Dean in his make-up; he still isn't tongue-tied nor a recluse, but he has the heart and build of a truly great pitcher. Pitching for a fifth-placer he tied Chandler of the champion Yankees for most victories, 20, and suffered 12 defeats. Trucks also showed further improvement, winning 16 and losing 10.

Uncle Sam bore down even harder on baseball in 1944, and the Tigers were one of the leading sufferers. Players called up included the new batting star, Wakefield; Second Baseman Jimmy Bloodworth; Outfielder Rip Radcliffe; Pitchers Virgil Trucks, Hal White, and even the 37-year-old Tommy Bridges. Again Jack Zeller had to scurry around for whatever material he could dig up. The Athletics released Second Baseman Eddie Mayo, a former National Leaguer with the Giants and Braves, to Louisville, but Jack put in an immediate draft for him and yanked Eddie back—and got himself the 1945 *Sporting News* most-valuable-player-award winner. Zeller was so short of outfielders that he signed a 39-year-old Kansas semi-pro, Chuck Hostetler, who had a brief trial with the Braves as far back as 1928. But the venerable Chuck proved a handy pickup, hitting .298 for 90 games. An assortment of sprigs and 4-F's, such as Rufe Gentry, Stubby Overmire, Zeb Eaton, Roy Henshaw, and Forrest Orrell were added to the pitching staff.

The season started "pretty gosh awful," and what made it worse was that the Tigers were at their very worst before the home customers. While the St. Louis Browns got off to an American League record by winning their first 9 games, the Tigers were making a strange record for ineptitude at Briggs Stadium, losing 12 of their first 13 games played at home. The Tigers were faring a little better on the road, but Harry Salsinger wrote sadly: "For the first time in their long American League history, the Tigers are threatened with a tail-ender."

The club still was seventh at the time of the All-Star holiday in early July, but the field was so closely bunched that Detroit was only eight and a half games from the top and a half game from the bottom. Then the Tigers got a most unexpectedly good break. Dick Wakefield had been in Naval Aviation, taking the preflight course in Iowa City, when the Navy decided it had an abundance of pilots. Dick reported back to his Chicago draft board, applied for a Navy commission, and was given a 90-day leave while a decision was being reached as to his next move in Uncle Sam's forces. And what an eventful 90 days that was for the 1944 Tigers!

Just before the break in the schedule, July 9, the Tigers were beaten twice by the Yankees. The day Dick reported back to Steve, July 13, the Tigers socked the White Sox, 9 to 1, with Dick getting two singles in four attempts. The next day, the Tigers had to work harder to win, 2 to 0, for Stubby Overmire, with Wakefield getting a homer and single out of Detroit's scanty six hits. On the fifteenth, the Tigers lost the first game of a double-header to Dykes's team, but they bounced back to victory in the second game as a double, homer, and single flew from young Dick's bat. The Tigers woke up to the fact that they now had a red-hot bat in their line-up, and the entire morale of the team was uplifted. They won eight games out of nine, and from being a half step out of the coalhole they suddenly found themselves in the thick of the race. Dick never slackened in his pace. He was the league's nominal batting leader with .355 for 78 games; Boudreau, the accredited champion, hit .327 in 150 games. And before the 1944 Tigers were through, they missed the pennant by only an eyelash.

Yet, good as Dick was, his hitting couldn't have made contenders of the 1944 Tigers if it hadn't been for the superlative pitching of the talkative right-hander, Dizzy Trout, and the home-bred southpaw, Newhouser. Dizzy had arrived in 1943 and now Hal joined him in stardom. Not since Mathewson and McGinnity won 68 games for the 1904 champion Giants did two pitchers sparkle with such brilliance on one staff.

Trout won 27 games and lost 14; Dizzy had the league's lowest earned run average; he pitched the most innings, 352; the most complete games, 33; the most shutouts, 7; and was second only to Newhouser in strike-outs.

Though Hal had been recognized as one of the coming stars of baseball, he had been unlucky, hot-tempered, and couldn't win. In the combined seasons of 1940-41-42-43, he had won only 34 games and never went over 9. Now he almost matched that in one season, winning 29 and losing 9. He was second to Dizzy in earned runs and the strike-out king with 187. The veteran catcher, Richards, had much to do with Hal's improvement.

Prior to 1944, his main trouble had been control and his disposition. A heart murmur had kept him out of service, and he was a rather irascible kid in the clubhouse, especially when things were going badly—which they were most of the time. In the 1943 season, Steve O'Neill frequently talked to the boy like a Dutch uncle, told him to stop fighting himself, and at times was almost discouraged with the lad. But late in the season, Hal came to his manager of his own accord and said earnestly: "Steve, you've treated me marvelously and have been most patient with me. And in appreciation I won't let you down. I'm going to win for you next year." And how that boy made good on his promise!

From seventh on July 13, the Tigers drove upward through the standing as did George Stallings' miracle Braves of 30 years before. Thanks to their spring winning streak, the Browns held the lead most of the season, and had a seven-game advantage in August. The Yankees then were their nearest rival. However, St. Louis went into an acute slump; the Tigers kept moving up, and on September 10 they reached the top for the first time, but held the lead for only a few hours. For the next week, the Browns, Yanks, and Tigers jockeyed in and out of first place.

The Tigers then took the lead, September 17, winning a Sunday double-header from the Indians, while the White Sox held the Browns to an even break and the Athletics handed the Yankees a humiliating double drubbing. Detroit then held first place alone until September 25, the final Monday, when the Browns tied them as Nelson Potter blanked Boston while Russ Christopher of the A's nosed out the Tigers, 2 to 1. The tie lasted two days, as both leaders won their games of September 26. But Detroit again held sole occupancy of the front seat after the games of September 27, for Newhouser blanked the Athletics, 4 to 0, as the Browns, insisting on playing in the rain, lost to Boston, 4 to 1. Prior to this game the weakened Red Sox had dropped ten straight.

It then looked as though the pennant was in the bag for the Tigers. They led by one full game, and the schedule was all in their favor. They were winding up with a four-game series with the tail-end Senators, whereas the Browns were called upon to face the Yankees, who still had an outside pennant chance. How could the Tigers lose?

But, in war baseball anything could happen, and did. The eighth-place Senators held the Tigers to an even break, while those damn fool Browns, feeling the scent of World's Series kale in their nostrils, downed McCarthy's season-long contender four straight, giving the Brownies the flag by a single game.

Both the Tigers and Browns were rained out on the 28th, necessitating double-headers on Friday, the 29th. St. Louis got back to a tie this day, when the persistent Brownies won from New York, 4 to 1 and 1 to 0. On the same day, Gentry and Gorsica won the first game from Washington quite handily, 5 to 2, but the tail-enders quickly drubbed out the overworked Trout in the nightcap to win, 9 to 2.

Both clubs won on the final Saturday of the race, Newhouser winning his twenty-ninth game as he defeated the Senators, 7 to 3, and Denny Galehouse shut out the Yankees, 2 to 0. That left the two clubs tied on the morning of the final Sunday, October 1, and the American League had arranged for a tentative play-off game in Detroit, October 2, if the race ended in a tie. But there was no need of a play-off.

Even on the last day, the odds still favored Detroit. It didn't seem in the works for the Yankees to lose four straight to the Browns, nor were the Tigers likely to lose another to the tail-ender. But the fates were riding with the Brownies. Before a 45,565 crowd, Trout blew his second game of the series, losing to Emil Dutch Leonard, a right-hander, by a score of 4 to 1. Prior to the game, the Tigers had beaten Leonard seven straight times. On the morning of the game, a stranger called up Dutch at his hotel and told the pitcher he would get a present of $1500 if he lost the game. The guy who did the telephoning later admitted he was inebriated and did it as a rib. However, it only made Dutch fighting mad. He told his manager, Ossie Bluege, and then bore down all the harder. He gave up only four hits. The Senators wrecked Trout with a three-run blast in the fourth inning, when Stan Spence hit a homer with Kuhel on base.

The St. Louis-New York contest was only in the third inning, when the Tiger game was over. But many of the fans remained in Briggs Stadium—stayed to watch the scoreboard. The Yankees had gotten off to an early 2 to 0 lead by scoring a run on Jakucki in each the first and third inning. But, thereafter, the scoreboard news was equally bad. In the fourth inning, Chet Laabs, a Detroit boy and a former Tiger, tied the score by blasting a homer with Mike Kreevich on base. St. Louis semed to like this act so well that in the very next inning, the fifth, Chet belted a second round-tripper, again after a single by Kreevich. For good measure, Stephens hit an eighth inning St. Louis four-bagger, and the Browns won, 5 to 2. It gave the happy Browns their first pennant in 43 seasons, but left a lot of headaches in the Briggs Stadium clubhouse.

There was a disposition, in some circles, to be rather severe on Steve for his handling of pitchers in the last week. Some felt, after winning the first game of his September 28 double-header, he should have gambled with a lesser pitcher in the second game. That would have given Trout three days of rest—instead of two, for a Saturday game, and enabled the manager to close with Newhouser on the final Sunday. But Steve played the hand as he thought the cards were dealt him, tried to push his advantage, and anyway no one ever heard of Dizzy complaining of overwork when a pennant was at stake.

⊗ XXV ⊗

HANK BATS THE TIGERS
TO TWO TITLES

I

ESPITE THE RETURN OF DICK WAKEFIELD TO THE NAVY, THE LOSS of Third Baseman Pinky Higgins and a few lesser lights to the Army, the Tigers generally were picked to win the fourth-war-year flag of 1945. People said that the Browns were a one-year club, and that if O'Neill's right and left bowers (Trout and Newhouser) followed their 1944 pace, they couldn't help but pitch the Tigers to a seventh pennant against the generally weakened opposition. However, Rufe Gentry, who had won 12 games in '44 and showed considerable promise, decided to stay out in 1945, but O'Neill got a good break in the return of big Al Benton from the Navy.

During the winter Jack Zeller traded Infielder Joe Orengo to the Sox for O'Neill's son-in-law, Shortstop Jimmy "Skeeter" Webb. Steve later said he didn't know of the deal until he awakened one morning to find Olive's husband on his roster. And, on April 30, after a fortnight of the season was gone, Jack traded Outfielder-Third Baseman Don Ross and Second Baseman Dutch Meyer to the Indians for Outfielder Roy Cullenbine, one of the Detroiters set free by Abe Lincoln Landis in 1940. The Judge then had stipulated that none of the players he made free agents could play for Detroit within a three-year period. That deadline now was well passed, and Roy proved a useful war pickup, especially as a stopgap for Wakefield.

With the European war over, good old Hank Greenberg, by this time 34, was let out by the Army. He had risen to the rank of a captain and saw a lot of interesting service in the India-Burma theater. With a reception committee of 47,729 on hand to greet him, Greenberg celebrated his return to the Detroit line-up, July 1, by hitting a homer in his first major-league game in four years. It helped beat the Athletics, 9 to 5.

260

Though bothered considerably with leg trouble, Greenberg returned to the old left-field pasture, and hit .306 for 78 games, exactly the same number Wakefield played in 1944. Hank still had the old home-run knack, driving 13 over the garden wall, while he batted in 60 runs.

While the 1944 champions, the Browns, proved troublesome in the late season and finished third, it was oddly enough the 1944 tailender, the Washington Senators, who gave the Tigers keenest competition and were a difficult team to shake off. Ossie Bluege tried to make the unprecedented leap from cellar to champion, and but for Newhouser and Greenberg would have gotten away with it.

However, unlike 1944, the 1945 Tigers never floundered in the second division, and were up or near the top all year. Getting off to a surprising early start, the White Sox led most of the time up to May 24, but Steve's boys never were far away, and moved into first place for the first time, June 8. New York then scaled the heights for a few days, but after the Tigers defeated the Browns, June 12, while New York was idle, Detroit took the lead again. Repeatedly Washington fought within striking distance of the lead, a game or a half game away, but they never quite could dislodge the Felines from their tenacious hold to the top rung.

The Tigers had to make a September eastern trip, and that seemingly favored the eastern contender. But, as with Jennings' Tigers of 1907 and 1909, the Felines weren't bothered with geography. Though the race lasted two weeks longer, the Tigers really gave the Senators their crippling blow in a Saturday twilight-night double-header, September 15. Leading the Senators by only a half game, the Tigers came into the capital city for a five-game series, including Saturday and Sunday double-headers. Greenberg was out of the regular line-up at the time with a charley-horse; Bluege had his pitchers primed for the series, and the Washington fans felt pretty cocky.

But the Tigers cooled them off in that Saturday twin bill, 7 to 4 and 7 to 3. Newhouser was knocked out of the first game, but Overmire and Caster brought it in, and Trout took care of the night struggle. The next day, the Senators tripped up Newhouser, 3 to 2, in the first game, but Benton, Bridges, Caster, and Trout all collaborated in fetching in the second one, 5 to 4. Washington's pent-up wrath boiled over in the fifth game, which the Senators won, 12 to 5, but the Felines left Washington with their lead increased to one and a half games.

There was a trick 1945 schedule, with Washington closing a week earlier than the Tigers. Being a 1944 tail-ender, and not expecting to be in on a hot finish, Griffith had asked for an early closing, so he could permit the Washington football Redskins to use his park. It brought about an odd situation; while the Senators were sitting the last week out, the Tigers could either win or beat themselves.

After leaving Washington, they didn't do so well; they lost two to the Indians and divided another pair with the Browns in Detroit. On Wednesday, September 26, they divided a double-header with Cleveland. By that time, they had won 87 games and lost 65; Washington had finished with 87 victories and 67 defeats. The worst the Tigers now could do was finish tied for the lead, but they still needed one victory to clinch it.

They were scheduled for final Saturday and Sunday games with the Browns in St. Louis. If they lost both, it would require a play-off with Washington to decide the pennant. Griffith sent his three top pitchers, Wolff, Leonard, and Haefner, to Detroit for such a tentative game, and the entire Washington team was packed on Sunday prepared for a quick dash for Detroit.

The Saturday game was rained out, and a double-header was planned for Sunday, September 30. But it continued to rain; the field was a quagmire; and it looked as though the Tigers would be the "Umbrella Champions." But the rain slackened; the ground keepers patched up the field, and the umpires got the first game started over an hour late. Virgil Trucks, discharged by the Navy, reported to Steve O'Neill in St. Louis; he told the manager he was in fine fettle and ready to work. Steve started him, with Newhouser in the bull pen.

With the Tigers leading, 2 to 1, Steve rushed Hal into the game as Trucks's relief in the sixth, but the Browns tied in the seventh and scored again to take a 3 to 2 lead in the eighth. Nelson Potter, St. Louis' No. 1 pitcher, was on the hill. Then came a dramatic Tiger ninth inning, which electrified not only rooters listening in Detroit but fans from ocean to ocean.

Hub Walker, batting for Newhouser, started it with a pinch single; on Webb's bunt to McQuinn, the first sacker threw to second too late for a force and every one was safe. Mayo advanced the pair with a sacrifice, and Manager Sewell ordered an intentional pass for Cramer.

That was the setting, a Tiger on every sack, when Hank Greenberg struck his historic thirteenth homer of 1945. On the misty field, with semidarkness already coming in, he met the ball flush on the end of his bat and the white sphere described a beautiful arc as it landed deep in the left-field bleachers. It was a grand-slam homer, the feet of Walker, Webb, and Cramer pattering happily around the bases as the grinning Hank followed in their wake. Benton retired the side in the second half; Detroit won, 6 to 3, and the Tigers were in possession of their seventh pennant. A second game was started, but it had gone only an inning when rain and darkness cut it short.

The pennant-winning game was credited to Newhouser; it was his twenty-fifth. He again was the bellwether of the staff. Dizzy Trout, bothered with a misery in his back and other ailments, wasn't as effective as in 1944, winning 18 games and losing 15. But on Detroit's last eastern trip, Diz was like Dizzy Dean of 1934, going in nearly every day. The 1945 Tigers probably would have won fairly easily but for a broken leg suffered by Alton Benton in June. Previously, Al had been almost unhittable, but when he tried to come back later in the season, he wasn't the same pitcher. Even so, he won 13 games out of 21. Les Mueller, a spectacled Illinois right-hander, and Stubby Overmire, the pony left-hander, had flashes of brilliance; and George Caster and Jim Tobin, veterans picked up for the waiver price, helped in the late summer and fall campaign. Caster saved a number of games with fine relief work.

They called the 1945 Tigers "the nine old men." Some of them, particularly forty-year-old Doc Cramer, tired at the end, but for most of the season the Jersey carpenter had an inspired season. Rudy York wasn't up to his usual form, but Eddie Mayo played better than he knew how and Paul Richards was a tower of strength behind the bat. Bob Maier was brought in from Buffalo to play third base; he hit .264 in 132 games, but in the last fortnight of the season and in the World's Series, little Jimmy Outlaw took care of the hot corner. Before Greenberg joined the team, Jim was the left fielder. And though Joe Hoover outhit Skeeter Webb, .257 to .199, the latter played 118 games at shortstop.

At a time when it looked as though the Tigers might blow the pennant, some of the fans were pretty severe on Steve. They found fault with his third-base-coaching, and intimated he used favoritism by playing his weak-hitting son-in-law at short. That got a rise out of the old warrior. "They can find fault with my coaching, and I can take it," he said. "I'm the man who sends runners in, and I've got to use my own judgment. And when I'm wrong, they can pan me. But, me playing Skeeter because he married one of my girls, well, that really makes me mad. Webb is in there because he covers more ground than any one I have and has one of the best arms in baseball."

And Detroit fans surged into the park as never before. Not only did the attendance go over the million mark for the fifth time, but it almost matched the twenty-five-year-record of the old Yankees by reaching 1,280,341. That topped the 1944 Tiger attendance by 357,165. And Frank Navin's spirit must be pleased that they did it without the aid of night ball. However, seven twilight games, one with each club in the league, drew 144,618, with the game of July 6 with the Yankees drawing a record twilight crowd of 31,567.

2

With a dramatic victory having been achieved in the American League, the next problem was the first postwar World's Series, the first in the reign of Happy Chandler. With hostilities having ended less than two months before, every one knew the interest would be intense. A nation grateful for victory was licking its wounds and seeking diversion in the old fall baseball drama. "We had 40,000 requests for reserved seats, with an average of four tickets per request, which meant we had 160,000 customers for our 54,000 seats," said Jack Zeller. "Naturally, it would have been nice if we could have taken care of all of them, not only for ourselves, but for baseball. But, we had to appeal to our people to spread around the tickets so that one fan could use a strip ticket one day, his friend or neighbor the next, and a third party the third day."

Contrast that demand for 160,000 reserved seats at Briggs Stadium and the Tiger request for voluntary rationing of the precious ducats with those World's Series crowds of 7,300 and 6,200 at Bennett Field in 1907 and 1908!

The National League opponents of the Tigers again were to be the Chicago Cubs, their opponents in 1907, 1908, and 1935. And as in the latter year, the effervescent Charley Grimm was in command of the Cook County team. By a curious shuffle of the championship cards, Detroit never has come up with a World's Series opponent from the East. The opposing club always has been a team from its own section. This has held true from the very first, 'way back in 1887 when the old Detroits played the Browns. Detroit has met Chicago four times, St. Louis twice, and Pittsburgh and Cincinnati once each. The nearest they came to playing a team from the East was in 1908, when the Giants blew their postseason play-off to the Cubs and Hugh Jennings lost the chance to meet his old New York crony, John McGraw, in the series.

In a way, the Cubs and Tigers were the World's Series Patsys of their respective leagues when they squared off in 1945. Since defeating the Tigers in 1908, the Cubs had lost six World's Series, while the Detroit record was one victory in six tries. Something had to "bust," and it was a slam-bang series of home runs, good pitching, bases on balls, misjudged flys, and many ball players.

3

The Series started out most dismally for the Tigers and a stunned crowd of 54,637 well-wishers on a cold, bleak day in Detroit on October 3. With Newhouser blown out in less than three innings, the Cubs won by the lopsided score of 9 to 0. It was the worst defeat suffered by a team in 42 World's Series openers, and, to make it worse, it was the first time the National League had taken the first game since the all-New York series of 1936.

"Of course, it had to happen in Detroit," grumbled some out-of-town American Leaguers. "Why do we always have to look so bad in a World's Series in this town?" They had happier days ahead.

But what added further salt to the wounds was that the Cub shutout was administered by the former Yankee pitcher, Hank Borowy, who went to the Cubs in a strange July deal, after the Tigers and all the other American League clubs had waived on him. And Hank further teased the fans by letting many Tigers get into scoring positions. In the first six innings, ten Tigers were left on base and two others were wiped off on double plays. That gave Hank the idea, "these boys just don't intend to get rough"; he blotted them out in order in the last three innings.

Newhouser got off to a rocky start in the first inning. Don Johnson and Cavarretta outfooted a pair of infield hits on close decisions which put Hal in an early hole. The first run leaked in on a passed ball; Nicholson belted in two more with a triple, and Livingston scored Nick with a solid single. Hal gave up three more runs in the third before Steve sadly used the derrick on his pitching prince. Cramer was slow in getting to Johnson's fly; Doc got one hand on it, but couldn't squeeze it, and it fell safe for a double. Cavarretta's single, a booming double by Pafko, and another single by Livingston brought the end of Hal. Detroiters sorrowfully rubbed their eyes; was this the man who had hypnotized American League batsmen for two seasons?

After that O'Neill called in a flock of pitchers: Benton, Tobin, and the spectacled Mueller. Old Jim was fluttering his butterfly ball to the plate in the seventh when the Cubs struck again with two out. Cavarretta wafted a homer against the screen in right field;

Pafko singled and stole and scored on Nicholson's single, which was the thirteenth and last Cub hit.

4

Steve gambled hard on the second game, calling on Virgil "Fire" Trucks, the recently discharged sailor, who had pitched the closing game in St. Louis. O'Neill won on this throw of the pitching dice; in fact they called the 4-to-1 second game the "Army-Navy victory" in Detroit. Bluejacket Trucks rolled his truck over the Cub batsmen, and former Air Force Captain Greenberg clinched matters by exploding a powerful three-run homer on the roof of the Chicago dugout.

The day, October 4, warmed up perceptibly from the near-freezing first-game conditions, and the Tigers thawed out with the weather. Hank Wyse, a twenty-two-game winner in the National League season, was the opposing pitcher and for four innings Wyse was as tough as Borowy had been the day before. The Cubs practically stole their run in the fourth inning. With one out, Cavarretta hit an ordinary single to center, and before the startled Cramer knew what was what, Phil had stretched the hit into a double. He came home on Nicholson's single.

That run made the Tigers mad, and after being blanked for thirteen successive innings they broke loose with one big four-run inning. It was the one big thrill for Detroit fans at Briggs Stadium in the three home Tiger games—the only scoring frame in twenty-six innings. But it was plenty fun while the shooting was going on.

The bottom of the line-up, Richards and Trucks, had gone out on easy chances in the fifth inning, and the storm broke out of a clear sky. Skeeter Webb started it by poking a single to left, and Mayo drew his base on balls, the little shortstop advancing to second. Cramer atoned for Cavarretta's stealing that extra base on him by lining a single to left on the first pitch, scoring Skeeter with the tying run.

Then Bronx Hank dropped his bomb. With the count one ball and one strike, Greenberg connected solidly with a fast pitch, and sent it hurtling for a home run into the left-field bleachers 375 feet away, Mayo and Cramer happily prancing around the bases ahead of Hank. The crowd let out such a terrific din that poor Charley Grimm couldn't hear what he was saying to himself and thinking about Wyse.

266

5

Claude Passeau's one-hit 3-to-o shutout in the third game, the first World's Series one-hitter since Ed Reulbach, another Cub, threw one in 1906, is a swell-looking job in the pitching records, but for Detroit fans on the afternoon of October 5 it was about as interesting as watching a dear friend being led to the gallows.

"When the hell do we start?" more than one Tiger fan yelled during the hitless afternoon. They never did. It rained before game time; the downpour delayed the start of the game eleven minutes and prevented batting practice. The Tigers certainly showed the lack of it. Only two Detroiters reached base. Rudy York cracked out his team's lone hit, a long single to left center with two down in the second inning. The only other Tiger to reach base was Catcher Swift, who walked in the sixth. However, Borom, Bill's pinch runner, was promptly erased when Hub Walker, batting for Overmire, grounded into a double play. Only twenty-eight batsmen, one more than the minimum number, faced the stingy Passeau, and though the dose of whitewash was bitter and hard to take, Detroit fans generously applauded the super pitching by the gallant Cub right-hander.

O'Neill pitched Stubby Overmire, and the midget southpaw did pretty well until he retired for a pinch hitter. He gave up only four hits in his six innings, but the Cubs crowded three of them in a busy fourth inning when they scored twice. Peanuts Lowrey started it with a double to left, and Cavarretta sacrificed. Pafko walked, and singles by the persistent Nicholson and Hughes banged in the runs. Passeau fanned in three of his four times at bat, but he drove in the third run with a long fly in the seventh after Livingston had doubled and taken third on Hughes's sacrifice.

That finished the business in Detroit, where the three games totaled an attendance of 163,773 and a gate of $665,174. Jack Zeller said it could easily have been twice that if he had had the space, but contrasted with 1907 and 1908 it was like big business and a peanut stand.

6

As the Series shifted to Chicago for the fourth game, October 6, the Cubs felt rather sure of themselves. Their pitchers had goose-egged the Tigers on Michigan soil in every inning but one, and the Wrigley team always has been known as a strong home team. "This time we're going to win; they can't stop us," said Charley Grimm, while many of the critics expected to see the Tigers go down in five games.

However, the spirit of the Detroit club remained surprisingly high, even after that futile club-swinging exhibition in the last game in Detroit. "We'll get going; we'll start hitting when we have to, just as we did so often during the season," was the Tiger watchword.

O'Neill had held Dizzy Trout back, as the big fellow had been ailing with a cold, sore throat, and that misery in his back. Steve asked him how he felt the morning of the game in Chicago, and Dizzy replied: "I'm fit, boss; I'm ready to pitch the game of my life."

"And you're the boy who can do it," replied Steve.

His faith in Trout was not misplaced, as the big Hoosier really poured in his fire ball and pitched one of the classics of his career. He gave up only five hits, walked only one batter, and twice swept third strikes across the chest of Cavarretta, the National batting champion.

The game was similar to Detroit's victory in the second contest. Again the Tigers struck hard in one inning, and for the second time they hung a big fat "4" on the scoreboard. This time they broke loose on Ray Prim in the fourth inning, after the veteran left-hander had set O'Neill's players down in order for the first three innings.

Prim got rid of Webb, Tiger lead-off man, for his tenth successive victim, and then Ray lost his faith in Santa Claus. Those Tigers weren't such tame little kittens after all. The spell was broken when Mayo walked and Cramer shot a single to right field. Greenberg propelled the first pitch into left field for a single, and Mayo ran home. Cullenbine selected this appropriate moment for his first hit of the series, a double down the left-field foul line which scored Cramer. That finished Prim, and Oom Paul Derringer, the Tiger-tamer of 1940, tried it. He filled the bases by walking York; a third run came in when Outlaw hit into a force play and the fourth on Richards' single, which also was his first hit of the Series.

The Cubs scored only once on Trout, and then on a queer antic by Outlaw. Don Johnson opened the sixth with a triple, and on Lowrey's jab to Outlaw, Don was trapped halfway between third and the plate. However, instead of running him down, Outlaw threw out the batter at first. In the meantime, Johnson was trying to scuttle back to third, and when York's return throw to Outlaw landed in a field box, the umpires waved Don home.

After four games, the Tigers had scored in only two innings; they had hit only .160, but they were on even terms with their National League foemen. "Say, this doesn't begin to look so bad," said Steve, after it was over. "From here on, I know we are going to win."

7

Everybody was saying that the fifth game, played in Chicago on a lovely Sunday, October 7, was going to be the all-important game. "Whoever gets this one will win the Series," Clarence Rowland, Frankie Frisch, and Bill Terry, former World's Series tacticians, were saying and they had the right slant. It again was the first-game pitchers: Hal Newhouser, who had worked only two and two-thirds innings, against Borowy, who had pitched the opening shutout. This time it was Borowy who was led away as hostile base hits whistled around his ears, and Newhouser who made a glorious comeback. Actually Hal pitched a much better game than the final 8-to-4 score indicates. In the late innings, Detroit fielders had a strange faculty of being in the wrong places when fly balls were hit. Mayo lost one pop fly in the sun, and Cramer and Cullenbine let another easy lift from Cavarretta's bat drop at their feet, the loose play helping the Cubs to two gift hits and three runs.

As Cramer came running over to take the Cavarretta fly, Cullenbine yelled: "All right! All right!" So Cramer stopped and the ball fell between them. "What the hell did you mean by that all right?" demanded Doc. "I meant it was all right for you to take it!" replied Cullenbine.

Mayo and Greenberg both took tumbles on the base lines, but misjudged flys and flip-flops on the paths were all forgotten in the joys of 11 hits, including 3 doubles by Greenberg. The boys really put the wood to Borowy and looked like the old slugging Tigers.

Both teams picked up a run in the third inning. Skeeter scored for the Tigers when he walked, sprinted to third on Mayo's single, and tallied on Cramer's long fly. Borowy got that one back himself, as he cracked out a double with two out and scored on Hack's single.

Detroit then salted the game away with the third of its big four-run blocks in the fifth. Great fielding by the nimble Pafko saved Borowy in the earlier innings, but Cramer opened the fat frame with a single to center and took an extra base on Andy's fumble. Greenberg reached out at the first pitch, caught the ball before it broke, and crashed it to left for a dynamic double, scoring Cramer. Cullenbine's infield hit and a robust single by York scored Hank and finished Borowy. Tall Hy Vandenberg took over, and Outlaw's sacrifice advanced the two runners on the bases. Grimm then ordered an intentional pass for Richards, filling the bases, but the strategy backfired when tall Hy also walked Newhouser, forcing over Cullenbine, and York tallied on Webb's force. Chipman, a left-hander, finally extinguished the fire.

However, to put Newhouser on the safe side, the Tigers picked up three more runs, built around Greenberg's second and third doubles in the seventh and ninth innings.

8

The Tigers now led, three games to two, and were ahead for the first time in the Series. Red Patterson, then the National League publicity man—perhaps hoping to put a jinx on the players from Detroit—passed around the information that in both 1934 and 1940 the Tigers had enjoyed a lead of three to two, but blew the Series by losing the sixth and seventh games.

The Cubs did tie up the Series by taking the sixth game, October 8, a crazy twelve-inning affair, in which everything happened. In actual time consumed, 3 hours and 28 minutes, it was the longest World's Series game ever played, and no screwier ball game ever was entered in the book. To begin with each manager tossed 19 players into the game—38 in all. Of this number 9 were pitchers, including 5 Tiger chuckers. Hostetler, with a chance to score a run which would have won for Detroit in regular innings, took a header between third and home as though diving into a tank, and it was necessary to wait four hours after the game was over to get the accurate Detroit error count.

Passeau started against Trucks, the second-game winner, and it probably would have been an easy Cub victory if the Chicago star hadn't had a finger mangled by Jim Outlaw's line drive in the sixth inning. It tore off the nail and otherwise bruised the digit. Up to that point Claude had been almost as effective as in his spectacular third-game victory, giving up only two hits, one a scratch. The Cubs were leading at the time, 5 to 1. The gallant Mississippian tried to carry on, but lost his effectiveness as blood from the torn fingernail smeared the ball. Neither Wyse nor Prim could check the Tiger bats, and with his lead frittering away, Charley Grimm eventually called on the hard-working Borowy to save the game. The former Yank held back the Tigers for four innings, worked his way out of several holes, and eventually triumphed in the twelfth when the breaks gave the game to the Cubs.

Trucks didn't follow up his great effort against Wyse on October 4. For four innings, he appeared to have his stuff, but Virgil ran into a squall in the fifth inning, when the Cubs rolled over four runs before Caster could retire the side. Tommy Bridges, the erstwhile World's Series ace, then tried it. The old heart was there, but the arm no longer would do Tommy's bidding. He retired in favor of Benton after walking three men and yielding two runs in the seventh. Dizzy Trout took over after the score had been tied in the eighth, and what started as a slugging match ended in a duel between Dizzy and Borowy in the extra innings.

For the Detroit contingent in the stands most of the excitement was crammed into the busy seventh and eighth innings. Two runs were scored in the seventh, though this rally was pretty well punctured when Hostetler took his historic spill. Chuck was on second with one out, when Cramer stabbed a single to left. Having considerable respect for Peanuts Lowrey's arm, Steve O'Neill flagged the veteran at third base. But Chuck ran right through the red light. Perhaps that disconcerted him mentally, but he still had a chance to beat the throw when to the amusement of the Chicago fans Hostetler's feet suddenly went from under him and a moment later he was sprawled on all fours on the base line.

However, there were no laughs for the vexed Chicago rooters in the eighth inning. Trailing by 7 to 3, the Tigers tied the score with their third four-run block of the Series. The Tigers might have won in this frame if Eddie Mayo hadn't tried to stretch a single into a double while the rally was going full blast. With three runs in and two out, faithful Hank Greenberg brought the American League contingent to their seats by booming a homer high and far over the left-field fence.

After that few on the Detroit bench, and only the most faithful Cub rooters in the stands, doubted that the Tigers would end the Series that day. Everybody in the dugout was yelling, dancing, mauling each other. "That's it; that's the pay-off," yelled the happy O'Neill from the third-base coach's box, but from then on Borowy blocked the way.

The tantalizing game, one of the most unforgettable of World's Series play, had a sudden and dramatic ending in the twelfth. Dark shadows were hanging over the park, and it could only have gone another inning at the most. With one out in the Cub half, Pat Secory, batting for Len Merullo, clipped a single to center, and when Dizzy buzzed a third strike over on Borowy, the danger seemed to be pretty well over. However, Hack hacked what appeared to be an ordinary single to left, and Billy Schuster, Secory's pinch runner, headed for third.

Then came the most discussed play of the Series. As Greenberg charged in for the ball, with the idea of cutting down Schuster at third, the sphere hopped over his startled head and rolled to the fence while Schuster scored the winning run with no play being made on him.

The first decision of the official scorers, Messrs. Martin "Mike" Haley, Harry Salsinger, and Ed Burns, was that Hack was credited with a single and Greenberg charged with an error for permitting Schuster to score. The author served as alternate scorer at the Series, but was not consulted until after the play, as the other three men were unanimous at the time that it was an error for Hank. However, from the start I felt no error had been made and expected the repercussion.

Losing the game was bad enough, but the usually affable Greenberg was burned up over the error. He hadn't been charged with one in 78 American League games after leaving the Army, and to get a boot on that one made him see red. He wouldn't even talk to reporters after the game. However, O'Neill and his teammates talked plenty. "How in hell could anyone give an error on such a play?" demanded Steve, as York, Cullenbine, and other angry Tigers echoed the same sentiments.

Downtown at press headquarters at the Palmer House, there was almost as much indignation. The writer has attended World's Series for over thirty years and was chief scorer at three of them, and never have I seen fellow writers more worked up over a scoring play. After most of the men had filed their morning stories, and during the height of the indignation, Marty Haley and Burns contacted "Sal" by telephone and the scoring play was reversed. Hack was given a double and a run batted in, and Greenberg's error was rubbed out. Even then the tall Bronx boy was not completely mollified.

9

They knocked off October 9 to sell tickets, and the final game was played on a fine sunshiny day in the Chicago park on the tenth. It was the fourth time that the Tigers had gone into a seventh game, and three times before they had been turned back, twice by humiliating one-sided shutouts. Was history to repeat?

As the final struggle approached, O'Neill had it all over Charley Grimm in pitchers. The Pennsylvania Irishman had Hal Newhouser, his southpaw ace, primed for the game, and behind the southpaw prince he had Trout and Trucks. Charley Grimm's staff had been so mangled that he had to gamble on Hank Borowy's being Superman. Borowy had pitched five and two-thirds innings in the fifth game, four hard innings in the sixth, and had had only the open date to get some badly needed rest. Borowy is not built along the lines of Ed Walsh and Walter Johnson; Grimm sent Hank to the well once too often.

In the first inning Webb, Mayo, and Cramer stabbed Borowy for quick singles, Skeeter scoring. Grimm realized the former Yank didn't "have a thing," and quickly summoned Derringer, who had won the deciding game for McKechnie over the Tigers five years before. But Oom Paul wasn't Grimm's answer, either. Greenberg sacrificed, and a pass to Cullenbine filled the bases. Paul got York on an infield pop, but a walk to Outlaw forced Mayo over the dish, and then Richards inserted one of the most damaging pokes of the Series, doubling to left to clear the bases. Following Cramer's single in the second, Derringer put on a base-on-balls parade, walking Greenberg, Cullenbine, and York, which forced home Doc and brought Vandenberg into the picture. By this time Detroit led, 6 to 0. Those Chicago rooters were as quiet as though they were sitting in a tomb, but for the Detroit bunch, what a lark, to be taking the deciding game and rubbing a little salt in the enemy's wounds!

Richards belted in a seventh run with a second double in the seventh, and soon thereafter left the game with a mashed finger. But Paul was so happy, it didn't even hurt. As for Newhouser, he breezed serenely along, permitted the Cubs to get 10 hits—3 by Cavarretta—but when the Chicagoans threatened to get obstreperous, he put on a little extra steam and fanned nine, most of the strike-outs coming with the runners on the bases. He won comfortably by a score of 9 to 3. No wonder, they again gave him most of the honors in the book, the new Kenesaw Mountain Landis award for most valuable A. L. player, the *Sporting News* award for outstanding pitcher, and the designation as "Player of the Year."

The Series set new attendance and receipts records of 333,457 and $1,592,454. The total crowds knocked the 1926 Yankee-Cardinals attendance out of the book, and the gate passed the Detroit-Cincinnati figures of five years before. As for each of the happy Tigers, they pulled down individual slices of $6,443.33.

The new World's Championship was fittingly celebrated at a

big dinner given by Owner Briggs to the entire club at the Book-Cadillac on the night of October 11. Several of the players orated, but Hank Greenberg spoke for the entire club when he said: "We won for Steve O'Neill. There was no man on the club who didn't want to win for Steve—a man who never second-guessed a ball player and always understood."

⊛ XXVI ⊛

A STILL BRIGHTER
FUTURE

A FLY IN THE OINTMENT OF WALTER BRIGGS'S JOY WAS THE RESIGNA-
tion of the veteran general manager, Jack Zeller, after the
winning of the 1945 World's Series. Zeller had tried to resign before,
but Briggs had talked him out of it. But this time, Jack really meant
it. His wife wasn't too well in Fort Worth, and he wanted to take
things a little easier. Before going, Zeller disposed of all the Tiger
farm clubs, blasted the entire farm system, and suggested that all
young players be put into a great pool, from which the sixteen clubs
would draft their material. The Tigers later rebuilt a new farm
organization with the Toledo Mud Hens of the American Association their top club.

Briggs filled Zeller's shoe by naming the capable George Trautman former president of the American Association, as Jack's successor. Trautman is a man of great energy, who has been a well-
known figure in the Columbus, O., sports world for the past quarter
of a century. At Ohio State University, he pitched for the baseball
team, and former Governor John Bricker was his catcher. Service
with the Columbus Chamber of Commerce, especially in promoting
sports events, and as general manager of the Columbus ball club,
paved his way to the Association presidency in 1935.

The new Tiger management didn't rest on its oars, and many
changes were contemplated for the 1946 club. It was figured that
only thirteen players of the 1945 club would survive the pruning
of the early season. Such veteran war pickups as Chuck Hostetler
and Jim Tobin were discarded. The former slugger, Rudy York,
was traded to Boston for Shortstop Eddie Lake, and Hank Greenberg returned to first base. And after remaining a "batch" until
he was 35, tall Hank took to himself a wife, Miss Caral Gimbel,
shortly before the 1946 training season.

After the 1945 season, Tommy Bridges decided he had had

enough of pitching, and that the old curve ball had lost its deceptive break. Briggs promptly made a place for him on the Tiger roster as a coach. But in the salubrious late winter climate of Lakeland, Florida, Tommy had a change of heart. Though 39, he decided to take one more whirl at pitching, and thought he might work a game a week. With 193 victories to his credit, he reasonably felt he might bring in seven more to make it an even 200 before he permanently closed his pitching books.

Along with Hank, Benton, and Trucks, servicemen who returned in '45, a whole brigade came tumbling back from the war—Dick Wakefield, Barney McCosky, Birdie Tebbets, Harold White, Freddy Hutchinson, Johnny Lipon, Pat Mullin, Bob Patrick, Johnny Gorsica, Hoot Evers, Jimmy Bloodworth, Pinky Higgins, and some present unknown youngsters who may be the Ty Cobbs and Bill Donovans of the future.

Unfortunately on the 1946 training trip, Evers, after hitting over .400, suffered a broken thumb and cracked ankle, which the Tiger club physician said would side-line him until July. Pinky Higgins didn't come back at third base as strongly as was anticipated, and Barney McCosky was traded to the Athletics for George Kell to strengthen the position.

As the new season dawned, the Tigers were more formidable than ever, and were classed with the Yankees, Red Sox, and St. Louis Cardinals as the cream of the postwar teams. And with a pitching staff topped by Newhouser, Trout, Trucks, Benton, and White, many fans and critics couldn't see how the Tigers could be kept out of the 1946 World's Series. Some even termed the 1946 team the best of all of Detroit's clubs.

However, after a strong April, in which the Tigers won five games of their first six and led for one day—April 25, the Felines couldn't hit the side of a barn in their late spring and early summer 1946 campaign and soon were well behind the fast-moving Red Sox, with their big service stars back from the war, and the Yankees, who were doing their best to make it a race. Even so, the Tigers, held up by brilliant pitching, were no pushover and ran third for weeks. But Steve O'Neill wasn't satisfied with that and wailed, "Can't we ever get out of that third-place rut?"

At that time the big guns, who were supposed to produce the runs, weren't functioning. The chap who fell down the hardest was the expensive young star, Dick Wakefield, who had a difficult time making his peacetime readjustment. There was talk during the training season of a thousand-dollar bet between Wakefield and Ted Williams

The 1945 World's Champions

Jimmy (Skeeter) Webb, Steve O'Neill, and Henry Nowak

© Sporting News

© George Dorrill

Detroit's Own Hal Newhouser

Paul (Dizzy) Trout

as to who would have the higher 1946 batting average, but after Commissioner Chandler had them call it off, the boys said it was all in fun anyway. It was a good thing for Dick that it wasn't on, for despite the fact that he perked up at the finish, Wakefield had to be satisfied with .269 against Williams' .342.

Greenberg hit in spots, but not consistently, and while he was getting his share of long hits, he couldn't pump the old batting average over .250. He was bothered with a back ailment, and Steve rested him in the second game of double-headers. When Hank was overlooked on the American League's All-Star squad, on which Rudy York and Mickey Vernon of Washington drew the first-base positions, there was some talk that the big Bronxonian was huffed, that he would retire and buy a ball club with his wealthy in-laws. At one time they were mentioned as possible purchasers of the Giants.

And just around the time that Hoot Evers recovered from his spring injuries, he had a head-on collision with second baseman Eddie Mayo in Washington, and both players were hospitalized. Evers suffered from a broken jaw, but eventually took part in 81 games and generally was regarded as the American League's rookie of the year.

In the meantime, the Tigers were drawing amazing crowds in baseball's lush postwar season, attendances which dwarfed everything else the Detroit club ever had done before on its busy turnstiles. Way back in early April fans lined up for blocks to buy opening day tickets, and the queues kept lining up all season. The opening game with the Browns attracted 52,118 fans, a new first-game Tiger record, and the first Sunday contest, April 28, with Cleveland as the opposition, drew 57,149, a new park record. The latter count was boosted to 57,235 in a later Sunday double-header with the lowly Browns. The club's first five games of 1946 at home played to 173,451 rootin', tootin' Tiger fans, and through good days and bad they kept piling into the Michigan and Trumbull arena. The Tigers eventually raised their home total to 1,722,590, the second highest in baseball history. It was topped only by the new record 2,309,029 fans who attended games at Yankee Stadium in baseball's banner year of 1946.

In the latter part of the season the loyal Detroit rooters were rewarded with the kind of baseball they expected to see all year. What had irked the faithful was the futile efforts of their beloved Felines against the Red Sox in the months when the powerful Bostonians swept everything before them. Steve's boys won only three of their first 18 games from the Red Sox, but the Tigers saved some shred of their reputation as the 1945 World's Champs by winning the last four contests between the two clubs, a pair in Boston and a final pair at Briggs Stadium. The Tiger clubhouse got quite a boot out of their 9-to-1 and 7-to-3 victories over Boston on September 10 and 11. The Red Sox were all set at the time for their pennant celebration, and Tommy Dowd, their traveling secretary, had the dinner ordered and the champagne on ice at the Book-Cadillac. But Tommy had to move his wine and order a new dinner in Cleveland. What a laugh that got out of Dizzy Trout, Roy Cullenbine, and other merry souls on the Tigers!

It was around this same time that the Tigers got out of their "third-place groove" and nudged the Yanks out of second place. They actually flew past the slumping New Yorkers, winding up five games to the good in the runner-up position, but still 12 in arrears to the new Boston champions. However, the club actually won four more games and finished 22 points higher than the champions of 1945—.597 to .575. The Detroits were the hottest team in both major leagues in the last six weeks of the season, winning 28 of their last 38 games.

The Tigers closed on high in all departments, even in batting, where they finished third after trailing in midseason. Greenberg spurted to a satisfactory .275, and despite tired legs and his ailing sacroiliac, he swung his home-run cudgel as he had when he was ten years younger. Detroit termed it a happy season when biffing Hank beat out Boston's The Kid, Ted Williams, for the homer crown, 44 to 38, and nosed him out in runs batted in, 126 to 123. And Hank was in eight less games. Roy Cullenbine, who couldn't beg a hit in the spring, zoomed from .165 to .335 and closed with 15 homers. Some of the bleacherites weren't too pleased with the Kell-McCosky swap when George Trautman made it, but it proved a great piece of work for George. Kell, a capable player in Philadelphia, became a whiz-bang in his new Tiger stripes; he was voted the outstanding third baseman of both majors; his fielding average was only one point behind Willie Kamm's American League record, and George hit a lively .323.

All season the pitching was superb. Some said Hal Newhouser wouldn't find the going so easy, when the pros got back from war, but they didn't know their Hal. He was as brilliant against the star-studded line-ups as he was against the 4-F's and war replacements of 1944 and 1945. Detroit's own home-grown left-hander won 26 games and lost only nine, and again was his league's leader in earned runs, keeping opponents under two earned runs per game for the second successive year. But for some midseason difficulty with his valuable left elbow he would have made it 30 victories.

Dizzy Trout had most of the tough pitching luck, and for weeks the gang just forgot to score whenever he pitched. Of the 11 shutouts pitched against the Felines in 1946, Dizz was on the wrong end of six of them. "What must a guy do to win in this league?" he asked. He did succeed in coming up with 17 winning brackets against 13 defeats.

Big Virgil Trucks, released from service just in time to finish the 1945 season, won 14 games and lost 9; Al Benton had an 11-7 record, and hefty Freddy Hutchinson showed better stuff and greater steadiness than before the war, finishing with 14 wins and 11 defeats. Two of the high pitching spots of the season were a pair of duels between Newhouser and Cleveland's Bobby Feller on the final two Sundays of the season. Hal won the first, 3 to 0, in the Indians' wigwam, September 22, the talented southpaw giving up only two hits. A week later, September 28, in the season's finale at Briggs Stadium, Feller reversed the order, winning by 4 to 1. Detroit fans got a big kick out of Newhouser getting more strike-outs than Feller, the new whiff king, in both contests, nine to seven in the Cleveland game and seven to five in Detroit.

Following the successful and profitable 1946 second-place season, several more changes were made on the Tigers. A new first lieutenant was selected for Steve O'Neill in Bill Sweeney, former manager of the Los Angeles club and for years a scrappy warrior on the coast. Paul Richards, who did such a swell job as a wartime fill-in catcher, was released so that he could take up the management of the Buffalo club, and Tommy Bridges finally said good-by to Detroit so that he could try to pitch for Portland in the more salubrious climate of the Pacific Coast League. The veteran relief pitcher, George Caster, was tendered his unconditional release, but a drove of newcomers had been brought up to fight for jobs at Steve's 1947 Lakeland training camp. First baseman Bob Moyer, formerly of Dallas and home-run king of the Texas League, and young Art Houtteman, standout pitcher of the Buffalo Bisons, allegedly were the picks of the crop.

Walter Briggs, Sr., lost more than a valuable player when the National Association, the governing body of the minors, drafted his comparatively new general manager, George Trautman, as its new head in the Los Angeles meetings in December 1946. After only one year in Tigerville, George succeeded the venerable Judge William G. Bramham as czar of the minor-league world. It left Briggs in something of a quandary, as he hadn't even known that Trautman was interested in the job. But it was the kind of a post few baseball men could turn down.

Jack Zeller, Trautman's predecessor, who had remained in the organization as scout emeritus, jumped in again and gave a helping hand, as Briggs searched the baseball ranks for a big man to handle a big job.

Owner Briggs found this man in two-hundred-pound Billy Evans, president of the Southern Association and one of the most capable, hard-hitting baseball men in the country. Billy went into his new job with a rich background of baseball experience, practically all of it in the American League. He was for years the loop's top umpire, and he served as general manager of the Cleveland Indians and then as head of the Red Sox's farm system. He was elected president of the Southern Association in December 1942 and served until his appointment to the Tiger job in December 1946.

Great things were predicted for the Tigers as they prepared for their 1947 season. The pitching staff still was young and seemingly the best in baseball, and there was plenty of dynamite in the batting order in August and September of '46. And the Cardinals proved in the 1946 World's Series that the Red Sox were not invincible. "They can be beat," was the slogan of Detroit fans, hungrier than ever for baseball, and the management already speculated whether the newly established attendance record of 1,722,590 would fall in '47.

It didn't! Plagued by foul weather in the spring and early summer, which wiped out several rich Sunday plums and curbed attendance at other week-end games, the 1947 turnstile count dropped to 1,398,093. That was a lot of people, and this number would have been terrific before the war, but it was 325,000 under 1946, and good for only fourth position on the league's attendance chart. Detroit trailed New York, Boston, and Cleveland in the important turnstile department.

The club continued to draw handsomely at its seven twilight games. These fine 5 o'clock turnouts, and the great crowds that flocked to night games in New York, Cleveland, Boston, and other cities, finally convinced Bossman Walter Briggs that there was no sense in further bucking the night-ball tide. He instructed Billy Evans to put in lights for 1948; the Detroit club was the last in the American League to yield to the new order, and that left only one major-league outfit, Detroit's old World Series rivals the Cubs, on an all daylight schedule. Evans, who had seen what night ball did for minor-league attendances, strongly recommended a limited number of nocturnal games.

"I'll put in lights on only one condition," Briggs told Billy, "and that is that we get the last word in lighting equipment. But, even though we've been late in putting in lights, let's give our fans a chance to say: 'Detroit has the best lighting system in baseball.' " Fourteen night games were scheduled for Briggs Stadium in 1948, and perhaps even the spirit of Frank Navin, in his lifetime the relentless foe of night ball, now is reconciled to the inevitable.

The 1947 Tigers finished in second place, yet it wasn't an entirely satisfactory season. The Red Sox, who had spread-eagled the field in 1946, suffered a severe reaction, and the club that beat out the Tigers was the "busts of '46"—the Yankees. As in 1946, Detroit snatched second-place money in a fighting September finish, when they ambled home thirteen points and two games ahead of the Red Sox. The position wasn't decided until the last day of the season, when Detroit nosed out Cleveland, 1 to 0, as Boston was losing to Washington. It gave Detroit one first and three seconds over a four-year span, but the 1947 runner-up lagged twelve games behind the Yankees as they passed the finish pole. That didn't give Tiger fans much chance to get excited over the race.

Things started well enough, and the Tiger team broke from the barrier on its right paw. While the 1946 champion Red Sox and the New Yorkers both started in a daze, the Tigers were the pace-makers in May and the first half of June. Shortly before Decoration Day, their lead was four full games, and everybody around the Jungle felt pretty good. It didn't take much imagination to see a Tiger World Series in the offing.

But just as everything looked brightest, the club ran into an unaccountable ten-game losing streak. It started with defeat in the last game of a successful home stand, when the Felines were blanked by the Athletics, 4 to 0. After that, the club's second eastern trip was an extended nightmare. It started ignominiously enough June 15, with the loss of a double-header to the weak Washington team, 1 to 0 and 7 to 1, and for the next ten days the drubbings became daily routine. The worst humiliation was the loss of a four-game series at Yankee Stadium by such tough scores as 5 to 3, 5 to 4, 7 to 4, and 6 to 5. The streak finally was broken on the last day of the trip in Boston, June 25, when the Tigers split even in a double-header, winning the first game, 4 to 2, before losing the second, 4 to 3.

"It was difficult to put a finger on what was wrong with us on that trip," said O'Neill afterward. "We didn't play bad ball, but no matter what we did, we couldn't win. If we had a well-pitched game, we'd lose, one to nothing. If we did our share of hitting, the other side hit just a little harder. Why, every one of the four games we lost in New York might have been changed by a single base-knock inserted in the right place."

That ten-game losing streak hung like a heavy load around the Tigers' necks for the balance of the season. What made it worse was that shortly after the Detroit losing streak was checked, the Yankees embarked on their sensational nineteen-game winning streak, which left the other contenders, Detroit and Boston, far behind. In fact, the Tigers ran third through most of the summer before overhauling the faltering Red Sox in the stretch.

Some attributed Detroit's failure to make more of a race to the sale of Hank Greenberg to the Pittsburgh Pirates, of the National League, the winter before. That was a real shock for Greenberg, also for most of the Detroit fans. They reasoned, how could the club strengthen itself by getting rid of the man who had led the loop in homers and runs batted in, in 1946. It was little satisfaction to be told by the management that Greenberg would not have been released to one of the Tigers' pennant rivals, but was disposed of to a National League club, where his bat could do the Bengals no harm.

The trouble between Hank and the club was that the front office couldn't reconcile the New Yorker's big-salary demands with the drying-up elastic in his legs. Yet, there was a poignant note to Greenberg's release after his years of faithful service to Detroit. He felt so badly that at one point he said he wouldn't report to Pittsburgh, but would retire from the game and go into private business. "Why, I felt I belonged to Detroit," he said; "I never dreamed I would end my career anywhere else." Adding to Hank's unhappiness in passing from Briggs Stadium was the fact that when George Trautman resigned as business manager, Greenberg had applied to the elder Briggs for the job, but he hadn't even received a reply. In the version of the No. 1 Tiger executive, a reply was sent, but he did not think Hank was the man for the job. Greenberg's mediocre 1947 season with Pittsburgh and his frequent absences from the regular Pirate line-up justified—in some measure—the Detroit club's action in separating this aging high-salaried star from its pay roll.

Even without any outstanding slugger, Detroit had fair scoring power in 1947. Along with the Yankees and Red Sox, they were the only American League clubs to score over 700 runs. Moyer, the Dallas home-run man, didn't make the grade, and Roy Cullenbine played first base most of the season. Roy's batting average tumbled to a lowly .224, but he managed to let 24 homers do a lot of talking for him. Kell, the fancy third baseman, was the Tiger batting leader with .320. However, it was well for the Tiger management that Kell hit so smartly; otherwise, it would have heard plenty from the fans on the Barney McCosky-Kell deal of the year before. Barney was runner-up to Ted Williams, the batting champ, with .328. In the spring, the Tigers traded their first-string catcher, Birdie Tebbetts, of the squeaky voice, to the Red Sox for Hal Wagner. That also came out fairly even, as Hal hit .273 to Birdie's .267.

The real failure of the Tigers to regain their 1945 heights in 1947 was the team's allegedly strongest department—the pitching staff. Most critics rated O'Neill's staff the strongest in the two major leagues, to which Steve commented: "What's the good of having the best staff on paper if they don't deliver on the ball field?"

With the exception of Freddy Hutchinson, little Stubby Overmire, and young Art Houtteman, who pitched brilliantly after being re- called from Buffalo, the staff buckled badly. Big two-hundred-pound "Hutch" continued to pay postwar dividends on his big purchase price of 1938; he won eighteen games and lost ten. Steve found spots for little Stubby, who was credited with eleven wins against five defeats, while the youthful Detroiter, Houtteman, with a fast ball that fairly jumped, won seven out of nine games after getting regular assignments in the late summer.

Otherwise, the pitching boys were full of frustration. Though Hal Newhouser pitched in some hard luck, and ranked fifth in low- earned runs, the left-handed Tiger pitching prince wasn't the Hal of the past three seasons. The Detroit homebred was credited with seventeen victories against as many defeats. Hal even had a few returns of earlier temperament, and O'Neill socked a fine on him when Newhouser failed to leave the mound in a game in which Steve signaled that he had seen enough—and that he wasn't pleased with that enough.

The other big names did even worse. Bothered with an assortment of ills, Dizzy Trout won only ten games and lost eleven. Big Virgil Trucks was no better, with a 10-to-12 showing, and he was with the also-rans in earned runs with 4.52. And Alton Benton could show only six wins against seven defeats.

Yet, Billy Evans and O'Neill felt the pitching letdown was only a one-year slump. While New York and Boston strengthened their staffs considerably for the 1948 pennant drive, Steve was relying on virtually the same staff he had in 1946 and 1947. One new acquisition,

Lou Kretlow, six feet, two inches of Oklahoma rawhide, supposedly was headed for stardom, but never lived up to his build-up.

Owner Walter Briggs made a move which cast its shadow on future events when he engaged the able Robert "Red" Rolfe, former Yankee third-base star, to head the Tiger farm organization. In the meantime, Billy Evans did a bit of house cleaning when he released Roy Cullenbine to the Phillies and Steve O'Neill's son-in-law, Skeeter Webb, to the Athletics. Faithful Roger Cramer, by this time forty-three, was retained on the active list, but his duties were largely on the coaching lines, with an occasional pinch-hitting assignment. For the first-base job, formerly held down by the sluggers Hank Greenberg and Rudy York, Billy acquired a big 200-pounder, George Vico, from Portland in the Coast League. To back up big George, Evans purchased Paul Campbell from the Red Sox organization. Paul had been quite a ballplayer at Louisville; he really could play the bag, but there was no authority in his bat. He had failed in several trials with the Red Sox. Vico showed some promise, and hit .267 in 144 games. But, he couldn't get that heft behind his powerful swings; he connected for only eight home runs and drove in a disappointing 58 runs. Johnny Lipon, who had rave notices as a nineteen-year-old shortstop before Pearl Harbor, was back for another trial, and did nobly, hitting .290. Johnny Groth, a dashing Chicagoan, showed a lot of stuff at the 1948 Lakeland training camp, but Evans thought the boy needed more experience and sent him to Buffalo. Back at the fag end of the season, Johnny exploded like a bunch of firecrackers, hitting .471 in six games. Some Detroiters then asked: "Why wasn't he with us all year?"

Yet, despite a new 1,743,035 attendance record, passing the 1946 top by over 20,000, 1948 proved a disappointing year for Walter Briggs and the Tiger fans. For most of the season, the American League had a great four-cornered race between the Indians, Red Sox, Yankees, and a surprise team, the Philadelphia Athletics. As late as August, only six points separated the top four, and in such a race Detroit could rise no higher than fifth. Actually, the 1948 Tigers won two more games than they lost and invariably gave all comers a rousing tussle. Their hustle and impartial battling against all four contenders, along with the novelty of arc light ball, kept the customers coming.

Lights were turned on at Briggs Stadium for the first time in a game with the Athletics on June 15. True to his promise, Briggs gave his fans the best in lighting equipment that money would buy, spending $400,000 on the new installations. That was about ten

284

times as much as the Tiger franchise was worth in the early years of the American League. If the wraith of Frank Navin was hovering over Briggs Stadium on that coolish late spring night, even he must have thrilled at the splendidly illuminated plant.

The money Briggs layed out for his "last-word" lighting equipment quickly started flowing back. The first night game drew an enthusiastic crowd of 54,480. They saw a good show, too, as Hal Newhouser threw a two-hitter against the Athletics for his seventh straight victory as the Tigers won, 4 to 1. A rather distressing play, for the visiting team, the Tigers, and the home folk, was Barney McCosky, the Detroiter and former Tiger, meeting with a serious injury when he crashed into the stands while trying to field Dick Wakefield's homer. With all the lights blazing as in an operating room, the crumpled Barney was carried off the field on a stretcher.

The first Detroit night show went so well that three days later, another 50,000 crowd braved showers and threatening skies to see more of it. But, these hardy fans and fanettes got nothing more than a good drenching for their pains, as the scheduled game with the Red Sox was rained out. Ever since, when the weather has been at all favorable and the competition other than Washington and the Browns, Detroit night games have averaged close to 50,000.

Back from their Lakeland training trip, the 1948 Tigers failed to thrive on home cooking when they were reunited with their spouses. The club suffered the same early-season ineptitude at their home grounds which characterized Steve O'Neill's 1944 club. The season was nearly a month old, May 15, before the Tigers treated a home crowd with a victory, and then they picked on the humble Browns, 4 to 1. The Tigers rallied somewhat from this poor start, ran fourth until middle June, but the Red Sox shoved them out of the first division when they started their upward climb, and from then on the Tigers ran in a fifth-place groove.

However, there was thrill for Tiger fans in the last week of the season, when the Detroits threw the American League race into a tie by winning two of their last three games from their old foes from across the lake, the Cleveland Indians. The Indians had a lead of a game and a half over Boston and New York—tied for second place, with only three home games with Detroit left on its schedule. The Indians were two putouts from a victory on October 1, when the Felines knocked out Bob Lemon in the ninth and pummeled Russ Christopher, his successor, for three runs to win by 5 to 3. Gene Bearden then blanked the Tigers, 8 to 0, on Saturday, October 2, as the Red Sox eliminated the Yankees. It reduced the

Cleveland lead to one game on the morning of the third, the last day of the season. It was Hal Newhouser against Bob Feller on this final Sunday. Bob had beaten Hal five times out of six, but on this crucial Sabbath, it was all Hal. The 1948 Tigers were only fifth in team batting, but they awed a Cleveland crowd of 74,181 with the ferocity of their attack. They were the reincarnations of Cobb, Crawford, Heilmann, and Veach. The Cleveland fans had poured into their huge Municipal Stadium in a holiday mood, intent on celebrating the Indians' second American League pennant; instead they saw Feller routed with a run-run fusillade in the third inning, while the Tigers climbed on six pitchers for 15 hits and an easy 7-to-1 victory for Newhouser.

How the Red Sox tied the race by beating the Yankees on the same Sunday and then, saved for a day by Detroit, lost to Cleveland in the play-off game in Boston is baseball history. But, after winning his Sunday game, Steve O'Neill had quipped, "Well, nobody can't say the Tigers didn't give them all they had."

Being a disturbing factor in the race wasn't enough for Walter Briggs. Like the late Col. Ruppert of the Yankees and Barney Dreyfuss of the Pirates, Briggs considers himself a first-division man. After one first and three seconds over a four-year span, a fifth-place finish meant the finish of the likable O'Neill as manager. Yet, things happened that were beyond Steve's control. His offense was badly disarranged when his best hitter, George Kell, was out of the line-up twice with serious injuries, first with a broken wrist and later with a fractured jaw. George played in only 92 of his team's 154 games and hit .304, well below the Kell standard.

On the defensive side, the hard luck that followed the young Detroiter, Art Houtteman, was almost unbelievable. Not only were all the evil gremlins in Michigan riding on his broad back, but he must have been jinxed by a chorus of cross-eyed girls. Everyone admitted Art was one of the best young pitchers in baseball, yet he couldn't win. The genial kid finally wound up with two victories and sixteen defeats, enough to break any youngster's heart. Not since Jack Nabors of the 1916 Athletics won only one game and lost nineteen did any American League pitcher show up worse in the won-and-lost columns. Most of the time, Houtteman pitched good ball. His June performances told the year's story. On the sixth, he lost a 1-to-0 decision to the mauling Yankees for his eighth straight defeat; on the sixteenth, he won one of his two games when he outlasted Lou Brissie, the Athletics' purple-heart left-hander, in an 11-inning, 2-to-1 duel. On the twenty-second, he lost a game to Washington before a 34,447 night crowd at Briggs Stadium, when Earl Wooten, a rookie Senator outfielder, chose Art as the victim for his first big-league home run.

Again Steve's pitching wasn't as strong as most of the experts figured. Despite a midsummer ailment, which limited Hal Newhouser's activity in the All-Star game to a stint as pinch-runner, lefty Harold checked in with 21 victories against 12 defeats, and ranked behind only the two Indians, Bearden and Lemon, in earned-run effectiveness. The rest of the staff was just so-so. Trucks won 14 and lost 13, but participated in only seven complete games. Hutchinson was about the same with a 13–11 rating, while Dizzy Trout had his troubles, and could post only ten victories to offset 14 defeats. Ted Gray, a Detroit home-bred left-hander, showed promise by winning six games out of eight. He was a comparatively little fellow, weighing 160 pounds, but Ted could get plenty on the ball. Big Kretlow did little, and there was some criticism of O'Neill for starting the huge Oklahoman against Bearden in the October second game with Cleveland. However, the carping subsided when the Tigers took the series, two games out of three.

The outfielders gave Detroit fans much pleasure. Hoot Evers had a good season and hit .314; Pat Mullin got a lot of mileage out of a .288 batting average and was death to the Yankees. While Vic Wertz batted only .248 in 119 games, Victor hit a long ball and gave all signs of developing into a real hitter. Dick Wakefield, the expensive University of Michigan boy, just couldn't get back into his 1943–44 wartime stride and came home with a .276 average for 110 games. With the American League outfield stars, Ted Williams and Joe DiMaggio, out of the annual St. Louis All-Star game with injuries, Evers and Mullin made Manager Bucky Harris's junior loop line-up and Hoot contributed a homer to the Americans' 5-to-2 victory.

When Briggs decided on a managerial change for 1949, Red Rolfe, 1948 farm superintendent, was a natural for the job. For years, the Dartmouth graduate had been recognized as one of the smartest fellows in the game. With a keen, analytical mind, the New Hampshire redhead had made a study of everything connected with baseball. And, like a lot of other former players, he had a yen to try his hand as field director of a club. The only seeming stumbling block to managerial success was the New Englander's health. At thirty-three an intestinal ailment had cut short his playing career with the Yankees, and for a while Red's physical condition was a cause for concern. It was feared the worries of running a top-notch major-league club would not be conducive to the smooth flowing of his digestive juices. However, Red overcame some real worries; he lifted the Tigers back into the first division and in the closing weeks of the season he had injected something of the winning spirit of the old Yankees into his charges. What's more, he surrounded himself with an aggressive, live-wire coaching staff in Dick Bartell, shortstop of the 1940 Tiger champions and former National League firebrand; Ted Lyons, the popular and canny former White Sox pitching ace and manager; and Rick Ferrell, former American League catching great. Rick landed in Detroit two decades late. In March, 1929, when Ferrell was a promising Tiger farmhand, Judge Landis made him a free agent and the catcher peddled himself to the St. Louis Browns for a $25,000 bonus.

It looked as though the fates finally had done their worst to Art Houtteman during the 1949 Tiger training season. The unlucky pitcher of the year before was badly injured in an automobile collision at Lakeland, March 6. He suffered a basal skull fracture and other injuries, and at first little hope was held for Art's recovery. So serious was his condition that the last rites of his church were given to young Houtteman, as Rolfe and his Detroit players went about their training with heavy hearts. But, at the age of twenty-one the human constitution can take a bad beating and show amazing recuperative powers. Art rallied from death's door to a point where physicians expressed the hope that perhaps he might be able to play ball again. They felt if he knocked off a year, and took a long rest, he might resume his pitching chores by 1950.

That didn't suit Art; he had other ideas and plans. By early May, he was back in his Tiger uniform, and by May 21, he returned to the mound as a relief pitcher against the Athletics at Shibe Park. The entire Philadelphia stands stood up to cheer the young pitcher as Houtteman walked to the mound, and fans thrilled everywhere when they heard the wonderful words on the radio: "Houtteman now pitching for Detroit." What's more, with the automobile crack-up, Art's bad luck seemingly came to an end. Despite missing the first six weeks of the season, the pitcher who won only two games in 1948 pitched 204 innings in 1949 for a credible 15–10 record. Houtteman's 13 additional victories were reflected in the Tiger percentage as Rolfe's team won nine more games than did O'Neill's 1948 aggregation.

After running second to the Yankees during most of June, Rolfe's cats suffered a pre-Fourth-of-July slump and slipped as low as fifth. But, just at a time when most of the interest was focused on the Yankees and Red Sox at the top of the American League ladder in late August, Red got his machine rolling and it finished in high. The Tigers reeled off 18 victories in 20 games and had a ten-game winning streak when they went to Boston, September 13, to start their last eastern trip. The Red Sox brought the winning romp to an end when they tripped the Felines, 7 to 4. The Red Sox were road blocks for Detroit all season, and it was through no fault of Rolfe that his old New York teammates got away with their sixteenth pennant. While Rolfe fought the Yankees to an even break in 22 games, his boys could win only seven out of 22 from Boston. The Tigers' late season upsurge almost enabled them to wrest third place from the 1948 World Champion Indians and they overhauled Cleveland by a game in the last week of the season. Then, to the distress of Tiger fans, the Indians rallied to sweep their last three-game series at Briggs Stadium to take third money by a two-game margin. The fans kept coming to the very end, and when the season was over the beaming Billy Evans was able to inform the Detroit sports writers that the Tigers had set another new attendance record. This time the turnstile count soared to 1,821,204, or about as much as the Tigers drew from 1901 to 1908, inclusive.

Highlighting Detroit's early 1949 fighting was the inspired play of Johnny Groth, the young Chicago outfielder, brought back from Buffalo late in 1948. As the Tigers opened the season, April 19, before 53,435 fans—the largest first-day throng in Detroit's history—Johnny set off his box of fireworks with two homers which were good for a 5-to-1 victory over the White Sox. The next day Johnny beat the Sox, 5 to 2, by exploding a 4-run homer in the eighth inning. In his first two games, Groth hit 3 homers, a double and single in seven official times at bat, and drove in seven of his team's ten runs. He kept it up at a somewhat slackened pace for another fortnight, and was the early rage of the season. People were speaking of him as Detroit's greatest hitter since Cobb, and magazine and syndicate writers were tripping over each other to write the modest Chicagoan's life story. However, whether it was a case of too much publicity, or the pitchers catching up with young Groth, Johnny's average suddenly took a nose dive. Rolfe eventually thought it advisable to bench Groth, but the youngster got back and wound up with a satisfactory .293 for 103 games.

The outfielder who really came fast for the Tigers in 1949 was

Vic Wertz, playing his third season in the league. The York, Pennsylvania, boy played in all of his team's 155 games, and slugged the ball with all the resolution of an old-time Tiger outfielder. While Wertz's batting average was .304, he hit 20 homers, and his 133 runs batted in were second only to the 159 driven in by the two clouting Red Sox, Ted Williams and Vern Stephens, tied for first place. Hoot Evers was just a point behind Wertz with .303, but Detroit's one-time top outfield figure, Dick Wakefield, slumped to .206 for 59 games. Though used largely as an outfield spare and pinch hitter, there were weeks when Dick couldn't beg, borrow, or steal a hit.

Detroit had its first batting champion since Charley Gehringer won the crown in 1937, but the new bingle king, George Clyde Kell, won his title by the width of one of his chin whiskers. George came back nobly after his mishaps of 1948, and finished almost in a dead heat with Boston's lusty Ted Williams. The league statistician had to carry out the averages to four figures to determine the winner, and Kell emerged ahead with .3429 to Ted's .3427. Kell also had come fast in his third-base play; he opened the sixteenth All-Star game in Brooklyn at third base for the American League, and easily won the third-base assignment on the Baseball Writers Association's All-Star team of the year. Making the 1946 Barney McCosky-Kell swap look even worse for Connie Mack, and better for Detroit, McCosky was incapacitated all through the 1949 season with an injured spine.

If Rolfe derived much satisfaction out of Kell's play at Red's old position, he wasn't so pleased with the rest of his infield, and blamed his inability to fight the Red Sox and Yankees for the pennant on the weak right side of his infield. Johnny Lipon did all right at shortstop, but everybody took a hand at first and second. Accustomed to seeing the hefty first sacker, Lou Gehrig, explode long-distance hits in the Yankees' heyday, Rolfe just couldn't look at the futile swings of the six foot, four inch California giant, George Vico. He yanked George after he hit a poor .190 for 67 games, well below his '48 freshman average. Paul Campbell, playing 87 games, hit .278, but he didn't come up either to Red's idea of a clouting first baseman. Early in the 1949 season, a "handy Andy" infielder, Don Kolloway, was procured from the White Sox in a trade for outfielder Earl Rapp. Don also worked 57 games at first base for Detroit, and spaced Neil Berry at second. The venerable Eddie Lake also took part in 94 games at second base and shortstop, but added little to the team's stickwork when he matched Vico's .190.

Before Rolfe was moved up to the management the winter before, Billy Evans procured the former Yankee catcher, Aaron Robinson, from the White Sox in a swap for southpaw pitcher Bill Pierce. Robbie helped, hit .269 in 110 games, but he was 33 years old, and Rolfe hoped to develop a younger and faster man to work regularly behind the plate.

Next to Art Houtteman's splendid recovery after his training accident, the most pleasant feature of Detroit's 1949 pitching was the superb chucking of Virgil Trucks, the big boy from Birmingham. Old Fire Trucks had the best season of his big-league career, winning 19 games and losing 11, while his earned-run average was second only to that of Boston's Mel Parnell, the league leader. And, to show he still had some of the steam with which he fanned 418 Alabama-Florida batsmen in 1937, Virgil struck out 153, which was the 1949 high for both major leagues. Newhouser wasn't quite as sharp as in some former seasons, as he won 18 games and lost 11 and had the doubtful distinction of being tagged for more hits than any pitcher in the league, 277. The other Detroit-bred lefty, Ted Gray, broke even in 20 games. Rolfe found spots for Hutchinson, and Freddy came up with 15 victories against seven defeats. Dizzy Trout, who won 47 games in 1943 and 1944, was used largely in relief.

At the end of the season, Rolfe told Billy Evans: "We just have to strengthen the right side of our infield. Our outfield is set; we have the pitchers; our catching is all right; and if we can get more power into the right side of our infield, we can make trouble for any of them."

Billy did good business on the trading marts. The St. Louis Browns, always in need of cash, were willing to dicker for second baseman Gerald Priddy, one of the few solid players on the Missouri club and an infielder much in demand. Originally Yankee property, Priddy had won fame with Norfolk and Kansas City, when he was coupled with Phil Rizzuto, the present crack Yankee shortstop. Both came up to the Yankees together in 1941, and Rolfe was Gerry's teammate on the Bomber Champions of 1941 and 1942. In fact, Gerry substituted for Red in one of the games of the 1942 World Series. In a war transaction, Priddy was sent to Washington by Ed Barrow, then the Yankee chief, and Griffith later traded Gerry to the Browns. His reputation went up considerably after the war, as he improved in batting and won acclaim as a "Take Charge Guy" on a ball club.

"If we could get Priddy, I know it would do us a great deal of good," Rolfe told Evans.

Billy arranged the deal, $100,000 and the promising Oklahoma pitcher, Lou Kretlow. That's what Mickey Cochrane cost Detroit sixteen years before, but player values zoomed after the war.

In another deal with the Yankees, Evans and Rolfe felt they strengthened the weak first-base spot by the acquisition of Dick Kryhoski, a 200-pound New Jersey collegian. In the early part of the Yankees' 1949 pennant drive, Casey Stengel used young Kryhoski at first base against right-handed pitching. The big Jersey Pole seemingly did all right, and in midseason was hitting .294 for 54 games when he was sent to Oakland, California for additional experience. In the Coast League, Dick hit .328. Billy had carefully watched his work in the Yankee chain through the postwar years, and decided Kryhoski, a war veteran, was ripe for big-league picking. To lure Kryhoski from the Yankees, the Tigers finally gave up on the expensive Dick Wakefield, the man they once thought might rival Ted Williams.

The Tigers made a few other changes. After the Yanks gave Charley Keller, former outfield slugger, his unconditional release, he was signed by Rolfe, his erstwhile New York buddy. Keller underwent an operation for a spinal disc following the 1948 season, but still suffered from back trouble in 1949 and no longer could hit the long ball that had made him famous. But Charley was only 33 years old and Rolfe was willing to gamble the man they once called King Kong would regain something of the old power.

A 31-year-old spectacled pitching veteran, Paul Calvert, was purchased from the Washington club despite Paul's 1949 6–17 record with the tail-end Senators and a 14-straight losing streak. But Calvert pitched a low sinker, frequently was most effective for a few innings, and Rolfe felt he might be just the man he needed for relief work. "Paul's no Joe Page," said Red, "but he can help us."

Little Stubby Overmire was released to the Browns, and Hal White was yanked back from Toledo. The club also brought up right-hander Saul Rogovin, a tall Jewish boy from Brooklyn, who had a good 1949 record with Buffalo. Rogovin once underwent the strange experience of landing in a Venezuelan jail for giving up too many bases on balls. Sol didn't have his range finder with him that day; the Venezuelan fans shrieked their protests; the gendarmes pulled him off the mound and tossed him into the hoosegow. That's one way of teaching a pitcher control. When Myron "Joe" Ginsberg caught Rogovin, Detroit had an all-Jewish battery. Though Ginsberg was born in New York, he grew up in Detroit and was plucked off the Automobile City's sand lots. After several trips to the minors, Joe completed his lower-league education with Toledo in 1949 and was adjudged ready. "Ginsberg will do a lot of catching from now on," Rolfe announced at the start of the 1950 season.

Red, however, had one of those bonus-problem children on his hands in a big catcher from Bessemer, Alabama, Frank "Pig" House. Steve O'Neill, the former manager and a specialist on catchers, went overboard on young House when Frank was catching for Bessemer High School and in North Carolina semipro circles. In August, 1948, the Tigers paid the husky youngster $75,000 and threw in a couple of automobiles for his father to sign a Tiger contract in Frank's behalf. House then was only 18 years old. The husky youth had only indifferent 1949 success with the Flint, Michigan, team of the Central League, hitting only .261, while reports reached Detroit that the big-bonus boy stuffed himself with the heavy sugar paid him by the Tigers and that he found training rules most irksome. Under the bonus rule in effect in 1950, the Tigers could send House to the minors for only one season, so Rolfe had to make a place for the youngster on his bench, or have the club lose its big investment in the catcher.

Sports writers liked what they saw of the Tigers at their 1950 Lakeland training camp, and while the majority picked the Red Sox to win the American League flag, as many picked the Tigers for first place as favored the World Champion Yankees. Practically all picked the Tigers to run one, two, or three. And they felt, if there was a dark horse, Detroit would be it. The only discordant note in the Detroit picture was Hal Newhouser complaining of an ailing arm and shoulder and pitching only a few training innings. However, medicos and bone specialists assured the crack left-hander there was nothing radically wrong with his valuable salary arm.

Still feeling the momentum of their strong 1949 finish, the Tigers tore open the western end of the league in the first fortnight of the 1950 race and sprang early into the lead. Even with Newhouser sitting out the cold early games, the Tigers cut quite a swathe as Houtteman won more games in April than he won in the entire 1948 season. Johnny Groth was the same spring meteor that he was in 1949, and in the first week of the season he dashed off nine consecutive hits. Young Kryhoski drove in his share of runs, and though Rolfe found it necessary to plaster a fine on Gerry Priddy for visiting Detroit night spots after the club's curfew, the "Take Charge Guy" of the infield was proving his worth. Young Ginsberg did most of the catching; Paul Calvert turned in several fine relief jobs; Vic Wertz, George Kell, Hoot Evers, and Pat Mullin were hitting; and the entire club was clicking. Like owner Briggs, Tiger fans were settling for nothing less than a pennant. The Detroit club's past was a brilliant and interesting one, but an even brighter future seemingly awaited Michigan's famous Tigers.

INDEX

Compiled by Bonnie Hanks

Heilmann, Harry: batting averages, 156, 170, 172, 174, 177, 178, 187; batting championships, 167, 172, 176, 184; career, 156, 189; early years, 156; as first baseman, 158; 1919 season, 160; 1920 season, 161; sold to Cincinnati, 189–90; Veach and, 168

Henshaw, Roy, 219–20, 256

Herman, Billy, 219, 221, 223–24

Herman, Floyd "Babe," 171

Herrmann, Garry, 94–95, 98, 144

Herzog, Charley, 157

Heydler, John, 126, 162

Higgins, Pinky, 238, 245–49, 251, 260, 276

Higham, Richard, 6

Highlanders, New York, 35–36

Hines, Paul, 24

Hinky Dink's saloon, 65

History of Baseball (Richter), 15–16

Hofman, Solly "Artie," 112–14, 116

Hogsett, Chief, 192, 206, 208, 214, 221–22

Holloway, Ken, 184

Holmes, Bill "Ducky," 29, 33, 73

Hoover, Joe, 263

Hornsby, Rogers, 62, 68, 74, 170

Hostetler, Chuck, 256, 270–71, 275

Houck, Sadie, 6

House, Frank "Pig," 293

Houtteman, Art, 279, 283, 286–88, 293

Howard, Del, 97, 103

Howe, Irwin, 170–71

Howell, Harry, 140

Hoy, Dummy, 25

Hoyt, White, 191

Hubbell, Carl, 178, 184, 187, 247

Hull, Cordell, 193

Hulswitt, Rudy, 50

Hurst, Tim, 64, 65

Huston, Tillinghast, 159–60

Hutchings, Johnny, 248

Hutchinson, Freddy, 243–44, 255, 276, 279, 283, 287, 291

Hyland, Robert F., 78, 209

Indians, Cleveland, 165

International Association, 19

International League, 19

Isaminger, Jimmy, 194

Isbell, Frank, 34, 42

Jackson, Joe, 53, 89, 118, 122, 140, 143, 145, 148–49

Jacobson, Bill "Babe Doll," 153

Jakucki, Sig, 259

James, Bill, 153–54, 183

Jennings, Hughie: American League pennant and, 88; at 1911 banquet, 144; Ty Cobb and, 70; contracts and, 106; death, 87; Detroit Tigers and, 84–86, 121; early years, 86–87; Giants and, 166; Herrmann and, 94–95; injuries, 87; Ban Johnson and, 84–86, 89, 125; military service, 159; Frank J. Navin and, 57, 84–86, 164; 1907 season, 90, 92; 1914 season, 150–51; 1918 season, 158–59; personality, 86, 87–88; players strike and, 146; as shortstop, 5; signing with Detroit, 84–86; World Series (1907), 99–100, 102; World Series (1908), 113, 115, 117; World Series

(1909), 127, 130, 132–33, 136; World Series and, 125–26

Johnson, Bob, 189

Johnson, Byron Bancroft "Ban": American League and, 29–31, 50; Baltimore and, 48; at 1911 banquet, 144; clean baseball and, 29–30; Ty Cobb and, 185–86; Cobb-Speaker case, 181; criticism of, 105; Detroit ownership and, 55; Herrmann and, 94–95, 98; investigations and, 140; Jennings and, 84–86, 89, 125; Lasker plan and, 162; Mays and, 159; McGraw and, 85; National League and, 29, 46, 50; Pittsburgh Pirates and, 49–51; players strike and, 146–47; retirement, 38; rules and, 63; Stallings and, 35–36; Sunday bootleg ball and, 37; Western League and, 20; World Series (1909), 129

Johnson, Don, 265, 268

Johnson, Jack, 81

Johnson, Roy, 189

Johnson, Sylvester, 169, 170, 172

Johnson, Walter, 69, 92, 188, 193, 201

Johnstone, James, 130–31

Jones, Bobbie, 158, 160, 167, 177

Jones, Davey: acquired by Detroit, 81; batting averages, 124; 1907 season, 91; as outfielder, 144; World Series (1907), 96, 102; World Series (1908), 113, 116; World Series (1909), 127, 129, 131–33, 135

Jones, Fielder, 60, 155–56

300

303

Reulbach, Ed, 97–98, 100, 111, 236–37, 267
Reynolds, Ross, 151
Rice, Grantland, 72, 73
Rice, Harry, 187, 191
Rice, Sam, 193
Richards, Paul, 255, 257, 263, 266, 270, 273, 279
Richardson, Hardy, 7, 10, 16, 17
Richardson, Nolen, 191
Richter, Francis "Frank," 15–16, 68
Rickey, Branch, 241
Rigney, Emory Elmo, 169, 172, 177
Riley, W. F., 6
Ripple, Jimmy, 251
Risberg, Charles "Swede," 182–83
Risberg-Gandil case, 183
Rizzuto, Phil, 291
Robinson, Aaron, 291
Robinson, Wilbert, 31, 86
Robison, Frank De Haas, 50–51
Rogell, Billy: batting averages, 216; Doljack and, 194–95; 1933 season, 195; 1934 season, 200; as shortstop, 238; traded, 242; World Series (1934), 205, 206, 208, 209, 210, 212, 213, 216; World Series (1935), 221–22, 224
Rogers, John I., 26
Rogovin, Saul, 292–93
Rolfe, Robert "Red," 284, 287, 291
Rondeau, Henri, 149
Root, Charley, 219–20
Ross, Don, 260
Rossman, Claude: batting averages, 109; contracts, 106; Frank J. Navin and, 88; 1907 season, 90–92;

traded, 121; World Series (1907), 97, 99, 101–3; World Series (1908), 111–12, 114–16
Rothrock, Jack, 205–6, 208, 212, 214
Rowe, Jack, 7, 10, 16, 18
Rowe, Lynwood Thomas "Schoolboy": acquired by Detroit, 194; injuries, 229, 235, 253–54; 1935 season, 217; sold to Brooklyn, 254; suspensions, 230; win-loss records, 201, 239, 243–44; World Series (1934), 204, 206, 211–14; World Series (1935), 219, 220–223, 232; World Series (1940), 246–47, 249–50
Rowland, Clarence, 152, 166, 269
Royston Rompers, 71
Ruel, Muddy, 192
Ruffing, Red, 218
rules, scoring (1887), 10
Ruppert, Jake, 159–60, 198
Rusie, Amos, 87
Ruth, Babe, 52, 68, 154, 161, 172, 175–76, 178, 198
Ryan, Jack, 29
Ryan, Tommy, 57

St. Louis Browns, 10–15, 49, 138–39, 259
St. Louis Republic, 140
St. Louis Star-Times, 76
salaries, player, 21, 41
Salsinger, Harry, 153–54, 157, 166, 204, 272
Sanborn, I. E. "Cy," 103–4, 118
Sargent, Joe, 167, 169
Schacht, Al, 62, 213–14
Schaefer, Herman "Germany": acquired by De-

troit, 62; Couglin and, 61; humor of, 61–65; 1907 season, 89, 91, 92; at second base, 62; traded, 121; World Series (1907), 96, 99, 102–4; World Series (1908), 110, 113–14, 116
Schmidt, Charley "Dutch": as catcher, 81; Ty Cobb and, 82–83; disposition, 78; 1907 season, 96–101; World Series (1908), 112–13; World Series (1909), 129–30, 135–36
Schreckengost, Ossie, 29, 63
Schulte, Frank, 96–97, 101, 112, 114, 116
Schuster, Billy, 272
scoring rules (1887), 10
Secory, Pat, 271
Sewell, Luke, 262
Seybold, Socks, 29
Shaver, Bud, 83, 168, 201, 204
Shawkey, Bob, 54
Sheahan, Arthur T., 41, 228
Sheckard, Jimmy, 97, 99, 101, 112–13
Sheridan, Jack, 48, 64–65, 94, 101, 117
Shettsline, Billy, 26
Shibe, Ben, 31
Shore, Ernie, 154
Shorten, Chick, 160
Siever, Eddie, 47, 88, 99
Simmons, Al, 184–86, 199, 228
Sisler, George, 69, 157, 161, 170
Slagle, Jimmy, 60, 97, 99, 101–3
Slapnicka, Cy, 253
Slocum, Bill, 54
Smith, Charles W., 17
Smith, Frank, 54, 108
Smith, Harry, 50